No masters but God

MANCHESTER
1824

Manchester University Press

Contemporary Anarchist Studies

A series edited by
Laurence Davis, *University College Cork, Ireland*
Uri Gordon, *University of Nottingham, UK*
Nathan Jun, *Midwestern State University, USA*
Alex Prichard, *Exeter University, UK*

Contemporary Anarchist Studies promotes the study of anarchism as a framework for understanding and acting on the most pressing problems of our times. The series publishes cutting-edge, socially engaged scholarship from around the world – bridging theory and practice, academic rigor and the insights of contemporary activism.

The topical scope of the series encompasses anarchist history and theory broadly construed; individual anarchist thinkers; anarchist informed analysis of current issues and institutions; and anarchist or anarchist-inspired movements and practices. Contributions informed by anti-capitalist, feminist, ecological, indigenous and non-Western or global South anarchist perspectives are particularly welcome. So, too, are manuscripts that promise to illuminate the relationships between the personal and the political aspects of transformative social change, local and global problems, and anarchism and other movements and ideologies. Above all, we wish to publish books that will help activist scholars and scholar activists think about how to challenge and build real alternatives to existing structures of oppression and injustice.

No masters but God

Portraits of anarcho-Judaism

Hayyim Rothman

MANCHESTER UNIVERSITY PRESS

The right of Hayyim Rothman to be identified as the author
of this work has been asserted by him in accordance with
the Copyright, Designs and Patents Act 1988.

Published by Manchester University Press
Altrincham Street, Manchester M1 7JA
www.manchesteruniversitypress.co.uk

British Library Cataloguing-in-Publication Data
A catalogue record for this book is available from the
British Library

ISBN   978 1526 14903 9 hardback

First published 2021

The publisher has no responsibility for the persistence or
accuracy of URLs for any external or third-party internet
websites referred to in this book, and does not guarantee
that any content on such websites is, or will remain,
accurate or appropriate.

Typeset
by New Best-set Typesetters Ltd

This book is dedicated to Esther, to Sadira, and to Kaddish

I remember your youthful devotion, how you loved me and followed me through the wilderness, through a land not sown. (Jeremiah 2:2)

Contents

List of figures

Acknowledgements

This book would not have been possible without the generous support of several institutions — first and foremost, the United States-Israel Educational Foundation (Fulbright) which, together with Bar Ilan University, has fully funded my post-doctoral studies. Recognition is also due to the Center for Christian-Jewish Learning and to the Clough Center for the Study of Constitutional Democracy, both at Boston College. Their support enabled me to do the preliminary research that got this project off the ground. I wish to extend special thanks to Anne Kenny and her staff at Boston College Libraries; without their determined efforts to secure many of the materials on which it is based, this book could not have been written. Of course, it is upon me to thank the many friends and colleagues whose questions, comments, criticisms, and also persistent faith in me and my work both enriched it and gave me the strength to persevere. In this respect, special thanks is due to Uri Gordon, whose dedication to the project was decisive in bringing it to print and whose insight and advice has been of inestimable value to me. I would also like to extend my thanks to Muslala, Jerusalem, for providing me a wonderful place to work on this book. Finally, I humbly acknowledge Yoel Matveyev, whose preliminary research on the subject constituted the starting point for my own efforts.

1

An anarchist *minyan*

A King who tells the sea: 'until here and no further!'
He shall rule as King!
A king who comes from a putrid drop
and ends up in the grave,
why should he rule as king?

(Eleazar Kallir)

In one of his lesser-known autobiographical vignettes, *Tate Vert an Anarkhist* (Daddy Becomes an Anarchist), Isaac Bashevis Singer recounts how, with 'blue eyes and fiery red beard glowing,' his father returned one day from Warsaw's Radzyminer *shtibl* (small synagogue) with news of a group 'whose members call themselves anarchists.' He recalls how till late into the night his father described 'the happy times to come, when there would be no need for money and everyone would work and study Torah,' concluding that though 'Jews long for the messiah … while we're in exile, it would be *quite* a good thing.' Yet, he reports, his father's ardor waned once he heard 'that their entire philosophy was incompatible with Judaism (Bashevis Singer 2000, 193–200).' Rabbi Singer's career as a religious anarchist was thus aborted before it began.

One wonders, however, what might have been had the impressionable Rabbi not rushed home but, after leaving the *shtibl* on Franciszkanska Street and crossing through Krasinski Garden on the way to Krochmalna Street, instead tarried at the Jewish library next to the Great Synagogue. If we consider the Warsaw of Eliezer Hirschauge's memory, he may have bumped into Aaron Pinhas Gross, known among the anarchist underground by his alias *Der Alter* (Hamburg 1977)[1] who, with a 'thick *sidur* or *mahzor* and a *talis* underarm (prayer books and a ritual shawl)' would have been making his way to synagogue 'with a lively step (Hirschauge 1964, 53–54).'[2] He may have come across 'more than a *minyan*,' a prayer quorum, 'of God seeking youth studying anarchist texts (Hirschauge 1964, 27–30).' He may even have heard one of the 'revolutionary sermons' that were 'more abundant than flowers' and thus learned of the 'religious-mystical views' that drove others 'to make human life more just' and 'the earth a bit more heavenly (Hirschauge 1964, 53–54).' Perhaps he would have persisted in the face of skepticism; perhaps the story would have ended differently.

So far as R. Singer *himself* is concerned, one can do no more than wonder. But this vignette confronts us with more fruitful threads of inquiry. For one, it seems difficult to argue with the claim that dampened Singer's fervor. Classical anarchists were notoriously anti-religious and militantly atheist. Their Jewish followers, men like Joseph Boshover, characterized anarchism as 'a world in which churches *and synagogues* become stables … a world of knowledge and not of faith (Boshover 1925, 94–95);' beyond *neglecting* tradition, they gleefully trampled it underfoot by hosting sacrilegious 'Yom Kippur Balls (Margolis 2004).' Therefore, the true wonder is that Rabbi Singer *could* have ambled over to Tlomackie Street and encountered what Hirschauge describes: a circle not simply of Jewish, but *religious* Jewish anarchists. Let us ponder for a moment the significance of this marvel.

In the long arc of Jewish history, many elevated souls have strayed from the fold. In describing such individuals, Isaac Deutcher retold the story of Elisha ben Abuya, the first-century rabbi-cum-heretic later known as Aher, and his last remaining student, R. Meir. As the talmud relates, the two would study together on the Sabbath while strolling outside the city. Upon reaching the *tehum*, the municipal boundary, which an observant Jew will not cross on the holy day, Aher would walk on while R. Meir would turn back (Hagigah 15b). On Deutcher's reading, the master's step beyond the boundary, the limit of tradition, was an act of bravery; accordingly, he praises the 'non-Jewish Jews' who later followed in his footsteps — individuals like Baruch Spinoza, Karl Marx, Rosa Luxemburg, and Emma Goldman. In contrast, he represents the student as a coward, as the progenitor of debased men like Uriel da Costa (Deutscher 2017), who could not bear the challenge of ostracism and accepted the humiliating terms of reacceptance presented to him by his Amsterdam coreligionists.

I see both men differently. There is a comfort in severing ties with the past and starting over with a clean slate. Likewise, there is a profound challenge in changing while yet maintaining old bonds and *taking responsibility* for them. If indeed there was something worthwhile across the *tehum*, who is more praiseworthy, the one who pursues it for himself or the one who fetches it and brings it home? I see in R. Meir someone who adopted the second alternative, someone who learned what Aher had to teach but then carried it into the *beyt midrash*, the study hall, enriching the tradition rather than wiping his hands of it. I aver that the *minyan* of which Hirschauge speaks was an example of precisely *this* type of courage. It was composed of individuals who, like R. Meir, ventured to the farthest extreme but somehow found a way to integrate it with their Judaism — this in spite of the sort of skepticism that discouraged R. Singer.

It is one thing to reverse our interpretation of a talmudic anecdote, to vilify the hero and heroize the villain, and quite another to *substantiate* that reversal. As R. Elazar once taught, one must know 'how to respond to an *apikoros* (M. Avot 2:14),' a skeptic. Simply to valorize R. Meir's return is insufficient. We must be able to explain what it meant and how he did it. By analogy, if we wish to imagine R. Singer's meeting with Mr Gross and his comrades, if we wish to imagine an alternate scenario in which *tatte* not only became, but also remained an anarchist, it is necessary to respond to the *apikoros* who told him that Judaism and anarchism are inconsistent. If not exactly the Warsaw *minyan*, we must imagine one like it. If not exactly *their* revolutionary sermons, others like them. In short, we must trace for ourselves a hermeneutic and historical *path* leading from the anarchist edge of the *tehum* back to the proverbial 'four cubits of Jewish law (Berakhot 8a)' — back into Jewish tradition.

The skepticism with which R. Singer was assailed is not merely a pious gesture, it also represents the prevailing scholarly orthodoxy according to which Jewish radicalism generally, and Jewish anarchism in particular, stood at the farthest distance from Jewish piety during the period in question. In many respects, this account is justified. Irving Howe, for instance, writes that while 'public avowal of agnosticism, atheism, apostasy, and backsliding was no new phenomena' in late nineteenth-century Jewish life, anarchists more so than other radical groups 'went far beyond secularism or anticlericalism in the bitter extremes of their antireligious struggle (Howe 2005, 105).' As Rebecca Margolis explains, if other groups held religion in disdain, they also tended to treat it as a private concern. In contrast, early Jewish anarchists saw religion as 'a fundamental evil … and sought to battle it directly (Margolis 2004).'

Their animosity represented a long tradition of anarchist opposition, not only to organized religion but to theistic faith itself. Pierre Joseph Proudhon, the father of modern anarchism, wrote that 'the first duty of man, on becoming intelligent and free, is to continually hunt the idea of God out of his mind and conscience (Proudhon 2012).' Anarchists in later generations largely agreed. Some went so far as to assert that anarchist libertarianism stops short at the freedom of worship. As Madeleine Pelletier wrote in *L'Encyclopedie Anarchiste*, there is no question of 'freedom and liberty' where religion is concerned, 'only war (Pelletier 1934, 2311–2315)' — both in figurative and literal senses.[3] Nevertheless, scholarship has long recognized a minority trend of religious and spiritual anarchist expression among writers, including Leo Tolstoy, Dorothy Day, and Mohandas Gandhi. Kropotkin (1995) already noted anarchist tendencies in both Reformation Christianity and Taoism. Lately there has been booming scholarly interest in religious anarchism, with several new monographs (Rapp 2010; Wiley 2014; Christoyannopoulos 2019) and the three-volume collection *Essays in Anarchism and Religion* (Christoyannopoulos and Adams 2017, 2018, 2020).[4] While the field has been dominated by Christian voices, others have also begun to make themselves heard: Muslim, Taoist, Hindu, Buddhist, and also Jewish.

The view that Jewish anarchism is inherently anti-religious has recently been challenged by appeal to historical shifts in the circumstances of European Jewry, both external and internal. Externally, as Paul Avrich (1990, 189) noted, the steep rise in antisemitic violence during the period surrounding the infamous Kishinev pogrom 'had a sobering effect, turning more than a few Jewish anarchists back to their roots.' At the very least, these tragedies prompted more nuanced reflection on the question of Jewish religion. Internally, Annie Polland (2007) argues that the waning of religious authority after the turn of the twentieth century created an identity crisis; a successful rebellion against tradition mean that secularism had to be redefined in positive terms; it also permitted a degree of tolerance towards religiosity that seemed impossible before. A later stage of the same phenomenon has recently been addressed in greater detail by Lillian Turk and Jesse Cohn, who document a lively debate that took place on the pages of the *Fraye Arbeter Shtime* between 1937 and 1945, wherein anti-religious conviction persisted but was also complemented by warmer attitudes (Turk and Cohn 2018).

From a theoretical standpoint, the non-dichotomization of religious and radical identities is explained in two ways. Polland (2007) argues that historians have taken their cues from 'the *rabbis* or the radical *leaders*'[5] who tended toward greater ideological rigidity, whereas at the popular level ideological fluidity prevailed. Turk and Cohn (2018) contend that it is not simply a matter of distinguishing between the elite and the masses, but also between different ways of understanding Judaism. A similar position is also adopted by Carolin Kosuch (2019). Among radicals, those inclined to reduce Judaism to orthodoxy (and certain forms of orthodoxy at that) tended to reject it altogether, while those prepared to tolerate or to embrace religion also understood Judaism in more pluralistic terms. Hence the secularized theologies of anarchists such as Aharon David Gordon and Martin Buber, who had exited the fold of traditional observance but continued to draw deeply on kabbalah and hasidism.

This approach accounts for the vast majority of what scholarship exists on the nexus of religious Judaism and anarchism. The contributions of the religiously observant to 'anarchist creativity' have yet to be recognized and appreciated (Goncharok 2011). Indeed, apart from Goncharok's weighty suggestions and my own work, extant scholarship in English is limited to

Tsahi Slater's work (2019, 2016, 2014) on R. Shmuel Alexandrov, and Anna Elena Torres' work (2019) on R. Yaakov Meir Zalkind. These are addressed in the relevant chapters below. In Hebrew, Amnon Shapira's voluminous *Jewish Religious Anarchism* (2015), as its full title suggests, takes a panoramic view of Jewish anti-authoritarian ideas extending from biblical times through the twentieth century. While it certainly breaks new ground, the book wavers between actually writing a history of Jewish anarchist theology and speculatively constructing one from 'anarchistic' or antinomian elements in the history of Jewish thought (Biagini 2008; Berti 2010).

This book attempts the former task. I show that there existed, from the late nineteenth through the mid-twentieth century, a group of rabbis and traditionalist thinkers who explicitly appealed to anarchist ideas in articulating the meaning of the Torah, of traditional practice, and of Jewish life. The book contends, first, that not only the rank and file, but also the elite demonstrated remarkable ideological fluidity; second, that if this fluidity was often underwritten by unorthodox interpretations of Judaism tendered by men who lived otherwise than traditional lifestyles, this was not *always* the case. Drawing on every available source — from forgotten books and pamphlets, to newspaper and journal articles appearing in long ago defunct Yiddish and Hebrew periodicals, to previous unpublished archival material — it probes the life and thought of long-forgotten figures, whose writings have gone largely unread since they were first published, but which demonstrate the resonance of anarchism with Jewish religion conceived along traditional lines. In sum, it argues for the existence of something that might be called anarcho-Judaism — a term which I use to highlight its specifically religious nature and to distinguish it from phenomena like Jewish anarcho-nationalism[6] or the simple participation of individuals with Jewish backgrounds in anarchist movements,[7] both of which might fit under a more general term like 'Jewish anarchism' — by laying the groundwork for a canon.

Canonization raises several problems worth considering. As Nathan Jun has pointed out, 'how we define the anarchist canon — let alone how we decide which thinkers, theories, and texts should count as canonical — depends very much on what we take the purpose of the anarchist canon to be. 'If a 'thinker, theory, or text must belong to an actually existing historical anarchist movement in order to qualify,' then this book is, for the most part, *not* a book about Jewish anarchists because very few of the figures discussed were actively involved in such a movement. If, on the other hand, *all* that is required is '*anarchistic* theoretical or philosophical orientation (Jun 2013)', then the present volume is much too narrow in scope and the premodern figures, ideas, and movements I shall later survey under the rubric of the theological foundations of anarcho-Judaism would simply become its expressions. I adopt a mean between these extremes. In my opinion, it is anachronistic to include pre-modern anti-authoritarian or egalitarian practices and ideas in a history of *anarchism* due to the concrete historicity of modern anarchist movements. Yet it also seems rather myopic to exclude figures promoting such practices and ideas during the period when those movements flourished, especially when they operated in an intellectual and cultural milieu in which revolution was an organic element of the *zeitgeist* (Rakovsky 2003, 70; Frankel 2009, 12). So long as it is limited enough in historical scope to be meaningful, and inclusive enough in other respects to encompass a wide spectrum of viewpoints, I believe that the process of canonization is a helpful heuristic strategy for facilitating reflection on a family of related figures, ideas, practices, and texts. In part, this book constitutes a twofold act of canonical revisionism; it aims to insert anarcho-Judaism into the canons of anarchism and of modern Jewish political thought, from both of which it has been largely excluded.

Yet, in expanding these canons, a new canon is being created — one that is subject to some of the same criticisms as that which it challenges; chief among them, its eurocentricity (Ciccariello-Maher 2011; Evren 2012) and its androcentricity (Kinna 2005, 13; Adams 2013; Campbell 2013). In the most general terms, this book focuses on Jewish men who began their lives in Eastern Europe during the last two decades of the nineteenth century. Some of them crossed the continent, some made their way to the UK, some to North and South America, some to Palestine and later Israel. But the Pale of Settlement (see below) was their point of departure, both geographically and culturally.

Earlier in the nineteenth century, Jews of Sephardic origin in France, the Pereire brothers for instance, were associated with utopian socialists like Saint-Simon (Davies 2016); later, Bernard Lazare, also of Sephardic background, became a prominent French anarchist and Jewish nationalist (Wilson 1978). These, however, were secular contributions. Anarchist movements existed in Alexandria and Constantinople during the period in question, but the Jews involved were Eastern European immigrant laborers (Khuri-Makdisi 2010), they did not hail from Sephardic and Mizrahi Jews indigenous to the region. Radical movements — led, for instance, by Avraham Benaroya (Starr 1945; Benaroya 1949) and Joseph Eliyia (Goldwyn 2015) — arose in Salonika among Sephardic and Romaniote Jews (Vassilikou 1999; Ilicak 2002), but these were both secular and social-democratic in character. While future research may uncover anarchist, even religious anarchist, material in the historical Ladino press, this possibility is not explored in the present volume (due, above all, to linguistic constraints).

Nonetheless, I resist designating anarcho-Judaism as a eurocentric (or Ashkenazi-centric, as the case may be) phenomenon. If Kropotkin, for instance, traced the birth of modern anarchism from the ancient Greeks through the Anabaptists, libertines like Francois Rabelais, the Philosophes, and William Godwin to Pierre-Joseph Proudhon — if, in other words, he ascribed to it a thoroughly European pedigree — the same cannot be said of the Jewish religious anarchists studied here. If Ashkenazic rabbis are shaped by ideas arising within the Sephardic or the Mizrahi world, is the result of their reflections strictly Ashkenazic? If for instance, a rabbi from Kobryn (who happens to have distant Sephardic and Mizrahi roots) living in London grounds his position on centralized government by appealing to a rabbi from Lisbon who wrote on that subject while residing in Venice, how do we categorize his views? To which congregation do they belong? If an Ashkenazic rabbi is influenced by philosophical texts composed in Egypt, or in Iraq, in whose ethnic box do his anti-authoritarian ideas fit? In other words, I believe that the nature of Jewish cultural transmission does not fit the eurocentric model of anarchist historiography even if the individuals of which the cannon is (thus far) composed happen to be of Ashkenazic origin.

In spite of the aforementioned androcentrism of classical formulations of the anarchist canon, it is well-known that women, especially Jewish women, played central roles in various anarchist movements.[8] In Warsaw itself, women such as Esther Rosiner, Hava and Rochel Zoyberman, and Gutshe Sabeh were all active in the anarchist underground (Hirschauge 1964, 55, 57). So far as I have yet to discover, however, women played no role in the articulation of anarcho-Judaism.

There are historical, cultural, and religious reasons for this absence. For one, the 'classical' anarchist tradition was itself largely 'blind to the existence of gender-based tyrannies (Gemie 1996).' This is especially the case when considering the theorists who most profoundly influenced them. Proudhon, Kropotkin, Landauer, and Tolstoy were politically radical but in many respects culturally conservative, even patriarchal (Haaland 1993, 8–13; Cohn 2009; Christoyannopoulos 2019; Garcia and Lucet 2019). These culturally conservative anarchists appealed to those who wished to uphold Jewish life-ways.

Another reason, and one more germane to Jewish heritage, involves the education of women, who were traditionally exempt from the precept of Torah study, a dispensation that generally functioned to *exclude* them from it. Educational opportunities for women slowly expanded over the course of the nineteenth and twentieth centuries (Eliav 1999; Adler 2011; Fuchs 2013). Pioneering institutions like *Bais Yaakov*, however, which normalized formal religious education for Jewish women, did not yet exist during the historical window — from the 1880s until World War I — within which *all* of the figures considered in this volume were radicalized. In this crucial period, women in traditional and 'enlightened' homes alike were seldom familiar with the languages of traditional Jewish scholarship, Hebrew and

Judeo-Aramaic (Parush 2004, 2–3), and even more rarely initiated into the most basic elements of the Jewish intellectual heritage that men inherited as a matter of course — an unfortunate fact that is graphically expressed in Emma Goldman's memoir, *Living My Life*. Aggressively dismissing her desire to obtain an education, she reported, her father remarked that 'all a Jewish daughter needs to know is how to prepare *gefilte* fish, cut noodles fine, and give the man plenty of children (Goldman 2011, 12).' According to Iris Parush, androcentric accounts of the Eastern European Jewish Enlightenment (Haskalah) enterprise — of which Jewish radicalisms were a product (Haberer 1992) — may be challenged by turning to the margins of Jewish society, and especially by questioning the elitist suppositions which male enlighteners (*maskilim*) themselves introduced; above all the superordination of the Hebrew language vis-a-vis the Yiddish folk-idiom (Parush 2004, 3; Trachtenberg 2008, 46–81). Yet, because anarcho-Judaism presupposes familiarity with the sources of a 'text-centered tradition (Halbertal 1997, 1)' and, therefore with the languages in which it is written, this option does not apply. As Naomi Shepherd explains, proximity to 'a powerful tradition of learning' from which they were barred sensitized Jewish women to ideologies promising radical deliverance from stultifying discrimination (Shepherd 1993, 62). For them, liberation meant *freedom from Judaism*, not its renewal. In spite of carefully sifting through both Hebrew and Yiddish language sources, printed and archival, my research thus far confirms this conclusion; I have not yet discovered female contributors to this field of discourse.[9]

The anarchist '*minyan*' constituting the basis for a canon of anarcho-Judaism was composed of eight individuals. R. Shmuel Alexandrov (1865–1941) formulated a synthesis of anarchism and Cultural Zionism that he promoted both through contributions to major Hebrew-language journals and via extensive correspondence with Jewish intellectuals throughout Europe. While functioning as a communal rabbi in a small Polish hamlet, R. Aaron Tamaret (1869–1931) published books and pamphlets promoting a diaspora-oriented form of anti-nationalist anarcho-pacifism after breaking with the Zionist movement early in his career. R. Yehudah-Leyb Don-Yahiya (1869–1941) was among the founders of religious Zionism which, in keeping with its initial revolutionary spirit (Schwartz 2000), he articulated in roughly Tolstoyan terms. Perhaps the most colorful of the group, R. Yaakov-Meir Zalkind (1875–1937) was highly active as a Zionist and a territorialist (territorialists sought to establish Jewish autonomy but not necessarily in Palestine); radicalized over the course of World War I, he took up cause with London-based Jewish anarchists, eventually assuming editorship of the *Arbeter Fraynd*, among the most important Yiddish-language anarchist journals of its day. Advocating a blend of Zionism and Tolstoyan anarcho-pacifism, enshrined in a collection of essays mostly published posthumously,

R. Avraham Yehudah Heyn (1880–1957) led several communities in Eastern and Central Europe before settling in Jerusalem, where he headed the department of religious culture for the Jewish Agency. Though better known for his voluminous commentaries on the Zohar (the thirteenth-century kabbalistic classic), R. Yehudah Ashlag (1885–1954) also adapted his kabbalistic insights into a social theology combining Zionism and libertarian socialism. Isaac Nahman Steinberg (1888–1957), a university-trained lawyer and talmudic scholar, was a prominent member of the Left Socialist Revolutionary party (heirs to the narodniks, pre-Marxist Russian libertarian socialists). Briefly serving as the first Soviet Commissar of Justice, he later promoted Jewish libertarian socialism through his journalism and, above all as head of the Territorialist Movement. Raised on a small farm in Poland, Natan Hofshi (1890–1980) emigrated to Palestine, where he became active in *ha-Poel ha-Tsa'ir* (an organization associated with Labor Zionism); taking A. D. Gordon's Tolstoyan ideals to heart, he participated in the establishment of Brit Shalom (a movement seeking to ensure peaceful coexistence through a bi-national Jewish-Arab polity) and founded the Palestinian (and later Israeli) branch of the War Resisters' International.

Although many of them shared a common commitment to some form of Zionism, as proponents of anarcho-Judaism they were not joined in a movement if, by that, we intend some sort of coordinated practical effort or a high degree of intellectual cooperation or mutual insemination. Several — Don-Yahiya, Zalkind, Steinberg, Heyn, and Alexandrov — were distantly related via complex (and questionably reliable) rabbinic genealogies. Don-Yahiya also became chief rabbi of Heyn's hometown after his father left for Palestine. There is evidence of limited cooperation. Hofshi occasionally cited Heyn and briefly collaborated with Steinberg on Yiddish translations of his essays. Steinberg intermittently referenced Zalkind's talmudic writings, while Zalkind contributed a few pieces to one of Steinberg's journals. Tamaret and Alexandrov corresponded briefly. More substantially, the majority of figures considered in this volume were alumni of the famed Ets Hayyim Yeshiva of Valozyn, an important center of Eastern European rabbinic learning. Though they did not attend simultaneously, the intellectual foment into which the institution entered in the decade prior to its 1892 closure left (as I shall later elaborate) an indelible and shared mark on their understanding of Judaism, most notably, their deep engagement with Zionism, either for or against.

Concretely, it would be more accurate to describe our '*minyan*' as an artificial grouping of individuals who, under common religious, intellectual, and historical influences more or less independently turned to the Jewish intellectual heritage with similar questions and arrived at analogous conclusions as to what Judaism should be and who Jews should become. They did not participate in a common movement; rather, to adapt a turn of phrase from Deleuze and Guattari, they took part in the creation of a minor theological literature. According to Deleuze and Guattari, one of the core characteristics of a minor literature is that 'in it everything takes on a collective value.' As they explain, this means that it is a literature in which marginalized authors attempt 'to express another possible community and to forge the means for another consciousness and another sensibility (Deleuze and Guattari 1986, 17).' The task of the minoritarian author consists not in 'addressing a people, which is presupposed already there,' but in 'contributing to the invention of a people (Deleuze and Guattari 1986, 217).' For our anarchist *minyan*, this was true in a twofold respect. The Zionists and Jewish nationalists among them were part of a broader ethnogenetic project initiated under conditions of persecution, an effort to create (or recreate) a Jewish people empowered to resist oppression. As marginal figures within this broader project, or apart from it, they aimed to summon into being another sort of missing people, an imagined community of religiously inspired radicals.

Matthew Adams (2015, 182–187) has argued that political traditions, like peoples, are always invented. This does not make them false — it makes them mythical. As Sorel contended, myths must be understood as 'expressions of a will to ac (Sorel 1999, 28),' a will to build. The tradition of anarcho-Judaism constructed in this volume is a myth of this sort. If the figures examined here failed in their aspiration to summon a missing people, it is no refutation. It merely implies, as Sorel put it, insufficient preparation and therefore constitutes a call to 'set to work again with more courage, persistence and confidence than before (Sorel 1999, 31).' Myths arrange masses into a 'coordinated picture and, by bringing them together,' give 'to each one of them its maximum intensity (Sorel 1999, 118).' The same can be said of texts and ideas entering an open canon and becoming-tradition — they intensify one another and thereby strengthen a will to action: to call into being the community to which a loosely connected group of minoritarian writers aspired over a century ago.

The course of the book

This study begins with a survey of the historical and theological background of anarcho-Judaism. Its main body is divided into four sections, in which the lives and work of the individuals who make up the anarchist *minyan* are examined in detail. The first section is devoted to figures who played an active role in actually existing political and social movements: Zionism, territorialism, socialism, and of course anarchism or libertarian socialism; divided into two chapters, it focuses on the contributions of R. Yaakov

Meir Zalkind and Isaac Nahman Steinberg. The second section is devoted to figures who integrated Jewish mysticism into their libertarian theologies. It is likewise divided into two chapters, one dealing with R. Yehudah Ashlag, the other dealing with R. Shmuel Alexandrov. The third section deals with anarcho-pacifism in Jewish tradition. It is divided into four chapters, devoted to R. Yehudah-Leyb Don-Yahiya, R. Avraham Yehudah Heyn, Natan Hofshi, and Aaron Shmuel Tamaret respectively. Tamaret takes the final position in this volume because I take his thought to be the most thorough and comprehensive expression of anarcho-Judaism. A concluding chapter is then devoted to highlighting central themes developed over the course of the preceding chapters and reflecting on their contemporary relevance.

Notes

1 Gross was an (apparently) influential but now mysterious figure. His name appears in less than a handful of sources. He taught at Warsaw's Hinukh Jewish gymnasium and his pedagogical talents extended to his activism — this, to the unfortunate exclusion of any written record. Worthy of note, Gross lived in a basement on Moranowska Street, which was connected by an underground tunnel to the bunker under 18 Mila Street; the complex would later serve as the base of operations for the Warsaw ghetto uprising.

2 Hirschauge's work is the only book-length history of Jewish Anarchism in Poland (Pawel Korzec wrote a history of anarchism in Bialystok in 1965). Sadly, it has fallen into obscurity because it is written in Yiddish. He emigrated to Israel and played a role in the anarchist scene in Tel Aviv (Gordon 2009).

3 Pelletier recommended suppression and expulsion. Anti-clerical violence during the Spanish Civil War is a classical example of even more extreme expressions of the same sentiment (Ledesma 2001). For an overview of classical anarchist critique of religion, see Barclay (2010) and Christoyannopoulos and Apps (2018). See also the brief bibliography appearing in the preface to *Religious Anarchism: New Perspectives* (Christoyannopoulos 2009).

4 Alexandre Christoyannopoulos, for instance, has produced a number of excellent studies on Christian anarchism generally and Tolstoyism in particular. A full bibliography of the (relatively) vast body of literature on Christian Anarchism is far beyond the scope of this introduction.

5 Emphasis added.

6 Regarding Jewish anarcho-nationalism generally, the most important text is Grauer (1994); see also Horrox (2009). On Moses Hess' anarcho-nationalism, see Abensour (2011, 50–52; 61). On Bernard Lazare, see Löwy (2004). Much has been written on Martin Buber: I direct the reader only to the most recent study, Brody (2018). On Gershom Scholem's political thought, see especially Jacobson (2003). Concerning the Jewish element of Gustav Landauer's work, see Mendes-Flohr and Mali (2015).

7 Several relatively recent studies have been devoted to the history of Jewish anarchism in Great Britain, the United States, and Latin America. See for example, Knepper (2008), Zimmer (2015), Moya (2004).

8 Scholarship on Emma Goldman is a case in point (Waldstreicher 1990; Reizbaum 2005; Berkowitz 2012). Other prominent examples include Rose Pesotta (Leeder 1993; Shone 2019), Marie Goldsmith (Confino and Rubinstein 1981, 1982, 1992), and Millie Witkop. See also Seemann (2008).

9 That being said, I find it necessary to clarify that anarcho-Judaism is not an *inherently* male undertaking, nor are the theological innovations of its historical promoters irrelevant to Jewish feminist theology (a subject later to be addressed). It is an undertaking requiring multiple linguistic and textual skills that are gendered only to the extent that, in spite of great strides, gender inequality persists in Jewish education (Hartman and Hartman 2003).

2

Historical and theological context

The past is a cemetery for dead dreams. The future is a nursery where fresh dreams grow. The present is like a volcano; from above, it is covered with extinguished dreams, underneath which rumble fresh, hot, boiling, lava which searches for an opening. (Zalkind 1920d, 3)

Historical context

It is well known that the nineteenth century was, for Jews in the Russian Empire, a time of great turmoil and even greater suffering. Repeated failure to cleanse Imperial Russia of its Jewish population led to the 1791 creation of the *Chertá Osyédlosti*, the so-called 'Pale of Settlement' in the Western part of the Empire to which almost all Russian-Jewish residency was restricted until 1917. During this century-plus period of confinement, Russian Jews were subjected to a brutal and lengthy process of social and political engineering functioning as a thinly veiled endeavor to destroy it both spiritually and materially. A sequence of discriminatory measures, ostensibly intended to 'productivize' them, had the actual effect of herding them into overcrowded cities while at the same time restricting already limited opportunities for economic and educational advancement. The result: the Jewish population of the Pale was largely transformed into a lumpenproletariat mass residing in a constellation of urban centers. Economic oppression was complemented by religious persecution. Traditional structures of Jewish political and cultural autonomy were systematically dismantled. A program of compulsory 'enlightenment' was instituted, involving not only what amounted to a hostile government takeover of Jewish education and communal leadership but, by removing Jewish youth from their homes for a period of military service lasting from the age of twelve until nearly the age of forty, during which time they endured both physical abuse and religious coercion (Ofek 1993), also of the Jewish family; the chain of cultural transmission was deliberately interrupted. Impoverished, geographically displaced, and under cultural assault, Russian Jewry strained, and in many respects buckled, under the weight of what Simon Dubnow would call a century-long 'administrative pogrom (Dubnow 1918, 277).'

This policy of forced assimilation, or Russification, was not entirely one-sided. Cognizant of their numerical inferiority but convinced of their ideological superiority over the traditionalist camp, proponents of Haskalah deviated sharply from the prevailing norm and called upon the authorities to interfere in the internal affairs of the community and institute reforms in Jewish life. In the naive belief that Russian authorities sincerely wished to improve the Jewish condition in the spirit of enlightened humanistic values, *maskilim* like Max Lilienthal became unwitting allies and agents of a government seeking to leverage reform for other purposes (Etkes 2010); namely, to eliminate a class of people deemed parasitic on account of their distinct collective identity (Klier 2005, 2). Working in collaboration with an oppressive government (Aronson 1966, 145–146) to undermine 'the old way of life without providing a satisfactory new one (Meyer 1990, 25–26),' *maskilim* were deeply distrusted by the Jewish masses.

In the second half of the 1870s the shades began to fall. Officially cast as a fifth column supporting the Ottoman Empire during the Russo-Turkish war of 1877–78, Jews were subject to intense persecution (Neuburger 1996), which touched not only those who had resisted acculturation, but also enlightened proponents of Russification (Etkes 2010). Waves of astonishingly violent, and government sponsored, attacks on Jewish communities throughout the Pale followed, lasting through the turn of the twentieth century. These culminated with the 1903 Kishinev pogrom, in which Jewish civilians were literally hacked to pieces. The imperial government responded, not by holding perpetrators responsible, but by punishing the Jews for atrocities committed against them; already crippling restrictions were tightened, thus leading to the 'complete economic collapse of Russian Jewry (Dubnow 1920, 22).' A mass exodus of Russian Jews to Western Europe, Great Britain, the Americas, and Palestine ensued; it included many figures discussed in this book. Kishinev became a turning point in modern Jewish history (Penkower 2004), not only because it led to this exodus but, more importantly, because a shift change in Jewish attitudes already underway crystalized thereafter: realizing the impossibility of merging with a people that 'appeared in the shape of a monster (Dubnow 1918, 324),' former proponents of acculturation or assimilation experienced deep disillusionment and returned to the fold, laying the groundwork for modern Jewish nationalisms (Salmon 1991; Berk 1977).

This shift had enormous repercussions for what, to distinguish it from medieval Jewish quietism (Lederhendler 1989, 58–83), was later called 'the new Jewish politics (Polonsky 2003)' characterized by agency and active resistance. Some of these ways are considered below, but for the moment, let us briefly consider what this shift meant for the longstanding divide between defenders of tradition and champions of modernization. If earlier in the century, the Jewish masses were hostile to the Haskalah, its Jewish turn, albeit largely secular in character, was an opportunity for rapprochement — not least because, as Strauss put it, when 'Cultural Zionism understands itself, it turns into religious Zionism (Strauss 1996, 6).' The rise of Jewish nationalism created dialectical space in the public discourse of Eastern European Jewry for a synthesis of enlightenment and orthodoxy, thus permitting the emergence of an 'orthodox modernism (Danzinger 1966)'[1] according to which knowledge of Torah and knowledge about the world at large could exist in organic harmony.

Although efforts to represent R. Elijah, the Gaon, of Vilna and his students as proto-*maskilim* because they embraced a certain synthesis of secular and religious study may be exaggerated (Nadler 1999, 127–150), relations between *maskilim* and the sober, rational, *mitnagdim* (opponents of hasidism) were generally warmer than those between either and the more exuberant *hasidim* (Etkes 2010; Shuchat 1998) — excepting, to a certain degree, hasidism of the Habad school, which was distinguished from the ecstatic mainstream by its intellectualism (Biali 2017, 297) and was therefore better received by both factions (Wolfson 2015; Meir 2017). The aforementioned Ets Hayyim Yeshiva of Valozyn became an important center for the fusion of these intellectual trends. Founded by the Vilna Gaon's successor, it attracted the most gifted Habad youth (Friedman 1994) and during the last two decades of the nineteenth century became, unofficially and perhaps in spite of itself (Schachter 1990), an important center of post-Haskalah efforts to integrate worlds old and new.

While this process of integration included coming to terms with modern science along the lines promoted by men like Hayyim Selig Slonimski, whose views were embraced by Valozyn students and alumni (Shapiro 2017), it also (and for our purposes, more importantly) extended to history, Western philosophy, politics, and social theory. In practice, this involved the blend of proto-Zionism and Russian narodism, or populist socialism that characterized the Hibbat Zion movement, for which Valozyn served as a major center (Kloyzner 1959).

Emphasizing cultural renaissance through the process of building up the land of Israel (Reinharz 1993) — as the slogan went, they sought 'to build and to be rebuilt' — Hibbat Zion represented a union of Practical and Cultural Zionism, two trends that would separate in the later development of the Zionist movement (Conforti 2011a; Firestone 2012, 179–200). One of the most important ways that Hibbat Zion can be distinguished from Theodore Herzl's Political Zionism is that, formulated along these lines, its proponents generally did not conceive of national rebirth in statist terms (Shumsky 2018). In contrast to Herzl's vision of a *Judenstadt*, their program could be squared with an anarchistic worldview (Goldman 1989; Grauer 1994). Thus, while the intellectual atmosphere permeating the study halls of Valozyn produced figures like Abraham Isaac Kook, who would become the first Ashkenazi Chief Rabbi of British Mandatory Palestine and whose conceptions of ethnicity and power firmly tended toward statism and militarism (Garb 2004; Persico 2017), it also produced many of the figures discussed in this volume.

In part, Hibbat Zion owed its anarchist features to the historical circumstances from which it emerged. Eastern European *maskilim* who returned to the Jewish fold, abandoning hopes of solving the Jewish Question via assimilation or acculturation, did not simply drop everything; rather, like R. Meir, they brought back to their communities what they learned on the other side of the proverbial *tehum*. Russian populist socialism (*narodnichestvo*) together with its notion of *sobornost*, the spiritual unity and spontaneous order achieved within living communities expressed in the slogan 'going to the people (Pedler 1927),' was perhaps the most important of these influences. Post-Haskalah Jewish nationalists 'went to the people' via the Jewish people (Kiel 1970; Bar-Yosef 1996; Tsirkin-Sadan 2012). More so than among their secular counterparts, the religious nationalists at Valozyn understood this calling in the religious terms that it was originally conceived (Golovic 2020).

The thread that leads from the Russian narodniks to Eastern European Jewish nationalism, especially its religious variety as developed at Valozyn, is crucial for explaining its latent anarchistic tendencies. Russian anarchism had deep narodnik roots that it never thoroughly cut. Kropotkin, Bakunin, and Tolstoy, for instance, all operated within an anarcho-narodnik frame (Carnochan 1980; Gamblin 2000). Functioning as agents of cultural transmission, *maskilim* returning to the fold brought with them anarcho-narodnik ideas that subsequently became an inseparable part of Jewish nationalist discourse in Russia (Kiel 1970; Tsirkin-Sadan 2012). In contrast to the Political Zionists, who would later assert that Jewish liberation from violence condoned or sponsored by the gentile state is predicated on the establishment of a Jewish state, many members of Hibbat Zion held that it depends on the abolition of the state and the creation of a system of self-governing agrarian communes — *obshchina*, or the more familiar Hebrew term, *kibuzim* (Frankel 1984, 33).

Jewish attraction to anarcho-narodnik thought and practice had causes beyond the simple fact of cultural transmission. While many early anarchist thinkers like Proudhon and Bakunin were unabashedly antisemitic (Krier 2009, 179–233; Wolff 2013; Wolf and Mümken 2014), the ones who exerted the most influence over Jewish anarchism and anarcho-nationalism were decidedly less prejudiced. Kropotkin strongly resisted both claims to the effect that pogroms (whether 'administrative' or physical) were due to Jewish exploitation of the peasantry and that popular antisemitism was somehow reflective of revolutionary spirit (Kinna 2016a). In exile, he also worked closely with the Jewish labor movement in London (Rocker 1942), exerting enormous influence on the circle surrounding the aforementioned *Arbeter Fraynd*. Tolstoy, though sometimes ambivalent about Jews, ultimately issued several statements denouncing their oppression and celebrating their heritage (Schefski 1982; Medzhibovskaya 2013). The Christian-anarchist followers of Vladimir Solovyov, 'God-seekers' like Nikolai Berdayev, were extremely vocal in their denunciation of antisemitism and published extensively on matters Jewish (Berline 1947; Berdyaev, Spears and Kanter 1950; Solovyov 2016).

Proponents of anarcho-Judaism were drawn to anarcho-narodnik thought, not only because some of its champions were sympathetic to Jewish people, but also (and more importantly) for philosophical and theological reasons. For instance, God-seekers of the Solovyov circle were deeply indebted to the philosophy of F. W. J. Schelling (Vasilyev 2019). Its neoplatonic elements fit long-standing trends in the orthodox theology (Lossky 1976, 29; Louth 1989, 20–21; Vasilyev 2019). Its engagement with parallel kabbalistic notions attracted Jews (Franks 2019), attracted Russian Christians to Jewish thought (Kornblatt 1991; Burmistrov 2007a, b; Daigin 2008), and attracted in tandem Jewish thinkers to Russian Orthodox theology and philosophy (Slater 2016, 2019). The notion of *sobornost* which, as indicated above, played a central role both in anarcho-narodnik and proto-Zionist thought continued, for the Russian God-seekers, to bear *religious* meaning (Rosenthal 1977, 1993, 2006; Nalimov 2001). In this sense, champions of anarcho-Judaism who adapted this concept to Jewish theology and did not desacralize it stood much closer to the source than their secular counterparts.

In a more general sense, anarcho-narodism and other pre-Marxist utopian socialisms appealed to religiously inclined Jewish radicals because they represented an alternative to Marxist materialism. Eliahu Stern (2018) has convincingly argued against the supposition that materialism and secularism go hand in hand by showing that many rabbinic figures during the period in question built on fundamentally materialistic theoretical foundations. Nonetheless, religious Jewish anarchists who addressed the issue explicitly rejected materialism; even when integrating it into a broader historical dialectic, they maintained that it would ultimately give way to a spiritual renaissance underwritten by new ideals. Their objections were religious in form, but more often than not moral in character. Surely the question of Marx's and Marxism's attitude to morality has long been a subject of dispute, both outside of and within the Marxist camp; here is hardly the place to resolve that question. What matters is that the proponents of anarcho-Judaism considered here attributed to materialism in general, and Marxism in particular, an amoral orientation inimical (in their view) to the revolutionary cause. They believed that without faith, egalitarian visions were ultimately groundless. They rejected the notion that radical social and political change is a natural outcome of economic laws, maintaining instead that it depends on human agency as motivated by moral conviction. They held that denying this ultimately serves to undermine individual liberty and to justify tyranny. While narodism and utopian socialism were hardly synonymous with religious conviction, their underlying idealism left room for faith and, with it (in the eyes of religious Jewish anarchists) ethical consciousness.

Thus, we find that religious Jewish anarchism first took shape in a period during which state-sponsored violence against Russian Jewry reached a crescendo, dashing naive hopes of liberation through accommodation. The return of assimilationist *maskilim* to the Jewish fold made reconciliation between tradition and enlightenment possible; if not religious *per se* the latter was Judaized to a degree and therefore had something to offer the Jewish community. Among other things, they brought with them anarcho-narodnik notions that reached even major centers of rabbinic learning like Valozyn. These appealed not only because they originated in the minds of figures who demonstrated appreciation for Jews and Judaism, but more importantly because idealist-utopian features of anarchism and narodism left room for Judaism or Jewishness in the articulation of revolutionary spirit. In this sense, anarcho-Judaism arose together with, and in many respects overlapped with, the cultural and practical foundations of Eastern European Zionism before they were annexed to the political movement later organized in Western Europe.

The centrality of narodnism to post-Haskalah Jewish nationalism is crucial for understanding not only the anarchist turn made by figures considered in this volume, but also for understanding relations between their anarcho-Judaism and other, more familiar, ideologies that took shape and attracted adherents during the same period. Above all, it formed the basis for links with the Socialist Revolutionary Party that sprouted directly from the earlier narodnik movement (White 2010, 7–14) and in which Jews like Isaac Nahman Steinberg and his somewhat better-known friend Chaim Zhitlovsky, played key roles (Chernov 1948). As we shall later discuss, Steinberg's engagement with anarchism grew from his role as a leader in that movement (and also along with his diaspora nationalism).

While I have emphasized the link between narodnism and post-Haskalah Jewish nationalism as embodied in Hibbat Zion, it was not limited to that movement. Hibbat Zion was Palestine-centric and, at least as indicated by its major propaganda organs, journals like *ha-Magid*, *ha-Meylits*, and *ha-Levanon*, Hebraic in linguistic orientation. Given that the people resided far from the holy land and that Hebrew, only revived as a spoken language in the 1880s, was hardly their mother tongue, I would argue that, if narodnik in spirit, the movement was less so in form. 'Going to' the people instead meant, at least in certain respects, *bringing* them somewhere — both spiritually and geographically. Meshed as they were with the language and culture of European Jewry, such as it was, diaspora nationalism or autonomism, which emphasized the cultivation of 'spiritual nationhood' and promoted the self-rule of Jewish communities in the diaspora (Kochan 1977; Gechtman 2011), and territorialism, which upheld both of those goals but considered them to be conditioned on territorial autonomy (though not in the form of a state and not necessarily in Palestine), were more natural outgrowths of Russian folk populism. Indeed, the historian Simon Dubnow, a key figure in proliferating autonomism, was deeply influenced by narodniks like Nikolay Chernyshevsky, Pyotr Lavrov, and Mikhailovsky (Seltzer 2013). Non-Zionist proponents of anarcho-Judaism like Isaac Nahman Steinberg and Aaron Shmuel Tamaret both directly and indirectly appealed to Dubnow's theories; after the decline of the Socialist Revolutionary Party, the former assumed leadership over the Territorialist Movement in its incarnation as the Freeland League.

To a limited extent, narodnik-inspired autonomism also served as an ideological link between these threads of anarcho-Judaism and the idea of *doikayt*, or 'here-ness,' promoted by the General Jewish Labor Bund (Gechtman 2005) together with a degree of national–cultural autonomy. However, what they shared was largely overshadowed by their differences. For one, Bund members did not view their organization as a specifically Jewish movement, but 'sought to integrate the Jewish worker into the general Russian proletariat (Blatman 2010).' More fundamentally, the Bund was a social-democratic movement, and later a Marxist, movement. Strictly materialist in worldview (Pickhan 2009), members of our anarchist *minyan* would have regarded it not only as intrinsically antireligious (not without justification) but also (as indicated above) as lacking in moral foundation. So far as my research has uncovered, there was no direct cooperation between them. This is not to suggest, however, that *minyan* members were totally disengaged from the broader labor movement. Some, like Natan Hofshi, were committed to the idea that the Zionist labor movement should become part of a binational Jewish-Arab cooperative project. Others, like Isaac Nahman Steinberg, were directly involved in agitations that led up to the Russian Revolution, in the early post-Revolutionary coalition government, and later in efforts to organize non-Marxist radical parties in Central and Western Europe in hopes of restoring the revolution to its moral foundations (or what he took them to be). Still others, like Yaakov Meir Zalkind, worked with unionists to stage strikes and other demonstrations and contributed to or edited periodicals serving as hubs for labor organization efforts both theoretical and practical.

Autonomism may even serve as a theoretical link — albeit a historically weak one — between anarcho-Judaism, with its modernizing tendencies, and the developing political ideology of the ultra-orthodox. Ultra-orthodox communities, which largely rejected Zionism and secular Jewish nationalism (Rabkin 2006), strenuously resisted acculturation and developed an essentially diasporic model for internal self-governance, however authoritarian in character (Katz 1997; Brown 2014). Arguably, they upheld the principle of Jewish cultural autonomy within a broader political and economic setting while dismissing the notion that Jewish culture is or ever could be secular in nature. To a degree, this is the approach taken by some members of the anarchist minya, only that they both denied the value of extreme strictures held sacrosanct within ultra-orthodox communities and rejected their hierarchical structure.

In sum, I situate anarcho-Judaism as a historical trend that began during the last two decades of the nineteenth century. One among several responses to the oppression of Russian Jewry, it was made possible by the nationalization of the Haskalah, which transformed modernization into a Jewish project of liberation where once it had, to one degree or another, been assimilationist in character. This shift opened certain elements within the traditional camp to decidedly non-traditional intellectual influences. Among them, narodnik ideology, the idealism of which appealed to their religious and moral sensibilities. Anarcho-narodnik principles fed both the rise of Hibbat Zion, which differed from the Zionist movement that took shape in the West insofar as it emphasized cultural and practical efforts and shunned politics, as well as autonomist and territorialist forms of diaspora nationalism.

Theological context

While the 'habit of tracing an anarchist tendency' through premodern sources runs the risk of 'ahistoricism (Adams 2013)', failing to acknowledge the ways in which such sources inform modern movements runs the opposite risk; it would give the impression that anarchism arose *sui generis* and without precedent. Anti-authoritarian and egalitarian notions predated modern anarchism; if we grant that these constitute core anarchist principles, then anarchism can be treated as an idea that 'has always existed in humankind and so is not temporally bound by any particular historical movement (Jun 2013).' This is not to suggest that premodern iterations of these principles were 'anarchist' in a historical sense; they existed in their own intellectual milieus. Rather, it is to suggest that they resonate with modern iterations of similar principles so that devotees of the latter draw inspiration from them or claim them as their own. That is, I regard anachronism as problematic only when it is blind: when modern ideas are *ascribed to* premodern people and texts rather than being *informed by* them. It is in this spirit that I trace what I take to be the historical theological underpinnings of anarcho-Judaism. A thorough survey of the relevant material along the lines attempted by Shapira (2015) lies far beyond the scope of the present volume. Instead it considers four primary themes: the idea of the messianic abrogation of the law; anti-authoritarian and especially anti-monarchist traditions; the imperative to neighborly love; and the prophetic vision of social justice and its messianic culmination.

The messianic abrogation of the law

Among the more pervasive theological themes in historical disputes between Judaism and Christianity concerns the role of the law. As the latter diverged from its roots, faith in justification by 'works of the law (Galatians 2:16)' ultimately disappeared and a perceived dichotomy between Christian grace and Jewish legalism appeared that, among Christians, has only recently been challenged (Klein 1978; Sanders 1983). In point of fact, however, questions as to relations between letter and spirit occupied Jewish sages from antiquity onward and persist until today.[2]

Classical rabbinic law is aptly described as flexibly nomian (Hayes 2017). That is, tactics for indefinitely suspending or even abrogating laws that cannot or should not be practiced are built into the legal system. Here, however, we are concerned with theological tendencies that break with the system entirely, either by anticipating the advent of a new law (neonomian),[3] or the complete abrogation of law (antinomian) — both being bound up in apocalyptic messianic speculation.

Neonomian themes often appear in midrashic literature. Several sources indicate that the messiah will abolish some,[4] or even all, of the Torah's prohibitions. A pun on Psalms 146:7 'the Lord sets prisoners free (*matir asurim*),' for instance, produces the striking contention that he will permit (*matir*) the prohibitions (*isurim*) in days to come (Scholem 1995a, 78–141). In this formulation positive duties remain intact but are not enforced and nothing is forbidden — there is a sort of law, but a new one. Such notions ground medieval disputes concerning the mutability of the Torah,[5] but truly flower in kabbalistic literature. The books *Sefer ha-Peliyah* and *Sefer ha-Kanah* (fourteenth century) attributed to the mishnaic sage R. Nehunyah ben ha-Kanah, for instance, anticipate the abrogation of many rules (Fishman 1992), but not of the law as such and not for everyone; only the elite are above the law.[6] This distinction was ultimately obliterated by the Sabbateans, who transformed *matir asurim* into a true *modus vivendi* (Scholem 1995a; Michaelson 2017). Yet in the end, it was a *modus vivendi* with its own structures of obligation and authority.

Truly antinomian visions are rarer, but I contend that they too existed. In the talmud there is a discussion of the authorized use of otherwise prohibited fabrics (*sh'atnez*) for burial shrouds. Punning 'abandoned (*hofshi*) among the dead (Psalms 88:6),' R. Yohanon contends that death liberates — makes 'free (*hofshi*)' — from the law such that *shatnez* garments will be permitted to those resurrected in the end of days. In this hypothetical scenario, the law as a whole is *suspended*; operative in principle, it is neutralized by the fact that in the era of resurrection it applies to nobody. In contrast, R. Yosef holds that '*this*' — the *shatnez* dispensation itself — 'means that the law will be *abolished* in days to come.' In other words, it is *not* that death and resurrection eliminate the community to which an otherwise operative system of law applies, but that *law itself is eliminated*; he intends its abrogation and not merely its suspension (Niddah 61b).

As with neonomianism, antinomian sentiments ripen within the kabbalistic tradition. One example can be found in the book *ha-Temunah* (fourteenth century, also attributed to R. Nehunyah ben ha-Kanah), which speaks of a series of cosmic cycles, or *shemitot* (Scholem 1995b, 178), each of which corresponds to a unique revelation of the Torah. In the present *shemitah*, the letters of the Torah are 'bonded together' into composites (Temunah 3:5) — that is, words conveying law. In *shemittot* to come, however, these bonds will dissolve and unite humanity with God directly (Temunah 3:21), being read as musical sounds and not practical instructions (Temunah 3:22). Likewise, the *Raya Mehemna* (an appendix to the Zohar) promises that the final *shemitah* constitutes a cosmic jubilee in which the distinction between prohibition and permission — and, therefore, law itself — disappears.[7] A more modern articulation of this same line of thought appears, finally, in Haskalah literature; most notably in the writings of Mordechai Schnaber-Levison (Pelli 1970; Ruderman 1997; Jutte 2015, 248–249; Schick 2017), who argued that intentionality, the rational love of God, supersedes practical adherence to the law.[8] During the messianic era 'the land shall be filled with devotion to the Lord as water covers the sea (Isaiah 11:9);' that, he argued, is the ultimate reason for the anticipated abrogation of the law (Schnaber 1784, 9b).

Thus, between 'flexibly nomian' and radical antinomian traditions, we observe a train of thought extending from antiquity through the modern period. Though authors considered in this book did not draw on *all* of these sources, they did appeal to an ongoing discussion as to the ultimate status of the law in formulating their modern anarchist theologies. They would, in this sense, be following Kropotkin's lead when he points, for instance, to Hans Denk who emphasized the intuited word of God over the letter of scripture.

The imperative to neighborly love

The imperative to neighborly care, the command to 'love your fellow as yourself (Leviticus 19:18),' functions as another important theme to which Jewish religious anarchists appealed. In talmudic literature, we find two variations of the same fundamental claim. R. Akiva called it the 'great general rule *of* the Torah (J. Nedarim 30b),' while Hillel the Elder paraphrased it as 'that which is hateful to you do not do to another; that is the *entire* Torah (Shabbat 31a).' Here, we discern a fine distinction. For R. Akiva, the principle is 'of the Torah;' this implies that the Torah circumscribes it. Moreover, it suggests that the imperative to love extends only to the people of the Torah.[9] For Hillel, however, it is the *whole* Torah; the Torah is circumscribed by it (Schneerson 1994). Accordingly, it extends to all humankind.[10]

Elsewhere, the embeddedness of the Torah in the imperative to love the neighbor is coupled with the love due God. R. Simlai taught *both* that 'its beginning is an act of kindness and its end is an act of kindness (Sotah 14a)' *and* that 'Amos came and established the 613 mitzvot upon one, as it is stated: "So says the Lord to the house of Israel: seek me and live" (Amos 5:4; Makkot 24a).' The Torah is contained within works of love toward others and stands on the love of God; for R. Simlai, the two function as synonyms.

Later, this synthetic conception of universal love came to constitute the core of the Christian teaching. In the book of Matthew Jesus teaches that 'the greatest commandment in the law' is a composite of imperatives to love God and the neighbor, which includes the stranger, the wrongdoer, and even the enemy (Matthew 5:43–45). Like R. Simlai, he contends that 'on these two commandments depend all the law and the prophets (Matthew 22:40).'

Here is not the place to exhaustively examine this synthesis as it developed either in Judaism, or in Christianity. However, that it poses a profound challenge to the normative law is evident. If neighborly love and the love of God circumscribe the Torah, then there is room at least to bracket the Torah in favor of that which it serves. Indeed, that is the basic thrust of Pauline Christianity. For our purposes, we set that consideration aside; this dimension of the principle is not made explicit in rabbinic literature and, furthermore, neo/antinomian tendencies in rabbinic literature have already been addressed. Rather, we skip ahead nearly two millennia to discuss briefly how Tolstoy received these teachings.

For Tolstoy, neighborly love as rooted in and derived from love of God includes the enemy and implies an ethic of non-violence. This led him to a robust critique of statism, militarism, and patriotism. To begin with, the exercise of authority means forcing others to act contrary to their will; this itself violates the imperative to non-violence. Moreover, even granting that it is exercised in good faith and that private violence is suppressed in service of the common good, maintaining a sovereign monopoly on violence itself demands violence, *new forms of violence* arising from the interests of the sovereign itself. Furthermore, the 'common good' is always partial, tied as it is to a definite and typically unequal regime of property relations that was itself established through violence. The minority attempts to secure its advantage through militarization: by enhancing its capacity to control the disadvantaged majority. Though motivated by *internal* tensions, this provokes neighboring countries and sets in motion a vicious cycle of military escalation. This, in turn, serves to manufacture consent within each society; external threats deflect attention from the true enemy and also evoke patriotic sentiments. Ultimately, so Tolstoy argues, the only way to destroy this system is to undermine its foundation: to refuse violence in any form through passive resistance and thus instigate a revolution of the heart.[11]

This train of thought exerted a profound influence on many of the figures studied in this book. Through Tolstoy's theological writings, the hermeneutic loop closes: the doctrine of radically loving the neighbor passes from the rabbis through Christian teaching, and then back to the Jewish religious imagination. For them, as for Tolstoy, this love implied an absolute commitment to non-violence that carried with it not only an opposition to militarism, but to statism and patriotism. It likewise implied for many the moral necessity of economic justice, leading to a Jewish articulation of the sort of religious agrarian socialism that Tolstoy's anarchism carries with it.

Anti-monarchist prophetism

The nature of sovereignty and the legitimacy of its exercise is a topic that concerned biblical authors from the first chapter of Genesis forward. On the one hand, humankind is granted dominion over the natural world. On the other hand, human caprice is limited by God's command; it is bidden to abstain from the tree of knowledge. While yet they heeded God's word, man and woman were 'one flesh' — undifferentiated and so necessarily equal. Neglecting it and thus rebelling against the divine sovereign, one came to rule over the other. Regarded from this vantage, the Torah announces at the outset a clear political message: so long as God reigns, human authority extends to things but not people; when God's regime is overthrown, inequality of power sets in and injustice prevails.

Arguably, the remainder of Genesis and the majority of the book of Exodus constitute a commentary on this single theme. God favors Abel's pastoralism over Cain's agriculture and the urban civilizations it fed, civilizations represented by Babel, which God destroys. God chooses Abraham and his family, who wander. Reciprocally, Abraham invokes God's name and refuses sovereignty when it is offered to him by the Sodomites after the war of the five kings, and by the Hittites after Sarah's death.[12] The family's woes begin when their wandering comes to an end in Goshen and they assimilate into a civilized nation led by a tyrant who enslaves them. The subsequent exodus is in essence a story about rebuke and restoration. God rebukes Pharaoh and the way of life he represents, destroying the 'idols of Egypt' and, in a desolate land where such political idols cannot grow, reinstates himself as the rightful King of Israel.

This is not to say that the text of the Torah is univocal where the question of human versus divine sovereignty is concerned. Indeed, the tension between these opposing sources of authority lies at the center of the dispute between Moses and Korah. Against Moses, who is called 'a king in Jeshurun (Deuteronomy 33:5),' Korah contends that 'all the community are holy, all of them, and the Lord is in their midst;' thus he demands 'why then do you raise yourselves above the Lord's congregation? (Numbers 16:3).' While the exact meaning of Moses' vindication and Korah's downfall is subject to interpretation, it at least suggests that the monarchy is not held in utter contempt.

This tension is most evidently in play between two crucial biblical texts dealing with laws pertaining to the king; namely Deuteronomy 17:14–15, where 'set as king over yourself one of your own people' appears as an imperative, and the eighth chapter of I Samuel, in which the Israelites implore their prophet to do just that and are rebuked for it; says God, 'they have rejected Me from reigning over them (I Samuel 8:7; Lorberbaum 2011).' These apparently conflicting messages are confronted in several rabbinic texts recording a dispute between R. Yehudah and R. Nehorai. R. Yehudah claims that the deuteronomic passage communicates a positive obligation to establish the monarchy, while I Samuel communicates an objection to Israelite *motivations* for doing so: not to fulfill the divine will, but to be 'like all the other nations (I Samuel 8:5).' In contrast, R. Nehorai contends that the deuteronomic passage communicates a qualified *option* — if a king is appointed, *then* he must be 'one of your own people' — while God's *opinion* on it is communicated in I Samuel (Sanhedrin 20b).

As other midrashim make clear, this dispute is not merely about monarchy as opposed to other forms of political sovereignty. Rather, it is about divine sovereignty in relation to human sovereignty *as such*. Enumerating the sins of even the best kings, the hermeneut concludes by quoting Isaiah 33:22, 'the Lord shall be our ruler, the Lord shall be our prince, The Lord shall be our king,' and envisions a messianic reversal of the demand issued in I Samuel (DR 5:11).

While a thorough review either of the rabbinic or of later medieval treatments of this dispute lies far beyond the scope of the present introduction, the classical proponents of each side may be noted. Representing (and in many respects establishing) the majority opinion, Moses Maimonides sided with R. Yehudah.[13] In contrast, the Renaissance philosopher and exegete Isaac Abravanel sided with R. Nehorai. Maimonides relies on the midrash already cited in support of this position. Abravanel, however, elaborates at length in his commentary on *both* biblical passages.

On Abravanel's reading, not only is the monarchy optional, but it is analogous to that of the infamous rule of the 'beautiful woman,' whom a soldier *may* take captive (Deuteronomy 21:10–14) but will, in doing so, be considered utterly despicable. He then proceeds to inquire whether societies need kings and, if so, whether that same necessity applies to Jews. Kings, he says, serve several functions, all of which can be fulfilled through other political structures — the Italian republics of his day being a case in point. On the basis of this reference, many scholars regard Abravanel as a *republican* thinker (Kimelman 1995). In doing so, however, they disregard his claim that for the Jews *God fulfills these functions through his Torah* — which means that, at least for them, human authority is rejected.

That Abravanel was ultimately hostile, not to the institution of the monarchy alone, but to centralized authority in general, we infer further from his commentaries on the stories of the Tree of Knowledge, the Tower of Babel, and the promised messiah. For Abravanel, the Tree of Knowledge represents the practical reason[14] that humanity, unsatisfied by the natural bounty God provided, used to manufacture artificial goods for himself.[15] The same error, he attributes to the builders of the Tower of Babel. It led them to devote:

> All their attention to innovating the skills required for building a city with a tower in it, so as to gather together therein and render themselves civilised (*medinim*) ... They strove only to found states (*kibbuts medinot*) ... believing this to be the highest human achievement while ignoring all that follows from it: titles, appointments, dominion, imaginary honors, the pleasure of accumulating property, violence, theft, and bloodshed.

Here, Abravanel expresses what could be described as an anarcho-primitivist viewpoint. The rise of the state is associated with a capriciousness that destroys natural human solidarity and also the human bond with God. Indeed, *that* is the meaning he ascribes to the dispersion: they 'withdrew from brotherhood' in order each 'to own things for himself' and likewise 'they migrated from the east (*mi'kedem*) (Genesis 11:2),' parting from 'the One who preceded the world (*Kadmono shel Olam*) (GR 38, 7).'[16] Here, there is no mention of kings, just statecraft. Yet, Abravanel's hostility is equally if not more palpable.

Accordingly, he goes so far as to reject the doctrine of the anointed 'king messiah (*Yeshu'ot Meshiho*, II.3).' In the end of days, he says *no one* shall 'serve any prince, king, or ruler; only God.'[17] Rather, 'everyone will be as equal as they were at the beginning of creation, in the generation of Adam;' then, 'the Lord will be king over the earth' and serve as its sole judge.[18] Presumably, by absolute language like 'no one' and 'everyone,' he means also to include gentiles. Thus, we find that Abravanel's vision is not republican, but positively anti-authoritarian, serving as an alternative to the Maimonidean norm that sided with R. Yehudah in interpreting the laws of the king, it later served as a primary resource for anarchistically inclined Jewish theologians wishing to side with R. Nehorai instead. Like Kropotkin, who began as a prince and became an anarchist, Abravanel may have filled the role of a 'Jewish aristocrat,' but his heart was filled with 'the deepest Jewish anarchism (Bick 1940, 74).'

Abravanel represents, for pre-modern Jewish thought, the epitome of the anti-authoritarianism that moved Jotham to tell the parable of 'the trees went forth to anoint a king' and, finding none that would agree, turned finally to the thornbush that said 'if you are acting honorably in anointing me king over you, come and take shelter in my shade; but if not, may fire issue from the thornbush and consume the cedars of Lebanon (Judges 9:15).' Like Jotham, he understood sovereignty as a threat.

Messianism and the prophetic voice of justice

A final positive influence on the thought of religious Jewish anarchists was the prophetic tradition and its messianic vision of ultimate justice. In this, they differed not greatly from religious socialists — indeed several, either directly or otherwise, give evidence of having been exposed to the ethical and religious reflections of philosophers like Hermann Cohen, who devoted his later years to articulating a Hebraic Kantian-socialism. Given that the individualist anarchism of men like Max Stirner was universally rejected by members of the group that concerns us, however, this should come as no surprise; as I noted earlier, their anarchism was very much a libertarian socialism. Thus, while they would clearly reject Cohen's idealized statism, his socialist reading of messianic prophetism was welcome.

Like Cohen, many operated on the supposition that Jewish monotheism
is *ethical* monotheism; they conceive of God not as an abstract ideal, but
as the concrete source of the justice pronounced by his prophets — a call
to justice that itself *constituted* prophetic religion. As Micha put it, 'what
is good, and what [does] the Lord requires of you: only to do justice and
to love goodness, and to walk modestly with your God (Micha 6:8).' On
Cohen's paraphrase: 'the politics of the prophets are nothing but what we
today call socialism. Their faith is to have justice done to the poor, and
their religion is morality (Schwarzschild 1956).' For them, messianism
represented a final abolition of social sin and the ultimate realization of
true faith in God: achievement of the ethical ideal.

Among the prophets, Amos and Isaiah impressed most deeply; Amos
both for his social origins and for his vicious critique of the ruling class,
Isaiah for his messianic vision. Amos was neither a prophet nor a 'prophet's
disciple' but 'cattle breeder and a tender of sycamore figs,' a peasant revolutionary from a village south of Bethlehem whom God 'took from following
the flock' and sent to denounce rampant violence and inequality (Amos
7:14–15). 'Ah, you who are at ease in Zion and confident on the hill of
Samaria (Amos 6:1)' he cries, woe to the fattened 'cows of Bashan (Amos
4:1)' who 'lie on ivory beds, lolling on their couches (Amos 6:4)' while
dining on 'the needy, annihilating the poor of the land (Amos 8:4),' trading
the one 'for silver' and the other 'for a pair of sandals (Amos 8:6).' The
Lord has sworn, he warns, 'never [to] forget any of their doings (Amos
8:7)' but to demolish 'ivory palaces' and 'great houses (Amos 3:15),' to
hasten the day when their owners are 'carried off in baskets (Amos 4:2).'
Thus, he advises: 'hate evil and love good, and establish justice in the gate;
perhaps the Lord, the God of Hosts, will be gracious (Amos 5:15).' Here,
the prophetic message is revolutionary upheaval: destruction of the prevailing
order, the reign of injustice.

Isaiah shares Amos' outrage and also his conviction that the substance of
God's word is justice. Through him, therefore, God rages: 'what need have
I of all your sacrifices?' Bring no more vain offerings, for your 'incense is
offensive to Me (Isaiah 1:11–13).' Instead, 'cease to do evil' and 'devote
yourselves to justice; aid the wronged. Uphold the rights of the orphan;
defend the cause of the widow (Isaiah 1:16–17).' Unlike Amos, however,
the prospect of restoration and revival is more than a 'perhaps,' a faint
possibility. Through him, God promises that while 'man's haughtiness shall
be humbled (Isaiah 2:17)' the prideful wolf will ultimately 'dwell with the
lamb (Isaiah 11:6).' A vision of peace and reconciliation prevails: 'nothing
evil or vile shall be done, for the land shall be filled with devotion to
the Lord as water covers the sea (Isaiah 11:9).' For the same reason will
all nations 'beat their swords into plowshares (Isaiah 2:4).' Then, alone

the 'Lord shall be Exalted (Isaiah 2:17)' — the proverbial kingdom of heaven is restored; 'peace, and justice' will serve as 'your officials' and the sound of violence 'shall no more be heard (Isaiah 60:17–18).' In Isaiah, therefore, Jewish radicals with religious inclinations — anarchists and also socialists — discovered a conception of Judaism wherein justice takes center stage. While this involves a revolutionary reversal of fortunes in which the mighty are humbled and the weak made strong, it ultimately becomes a vision of equality, harmony, and peace in which God alone reigns over mankind.

As indicated earlier, Jewish religious anarchists were invariably philosophical idealists. For them, libertarian socialism was above all a *moral calling*. For some, this implied a revolution of the heart in lieu of *any* violent means. For all, it meant rejecting socialist, especially Marxist, materialism. As they understood it, once progress is reduced to a historical dialectic of which moral ideas are but epiphenomena, a dangerously irresponsible fatalism sets in. Then, not only is concrete agency neglected so that excesses of violence become inevitable, but an obedient attitude toward external authority is cultivated. When the proverbial 'thin still voice (I Kings 19:12)' of moral insight is silenced, the difference between natural necessity and party interests becomes blurred. These convictions also arose from prophetic literature, with its emphasis on rebuke and penitence on the one hand, and reliance on God over men on the other.

For instance, Joel instructs the people to 'rend your hearts rather than your garments, and turn back to the Lord your God (Joel 2:13),' promising that whoever 'invokes the name of the Lord' will achieve salvation (Joel 3:5). Indeed, Ezekiel promises in God's name 'I will remove the heart of stone from your body and give you a heart of flesh.' Then, they will 'follow my laws and faithfully to observe my rules (Ezekiel 36:26–27).' Justice ultimately comes through a change of heart of which *all* men are capable. 'Is it my desire that a wicked person shall die?' Ezekiel has God ask. No, he answers, let the wicked one 'turn back from his ways and live (Ezekiel 18:23).' Thus if some trust in 'chariots' and 'horses,' the prophets instructed their followers instead to 'call on the name of the Lord our God (Psalms 20:8)' because it is this inward change that produces a lasting revolution: 'not by might, nor by power, but by my spirit (Zechariah 4:6).'

Proponents of anarcho-Judaism understood that in essence Jewish religion is about 'the law' broadly construed. That is, the imperative concretely to realize justice. Thus, they drew on sources like Amos' rage to express their own, and drew inspiration from Isaiah's faith in the messianic restoration of justice and social harmony. The prophetic voice, as they understood it, called for a revolution of the heart, through penitence, through the divine spirit — not because human agency was submitted to God, but because they saw in the idea of God one's ability to assume responsibility for *changing himself* and, in doing so, to change the world.

In sum, the claim made here is *not* that theological concepts tracing back to antiquity and developed over the course of two millennia were expressions of anarchism before the fact. I contend instead that each generation interprets the ideas it receives in keeping with its own distinct character. Recurrent anti-authoritarian and egalitarian themes — antinomian or neonomian ideas, anti-monarchist traditions, the imperative to neighborly love, and the prophetic-messianic vision of justice — were not expressions of any latent anarchist ethos. Rather, they assumed that sense in an intellectual milieu suffused with populism, utopian socialism, and anarchism.

Notes

1 See also Leigh (2013). Regarding the issue of the bifurcation of the Torah and secular knowledge in Modern Orthodoxy, see Brill (2004).
2 See, for instance, midrashic interpretations of 'you shall be holy, for I the Lord your God am holy (Leviticus 19:2)' — the Midrash Tanhuma contends that this verse contains the whole Torah; the Sifra understands by sanctity (*perishut*), i.e. piety beyond the letter of the law. See Gudemann (1892).
3 This notion was first conceived by Edward Fisher (1828, 5–6, 158, 326) and recently applied to Jewish sources by Shaul Magid (2004, 210–211).
4 Leviticus Rabbah 9:7; Midrash Tanchuma Emor 14; TB Kiddushin 72b.
5 Maimonides unequivocally rejected the notion (Laws of Kings 11:3). Joseph Albo relegated the immutability of the Torah to the status of a doctrinal 'branch' the denial of which is sinful but not heretical (Ikkarim 1:15). Isaac Abravanel conceded the possibility of moderate reform but believed this to arise from the immutable law itself (Rosh Amana 13). David Kimhi conceived of true innovation (Commentary to Ezekiel 46:4). In the early-modern era, R. Jacob Emden vehemently rejected Maimonides' view (Shapiro 2011, 125).
6 See *Sefer ha-Kanah* 93, where (in the context of a discussion concerning who is permitted to eat meat) it is stated that 'to the masters of the mishnah and the teaching [of talmud] meat is given to eat since they are the form and image of God and [thus] negate all God's decrees, for they are [like God] sovereign over every ruler.' This distinction between the elite and the masses appears also in Izbica-Radzin hasidic thought as documented by Magid (2004, 216).
7 See *Raya Mehemna* on Parashat *Naso*.
8 His position here constitutes a minority view (Berachot 13b; Pesahim 114b; Rosh Hashanah 28b). There are, however, instances in which it determines the norm; e.g. when the observance of a positive command would interfere with the study of Torah (Menahot 110a; Megillah 31b). It is also suggested that God values even unrealized good intentions (B Kiddushin 40a) and well-intentioned misdeeds (B Nazir 23b).

9 For Maimonides, this implied not only that the imperative to love applies only to Jews (*Sefer ha-Mizwot. Mitzwot Asei*, 206; cf. *Mishneh Torah. Hilkhot De'ot*, 6:2), but specifically to Torah-observant Jews (*Mishneh Torah. Hilkhot Evel* 14:1; cf. *Avot d'Rabi Nathan*, 16.5).

10 See Sifra on Leviticus 19:34: 'just as Israel was told 'and you shall love your fellow as yourself,' so too is it said concerning the stranger 'you shall love him as yourself (Leviticus 19:34).' See also Ben Azzai's reply to R. Akiva's dictum: '"this is the book of the generations of Adam" (Genesis 5:1) — this is the great general rule of the Torah (J. *Nedarim* 30b).' Presumably, Ben Azzai was not shifting from neighborly love to some other topic, but indicating that it applies to mankind as a whole because all children of Adam are kinsmen.

11 There is a fairly extensive literature on Tolstoy's political theology. The most prominent contemporary scholar working on the subject is Alexandre Christoyannopulos. See, for instance, Christoyannopoulos (2008).

12 See Midrash Rabbah on the portions of Lekh Lekha and Hayeh Sarah.

13 *Sefer ha-Mizwot. Mitzwot Asei.* 173; *Mishneh Torah. Hilkhot Melakhim* 1:1. See also the commentaries of Rashi and Ralbag on 1 Samuel 8:6; and the commentaries of Sforno, Ramban, Ohr ha-Hayyim, and Kli Yakar on Deuteronomy 17:14–15.

14 See his commentary on Genesis 2:9–17.

15 See his commentary on Genesis 11:1–9.

16 See his commentary on Genesis 11:1–9.

17 See his commentary on Isaiah 2:17.

18 See his commentary on introduction to the book of Isaiah: *Behina 5, Shoresh* 12.

The activists

3

Yaakov Meir Zalkind (1875–1938)

DR. J. M. SALKIND,
New Minister of the Cardiff Jewish
Synagogue.

1 Rabbi Yaakov Meir Zalkind in 1907, photographed upon assuming a pulpit
in Cardiff.

[There are many individuals who hold several radical divergent views all at once, but] in all such examples, we are able to locate the central point of that person's thought in which its roots burrow and from which its fundamental stem grows ... [His thought] had no such point. Rather, it had many centers at once ... He was a man of contradictions who breached every boundary ... or so it appeared to us; he himself saw no contradiction at all. For him, everything grew from a single stalk ... He passed not from camp to camp, from Zionism to Socialism and Anarchism, from Hebraism to Yiddishism, from faith to heresy, from piety to libertinism ... rather, he inhabited all these camps at once, he thought every thought at once, entertained every belief at once, inhaled every atmosphere in a single breath and perceived no inconsistency in it. (Kleinman 1938)

The man referred to is Rabbi Yaakov Meir Zalkind (1875–1938), whose journey across Europe and ultimately to Palestine passed through all the major ideological trends of his day — trends which, for him, were not sequentially absorbed and then eliminated, but subject to a bewildering and fascinating process of gradual accretion. Blurring the 'binary of religious conservatism versus leftist atheism (Torres 2019),' he proved that one *can* be 'a rabbi and an Anarchist (Berti 2010)' and also a communist and a Zionist, a Hebraist and a Yiddishist, a scholar, a journalist, an educator, and an artist; one can do and be all of these things, think each of these thoughts all at once. It is Zalkind's consistent refusal of apparent consistency that makes him so intriguing. It is not the case, however, that Zalkind's thought lacked a unifying measure. This chapter highlights it by briefly tracing his ideological development through World War I and then elaborating in greater detail on his reflections on anarchism and Jewishness as he articulated them during the early 1920s.

Zalkind's early life through the end of his Zionist period (1875–1914)

Born in the White Russian city of Kobryn, Yaakov Meir Zalkind entered the world with a pedigree that included such luminaries as the famed Baal Shem Tov, Tzvi Hirsch Ashkenazi (the Hakham Tzvi, a talmudist whose scholarship is still revered), and R. Shlomo Yitshaki's (Rashi), the classical eleventh-century exegete. Widely recognized as an *ilui* (talmudic genius), he left home in 1890 to continue his studies at the Ets Hayyim Yeshiva of Valozyn, Belarus.[1] As noted earlier, Valozyn was a center for orthodox modernism and for the religious faction of the Hibbat Zion movement. Both aspects of the place gave direction to Zalkind's path in life — openness to modernity led him west to pursue a secular education, while exposure to Hibbat Zion profoundly shaped his ideological outlook.

Students at Valozyn, Zalkind included, were deeply influenced by the work of Asher Zvi-Hirsch Ginsberg, Ahad Ha'am, a major intellectual force within Hibbat Zion, according to whom the goal was national-cultural revival, not politics. Mediating between the division of so-called 'ethnic' and 'civic' nationalisms — the former legitimated by common ancestry, culture, and land, the latter by the will of a (potentially) diverse population as embodied in a shared constitution (Kohn 1946, 330–331; Meinecke 2015, 10) — he represented the fullness of human life in ethnic terms, while at the same time identifying 'Jewish spirit' with the grand moral vision of the prophets, who taught Israel to 'respect only spiritual power' and 'not to seek glory in the attainment of material power and political dominion (Kohn 1951).' In Fichtean fashion (Kohn 1949b), he defined Jewish national particularism in universal terms and rejected Zionist aspirations toward 'normalization,' insisting that the Jews not 'become like other peoples' but serve as a beacon illuminating a higher mode of life. Thus, in contrast to Western European Zionists, who sought to erect a Jewish state (Shumsky 2018), Ahad Ha'am and other key figures in Hibbat Zion aspired to create a 'spiritual center' that would serve as 'a refuge not for all Jews who need peace and bread but for the spirit of the people (Kohn 1951).' In this way, they responded more to internal *questions of Jewishness* than the external *Jewish Question*. The potentially anarchistic resonances of this goal, which were not lost on more familiar anarcho-Zionists like Martin Buber (Silberstein 1990, 79) and Gershom Scholem (Jacobson 2003), would later play a crucial role in Zalkind's anarchist turn.

Following Valozyn's 1892 closure, Zalkind joined the westward migration of Russian-Jewish youth then underway (Wertheimer 1987, 63–71), eventually matriculating at the University of Bern, where he joined the department of philosophy and ultimately completed a dissertation on the Song of Songs. His role as a Zionist activist on campus, however, is more important for our purposes. Bern served as a major recruiting ground for many ideological movements (Mase 2012) and, therefore, as an epicenter for the 'new Jewish politics' then taking shape. As the founder of two campus organizations for Jewish students, Zalkind was very much a part of this process. One of these, formed after the Kishinev pogrom, aimed to ready Russian-Jewish students to form communal self-defence units upon returning home. This serves to foreshadow later developments in Zalkind's ideological evolution, but for the present we attend to his overall goals: to inspire his fellow students with 'the Zionist idea,' to prepare them for 'collective and idealistic life,' and thus to transform each into 'a healthy and perfect limb of the national body of Israel (Anonymous 1901).'

By unpacking this remark, we gain insight both into his frame of mind at this time and also an additional clue as to the ideological underpinnings of his later anarchist turn. It draws on Ficht's notion of the 'national' or 'corporate' body, its instantiation in limbs or cells, and its health as represented by their soundness and unity (Turnbull 1923), or its illness as represented by their disunity (Fichte 2008, 46). This thread of Fichtean influence reached Zalkind from two sources. First, through Ahad Ha'am (1922, 8, 123, 180), who spoke of the 'scattered limbs of the national body' and of the pressing need to revive its cultural anemia by reuniting them in spirit. Second, through Max Nordau, whose writings exerted tremendous influence on him (Hermoni 1948). The latter source demands further elaboration.

Fichte implied that his corporate metaphor is reflexive, such that physical and national-cultural health go hand in hand (Fichte 2008, 127–128). This notion moved Friedrich L. Jahn to found the *Turnbewegung*, which sought to cultivate a virile and 'soldierly' national body (Kohn 1949a) by German nationalism with gymnastics (Hollerbach 2006). Nordau — who was called the 'Hebrew Jahn (Nordau 1913)' — founded the Bar Kokhba Association with the same goal in mind: to recondition the 'degenerate' Jewish body (Nordau 1909, 379–380)[2] and rehabilitate the Jewish national character (Nordau 1909, 93–111), transforming Jewish 'Helots' into 'Jewish Spartans (Nordau 1909, 376–377; Presner 2003),' thus producing 'a bellicose, militant Jewry (Mendes-Flohr, Mali, and Reinharz 1995, 547).' In brief, Nordau (among others) anticipated the radical transformation of Jewish modes of being: the creation of the so-called 'new Jew (Conforti 2011a; Firestone 2012, 179–200).' This element of Nordau's thought then took precedence for Zalkind; indeed, his organizations were described as 'junkerish (Mokdoni 2019)' right-wing fraternities (Mase 2012).

However, there is another side to Nordau's work, which is quite important for understanding Zalkind's later ideological evolution. While Nordau is often described as a classical liberal (Baldwin 1980; Mosse 1992), he had — for good reason — an influence in certain anarchist circles (Stanislawski 2001, 19–35; De Oca 2019, 47–48). The primary difference between anarchists and liberals is that the latter believe the state exists to protect most freedoms by restricting some, while the former adopt the Hobbesian view that it exists mainly to perpetuate itself and is therefore antithetical to freedom (Buchan 2018). With *modern warfare* as his central counterpoint, Nordau contended that 'civilized' people are both less free *and* less secure than 'savages (Nordau 1887, 146–192).' Thus, he rejected the liberal exchange and described the modern state as a sort of parasite (Nordau 1922, 144–184). In the belief that the state is dominated by hegemonic forces that monopolize moral and cultural agency at the expense of the average citizen, he also saw it as an 'annihilator of character (Nordau 1896, 330–343; 1922, 157),' contending that representative government merely veils this dynamic (Nordau 1887, 146–192). Thus, we find that even as Zalkind embarked on his career as a Zionist activist, pacifist and anti-authoritarian threads tracing back to Ahad Ha'am and Max Nordau were woven into the very fabric of his way of thinking. For this reason, it is less surprising to discover that as an anarcho-pacifist, he could still speak of the latter as 'one of ours' and a 'chain breaker (Zalkind 1923a).'

After defending his dissertation in 1903, Zalkind emigrated to the UK. There, he began his career as a public intellectual, journalist, and Zionist activist. He assumed leadership positions in a staggering number of Zionist organizations, participated in the congresses of the World Zionist Organization (WZO), and lectured frequently on Hebrew language, Jewish thought, and Jewish history. Serving (in varying degrees of formality) as a congregational rabbi, he also played a crucial part in the reform of Jewish education in the UK and made significant contributions in the then-nascent field of Jewish children's literature.

Around the time of Zalkind's emigration, the Zionist movement was split between Practical and Political factions. As indicated above, Practical Zionism arose largely from the Eastern European Hibbat Zion movement and emphasized cultural renaissance through building up the land of Israel irrespective of diplomatic developments (Reinharz 1993), while Western Political Zionists aspiring to establish a Jewish state turned to diplomacy. This divide had important geographical implications. Political Zionists recognized that achieving political autonomy and doing so in the ancient Jewish homeland were *not* the same thing. Therefore, they were open to 'alternative Zions (Sinclair 2009),' while Palestine-centric Practical Zionists were not. This debate came to a head in 1905 after one such alternative — the so called 'Uganda Plan,' which would have created a Jewish polity within the East Africa Protectorate, then under British administration — was declined by the WZO Congress (Alroey 2008). A splinter group, the International Territorial Organization (ITO), was then formed to carry on strictly political efforts to establish a recognized place of Jewish refuge wherever one might be secured. Within the WZO, the conflict was resolved (or, perhaps better put, glossed over) with Chaim Weizmann's formulation of 'Synthetic Zionism' in 1907: concurrent action in both Political and Practical arenas, with *all* such efforts being focused on Palestine. More than anything else, this compromise is the reason Zalkind ultimately broke with the Zionist movement.

Active in Russian-Jewish affairs since his student days, Zalkind asserted that there could be 'no policy in waiting for Palestine (Anonymous 1905)' and that immediate solutions had to be found for Jews languishing in the Pale of Settlement. Therefore, he initially took the side of the ITO, assuming several key leadership roles therein. For reasons that are not yet clear, however, the affiliation did not last and he returned to the Zionist fold shortly thereafter, remaining highly active for the next decade. The zenith of his activities during this period, which lasted until the outbreak of World War I, was his central role in founding Pardes Hannah-Karkur, now an Israeli town near Haifa; Zalkind's Zionist efforts bore concrete fruit.

Zalkind's break with Anglo-Jewry, his transition into radical politics, and his retirement: 1914–37

World War I proved a major turning point. A Jewish refugee crisis of unprecedented proportions was created through the combination of fighting along the Eastern Front and a concerted project of ethnic cleansing initiated by the Russian government (Sanborn 2005). As Zalkind saw it, Anglo-Jewry responded with appalling apathy both to this tragedy and to conflicts involving Russian Jewish refugees in the UK. He interpreted these failures as signs of moral and spiritual degeneracy, framing his response in a twofold fashion, appealing both to his Nordau-inflected form of Practical-Cultural Zionism and to the purely Political 'Zionism' championed by the ITO.

Nordau's ideas about the Jewish body were always threaded with notions of racial hygiene (Presner 2007, 48). Not all bodies are fit for rehabilitation, he believed; these should be left to expire (Nordau 1895, 540, 551, 556), thus enabling the rest to enter the 'new world (Presner 2007, 37).' Zalkind adopted an analogous position. 'The whole world,' he wrote, 'becomes a ruin, the existence of whole peoples hangs on a hair,' the Jewish people in particular. Yet, the 'white sheep' flocked calmly and the 'dead' did not stir; they remained the 'same petty people' they were before. Thus, Zalkind spoke with bitter contempt of the 'Mikes and Montys ... the painted Millies and Janes who all shared the same hope: to have a new apartment in Hyde Park (Zalkind 1914).' Unlike Moses, who defended his backsliding congregation when God proposed to destroy them and build Israel anew (Exodus 32:10), Zalkind compared Mike, Monty, and Millie to a ship's ballast and to a tree's diseased branch, arguing that they should be dropped and left to assimilate peacefully (Zalkind 1914). In contrast, he called upon the blessed remainder — those 'who love the Jewish people above all else, who love and dream about its past golden age, who believe it has the ability and the will to revive that past' — to build 'a new people and a new Judaism greater, more beautiful, and more holy than that which had existed previously' through the process of 'building up a new life,' a spiritual center, in Palestine (Zalkind 1914). Here, we see how a blend of Practical and Cultural Zionisms with Nordau's notion of degeneracy and his vision for the birth of a 'new Jew' were combined in Zalkind's assessment as to the moral condition of Anglo-Jewry: their acculturation and their decadence left them unequal to the Jewish renaissance he anticipated.

His frustration was exacerbated by the Anglo-Jewish response to a conflict between Russian-Jewish refugees over conscription. Like other working-class people, immigrant Jews objected to serving a nation that denied them the franchise.[3] More importantly, they had emigrated to escape a history of persecution that included forced conscription (Anonymous 1917a)[4] and developed a sense of national identity in opposition to it (Auerbach 2007).' As Zalkind expressed it, they held that the 'Torah forbids blood[shed]' and rejects salvation through war. To participate in the 'most brutal of all crimes' would 'betray our mission, betray the Jewish God, and disrespect our history (Zalkind 1916b).' It would put Jews in service of Ashmedai, king of demons, whom others released in the name of 'order' and to whom 'millions of sacrifices' had already been offered (Zalkind 1914).

Zalkind himself was charged with draft evasion, but ultimately obtained a clergyman's exemption (Anonymous 1917c). However, refugees without the same legal protections were confronted with a choice between conscription or deportation (Bush 1980; Cesarani 1989; Lloyd 2010). Intimidated by rising antisemitism (Tropp 1988), and also motivated by sincere patriotism, the Anglo-Jewish community sided largely with the British government against Russian-Jewish refugees, supporting the policy, castigating their brethren, and withdrawing charitable support for non-compliance (Lloyd 2009, 12, 128, 134, 151). Earlier in his career, Zalkind called radicals to task for standing in solidarity with oppressed groups of all sorts while conveniently ignoring the Jews, the 'classical pariahs ... proletarians of proletarians' who are 'persecuted and covered with ignominy (Zalkind 1900).' Crucially, his experience at this time was quite different; unable to rely on support from seemingly natural allies (Zalkind 1916a; Zalkind 1916e), he turned elsewhere. The Foreign Jews' Protection Committee Against Deportation and Compulsion, in the formation of which he had a hand, situated itself within the broader anti-war cause.

Bringing him into contact with the anarchists, dissident socialists, and a range of unionists committed to this cause (Lloyd 2009, 151; Anonymous 1916), this tactical decision proved personally transformative.

As Zalkind would later articulate at length (see below), a war effort relies on the compliance of industrial workers who supply it. Organizing them therefore becomes the most direct means of impeding it; for this reason, radical pacifists have historically relied on the general strike (Bennett 2001). The alliance between the Protection Committee and the anti-war cause therefore drew Zalkind into the labor movement (Kaddish 2013, 199–200). He stood trial in January 1917 for abetting strikers at a uniform manufacturer and later participated in a number of labor protests. By March of that year, he presided over Protection Committee meetings, passing not only motions concerning conscription, but also hailing the Russian Revolution as a beacon of 'justice, of humanity, and of fraternal cooperation' for lovers of freedom of all countries (Anonymous 1917b).' Thus, his path into the world of the radical left was laid on a sense of solidarity with his Russian-Jewish brethren and paved with pacifism.

The war impacted Zalkind's affiliations in other ways too. However tenuously, he continued to identify as a Zionist as of 1916 (Zalkind 1916c). But as the war wore on, he became increasingly alienated. For one, his developing pacifism set him at odds with the Zionist leadership, several members of which contributed directly to the war effort — for instance, Chaim Weizmann, whose scientific discoveries led to advancements in weapons manufacture, and especially Ze'ev Jabotinsky, who founded both the Zion Mule Corps and the Jewish Legion.[5] More importantly, the very ideological makeup of the mainstream movement became problematic for him. As I noted earlier, it was by way of the Synthetic-Zionist compromise that the WZO reconstituted itself after upheavals surrounding the Uganda Plan. As Zalkind came to see it, this compromise came at the expense of core Zionist principles. Operating within a European political context, he considered Zionist diplomacy to be inconsistent with the cultural revolution the movement was supposed to foment (see my discussion of *shtadlanus* below). Focusing on Palestine to the exclusion of other suitable places of refuge meant ignoring ever worsening conditions for Jews residing in the Pale of Settlement. In other words, attempts to conflate the 'question of Jewishness' with the 'Jewish Question' by attempting to answer them within the framework of a single movement meant betraying both. In spite of the fact that he left the ITO soon after joining it, I would suggest that Zalkind ultimately held the split to be optimal: the ITO should have handled the second question, while the WZO should have handled the first. Seeing that this was not how things turned out, he became disillusioned. These issues are addressed in detail below in a section devoted to Zalkind's mature reflections on Zionism. My account will encompass Zalkind's contributions, both to the *Idishe Shtime* — a 'radical-national and anti-militarist (Reisen 1926a, 1032)' paper that he edited from 1916–1917 — and to the *Arbeter Fraynd* (see below), his views as represented in both organs being substantially identical.

Zalkind's anarchist turn

Zalkind's impressions of East-End Jewish anarchists during his first years in London were far from positive. In an early letter to *ha-Zefira* (a Warsaw-based Hebrew-language journal), he complained of severe harassment, especially during the holidays (Zalkind 1904) — this still being peak season for antics like the aforementioned 'Yom Kippur Balls.' However, the community matured and Zalkind's own views also evolved.

The exact circumstances under which Zalkind found himself at the center of London's Jewish-anarchist scene are yet unknown. However, we have already observed anarchistic threads latent in his thinking as well as the way that a robust commitment to solidarity with his fellow Jews both pushed him out of the Zionist movement and into the world of the radical left, which stood up when his brethren stood down. Zalkind was also an ideal recruit. Once a strong and dynamic political force, their popularity declined after World War I, both because the traumatized Jewish community sought religious succor and could not tolerate their militant atheism and also because Rudolf Rocker was deported, creating a gap in leadership (Fishman 2004, 302–303). With charisma, organizing skills, and Jewish credentials, Zalkind represented exactly what they needed.

Zalkind's role among London's Jewish anarchists roughly parallels the one he played in Zionist circles and within the Anglo-Jewish community: he served as a public educator and organizer. After reviving the then-defunct *Arbeter Fraynd* in 1920, he lectured constantly and published furiously. As the editor of a major anarchist publication, he also served as a hub for the international movement. His correspondence with anarchists, both Jewish and not, throughout Europe as well as North and South America can be found in several archives in Israel and the United States. For many of his correspondents, he was a prime point of access to the Yiddish-speaking anarchist public, translating their works in installments for publication in the *Fraynd*. Zalkind's theoretical contributions, so far as they appear in that organ, fall under four general headings: determining anarchist principles and methods; defining the role of religion and spirituality; distinguishing Jewish anarchism; and articulating an anarchist comportment toward Zionism.[6]

Anarchist principles

Early in his editorship of the *Fraynd*, Zalkind wrote as follows: 'an ideal is the opposite of reality, something that we aspire toward but which does not yet obtain.' This means, he continues, that 'an ideal is a lie' and the idealist a great liar. But, he wrote, he is also an artist; artists strive to disclose 'concealed secrets' and the idealist composes 'the music of the future (Zalkind 1920v).' The anarchist, in his view, is an arch idealist (Zalkind 1922a).

Zalkind was an idealist, not just in the colloquial sense of the word, but also philosophically. Action, he held, is 'the *continuation of an idea* after it passes through some organ of mediation (Zalkind 1922e)' — not, the reverse. Therefore, he held, a group undertaking 'must be based on clearly defined principles (Zalkind 1921e),' this being 'the only sure guarantee of its ability to live, of its potential for development.' For Zalkind, anarchism was rich in consequence, representing 'the highest level of social and spiritual order' and the peak of 'human ideals (Zalkind 1921l), but poor in clarity and coherence, lacking both a systematic worldview and comprehensive conception of 'what society will look like once it is liberated from the stewardship of the state and thus becomes "free."' Each teaching from its own starting point, competing factions were guilty of 'marching separately' and merely 'striking together' and therefore of compromising the vital force of the movement (Zalkind 1921f). Thus, he proposed to determine for anarchism an 'ethical point of departure' and the tactics coherent with it (Zalkind 1921e; Zalkind 1920c). In this respect, he can be regarded as an early contributor to the debate that led to the divide between Platformists — who released the 1926 *Organisational Platform of the General Union of Anarchists*, in which an absence of organizational principles and practices was blamed for the weakness of the movement — and Synthesists, who promoted an 'anarchism without adjectives,' which was naturally more pluralistic in character. His position in it is clear.

According to Zalkind, anarchism entails both destructive and constructive elements (Zalkind 1920w). Positively, he held that 'anarchism clarifies the rights of the human as such (Zalkind 1920n).' To him, this means that it opposes the 'principle of authority, which is the source and origin of all social suffering and injustice;' it 'rejects the notion that any organization, union, or other human association has the right to force its authority and power on any individual person, for sovereignty lies with every individual (Zalkind 1920k).' This implied also an 'absence of social hierarchies (Zalkind 1922g)' the effort to bring about 'a society of brothers (Zalkind 1920c),' a 'social order in which the individual and the collective alike are both free and happy (Zalkind 1920c).' Often referring to anarchism as 'libertarian (*hershaftslozen*) socialism,' he contended that 'today's tragic material and spiritual conditions are a direct result of the 'criminal politics of the bourgeois' and its ideas about property (Zalkind 1922i). If the individual remains sovereign, Zalkind maintained, his freedom is ultimately to be realized *within the collective* — in short, the positive program of anarchism spelled anarcho-communism.

Naturally, Zalkind believed that this 'society of brothers' is possible only by doing away with 'force in all its forms, especially by 'destroying the state and everything that goes with it — institutions like militarism, bureaucracy, justice, power (Zalkind 1920c).' His account of law and justice represent a case in point. Channeling both Nietzsche and Maimonides, he wrote that the origin of justice is 'so disgusting that it had to be concealed in legend

(Zalkind 1920d)' — the biblical story of the fall, according to which mankind is tricked into distinguishing between good and evil (Zalkind 1921o). Equating this distinction with law and right, he concludes that they are established via deceit and maintained by force (Zalkind 1920v). As the 'sum of all rights, and powers,' the state appears as 'nothing other than masked force, a thief with a halo,' the justice it mediates as a 'blind and bloodthirsty' goddess (Zalkind 1921o). The world, Zalkind once wrote, is 'like a massive insane asylum,' only that 'the real crazies are not the patients, but the officers who keep them in order.' Justice is the guiding principle in this madness of order, but we do not see it that way because we have been raised inside (Zalkind 1922e).

Zalkind's distinction between positive and negative aspects of the anarchist program served to frame his understanding as to its limits and also its relationship with other radical ideologies — primarily individualism and socialism. As he understood it, anarcho-individualism and anarcho-communism agree on the *negative* side of the anarchist program; 'like us,' he wrote, 'they want to be exempt from the tutelage of the state and from the rule of one person over another.' However, their vision of the 'new order' to replace the old had nothing in common (Zalkind 1921g). Like Proudhon, however, Zalkind regarded private property as a form of theft (Zalkind 1921o) and, therefore, of violence and domination. Individualists rejected socialist elements of the anarchist program. For this reason, Zalkind recommended finally doing 'away with the illness that is "individualism" (Zalkind 1922c).'

If Zalkind rejected individualism on socialist grounds, he ultimately saw socialism as an element of pure anarchism. He regarded socialism in itself as too materialistic in its vision, limiting its focus to economic exploitation (Zalkind 1920k) and restricting its ambitions to goals like abolishing poverty and improving working conditions he considered 'all too human (Zalkind 1921n).' Anarchists, in contrast, 'seek more than their portion of bread;' they are people 'who suffer from lack of freedom, independent spirits who cannot submit to the will of another, stormy souls who find themselves in rebellion against everything and everyone.' While the socialist refuses the unfreedom of economic inequality, the anarchist refuses unfreedom in all its forms; 'there is no repression such spirits will not break.' Accordingly, Zalkind Saw anarchism not as a final *telos*, but as a 'perpetual struggle' that would continue even after the revolution; striving for 'what is new and different' against the 'dead dreams (Zalkind 1920v)' of the past will still require firm resistance. For this reason, 'the anarchist is an eternal wanderer into infinity (Zalkind 1921n).' In essence, Zalkind regarded socialism as a program of liberation, but an incomplete one.

The tactics of anarchism: what it rejects and what it embraces

Like many anarchists, Zalkind insisted on ends-means correspondence, or what is today called an ethic of 'prefiguration (Franks 2018; Gordon 2018a);' as he put it, 'means are equivalent to ends (Zalkind 1921n).' So he explained elsewhere, 'from equal causes come equal effects.' Accordingly, freedom cannot exist '*after* a good order is put in place' unless 'people are *first* free' in the process of instituting it. The fundamental principles of anarchism 'cannot be eliminated on *any* grounds or for *any* reason.' For this reason, 'anarchist revolution must ... be carried out according to the principle of justice and *not* power, vengeance, or by posing one class over another (Zalkind 1920e).' In essence, this boils down to two convictions. One, that class-based revolutionary agitation is ultimately inconsistent with anarchist humanism. Two, that 'political revolution' is rejected in favor of 'social revolution.' In the spirit of constructive and friendly criticism (Zalkind 1921m; Zalkind 1921p), he articulated his views as of 1920 by posing it against Bolshevism which, for obvious reasons, had become a major force in the international left in spite of the relatively marginal position the party occupied earlier.

The Bolsheviks defended the dictatorship of the proletariat as a means of abolishing 'exploitation of one person by another' and transitioning from the bourgeois order to socialism. According to Zalkind, anarchists hold that 'one dictatorship calls for another, never freedom' so that 'in order to have no classes, one must do away with class politics (Zalkind 1920e).' Therefore, he refused 'to carry on the class war such that the oppressed of yesterday become the rulers of today;' that, he held, would not mean '*creating a new order, but continuing the old rotten order with reversed roles* (Zalkind 1920b).' Condemning the politics of revenge that came to prevail in Soviet Russia, he therefore wrote elsewhere that it is 'incorrect to turn masters into slaves,' insisting that 'there should be neither masters nor slaves (Zalkind 1920s).' A classless society, in other words, is accomplished only by way of a classless revolution — this being the only true liberation of 'man as such.'

Bolsheviks wished to replace one state with another, not to simply abolish centralized state power but to transfer it (Zalkind 1920n). For their purposes, therefore, 'political revolution' sufficed; 'political revolutions have force as their means,' force being 'the means of the state,' which merely reproduces relations of 'servitude that obtains between the state and the people (Zalkind 1922g).' Bolshevism undertook '*to arm the workers, transforming them into a red army of socialist workers and farmers*' in order to 'take power from the exploiters and place it in the hands of the working masses' — that is, form a worker's state but a state nonetheless (Zalkind 1920j).

Because an anarchist revolution differs absolutely 'with respect to its purpose ... it must,' Zalkind explained, 'differ too with respect to its means and methods (Zalkind 1922g).' Insofar, he wrote elsewhere, 'as they interfere with perfect human freedom, anarchism negates all instruments of force and all forms of power and rule;' therefore, it 'admits neither army nor police and, above all, no organization entrusted with transcendent authority over people (Zalkind 1920j).' Accordingly, 'there is simply no place for war' in an anarchist model; 'war is impossible when there is neither ruler nor ruled, no armies to strike one another, and no generals to command them to do so (Zalkind 1920h).'[7]

Because anarchists aim to 'negate and destroy the state,' they must 'destroy its means: force, weapons.' As he explains, weapons and the power they represent, he wrote, 'cannot be destroyed by using other weapons.' They can be destroyed only 'by refusing military service together, together refusing to produce tools of murder, destroying weapons, and by providing help and nourishment to weary bodies' — in short, 'by means of social-economic action (Zalkind 1922g).' This is what he intends by 'social revolution.' Let us explore its forms so far as Zalkind elaborated them.

Zalkind placed education at the core of any constructive revolutionary program. Because 'youthful impressions leave a mark for a lifetime,' he considered it necessary to 'remove this weapon from the hands of the reaction.' More than 'rousing the masses to fight,' he argued, they must be freed from prejudice (Zalkind 1920c) by way of an education purged from the 'idolatries of militarism, nationalism, and egoism (Zalkind 1920s).' They need, he explained further, to learn 'self-understanding and independence,' so that 'each person is entitled and able to manage his own affairs without the help or the guardianship of the state or any other institution,' without 'force or hierarchy, but through commonality of interests and understanding.' When building in this way, he argued, 'one destroys much more than when only destroying (Zalkind 1920c).' To this end, he called for the creation of quality teaching materials and himself responded to it by including a youth insert in the *Fraynd*, in which anarchist values were conveyed in an age-appropriate manner.

Zalkind also recommended solidarity. 'Just as a musical instrument lies idle and can give no sound unless one strikes it,' he wrote, 'so too the holy spirit dwells not on he who has a full belly and who has never tasted suffering (Zalkind 1920v).' This 'holy spirit' is the sense of mutual responsibility. Thus, 'from the tremendous sea of human suffering,' he wrote elsewhere, 'we derive the necessary solidarity.' Through shared suffering, 'one feels himself the brother of all people and senses intuitively the imperative to stand in resistance together with them. Facilitating the overcoming of differences and, therefore, affective preparedness for cooperative endeavor, he considered it anarchism's 'finest and most real tool (Zalkind 1921n).' As he argued earlier regarding the Zionist movement, he also held that anarchists must stand for and with the oppressed.

Effective solidarity demands organization. Here, we have in mind not only ideological clarity, but concrete cooperation. Writing after World War I, when the movement was already in decline, Zalkind wrote that 'as long as our forces are split,' its influence will continue to wane. Thus, he sought to establish the 'Jewish Anarchist Organization of England,' which would include any Jewish worker with 'a connection to anarchism' and proposed for it a provisional 'constitution.' It included the creation of a 'legislative and executive' council (consisting potentially of all organization members) charged with coordinating movement activities. This council would then delegate tasks to a number of smaller commissions authorized to act autonomously while remaining answerable to the council. Among the more interesting of these commissions — a Jewish equivalent to Anarchist Black Cross (Zalkind 1922d), a group dedicated to aiding political prisoners (Hackett 2015).

Direct action in the form of the general strike was undoubtedly the most important tactic Zalkind championed. Expanding on the rabbinic notion of '*shev ve'al ta'aseh* (sit and do nothing),' according to which passive violation of the law is permitted in order to preserve human dignity, he recommends 'passive sabotage ... declining to help capitalism in its shameful undertakings.' Pointing to the way the (mainly syndicalist) Trade Union Congress effectively leveraged the threat of a 'general strike' to prevent the UK from intervening in the Polish-Soviet war (White 1974; Crosby 2014, 279–280), he concluded that by dealing 'the death-blow to their [bourgeois] interests,' direct action constitutes 'the most real means for destroying the dark powers of capitalism (Zalkind 1920o).'

For Zalkind, the general strike was more than a labor protest. It involved the formation of heterotopic sociopolitical networks. He affirmed 'communism through free association (Zalkind 1922g)' governed by the principle of 'from each according to his ability and to each according to his need (Zalkind 1920b).' This would involve the creation of labor syndicates 'with the power to supply for common needs (Zalkind 1920j)' — that is, with freedom to exploit communal means of production for the general good — and to manage distribution. Such groups, governed by consensus (Zalkind 1922g), he contended, represent 'the system of economic organization that impinges least on human sovereignty.' On this basis, he continued, life could 'develop in a harmonious relationship with justice and independently of the authority of the majority over the minority or the reverse (Zalkind 1920n).' The 'sovereignty of a human as a human would coincide with the interests of 'the general collective (Zalkind 1920e).'

If communities arising from 'affinity and communal interest' exist only so long as necessity and will demand it (Zalkind 1920n), Zalkind contended like many other anarchists before him, they may be federated along similar lines. The constitution he proposed roughly followed the model of the Jewish Anarchist Organization of England. A federal congress or council composed of community delegates (Zalkind 1920f) would be assembled as needed in order to 'coordinate' their independent efforts (Zalkind 1920e) and address shared concerns. As 'the group is free in the federation (Zalkind 1920f),' this body would lack 'sovereign power;' its resolutions being accepted by constituent communities on a strictly voluntary basis (Zalkind 1920e). As with the Jewish Anarchist Organization of England, this congress would charge separate commissions with carrying out its resolutions. Zalkind also recommended the establishment of a 'permanent federal commission' serving neither executive nor legislative functions, but as a 'way for the various regions to exchange ideas (Zalkind 1920f).'

Like Alexander Berkman (2003, 217–218), he held that economic transactions among 'free laborers' and voluntary 'trade associations' within the federation should involve '"productive means of exchange" only — that is, goods — money being unnecessary (Zalkind 1920j)' or inherently 'authoritarian and monopolistic (Zalkind 1922g).'

For Zalkind, these communities in federation were not simply an end goal. Rather, in the cooperative community, he claimed to see 'the means to destroy the present order and build a new society (Zalkind 1922g).' Thus, he wrote:

> As the individual understands the present social order, he must free himself and his creative powers from their institutions. It is not necessary to wait until the whole proletariat is free. The individual strives to free himself from slavery through his own production. As soon as he is able, he links up with like-minded people and, in this manner, begins an anarcho-communist production cell which provides for their nourishment, clothing, and shelter. What is left over can be used to expand, to help other, perhaps weaker, production communes or for propagandizing our ideas in the struggle against the present social order … Every production cell must, as far as possible, refuse the requirements which the state provides with relation to things material and spiritual, with which it suppresses freedom in the interest of capital and monopoly. Only in this way can the power of the state be destroyed, which the free individual takes as his duty. Only in this way can the developing social revolution begin. (Zalkind 1920h)

The creation of a new world within the old, to displace the old and render it superfluous, he regarded as the epitome of the general strike — it would constitute a near total boycott of society as a whole (Zalkind 1920l).

As noted above, Zalkind articulated his ideas about anarchist tactics largely in a dialectical manner, posing them against Bolshevism. This raises the question of alliance with other radical movements as a tactic in itself, which would likewise be subject to the law of ends-means correspondence. Zalkind recognized both the need for and the value of a united revolutionary front, regarding it as something that anyone 'who sees all the sickness and injustice of the present social order and strives to make better and more just forms of life' should welcome (Zalkind 1922h).' Thus he extended a hand to kindred movements; for instance, guild socialists (Zalkind 1922j)' and especially syndicalists (Zalkind 1920f; Zalkind 1922f).

However, there were limits — when cooperation meant turning a blind eye to oppression. Initially, Zalkind supported the revolutionary alliance between anarchists (among other parties) and the Bolsheviks (Zalkind 1920c).' Appalled, however, both by their utter insensitivity to the lasting effects of Russian antisemitism (Zalkind 1920b; Zalkind 1921j) and especially by their merciless suppression of anarchists and other competing parties in the wake of the 1921 Kronstadt Rebellion, he ultimately denounced the Bolsheviks as 'wild beasts in the shape of men who have abandoned all human feeling and lack even the most elemental notion of justice (Zalkind 1922k)' and renounced 'every sympathy' he once had for them. (Zalkind 1921h).

Religion and Jewishness in Zalkind's thought

Like many in his generation, the carnage of World War I profoundly challenged Zalkind's faith. The war, he wrote, 'utterly destroyed the foundations of our material and spiritual lives' so that 'we seek out of real hunger, as beggars who have nothing and scrounge for the most primitive and elemental necessities of life.' Under such circumstances, he felt it necessary to 'start over with the *"alef-beyt"*' and rebuild what was lost from there. For him, this meant embracing a 'religion without religion (Zalkind 1920x).' Hostile not only to official clergy — whom he regarded as 'instruments and tools of murder and branches of the states' — but also to 'theology, revelation, mythology, and mysticism,' he embraced what he called 'ethical-cultural expression of human being-together with the All, infinity, the eternal, spirit-wave of the origin (Zalkind 1922g).'

Such expressions could take the form of 'folk law,' one among other voluntary social institutions the sum of which would replace the state as a regulatory institution (Zalkind 1921o). Like Kropotkin before him (Morris 2018, 173–190), Zalkind believed these norms capable of securing 'harmony without force (Zalkind 1921o).' Presumably, he regarded his Yiddish and

Hebrew-language mishnah and talmud translation-commentaries as a contribution to such harmony. It is in *this* sense that I understand the claim that 'his anarchist ideology was deeply connected with his talmudic ethic (Hein-Shimoni 1968; Zalkind 1921a).'

Thus, he considered religious practice to be legitimate and even salutary, though not obligatory. It is possible that he based his position here on a passage in *Yalkut Shimoni* (Isaiah 443:34), in which a dialogue between God and Israel is represented. Exiled to Babylon, Israel questions the observance of the law. Zalkind explained that the challenge is based on the following: 'He gave them the lands of the [Canaanite] nations ... that they might keep his laws and observe his teachings (Psalms 105:44–45)' — if the second clause depends on the first, then 'the law is conditional' and 'no longer obligatory' when the gift is retracted (Zalkind 1917, 161). Obligatory or not, he saw it as valid and voiced outrage over Soviet efforts to eliminate it — especially when Jewish communities were singled out (Zalkind 1921b). This, of course, brings us to the question *Jewish* anarchism as Zalkind understood it.

Anti-authoritarian elements appeared in Zalkind's theology long before his anarchist phase. During the Passover seder he led while serving as rabbi in Cardiff, for instance, he spoke of the 'duties and solemn obligations' conferred upon Jews by their heritage and contrasted it with the way that nobles boasted of 'better blood' when in fact they owed their station to the fact that their ancestors 'were pirates or highwaymen, or people rich in the distinction of having trampled underfoot others or ground down the poor and robbed the helpless.' He likewise represented Moses' mission as a struggle for 'independence and liberty' against a culture in which the 'individual had no rights and everyone was a cypher, a slave under the rule of the despot' — this mission representing the essence of Jewish faith in 'a better and freer future (Anonymous 1907)'

In his 1917 collection of novellae, *wa-Yomer Yaakov*, Zalkind offered a radical interpretation of Korah's rebellion against Moses. Referencing a midrash according to which Korah relied on the fact that Samuel would descend from him (LR 18:1), he averred that the rebel was essentially correct when he contended that 'the community are holy, all of them, and the Lord is in their midst' and asked Moses 'why then do you raise yourselves above the Lord's congregation (Numbers 16:3)?' Echoing Abravanel, Zalkind elaborated:

> He saw that Moses and Aaron made themselves rulers over the people. He thought that this was contrary to the interests of the people, for it does not need leaders standing over them like a father standing over his child ... He opposed the authority of masters and desired to establish for the people unmitigated freedom.

Therefore, Zalkind explained, Korah relied on Samuel, who is 'weighed against Moses and Aaron (Taanit 5b)' — that is, he was their ideological 'counterweight, refusing to assume sovereignty over the people like they did (Zalkind 1917, 43–44).' While Zalkind ultimately impugned Korah's *motives*, that does not change his judgement as to the claim itself.

While Zalkind announced a significant thematic shift upon assuming editorship of the *Fraynd*, vowing to focus more 'on the life and the struggles of the Jewish proletariat than was previously the case (Zalkind 1920y),' his reflections therein were — likely owing to his largely non-religious audience[8] — decidedly less theologically substantial but no less important. Two primary issues occupied his attention: the Jewish character of Jewish anarchism, and the question of Zionism.

Concerning the first topic, Zalkind identified three alternatives. Members of the *Fraynd* circle were simply anarchists, Yiddish-speaking anarchists, or *Jewish* anarchists. Because it implied the superfluousness of a separate group such as their own, the first was rejected outright. The second was reduced to the third. Zalkind reasoned that language is either accidental or culturally significant, that only the latter would justify a distinct organization, and that it amounted to an affirmation of Jewishness. 'We regard language as something more than incidental, as a spiritual good for the Jewish masses,' he wrote; 'so why use a description as blasé as 'Yiddish speaking' when we are far more than that?'

This, however, raised a fundamental problem. While, owing to their essentially economic concerns, socialists could (in his view) bracket questions of culture, anarchism is a worldview from which 'nothing that is human is foreign.' Jewishness would have to be squared with anarchism. He begins by gesturing toward traditions of iconoclasm pluralism. Judaism, he argues:

> Is a broad river carrying along in its current many things from which everyone selects what seems best to him. For us, there is in Judaism precisely what is good in anarchism: destroying and building at the same time, the perpetual effort and endeavor to improve and elevate things, breaking old gods and accepting a new one.

Here, Zalkind presented his readers with a glimpse of what a positive theology of Jewish anarchism might look like. However, he dropped this train of thought completely, arguing instead that even as internationalists without religious commitments, members of the *Fraynd* circle were raised and continued to operate within a Jewish milieu that conferred definite physical, psychological, and cultural forms. For *this* reason, he concluded, 'we are Jewish anarchists (Zalkind 1920a).' With this response, Zalkind was forced to confront the fraught relationship between anarchism and nationalism.

Zalkind held that 'anarchism recognizes only human beings' and that 'human beings belong to *no nation* or race (Zalkind 1920h)' — like Rocker

(1998), he considers it an artificial construction; indeed, a largely harmful one (Zalkind 1922i). But not every artifice is objectionable in every respect; Zalkind thus distinguished between 'pure' and 'tainted' forms of nationalism (Zalkind 1920p).' In 'the hands of the filthy imperialists and capitalists' he condemned it, but at the same time saw no objection in a form of nationalism:

> Based on the principle of the brotherhood of humanity and which begins to dissolve the hatreds that exist among peoples together with the idea that one people is better than and thus has a right to rule another, which teaches that humanity arises from a federation of people-families equal in right if different in historical development, life-ways, and so on, and that peoples are but chords in a human symphony which is more beautiful the more diverse it is. (Zalkind 1920a)

When nationalism means cultural autonomy and the 'organization of groups for affinity and communal interests (Zalkind 1920n),' when it is about *peoples* that stand in solidarity with humanity as a whole, then it has a place in anarchism. Zalkind affirmed a sort of 'reticulated' humanism which admits of and celebrates difference while affirming mutual responsibility: a 'true man of the [Jewish] people' strives to uplift them morally and materially; his nationalism existed within the framework of 'a brotherly and intelligent human society (Zalkind 1920a).'

Articulating his position in this way, I would suggest that Zalkind drew on the radical republican roots of modern anarchism (Levy 2004; 2011; Forman 2010, 19–66). Giuseppi Mazzini, for instance, claimed that each nation, like each individual, 'performs its special mission' while also promoting 'the progressive advance of humanity (Gangulee 2006, 147–148).' Perhaps in spite of himself, Bakunin was deeply influenced by Mazzini's thought (Prichard 2010) and spoke in explicitly nationalist terms of his beloved Slavs as late as *Statism and Anarchy* (Forman 2010, 40). He was not alone, and Jewish anarchists like Zalkind picked up the suppressed threads of this tradition for their own purposes. While his exact position is not clear, it seems to me that by reducing language to culture and deemphasizing geography (see below), while at the same time gesturing toward concrete ties of kinship, he hovered between naturalist and culturalist approaches to anarcho-nationalism, thus synthesizing in a rather idiosyncratic way the views of Kropotkin and Rocker (Gordon 2018b).

Zalkind's reflections on Zionism

Zalkind's unique approach to the synthesis of Cultural and Practical Zionism grounded his break not only with the Anglo-Jewish community, but also with a Zionist establishment primarily focused on *political* methods. One must, he argued, not love a land 'platonically, from a distance, but tenderly' by working it 'until one's back aches.' Freedom, he continued comes 'with every small tree that shoots up from the earth that you, with your own hands, woke from a two-thousand year long slumber, when you subordinate all of your thoughts, your very being, to the land and its caprices.' Interpreting the verse 'the Lord God took Adam and placed him in the garden of Eden, to till it and tend it (Genesis 2:15),' he explained that the second clause implies working the land with the same 'love that a mother has for her child;' *then*, he promised 'the world, your land, will then be a paradise for you (Zalkind 1916c).' Accordingly, Zalkind demanded of the Zionist establishment an '*al heyt*,' a moral accounting (Zalkind 1916d), for failing to realize that via 'secret meetings, conferences and congresses, presidents and directors, societies and orders, golden books, and National Fund stamps' it might 'merit to throw off the tyranny of Sir Edward Gray and establish justice from London to Paris and vice versa' but would not achieve that true freedom sought through return to the land. Zalkind's rejection of Political Zionism was in this sense a matter of tactics, 'a land is not given as a gift' through 'the kindness of other nations,' he held, but gained by the 'hand that works until it is bedecked with callouses.' That is 'real politics,' the rest is 'whining (Zalkind 1916c).' Yet, it also involved his understanding of the moral and spiritual rehabilitation that Zionism was supposed to accomplish.

This, in two related respects. In the first place, he felt that emphasis on diplomacy created an internal divide between the elite and the rank-and-file that served to suppress dissent and cultivate submissiveness. The movement, he wrote, 'should become a folks-organization based on the people and which lives for the people (Zalkind 1916d)' but it is 'making us infantile or spiritually castrating us (Zalkind 1916c).' Its meetings, he contends, had been reduced to bourgeois social engagements at which to enjoy 'music, speeches, and dancing,' light conversation and plates 'full of sandwiches' to be eaten 'with relish (Zalkind 1916c).' Accordingly, they became conclaves of 'holy sheep who cry 'meh!' at every word that emerges from the mouth of the leaders' and thus follow 'the precedent of the [worshippers of the] golden calf (Zalkind 1916d).' Its 'whole history,' he claimed, is 'an unbroken chain of small ambitions, small people, and small intrigues,' an extended effort to 'drive away' the 'honest people' who refuse to 'obey every order that comes from the *gedolim* (bigwigs)' but instead 'have tried to drag the wagon from the mud and have dared called out 'hands up!'' to leaders under whom it 'has become bloodless (Zalkind 1916d).'

If the collective body of Israel had two phalli, Zalkind would have ascribed to Political Zionist 'scheming-finger-niks (Zalkind 1916c)' a double castration.

In his view, diplomacy was problematic, not only because it created conditions for stifling internal dissent, but because it was objectionable in and of itself. It smacked, he contended, of *shtadlanus*. The *shtadlan*, or court Jew, combined the roles of diplomat, advocate, and intercessor for medieval and early-modern Jewish communities. If the *shtadlan's* efforts were respected and appreciated, the institution itself was in every respect politics for the powerless (Klieman 2008). Therefore, Jews battling the degrading status quo came to hold it in disdain.

Initially, Zalkind used *shtadlanus* as a term of abuse against Jews who doubted the Zionist cause (presumably, seeking to further Jewish integration itno gentile society). In a particularly vehement piece from 1903, he tells 'little Moses' in every land 'who slither on their bellies and, with fear and terror, do what their masters tell them to' that times have changed; the upcoming generation 'hates slavery and groveling.' Appealing to the talmudic reading of 'it is to *me* that the Israelites are servants (Leviticus 25:55)' — 'and not slaves to slaves (Kiddushin 22b)' — he instructs these 'court Jews' to inform their 'nobles in their various clubs: the Jews have changed, they have stopped singing '*Mah Yafis*' as they did before!' *Mah Yafis* was a popular sabbath song that Polish nobles would often force their Jewish subjects to perform; to call someone a singer of *Mah Yafis* is the Yiddish equivalent of calling him an Uncle Tom — and that is precisely how Zalkind regarded his targets in this essay (Zalkind 1906).

Later, Zalkind cast the same slur on mainstream Zionism. I believe that his views on the matter were formulated during his short tenure as editor of the *Shtime*. However, record of their explicit articulation begins only after his anarchist turn. It is therefore to this period that we now direct our attention.

The question of Zionism appeared in the *Fraynd* prior to Zalkind's tenure as editor on at least two occasions. In 1903, Rocker published an open letter soliciting debate on the subject. A reader identifying himself as a 'Zionist anarchist'[9] responded that Zionism sought to settle 'homeless Jewish workers,' not to establish a state, and that both movements oppose capitalism while promoting liberation and emphasizing human agency in achieving it (Zionist Anarchist 1903). This claim was promptly dismissed by other contributors, who regarded Zionism as absurd, confused, or in conflict with anarchist internationalism. Several years later, however, a Yiddish translation of Kropotkin's more sympathetic response appeared. He saw national liberation movements as elements of an international struggle and defended Zionism on this account. However, he opposed Zionist palestinocentrism for two reasons. First, because Palestine was, in his estimation, too resource-poor to support a mass population influx. More importantly, because he felt that the Jewish national cause belonged in Europe and would do more good there (Kropotkin, 1907). When Zalkind stepped in as editor, this peripheral debate became a central focus. With an intimate understanding of the plurality of Zionist ideas, he distinguished between useful and harmful elements, supporting the former and fighting the latter (Zalkind 1920p). As we have already observed, he shared Kropotkin's view on the congruence of national and international liberation movements. His other reflections on Zionism likewise parallel Kropotkin's.

There is a deep affinity between the emphasis that, as an anarchist, Zalkind placed on direct action and his earlier rejection of Zionist *shtadlanus* in favor of a more practical approach. The same goes for the relationship between anarchist anti-authoritarianism and his assessment of Zionist *shtadlanus* as a contemptible act of submission (Zalkind 1921i). 'It must be the responsibility of the Jewish masses,' he wrote in 1920, 'to ensure that what the Jewish people yearn for should be articulated openly and proudly and *not* through the back-room politics of small men who do not understand that the honor of the Jewish masses is ... everything (Zalkind 1920u.' Who were these small men? The Zionist leadership because, as he put it, *shtadlanus* has become 'an organic part of modern Zionism, a heritage it has inherited together with all the old filth of exile. The "lowlives" are dragged to the head of the table, darkness falls, and we serenade them with *mah yafis* (Zalkind 1923b).' Thus, if once Zalkind regarded the movement as a source of national pride, the diplomatic direction it took transformed it, in his view, into another example of national debasement. For this reason, he described it as undergoing a process of senescence, comparing it to late August, when the grass begins to brown, the sun shines less brightly, the sharp taste of summer fruit mellows, and birdsong reminds one of 'penitential prayers' yet to be recited during the days of awe to come (Zalkind 1916c).

Zalkind's anarchist insistence on ends-means correspondence further informed his criticism of *shtadlanus*. Diplomacy, he argued, means throwing principle to the wind, based as it is on the idea that 'ends justify means.' Employing admittedly misogynistic language,[10] Zalkind describes the diplomat as a prostitute who 'throws flirtatious glances at whomever can be more or less useful (Zalkind 1920q).'[11] He or she weighs decisions 'not according to their ethical content, but according to their superficial results (Zalkind 1922b),' forging alliances at the expense of ethical consistency and moral principle.

This conclusion added a new dimension to Zalkind's critique of Zionist diplomacy. He denounced the movement's leadership for 'walking hand in hand with the blackest reactionaries rather than acting as a factor in the new life now being created (Zalkind 1920f).' Jabotinsky's 1921 military agreement with the Ukrainian patriot and pogromist Symon Petliura (Zalkind

1921c; Schechtman 1955)[12] and Chaim Weizmann's 1923 audience with Mussolini (Zalkind 1923b) served as cases in point. As Zalkind saw it, these undertakings were merely extreme examples of an approach which characterized and therefore tainted the movement (Zalkind 1921d; Zalkind 1921k). 'No good,' he insisted, can come of it when the sort of people 'who destroyed the world are the same ones entrusted to its rebuilding (Zalkind 1920t).'

As Zalkind represented it, the problem was threefold. He contended that collaboration with the 'blackest reactionaries' cannot be a neutral undertaking. Quoting an old Yiddish aphorism, '*vi es kristelt zikh azoy men yidelt zikh* (as with the Christians [gentiles] so with the Jews),' he argued that thereby the Jewish liberation movement 'absorbed the "forty-nine impurities" of modern political life (Zalkind 1922b).'[13] It became 'a capitalist institution responsible for all of the same old sins as capitalism — imperialism, militarism, bureaucracy, and so on (Zalkind 1920q).' Worse, Zionist 'leader-seducers' dragged the folk into 'a political swamp (Zalkind 1920g).' Infecting it with the 'thought of Jewish self-rule,' they contracted these and other related 'social illnesses (Zalkind 1920m).' In short, Zalkind believed that Political Zionism spread 'political relations' across the Jewish street (Zalkind 1922b)' and that this had a corrupting effect on the moral fabric of Jewish communities.

Thus corrupted, the movement came to bear the stamp of its time: a juncture in which human life 'reached the lowest depth of value and the most basic ethical notions are trampled (Zalkind 1922b). In other words, it put political objectives before human life. According to Zalkind, this was expressed in two ways. In the first place, he argued that by transforming into a political movement and focusing solely on Palestine, Zionism would work to solve the Jewish refugee by displacing the local Arab population and turning *them* into refugees. Thus, he wrote that 'our first step into the realm of colonialistic ethics' is 'a mark of shame for the Jews which can never be washed off, it is the blackest blood to have been written into the black history of colonial politics, a crime of which the conquistadors of America ... would barely have been able (Zalkind 1920m.'

Returning to themes first developed as a member of the ITO and later influenced by Kropotkin, Zalkind accused the Zionists of a 'crime against the suffering Jewish masses.' By placing 'Palestine at the center of Jewish politics' despite its small size and dearth of resources, he felt that they neglected the pressing Eastern European 'immigration problem (Zalkind 1921q)' and thus failed to stand 'on the side of the oppressed (Zalkind 1916d).' Palestine, he maintained, should have been regarded 'in the same way as any other place: from a practical and realistic and *not* from a romantic standpoint,' the sole question being 'can Palestine take them in and give them bread (Zalkind 1921h)? Writing during the twelfth WZO congress in 1921, he put the issue as follows: 'when this congress ends, everyone will cry out 'next year in Jerusalem! next year in Jerusalem!" while, in the meantime 'people will drown in blood, a million people will flee as from fire but know not where to go (Zalkind 1921i).' According to Zalkind, an adequate response would mean seeking out *any* suitable site of refuge; Palestine might serve as one such place able to absorb *some* immigrants, but not as the answer to the whole question (Zalkind 1921h).

In point of fact, Zalkind returned to Ahad Ha'am's vision for a spiritual center in Palestine, arguing that it should serve to absorb ' a special sort of migrant up to the task of building from the ground up, but not for the broad masses and ... never for the majority of the Jewish people (Zalkind 1921h).' This brings us to Zalkind's conception of 'pure' Zionism. Jewish life, he wrote, is like 'a wide sea,' flowing with strong currents atop which float 'fragile bubbles of soap.' Among them: 'government games and adventures.' He believed that in the ongoing struggle for true liberation within the brotherhood of peoples, these bubbles would burst, just like others that preceded them (Zalkind 1920r).

Thus, while Zalkind did not look at Palestine through the eyes of 'chauvinist charlatans who dream of a state with all the fixings of a Jewish imperialism,' and vowed to battle this perspective 'until it disappears from Jewish life like a bad dream,' he held Palestine to be an 'integral part of *Judaism* (Zalkind 1921h).' It is, he wrote, 'the only place never abandoned by Jews' throughout centuries of displacement and cultural evolution Zalkind 1921q).'

Accordingly, he argued that anarchism does not necessarily exclude Zionism as such and, more pointedly, that 'anarchism is expressed in groups who share certain affinities' not only economic, but also cultural and spiritual. These Jews, he continued, tend to share with other Jews more so than with others. Since 'no anarchist with a healthy human intelligence will' therefore 'deny that Jews ought to live by productive work or that they may live together in some land (Zalkind 1920p),' he therefore asked, 'if Jewish workers strive in order to establish and begin a new life on the basis of anarcho-communist or socialist-communist foundations why not help them and strengthen them? Why is Palestine invalid (Zalkind 1920a)?' The continuity between this claim and the program of Cultural-Practical Zionism he defended in 1916 is evident; Zalkind found acceptable forms of Zionism that do not 'connect the fate of the Jewish people with the dark powers that now rule the world and make the Jewish future dependent on what follows from the most reactionary movements in our society.' Indeed, he believed that in time autonomous anarcho-communist Jewish communities in Palestine could become the 'cradle of a new society that lives from the most noble ideals of Judaism and humanity (Zalkind 1921q).'

The demise of the *Arbeter Fraynd* and Zalkind's retirement

In spite of his tremendous productivity and the novelty of his contributions, both as a journalist and also as a scholar, Zalkind struggled to keep the *Fraynd* in circulation, and it folded in 1923. Thereafter, he maintained some connections in the anarchist world — for instance, by mentoring Sholem Schwarzbard, the Yiddish-language anarchist poet and the assassin of the Ukrainian patriot and pogromist, Symon Petliura (see below). Mainly, however, he devoted himself to what was to be his magnum opus, a monumental Yiddish (and later Hebrew) language translation of and commentary on the talmud. It was intended to democratize access to the rabbinic tradition for Jews uprooted both physically and spiritually from major centers of Jewish learning in Eastern Europe.

This project, which he began while still editing the *Fraynd*, he continued in Palestine after emigrating there in the early 1930s. Settling first in Tel Aviv and ultimately in Haifa, he wrote, taught, and hiked Mt. Carmel, lingering there with the 'spirit of Elijah,' and awaiting his own fiery chariot to heaven (Hein-Shimoni 1968). Though without chariot, Zalkind's time came on December 25, 1937 (Anonymous 1937). Eulogized a few days later before a large crowd, he was interred in a section of the old Haifa cemetery designated for great rabbis and scholars. A man whose fascinating life fit no neat narrative of modern Jewish identity, thenceforth fell into obscurity. As Zalkind once put it:

> My thoughts must be authentically Jewish, actually from the same country as the Jews, since they have the same *mazal* as the Jews in general. They cannot be found in any one place, but wander from place to place. A bit like the mark that was engraved on Cain's forehead: 'you shall become a ceaseless wanderer on earth.' (Zalkind 1922c)

Every wanderer eventually turns in circles. Perhaps the circuit of Zalkind's wandering thoughts has been completed; perhaps now there are attentive ears to receive them.

Conclusion

Let us now return to a claim made at the outset. It was said that Zalkind seemed to be 'a man of contradictions who breached every boundary,' inhabiting all 'camps at once,' while perceiving in this 'no contradiction at all.' Our survey of Zalkind's life and thought both simplifies and complicates this characterization. Throughout the course of his career, Zalkind remained devoted to two basic commitments: revitalizing Jewish culture and alleviating the plight of European, especially Russian, Jewry. While Chaim Weizmann explicitly conflated these two objectives, Zalkind did not. I argue that he defected to the ITO, not in rejection of Cultural-Practical Zionism and its attempt to respond to the question of Jewishness that modern Jews pose to themselves, but in the hopes of disentangling it from Political Zionism as embodied by the splinter group and its goal of responding *solely* to the Jewish Question created by gentiles. If the Synthetic Zionism formulated in 1907 facilitated his reintegration into the Zionist mainstream, its underlying weaknesses were exposed after 1914. Deeply disappointed both by the Anglo-Jewish community for its acculturation and its bourgeois mediocrity, its apathy toward national cultural renaissance, and also by the fact that Russian Jewry was, in his view, abandoned in its time of need, both domestically and internationally, by the Zionist movement, which did not alter its Palestine-centric policy to demand refuge wherever it might be obtained, Zalkind rejected them and sought solidarity elsewhere. Hence his work within the anti-war movement and consequent pacifism: no war, no refugee crisis in the Pale. Hence his ultimate anarchist turn: it was only natural for him to join a movement emphasizing solidarity with the oppressed, Jews included — especially given that his Zionism was itself inflected with anarchism and he held anarchism to be consistent with this 'pure' form of Zionism. Thus, while Zalkind passed through many ideological phases throughout his career and in this respect appeared to 'dance at many weddings (Zalkind 1920q),' it turns out that, in fact, he was always dancing at the same one; it just happened to have many venues.

Notes

1 For a far more elaborate version of Zalkind's biography (including bibliographical sources), see my forthcoming article 'Dancing at Every Wedding: The Biography of Rabbi Yaakov Meir Zalkind, a Religious-Zionist, Pacifist, Anarcho-Communist,' which will soon appear in the *AJS Review*. I refer the reader to this text for biographical references, as they are extensive and cannot be incorporated into the present volume.

2 Notions of degeneracy and regeneration were central features of Nordau's thought (Nordau 1895).

3 The Representation of the People Act, which gave the vote to all male citizens over 21, whether they owned property or not, was not passed until 1918 (women were not fully franchised until 1928).

4 Here, I refer to the history of the cantonist decrees according to which Jewish boys 12 years of age and up were conscripted for a 25-year period with the *express* aim of de-Judaising them (Ofek 1993).

5 For this father of the Zionist right, who stressed statism, militarism, and territorial maximalism (Kaplan 2005a), Zalkind reserved special disdain, referring to him derisively as the 'Jewish Garibaldi (Zalkind 1920i).'

6 Here, it is necessary to address a problem of authorship. Tidhar (1958) and Reisen (1926a) have indicated Zalkind's excessive use of pseudonyms. In the microfilm copies of the *Arbeter Fraynd* held by YIVO, a librarian labeled several articles with Zalkind's initials (J. M. S). Many of these 'pseudonyms' are in fact the names of other authors (Kropotkin, Rocker, De Likht, Schwarzbard, Volin, Barret, Volodin, Ramus, Mratchny, Yarchuck, and Shlomo ben David). Other bylines may be misprints and, if so, can also be identified with known authors: if the final *mem* of M. A. M is actually meant to be final khaf, it would refer to Chaim Eliezer Moshkat. If the letter *het* of H. Potashnik is meant to be a *khaf* (the two letters make similar sounds), it would refer to Kh. Potashnik, author of *Bukh funem farsholtenem amal: Zikhronos fun an altn arbeter* (1939). 'Le Libertaire' was actually a contemporary anarchist newspaper — presumably, Zalkind is being credited with translating from the original French into Yiddish. Internal evidence excludes other supposed pseudonyms. For instance, a letter from France by 'Gracchus' appeared in August of 1920, whereas Zalkind was lecturing in London at this time. Likewise, a column by Jay Emes, *Royte Peperlakh*, sometimes appears under the byline of Reuben ben Yitshak. Presumably, Zalkind's name is appended to these articles because he *translated* them. I take to be evidently pseudonymous bylines built from Zalkind's initials: Y. M. S., M. Y., Mizeh, and S. Zalkin. I take to be probably pseudonymous names that all extant secondary sources agree on and which are not evidently erroneous: Dr. Salifanto, Mibnei Hekhala, B. Meyer, and Heinrich Schmidt. I take to be *possibly* pseudonymous other bylines next to which J. M. S. appears but which do not refer to a known author: A. And, A. Aner, V. V. L-R., Dr. Gozdberg, A. Berezniak, Lisa S., Sasha Peter, and S. Cahill.

7 As observed in the account of Zalkind's career between 1914 and 1918, his reflections on the carnage of the Great War proved transformative, pushing him into the pacifist camp and allying him with a spectrum of radical groups. His visceral description of the tragedy in the *Fraynd* makes clear that this experience remained fresh and likely constituted the affective core of his anarchism. It is easy, he wrote 'to awaken the animal in men and evoke a hatred that can be stilled only by seas of blood from ten million human lives. It is easy to destroy in four years the treasuries that generations of diligent men created in hardship.' But healing these wounds to the 'collective social organism' proves much more difficult. 'Today's tragic material and spiritual conditions,' he continued 'are a direct result of the criminal politics of the bourgeois and their ideas of state, property, capital, militarism, nationalism, religion, and so on.' Anarchist rejection of 'parliaments and politics' represented, for him, the remedy (Zakind 1922i).'

8 For this reason, he condemned the Third International, calling it a 'Purim Shpiel — a play for fools.

9 Zalkind first raised the question in the June–July 1920 edition of the *Fraynd* but let it stand until December due to lack of certainty as to what an adequate reply would entail (Zalkind 1920a). In my view, the challenge consisted in discerning how to talk about Jewishness to a circle of readers that had until recently been extremely hostile to it.

10 This is almost certainly not Zalkind; the writer is later described as a critic or a lecturer from Glasgow, where Zalkind did not reside until a much later date.

11 This was not an isolated instance. Zalkind used similarly degrading and dismissive language on a number of occasions (Zalkind 1920d, 1921g, 1921j). That being said, he did explicitly include women in his call for equality in all respects as a basic value of Anarchism (Zalkind 1920s).

12 As Jabotinsky was then serving on the WZO executive committee, Zalkind held the movement as a whole to be complicit in this deal with the devil. In point of fact, he was removed from the committee in consequence of his actions.

13 Here, Zalkind draws on the kabbalistic notion that there are fifty degrees of impurity. To reach the last is to be beyond hope of salvation. The forty-ninth degree is therefore a precarious one. This tradition has it that under Egyptian domination the Israelites stood there just prior to the exodus. Zalkind therefore implied both that true liberation remained possible and also that it could be completely destroyed.

4

Yitshak Nahman Steinberg (1888–1957)

2 Yitshak Nahman Steinberg in 1917, in his role as the People's Commissar of Justice.

Many people would have called him a dreamer or a visionary, and yet he was one of the true, and unfortunately few, realists of our time. He was a realist because he could visualize a flower when he saw a seed; because he was not impressed by what generally appears powerful today, and yet in the light of history will have vanished tomorrow. (Fromm, undated)

He was a problem. A *frum yid* (pious Jew), not one who was a *baal teshuvah* (penitent), but a *frum yid* all his life, who was not in the organized orthodox movement; a Jewish socialist who was not in the Bund and not in Poale Zion ... He was a brave fighter for ethical socialism, liberty of thought, and Jewish existence. (Leftwich 1958)

The dreamer referred to is Yitshak Nahman Steinberg (1888–1957), a man who Zalman Shazar, the third president of Israel aptly called 'the saint of the Revolution and a good Jew (Ravitch 1960, 586).' Like Zalkind, he straddled worlds. He was a radical and also a man of faith; for him, these were not opposing designations, or even distinct ones. The struggle for social and political justice was part and parcel of what it meant to be Jewish; he understood his libertarian socialism through the lens of his Judaism and vice versa.

Born in the Latvian city of Dvinsk, Steinberg was — like Zalkind — born into a rabbinic family, one that traced its lineage to R. Moses Isserles, the revered halakhist whose rulings appear in all standard editions of the *Shulkhan Arukh* (Code of Jewish Law). The Steinberg home was suffused with traditional Judaism and the humanistic spirit of the Haskalah alike. The poetry of Micah Joseph Lebensohn was read alongside Maimonides. Russian literature and European philosophy were studied together with the talmud and its commentaries. As Aaron Steinberg later put it, 'never was there dissonance between the melancholic sound of talmudic chanting' and 'the music of Tchaikovsky.' For the time, the family was highly egalitarian as well: Steinberg's mother was well versed in rabbinic literature and fluent in Hebrew, while his aunt had a doctorate in philosophy.[1]

Steinberg drew influences from across the religious, cultural, and political spectrum represented within his closely knit extended family. He was deeply impressed by his grandfather's pious devotion to the ideals of the Musar movement,[2] but also inspired by the narodnik folk-socialism he studied with an uncle. From another uncle — Baal Mahshoves (Israel Elyashev), the first Yiddish literary critic— he learned to appreciate both the rich world of modern Yiddish literature and also the Hebrew cultural renaissance that Hibbat Zion sought to realize, composing plays and essays in both languages from a young age. During his gymnasium years — which coincided with the 1905 Russian Revolution — these influences coalesced. Caught up in the rising revolutionary fervor, Steinberg vowed to 'show through his actions that there is no contradiction between Judaism and revolutionary socialism (Ravitch 1960, 45).' He was aided in this goal by his talmud tutor, the mysterious R. Zalman Baruch Yehoshua-Heschel Rabinkow. Known as the 'Genius of Sosnits,' Rabinkow was the top student of R. Eliezer Gordon of Telz.[3] A prodigy in more ways than one, Rabinkow was an expert, not only in talmudic and post-talmudic rabbinic literature, but a Habad hasid, a kabbalist intimately familiar with the canon of Western philosophy ancient and modern, a supporter of Ahad Ha'am, and a libertarian socialist.[4] Under Rabinkow's influence, Steinberg became part of the wave of young Jews joining the Socialist Revolutionaries — a party with deep narodnik roots that largely overlapped with those of Russian anarchism (Gamblin 2000) — at the turn of the twentieth century (Reisen 1926b, 604–608; Schapiro 1961; Kiel 1970).

Steinberg subsequently entered the University of Moscow as a student of jurisprudence and became highly active in student politics. This brought him to the attention of the authorities; before Passover he was arrested, imprisoned, and threatened with Siberian exile — a sentence that was fortunately reduced to two-year exile in any destination. Officially freed two months later, on Shavuot, Steinberg refused to sign his release papers (writing being religiously forbidden on Jewish holidays), relenting only after a *beyt din*, a religious court, of Muscovite rabbis declared it obligatory on the grounds of *piku'ah nefesh* (mortal danger) — not an unfounded concern; several of his comrades were murdered a few days later.

Steinberg departed for Germany, continuing his talmudic and legal studies, as well as his political activities as a Socialist Revolutionary operative, in Heidelberg. Together with Rabinkow, who followed him west, Steinberg organized a group dubbed the 'Heidelberg school of talmudic science,' which included also Erich Fromm, the better-known psychoanalyst and political philosopher. With Rabinkow's assistance Steinberg composed a doctoral dissertation on criminal law in the talmud. Degree in hand, Steinberg returned home and began his legal career — most notably working on the defense of Menahem Beilis, the last Jew to stand trial on charges related to the infamous blood libel.

During the war, Steinberg worked first for the Jewish Aid Committee (Ravitch 1960, 111), assisting war victims in the Pale and then later as a representative of the Socialist Revolutionaries in Central Asia, return-ing to Moscow in 1917 (Reisen 1926b). Siding with the left wing of the Socialist Revolutionaries — which had splintered into an independent party internationalist in spirit and supportive of a united socialist front — he joined the coalition government as the Folks-Commissar of Justice. Thus began the short but striking foray of a traditionally religious Jew into the nascent Soviet regime.

Steinberg did not fail to appreciate the significance of this development. In his *Zikhronos fun a Folks Kommisar*, he marvelled that in the very office that 'rang with Jewish groans, that was 'permeated with Jewish terror' — where the Beilis trials were masterminded, where the May Laws[5] and Jewish quotas were drafted, where the very idea of the Pale of Settlement was conceived — sat a Jew, not as a guest, but as the agent 'of a new world order' intent on purifying the office of 'falseness and cruelty (Steinberg 1931, 150–151).' Many anecdotal reports highlight the peculiarity of a high-ranking Soviet official donning tefillin each morning, or interrupting Lenin's council meetings in order to recite the afternoon prayers (Ravitch 1960, 104).

The real substance of his contribution during this period consisted in his persistent effort to keep the revolution within moral bounds. He drafted a judicial code for the revolutionary tribunals then being assembled to try suspected counter-revolutionaries (Rendle 2013; Huskey 2014, 44–45). Placing himself in the fraught position of prioritizing 'law and justice' over the 'security of the revolutionary regime (Steinberg 1953a, 64)' he himself represented, Steinberg largely functioned as a Soviet gadfly. Nowhere was this more evident than in his vocal resistance to the government's efforts to outlaw the regime's defeated class opponents (Steinberg 1953a, 76–83; Lenin 1977a, 592, 1977b, 46–47). Referencing the ethnic cleansing of Jews in the Pale during World War I, he unsuccessfully petitioned the Council of Commissars to consider what happened when 'an entire people' was 'placed beyond the law (Steinberg 1953a, 65, 99–101).'

The deep gulf separating Steinberg and the Left Socialist Revolutionaries from the Bolsheviks peaked after the Treaty of Brest-Litovsk, which the former regarded as a retreat from socialist internationalism. In March 1918, they quit the government in protest and planned an uprising (Hafner 1991). Steinberg was appointed Left Socialist Revolutionary Military Chief of Staff in the southern Russian city of Taganrog (Avner and Prat 2001, 331–333). For this reason he was not part of the revolt in Moscow that July and thus escaped arrest until February 1919, at which point he was imprisoned for four months (Ravitch 1960, 94–95). Arrested again in late 1921 for continued underground activity, he found himself under threat of assassination (Steinberg 1935a, 281) and finally left for Germany after the 1922 Moscow Trial of Socialist Revolutionaries, when point the party's Russian core was thoroughly dissolved.

Active in revolutionary circles into the 1930s, he worked closely with anarchists and non-Marxist radicals — for instance, on the United Committee for the Defense of Arrested Revolutionaries. Over time, however, he shifted gears. Focusing his energies on the Jewish community, he published frequently in Yiddish-language radical journals and also founded his own:

the *Fraye Shriftn farn Yidishn Sotsyalistishn Gedank*. This shift is expressed most concretely in his turn to territorialism after fleeing Germany for the UK in 1933, assuming leadership of the Freeland League a decade later (Salant 2010).[6]

Steinberg's remaining years were singularly devoted to the goals of this organization as he understood them. Convinced that 'acting out of statism will lead into sin,' he posed 'spiritual Judaism' against 'state Judaism (Ravitch 1960, 126, 205).' He sought Jewish cultural and territorial autonomy, but not sovereignty, in sites as far-flung as Tanzania, Alaska, French Guiana, Uruguay, Brazil, Costa Rica, and especially Australia (Steinberg 1944; Steinberg 1945; Steinberg 1948). Vociferously opposed by the Zionists, even after the 1939 White Paper closed Palestine to Jewish refugees from Nazi Europe, he (like Zalkind) did not oppose Zionism per se. Rather, he emphasized the Jewish need for refuge, wherever it might be found, and also objected to the moral and cultural effects of mainstream Zionism on Jewish consciousness.

Steinberg emigrated to the United States in 1943. There, he continued his work with the Freeland League, lectured frequently on his personal history in radical politics, and served as chief editor of and contributor to *Afn Shvel*, a Yiddish-Language journal still in publication. However hopeless it seemed, he remained active in the cause until he died of heart failure on January 2 1957. He was buried in Mt. Carmel Cemetery in Queens, New York, and publicly mourned from Mexico City to London. After that, however, the name of this 'Don Quixote of history (Ravitch 1960, 197),' a man of letters, of action, and of faith,[7] fell into obscurity and has only recently come to attract scholarly interest (Wallat 2013, 2014; Grill 2014, 2015).

Mutability and moderation: morality, Judaism, and politics

At the outset, it is perhaps worthwhile to consider the foundations of Steinberg's thought. Here, three features are key. One, his understanding as to the ground of morality. Two, how morality relates to politics generally and to socialism in particular. Three, his conception of law as the concrete embodiment of a moral code. The first of these features, we discern in an unpublished essay entitled *Concerning the Source of Morals* (Steinberg, undated A), in which he proposed to synthesize opposing grounds of morality. One, the theological, according to which God determines what is good. Another, the 'humanistic,' according to which man is the measure of all things. The former is absolute but immune to change, the latter mutable but relativistic. To retain the virtues of each approach while escaping their drawbacks, Steinberg gazed through Kantian and Bergsonian lenses at a kabbalistic reading of Job 31:2, according to which the 'divine soul in a person is a portion of God above (Luzzato 2003, 24):' practical reason, or what he called 'moral consciousness' is an 'organic part of our being,' a striving for goodness that 'cannot pause midway' but must be oriented toward 'the idea of absoluteness, or the highest good' even if the latter cannot actually be reached. In this way, he argued, 'the source of morality lies in humankind' but he relates to it as something beyond himself; it is thus firmly grounded while yet free to function as a 'creative force' in progress toward perfection. This is how Steinberg understood the rabbinic doctrine of 'Torah from Heaven (*Torah min ha'shamayim*)' — 'moral truth stems from God' but it is articulated through historically contextualized interpretation and interpolation of God's will as manifest in scripture.

The 'creative evolution' toward moral ideals in Jewish tradition appears also in another unpublished essay entitled *Concerning Jewish Religiousness* (Steinberg, undated B). In it, Steinberg interpreted Proverbs 3:18, which asserts that the Torah is a 'tree of life,' to distinguish between religion and 'religiousness,' the former representing a 'stable, concluded whole,' the latter an 'organic permeation of human life and human community with religious value ... pairing prosaic needs and duties with eternal life.' The eternity and absoluteness of the Torah, he maintained, is expressed in the claim that all Jewish souls were present at Sinai (Shevu'ot 39a) and that each generation claims this revelation anew, inserting it into the 'actual historical flow' of experience as a response to the holy with a call to '*be* holy ... within a living human society.'

This evolutionary approach to morality and its expression through tradition shaped Steinberg's conception of the relationship between morality and politics (Steinberg 1966). Proceeding dialectically, he distinguishes between 'positivism' and 'idealism.' The former 'separates politics from morals' because it represents progress as the expression of 'unchanging laws that embody no human dream, line, or ideal, but which flow of necessity' without any 'moral objective' — vital but undisciplined, politics 'rolls about in the filthiest streets.' The latter, 'separates morals from politics' because it does not really try to translate them into a concrete historical program — pure but bloodless, morality resides on snowy mountain peaks 'so that the sinful earth not brush against the hem of its skirt.'

These antitheses, Steinberg attributes to Bolshevism on the one hand and Tolstoyism on the other. This distinction is considered below. For the present, their synthesis in libertarian socialism — that is, anarchism — is more important. Libertarian socialism, he wrote, 'does not recognize a separation between politics and morals.' The socialist revolutionary must, on the one hand, always be guided by 'a spirit of decision and rebellion that flows from' a 'powerful moral idea that is perpetually renewed,' and never come to terms with human suffering or treat it as inevitable. On the other hand, this moral ideal must not float 'above people and their history but [be] really connected to the concrete development of humanity;' the revolutionary must take 'personal responsibility for the course of history' and bind his or her ideal with political action, working *with* 'suffering people' struggling to 'liberate themselves.' We shall later examine Steinberg's understanding of libertarian socialism in greater detail, but it suffices to note the way it plays into his general moral-political world-view.

For Steinberg, this synthesis is expressed through law, which draws the line between legitimate and illegitimate use of forceful means to realize moral ends. His master work in this field was his doctoral dissertation, *The Doctrine of Crime in the Talmud* (Steinberg 1910). A thorough elaboration of this text is beyond the scope of this chapter but, stated in brief, it is dedicated to precisely determining the nature of crime and the limits of culpability. He explains that to be subject to criminal law, an act must be *performed*, which excludes thoughts and feelings. It much be *successful*, which excludes attempts. Finally, it must be the *sufficient* and *immediate cause* of an injury. Its perpetrator must *intend* to violate *a definite norm of which he or she has been made aware*. These carefully constructed limits to punitive force — together with the theology of mutability and moderation on which they are based — become an important point of reference when we consider Steinberg's critique of revolutionary violence in the context of the Bolshevik-led 'Red Terror' to which we shall turn shortly.

A moral revolution

Steinberg's account of the Russian Revolution was profoundly shaped by his belief that ideals must inspire and guide (if not govern) political action. External material factors alone, he wrote — servitude, exploitation, war, and so on — are insufficient to motivate an uprising. People 'fight not only to gain freedom *from* something, but also to gain freedom *for* something (Steinberg 1953a, 11).' Leaning on the vision of 'a new heaven and a new earth (Isaiah 65:17),' he explained that the people of Russian wanted the revolution to 'assure … a chaste and decent life, to revive prostrate truth, to banish sin from the earth' and in this way bring about 'far reaching changes in the structure of society, changes that would alter the relationship between one person and another *spiritually* and *morally* as well as governmentally and economically (Steinberg 1953a, 12–13).' More than that, because they held that 'all aspects of existence — social, economic, political, spiritual,

moral, familial were opened to purposeful fashioning by human hands'
they also believed that 'everything is possible for people (Steinberg 1953a,
44–45)' and that these changes *could* be made — and comprehensively
so. This meant, first, that in striving to institute the proverbial 'laws of
truth and equity (Psalms 11:8)' the people recognized 'no contradiction
between the human, universal human, morality and the "morality of the
revolution" (Steinberg 1927a, 16).' It meant, second, that the 'regeneration
of life itself' that they sought to realize might dawn in Russia but 'could
not be checked by national frontiers' — the revolution 'became part of the
great desire for world peace, for "the friendship of all peoples" (Steinberg
1953a, 13).' In this way, the populist call for 'liberated humanity, liberated land, liberated labor (Steinberg 1953a, 20)' represented a call for
more than bread and physical freedom; it was a 'moral goal, a life-work
(Steinberg 1935a, 16)' undertaken not only with 'joyousness and resolve
(Steinberg 1953a, 13),' but with religious solemnity — at least as Steinberg
understood it.

It is with these sentiments in mind that Steinberg described the narodnik
(and consequently the Socialist Revolutionary) conviction that 'the process of
change could not but go through the individual conscience of each revolutionary fighter (Steinberg 1953a, 118)' and, therefore, that the 'critically thinking,
and deep-feeling person' is the true agent of history (Steinberg 1953a, 117).
Because it is so prominent in his account of the original 'spirit of October,'
let us begin with the affective aspects of revolutionary consciousness.

Clearly, not all revolutionary sentiments are equal or good. Steinberg
identified three which, in his view, followed the dark pattern of 'humanity,
power, violence, cruelty, [and] inhumanity.' Some acted out of rage and
despair. Mired in the psychology of the 'upstart slave,' they used their
newly acquired power to wreak vengeance rather than to transform social
institutions; thus, liberation concluded with 'renewed enslavement (Steinberg
1953a, 196–200).' Others had aesthetic motivations; they were intoxicated
by the 'brutal spectacle' of the struggle. Referencing a rabbinic teaching
which states that the traveller who interrupts his learning to remark on the
beauty of the landscape takes his life into his own hands (M. Avot 3:8),
Steinberg explained that nature is sublime but neutral, while the law separates
good from evil. He who conflates the two, the Good and the Beautiful, he
continued, risks indifference to human life and human dignity and thus
puts the revolution at risk. Still others stood up out of pity — according to
Steinberg, an intrinsically paternalistic sentiment giving rise to the impression
that one knows what is best for others and ultimately to the conclusion that
one can coerce them for their own good. As he strikingly put it, 'pity hides
the sting of dictatorship (Steinberg 1953a, 206–212).' These sentiments,
Steinberg ascribed to the Bolsheviks.

Love was something else. A loving relationship, Steinberg explained, is egalitarian in character and focused on building together a shared life (Steinberg 1953a, 212). Accordingly, revolutionaries guided by love are concerned less with destroying what was than with constructing, in a spirit of 'harmony' and 'brotherhood,' what should be. Therefore, they are suspicious of power, understanding that 'in the violent flood of state coercion not only the rights, but human being itself, would drown (Steinberg 1953a, 217).' This is the revolutionary sentiment that Steinberg ascribed, not only to the Socialist Revolutionary and the narodniks before them, but to the people as a whole. Moved 'by love for the neighbor far more than by hatred for the enemy,' by the desire to liberate the oppressed and redeem the downtrodden than any ambition to topple the 'mighty and proud (Steinberg 1953a, 11),' they rose up in a 'historic love-storm' so as to bring about 'a new moral world order (Steinberg 1953a, 14)' and 'change everything so that our mendacious, tedious, miserable life may be come just, joyous and beautiful (Steinberg 1953a, 299).'

For Steinberg, this 'loving' approach was intimately tied to a moral theory of revolution, which brings us to the critical aspect of revolutionary consciousness. Emphasis on the *moral* motivations of the revolutionary implies that the revolutionary is a real moral agent. Progress, he held, is achieved not via 'obedience to the historic *fatum*,' but through a 'moral law' adopted by 'free decision (Steinberg 1953a, 117).' We are not, he contended, merely the dice 'which history tosses into the arena of its cold and deadly game.' Rather, 'we are the creators of the revolution' and therefore *responsible* for it. If it constitutes a sort of 'a social earthquake (Steinberg 1927a, 9–10)' over which total control is impossible, this does not absolve its participants from guiding its progression so far as possible. The masses, he wrote, are not 'human avalanches' or 'blind historical blocks of stone in which the individual worker … is as lost as a pin in a field.' Rather, they are 'free, unions of people who group themselves together, one next to the other, such that each feels his neighbor's warmth and … drives the soul of the other forward (Steinberg 1927a, 9–10).' Revolutions are made by moral agents working collectively toward 'the spiritual and moral liberation of humanity;' therefore, they must 'remain under the constant control of moral ideals (Steinberg 1953a, 116–117).'

As Steinberg addressed it, this involved a synthesis of utopian and scientific socialism capable of overcoming the weaknesses of both. If utopian socialism itself was 'a head without a body,' he wrote, scientific socialism became a 'body without a head.' The former 'strummed the strings of the human soul,' inspiring it with ideas of justice and uprightness, but neglected 'realistic paths (Steinberg 1927a, 286)' to their concretization and so 'forgot the means for the sake of the ends (Steinberg 1927a, 295).' Scientific socialism did the opposite. With what he called 'synthetic socialism' Steinberg aimed to furnish the revolutionary body with a head, taking a sober account of means without losing sight of moral ends.

In essence, synthetic socialism represented Steinberg's attempt to defend certain forms of revolutionary violence without writing a blank check. For instance, he justified the use of violence to negate a 'fiendish *order* together with its *institutions* (Steinberg 1927a, 49)' but not to 'annihilate the counter-revolutionary camp (Steinberg 1927a, 60).' Individuals or groups *actively* working to undermine the revolution could likewise be neutralized. But to hold 'innocent people responsible for their ... incidental class origins (Steinberg 1927a, 53)' or to criminalize a 'political abstraction (Steinberg 1931, 46)' he regarded as anathema (in keeping with his talmudic research) — hence his defense of the Kadets and of the Estonian upper classes. Similarly, the Left Socialist Revolutionaries 'did not see themselves as the only prophets and interpreters of history' and did not feel entitled to 'force their will on the masses of the people.' Rather they strove 'to realize their program of social transformation and personal liberation with the knowledge and the will of the people themselves (Steinberg 1953a, 121),' weakening ideological opponents by *'attracting* them to our side with spiritual force (Steinberg 1927a, 60)' alone. The point, of course, being to cultivate 'universal human brotherhood according to which each individual person who has removed the class-mantle from himself is dear,' not to empower a 'new despotic class (Steinberg 1927a, 60).' If for the Bolsheviks violence 'became a principle,' for the Left Socialist Revolutionaries it was never more than a bitter necessity (Steinberg 1953a, 125–126).' A necessity it was though (at least as Steinberg saw it), which brings us to the question of *how* he justified it. As with his efforts to establish the relationship between morality and politics generally, he proceeded dialectically.

Revolutionary violence: thesis (Bolshevism), antithesis (Tolstoyism), synthesis (the Left Socialist Revolutionaries)

Steinberg wrote that the 'naive and faithful open soul' of the people that 'was, not long ago, in harmony with the stormy-spirited expression of struggle had been shaken to its foundation (Steinberg 1927a, 18)' — 'the moral content of October' having been 'enslaved to a ... state-party' that regarded itself as 'sole embodiment of historical reason' and which was prepared to lift the proverbial tablets of the revolution 'over the heads of the people' and strike them with those same tablets. Thus, a 'sanctification of God's name thus becomes a desecration thereof (Steinberg 1951a, 156).' Let us examine Steinberg's account of the Bolshevik thesis on which this shift was based.

As indicated already, Steinberg regarded Marxism as a form of economic determinism according to which 'human will' is treated as an emissary 'through which natural laws are revealed' — merely 'a link in a chain, that evolves on its own.' One's 'thoughts and ideas, his hopes and dreams, his moral and religious beliefs' are not 'freely adopted' ideals, but merely the results of 'social evolution.' The individual may aspire to discover 'the mechanism of the chain and helping it to develop (Steinberg 1927a, 280–82),' finding a shadow of freedom in 'submission to historical necessity (Steinberg 1927a, 290).' Accordingly, there is room neither for selecting a course of action 'in agreement with freely adopted objectives' nor for rejecting one 'in agreement with a moral ideal.' The 'subjective moment' is simply absent (Steinberg 1927a, 282). Thus, Marxism is unable to 'pose moral questions as free tasks and creative motions of consciousness and will' — it 'is not so much anti-moral as *amoral* in a way that leads to anti-moralism (Steinberg 1927a, 288–289).'

As Steinberg goes on to explain, this is not merely a theoretical problem, but one with significant practical consequences. For one, it implies that 'every action is necessarily sanctioned a priori as a consequence of historical necessity (Steinberg 1927a, 283).' In this way, he continues, the moral conundrum of violence and its justification simply cannot be posed. 'Just like a stream of water ... does not choose the "best" path,' a Bolshevik whose ideology leaves no room for moral ideas and 'human feeling' does not deliberate about the justice of revolutionary means (Steinberg 1966). Appealing to the mixture of admiration and horror which the ancient rabbis had for R. Meir, who was clever enough to convincingly declare the pure impure and vice versa (Eruvin 13b), Steinberg wrote that 'there exists not a single *sherez* (impure thing) in world history which it [Marxism] is unable to scientifically purify (Steinberg 1925, 5).' Efficacy is the only question.

The second consequence of this amoralism is totalitarianism. In contrast to Left Socialist Revolutionary narodniks, the Bolshevik idea of '"the masses" is almost geological ... not connected with free people, personalities, but different *land masses* which, in order to be moved, must be penetrated with explosives (Steinberg 1925, 6)' wielded by the 'conscious tools of historical providence,' a self-appointed priesthood alone able to discern the '"historical laws" and operate according to them (Steinberg 1927a, 190).' Thus, Steinberg wrote, they turned to the suffering masses in a paternalistic spirit:

> They do not say 'come, let us destroy this hell together,' but 'we will save you from it, we will bear the weight of history and you will obey the commands of history.' You do not need freedom in the simple sense, your freedom is expressed in deference to the dictator. It is upon you to gratefully follow the path we show you as representatives of historical reason.

Perversely, liberty and subjugation become synonymous; the masses serve as 'material for the use of their exalted rulers' — and *this* is their freedom. Like Pharoah, who sought to realize certain 'exalted ideas about religion or the state' but 'actually built memorials to slavery (Steinberg 1966),' the Bolsheviks nationalized 'not only the material wealth of the bourgeois, *but also the free will of the workers* (Steinberg 1966).' Referencing an ancient midrash (ER 5:21–22), he comments that 'they repeat the old legend of Pithom and Raamses: social walls are built with the souls of living children (Steinberg 1925, 6).' In the name of freedom, the Bolsheviks constructed a regime based 'on the old pattern, with a centralized machinery of government (Steinberg 1935a, 203)' — indeed, one far more brutal than that which preceded it.

The 'logical conclusion' of this train of thought, so Steinberg explained, is that every deviation from the party line is also a deviation from the 'dictates of history' that 'must be removed unhesitatingly and ruthlessly (Steinberg 1953a, 119).' From here, he asserted, 'flows the [state] terror that permeates its [Bolshevism's] whole being (Steinberg 1966)' like a 'sort of social sap that oozes from the living orifices of the revolutionary organism (Steinberg 1927a, 166).' The 'organized conscious minority' that stands in for 'the collective, the naturally developing creation of the masses (Steinberg 1927a, 110),' aiming to force the latter toward a certain end, is isolated and vulnerable. The so-called 'enemy of the revolution' eventually comes to include 'everyone outside of power (Steinberg 1927a, 21)' — identical with the people itself, it 'becomes infinite.' If Marxist amoralism means that 'all is permitted' in the struggle against enemies of the revolution, it turns out that 'every means of violence and coercion against *everyone* (Steinberg 1953a, 134–135)' is permitted.

The problem, as Steinberg saw, it extended far beyond the creation of a new hierarchy to replace the old class system. The revolution was not just political, but extended to 'all fields of personal, economic, and social life;' all of them, therefore, came 'under the supervision of the state power (Steinberg 1927a, 25).' Terror therefore became a '*system* of violence' involving 'the whole of one's life' under which the entire population suffered. Physical and psychological, direct and indirect, it functioned to intimidate people into submission and bend them to the 'absolute will' of the regime (Steinberg 1927a, 19–20).

Because the reach of state terror was so wide, it extended its 'roots even into relations among subjects (Steinberg 1927a, 25)' and thus had a profoundly corrupting effect on society as a whole. So Steinberg contended, 'if all are slaves in relation to the state, then among the slaves each will turn on his neighbor;' terror from above is paralleled by 'terror from below among the citizens (Steinberg 1953a, 139).' Under the weight of 'mutual suspicion and distrust (Steinberg 1927a, 25),' solidarity disappears and 'society is shattered into millions of kernels (Steinberg 1927a, 105–106).'

This state of affairs kills 'the soul of the people (Steinberg 1927a, 26).' It is, Steinberg taught, in 'the nature of human genius to pronounce the defiant, "I cannot be silent."' When it is silenced nonetheless, genius dissipates; 'active will turns into human dust' and 'thought either freezes into icy silence or degenerates into slavish obedience (Steinberg 1953a, 136).' According to Steinberg, the most terrible expression of this moral deterioration was the way in which popular wrath was transformed from a spontaneous outburst into a *modus vivendi* through the revolutionary tribunals. In the 'oppressed slave, there often resides a master waiting for his moment (Steinberg 1927a, 160),' Steinberg wrote. Rather than serving as a 'moral center of gravity' and awakening more altruistic instincts, however, the Bolsheviks flattered their passions, directing popular wrath against class-scapegoats (Steinberg 1927a, 28–29). Thus distracted from the real task of building up institutions of justice and self-governance (Steinberg 1927a, 32), the infantalized population became that much easier to rule. In brief, Steinberg objects to the Marxist thesis on the grounds that its materialism and its determinism preclude moral reasoning and lead the way both to unbridled violence and to the concentration of power in the hands of a revolutionary vanguard.

His outrage and disappointment, however, did not permit him to accept the Tolstoyan antithesis. As he represented it: terror contradicts 'divine and human justice.' In spite of whatever efficacy it may have, it evokes 'lively human feeling of protest, the feeling that divides us from beastiality.' While acknowledging that moral sentiment is the 'subterranean spring that waters the whole moral field of the soul (Steinberg 1927a, 71–72),' alone he regarded it as an insufficient response to violence and injustice.

In Steinberg's view, sentiment is haphazard. First, 'it may condemn [today] what it will praise in the morning.' Second, there is no 'universal barometer of moral feeling,' and different people 'have different moral sensitivities' so that 'a more refined soul cries out bitterly and sharply in response to deeds that other souls do not even notice (Steinberg 1927a, 73–74).' Tolstoyism represented, for Steinberg, the extreme of such sensitivity. As he described it: 'never and nowhere, without any conditions may one force the human will' or resort to violence, even in response to the 'greatest and universally recognized evil.' Because resistance focused on 'social labor … eventually becomes social conflict,' all effort must be directed toward 'an interior struggle, in one's own personality, against evil passions (Steinberg 1927a, 75–76).'

At the outset, Steinberg points out that this approach assumes 'the just, morally healthy, happy human' as the point of departure toward rather than the result of a just social order (Steinberg 1927a, 75). More importantly, he argued that to rely solely on 'peaceful preaching' in the socialist struggle for human liberation is to transform the effort into a 'spiritual-utopian ideal … a regulative idea and nothing more (Steinberg 1927a, 78).' This is because failure to take account of the realistic means toward an end 'ultimately means abandoning the end (Steinberg 1927a, 82).' Awaiting 'millions of personal transformations' and 'transferring the whole task to the individual soul,' he argued, 'means yielding to the evil in the world.' Thus, 'freeing people, the Tolstoyan doctrine let humanity go under.' Paradoxically, the warm moral sentiment of retreating from *all* violence becomes 'the cold frost' of tacitly sanctioning it, something which only 'cruel souls' can accept (Steinberg 1927a, 79).

Marxists and Tolstoyans alike yielded passively to laws they regarded as inexorable — be they historical or moral. Steinberg believed, on the one hand, that history supplies but 'general lines of necessity and 'abstract schemes of inevitability (Steinberg 1927a, 169);' on the other, that an end is not a hard and fast rule, but an 'unclear silhouette (Steinberg 1927a, 89).' Mankind, he wrote, 'stands above the laws of nature, but below the *self-given ethic of his own spiritual life*' and 'writes his laws' accordingly (Steinberg 1927a, 329). In essence, Steinberg upheld the freedom to 'morally *evaluate* our deeds (Steinberg 1927a, 90)' and called for *deliberation*. Treating violence as an inescapable evil, but an evil nonetheless, he demanded a synthesis between Marxist and Tolstoyan antinomies reflecting his rabbinic faith in the mutable expression of a law oriented toward a moral absolute. Only by accepting the burden of violence *as a burden*, he maintained, would socialism proceed from 'pure and sterile ideal spheres to a place of imperfect but real actualization (Steinberg 1927a, 80).' This balancing act is what Steinberg called 'moral sense,' which he poetically described as 'an ethical musicality of human spirit,' a 'permanent unrest [that] strums the strings of the human soul' in which consciousness as to 'the sinfulness of violence' tempers 'the devilish evil inclination of violence (Steinberg 1927a, 329).'

Insisting that socialism is 'a moral objective according to its essence (Steinberg 1927a, 126),' Steinberg cautioned that in 'chasing after the external embodiment of the goal (Steinberg 1927a, 85),' as it were building 'the walls and domes of the [revolutionary] temple,' it is possible to abandon the 'inner spirit and pathos, which embody the soul of the temple (Steinberg 1927a, 87).' At the same time, he maintained that in seeking 'pure means, we do not throw away the substance, the end' for their sake, asserting that there must be 'harmony between means and ends (Steinberg 1927a, 82–83).' This requirement, Steinberg takes to a necessary extreme: were there '*no* paths to socialism but amoral ones' he asserted, it would be necessary to 'turn back with shattered hopes, but not shattered ideals.' Appealing to biblical precedent, he wrote that by 'smashing the tablets [of the revolution] on the earth,' *true* revolutionaries would 'preserve the commandments' engraved thereon, thus ensuring 'victory over the land of the future,' if not of the present (Steinberg 1927a, 96).

In substance, this is Steinberg's Kantian 'critique of pure violence.' Its 'categorical imperatives' run as follows: 'use violence only when you have no other available means in your arsenal. Use it only such that it does not destroy the upbuilding of a society of equal and pure people (Steinberg 1927a, 310).' Expressed otherwise, he proposed to replace the bloody formula 'the end justifies the means' with another: 'the end justifies *through* the means' that are 'inwardly, intimately, its own blood relation (Steinberg 1927a, 89).' By 'blood relation,' I understand him to suggest that means and ends need not be *identical*, but they must belong to the same 'family;' the former must closely approximate the latter as siblings or cousins resemble one another.

With these guidelines in mind, Steinberg redefined the idea of the 'transitional period' to socialism on the basis of which Bolsheviks justified a system of terror; it must, he asserted, 'entail no transition *from* the old world, but only a transition *to* the new (Steinberg 1927a, 182).' Concretely, this was taken to imply a 'socialist-maximum program' according to which 'elements of the era of realization' are maximized 'in a rudimentary form' while 'elements of the old world' are minimized so far as possible. Concretely, Steinberg insisted that socialism is an effort to 'liberate not simply an oppressed class, but to liberate *human beings* (Steinberg 1927a, 133–134).' As he saw it, this meant 'rooting out, from within, the old world of violence and evil' by doing 'everything in our power to preserve the ideal of humanity (Steinberg 1927a, 340–341)' — above all, by distinguishing 'between the [old] social order and its living bearers' and thus striving not to 'kill the human being in the class enemy, but kill the class enemy in the human beings (Steinberg 1927a, 134).' Abstracting from the rabbinic principle that 'the Jewish people are guarantors for (lit. 'mixed together' with) one another (Shavuot 39b)' Steinberg contended that socialism 'strives to negate the social class-blemish and tries to replace it with mankind in general (Steinberg 1927a, 308).' If the 'cultural ideal of socialism' is the liberation of an 'isolated I' and its free transformation into a 'collective we (Steinberg 1927a, 139),' then it is undermined by 'hatred and vengeance (Steinberg 1927a, 142).' Thus, Steinberg concluded, 'in order to have free and good people in the future, it is necessary to have love and care now, to extend these feelings to real people, to everyone' — the new world is built on 'mercy, soft-heartedness, self-sacrifice … mutual understanding (Steinberg 1927a, 140).'

Here, a brief post-Soviet coda is in order. As Steinberg gradually came to articulate his political ideas with exclusive reference to the Jewish community, his pacifism became more pronounced. He wrote that 'in Jewish consciousness, every war is a crime' — not least because they tend to 'play out at the expense of the Jewish masses.' Thus, he asked rhetorically, 'can a religious [Jewish] person take part in any war, assisting the effort either actively or passively?' With 'religious self-understanding,' he explained, a Jew called to service must reply 'I refuse *because I am a Jew*,' because the Torah teaches 'do not kill' and demands self-sacrifice over transgression (Sanhedrin 74a). He remarks furthermore that Isaiah's vision for the 'end of days is not in conflict with the present;' rather, it will be fulfilled '*thanks to* the world-changing deed of today.' Indeed, he saw the Jews as occupying a unique position of resistance. Invoking scripture, 'there is no peace … for the wicked (Isaiah 48:22),' he remarked that 'Christian peace efforts are too connected with present states in the culture-world to function as an independent factor in the anti-war struggle.' But as a people apart, the Jews have the ability to 'conduct a principled battle against the angels of destruction (Steinberg, undated B).' In this spirit, he dispensed with peace manifestos and parliamentary votes, recommending instead direct action through a general strike and writing of the duty 'not, in any way, to take personal part in preparation for any future slaughter: neither institutions in which material tools, nor in which the human material, are prepared (Steinberg 1952, 149).' Not without justice did Natan Hofshi (1966) write that over time Steinberg 'lost his faith in the ability of violence to establish the kingdom of heaven on earth and to remove violence from the earth.' While in other post-Soviet sources, Steinberg persisted in the position on violence described in this section, it is clear that he came to lean further toward the Tolstoyan worldview than he had before.

Socialism and anarchization

We have already taken note of Steinberg's conviction that socialist efforts to liberate oppressed people from exploitation are merely a means to the higher end: 'restoring inner and outer freedom,' via the 'revolutionization of society and of the individual (Steinberg, undated C).' As he expressed it elsewhere, this meant that the individual must buck supposed necessities natural and artificial and instead place himself 'under his *own freely recognized moral laws*.' Socialism, he held, will either liberate mankind in this way, 'or it will not free him at all (Steinberg 1927a, 346).' Fundamentally, Steinberg's socialism was suffused with an anarchist ethos.

This fusion of socialism and anarchism dates to Steinberg's days as a leader in the Left Socialist Revolutionary Party. In contrast to 'state-obsessed Bolsheviks (Steinberg 1953a, 60, 64)' the Socialist Revolutionaries 'went to the people' and sought to develop a program informed by peasant traditions embodied in the common ownership and administration of the land commune (*mir*). They held a federation of such collectives to be 'consonant with the freedom of the individual (Steinberg 1935b, 18).' A comprehensive account of the official Left Socialist Revolutionary position can be gleaned from a document appropriately entitled *Theses Concerning the State* (*Tezisy o Gosudarstve*), which Steinberg (1921) published in *Znamya*. Affirming the necessity of nourishing the 'revolutionary creativity of the masses' by instituting modes of self-governance conducive to the 'simultaneous development of a social group and a free person,' he opens by rejecting democracies bourgeois and proletarian alike. Both, he argued, alienate the masses and cultivate complacency by appealing to the fiction of representation — albeit in different ways. Liberal democracies through the illusion of inter-class solidarity via universal suffrage (Steinberg 1921). 'Proletarian democracy' through the idea of a 'transitional period' between the end of revolutionary hostilities and the ultimate 'withering away of the state' — an indeterminate interval during which a 'conscious avant-garde' exercises power on behalf of the passive multitude and leverages 'the most severe compulsion' to reeducate mankind from above in the paradoxical hope of thereby creating a 'free stateless life.' In contrast, the Left Socialist Revolutionaries believed in a 'conscious *majority*' capable of acting as its own agent in the social revolution and considered this to be the only approach consistent with the revolutionary goal of freedom (Steinberg 1921).

Steinberg's solution consisted first in distinguishing between political and socio-economic aspects of the state. Transferring power to the workers *might* eliminate class-exploitation, but not political domination. Being 'a certain kind of social and psychological relationship,' the state is fed by the 'subtle and hellishly multifaceted poison of power' pervading other relationships — e.g. that of family, church, and community. Thus, realization of 'ideal-anarchism' in the fullest sense would necessarily entail a gradual process of social and cultural change. While these changes were underway, Steinberg proposed a paradigm shift vis-a-vis political and economic power: rather than merely transferring it, or dreaming of its elimination, socialists ought to seek to reduce its *volume*. That is, mitigating the power of the state by limiting its functions, its geographic scope, and the intensity of its coercive force while also cultivating the administrative competencies of the masses (Steinberg 1921). 'The idea of the people's power,' he contended elsewhere, was in the air at an early stage of the revolution, when local councils originally formed to control 'the actions of the Provisional Government showed an ever-increasing tendency to evolve into direct government organs (Steinberg 1953a, 20).' However, as the Bolsheviks consolidated their power these institutions were quickly emptied of any meaningful agency.

He recommended a 'bicameral' system of councils (*soviets*) and worker-syndicates. The former being populated by freely elected and recallable deputies appointed by the latter. This would ensure a 'vital labor connection' between voters and delegates and allow for the 'counterbalancing of forces,' or a separation of powers extending beyond the 'constitutional architectonics of the state' and into the concrete life of the populace. This democratic system — inclusive of de-classed former bourgeois and nobles — would be organized along federative lines. Evoking Proudhon's (1863) *Principle of Federation*, Steinberg envisioned a 'union of unions' in which local autonomy could be preserved and yet general resolutions could be reached through a 'bottom up' approach by dint of which the 'manifestation of power comes closest to the will of the individual citizen (Steinberg 1921).' This same approach, he pointed out, also being a key element in the 'education and the character' development of their members, facilitating the sort of personal transformation that allows for libertarian structures to function as decision-making bodies (Steinberg 1953a, 123).

Within this system, he continued, government functions should be carried not by 'physical violence' but through 'spiritual influence' channeled via 'cultural alliances, ideological and political parties, and economic agreements.' A 'truly non-state public' consisting in such 'free unions' would become a social force in its own right. The 'free habits of a stateless community' would accumulate; 'laws ... and emerging customs, rites, and precedents' would take shape and collectively make for a 'gradual softening, weakening and, in this sense, "withering away"' even of the mitigated state apparatus. This moderate approach, he felt, would move society in the direction of 'ideal of freedom, the liberation of external and internal servitude,' while giving it time to adapt (Steinberg 1921).

It is important to note that throughout the Left Socialist Revolutionary manifesto, Steinberg repeatedly insisted that his platform be distinguished from anarchism. Proceeding in his customary dialectical manner, he posed socialist mutuality against anarchist freedom. Anarchism, he wrote, emphasizes 'the liberated personality on the background of society;' as expressed by the formula 'I+I+I,' he ascribed to it a granular conception of social life and reduced it to pure individualism. Socialism, in contrast, emphasizes 'brotherly society on the foundations of the liberated personality (Steinberg 1935b, 23).' While acknowledging that many anarchists supported programs roughly similar to his own, Steinberg considered these to be inconsistent with *anarchism as he represented it*. Thus, the Left Socialist Revolutionary synthesis of these antithesis — mutuality and freedom — is essentially an appropriation of anarchism *as it was actually conceived* (Steinberg 1952, 49–74).

In *The Role of Anarchist Principles in Revolutionary Socialism* (Steinberg 1929a), Steinberg openly embraced the anarchist core of his socialism. Drawing on Lavrov's assertion in *The State Element in the Future Society* that 'in the future society, not only can the element of the state be reduced to a minimum, it can actually disappear' he set out first to distinguish 'revolutionary folkism (narodism)' from state socialism and then to demonstrate that it and anarchism are not 'distinct systems.' Rather, 'in its veins flows also the blood of Bakunin' — that is, an 'elemental and infinite struggle for absolute freedom.' Most striking in this text is Steinberg's account of the circumstances leading to this shift. Having 'peeked behind the curtain of dominion' and 'experienced the true nature of power,' he wrote, he and his comrades concluded that 'all monopolistic state organs' are dangerous. Thus, he later wrote that:

> The state, the conscious machine that completely encompasses the life of the citizen, that is centralistic by nature and power hungry in essence … evokes in us … feelings of wrath and opposition … Our objective is to eliminate this idea, to stuff it down into the abyss of history … We want to turn the shocked world away from the psychological and the whole condition of statehood and spiritual servitude. (Steinberg 1952, 115)

That is, he ascribes to the Left Socialist Revolutionaries an interest in cultivating the self-governing capacities of the individual. Accordingly, he proceeded to outline a plan for socio-political organization substantially identical to that found in his earlier *Theses on the State* as well as several other texts (Steinberg 1925; Steinberg 1932) — the only difference being that he adds consumer cooperatives to the 'bicameral' system and acknowledged the impact of 'revolutionary [anarcho-]syndicalism (Steinberg 1952, 116)' on this train of thought. While Steinberg believed this plan would ensure that 'state organs will *functionally* disappear, he also persisted in the claim that such an organizational plan is *not* anarchism. 'Just as one can cut an earthworm into tiny pieces and yet, in each piece, the same worm remains, so too,' he maintained, 'dominion, even when it is in many hands, when its content is divided into many pieces, remains dominion all the same (Steinberg 1929a, 323).'

This brings us to the real crux of Steinberg's relationship with anarchism. To him, anarchism represents not simply a society in which power is radically democratized, but a *powerless* social system; in this sense, it is not a system at all, but 'a social-psychological category' denoting 'the deepest transformation of human consciousness (Steinberg 1929a, 331).' Conceived in this way, he critiqued anarchist thought *not* so as to reject it, but so as to deny that it is truly anarchistic and then to claim its basic ethos for revolutionary folkism. This critique focuses on three arenas in which hierarchical relations persist even granting the abolition of the state: in mass production, in modern consumerism, and in the tyranny of custom.

Steinberg's political-economic critique contends with Kropotkin's *Factories, Fields, and Workshops*, a text in which the author described a system of economically and politically integrated but nonetheless autonomous municipalities. Placing a high value on agriculture and handicraft, Kropotkin nonetheless acknowledged the inevitability of mass production. To mitigate its negative effects, he proposed to decentralize heavy industry, to improve factory conditions, and to pass saved labor time on to workers who might then use it to exercise creative freedom. This is where Steinberg's critique picks up. In the factory, he explained, 'human material is always divided into two castes;' the relations between them being represented 'by an order and not by an agreement;' thus, it functions like a small state. He maintained that this state of affairs could not be isolated and that it would leave 'its mark on society as a whole (Steinberg 1929a, 325).' Because the 'feel for power (*makht-gefil*)' is mainly nourished by the conditions of mass production (Steinberg 1929a, 327),' he proposed instead to 'submit the capitalist order to folk-industry (Steinberg 1925, 12).'

Steinberg's critique of consumerism contends with Kropotkin's *Conquest of Bread*, wherein the author affirms that the good life involves a measure of luxury. Steinberg countered that 'a substantial reduction of dominion goes hand in hand with readiness for a degree of primitivism, a free-willed simplification of life (Steinberg 1929a, 327).' One cannot 'exit the hidden system of the present society as long as he is enchanted by the countless achievements of modern economics and technics,' Steinberg wrote. For one, the cacophony of experience drowns out the proverbial 'thin, still voice' that keeps him aware of his 'brother who falls next to him (Steinberg 1952, 333).' Secondly, consumerism serves to render the working class 'spiritually dependent on the old bourgeois way of life (Steinberg 1925, 5),' assimilating a revolutionary force into bourgeois society. For the worker to 'rise above his prosaic interests, for him to fight not only for himself and his family, but for a new world and a new generation,' Steinberg contended, 'he must delay his material interests (Steinberg 1927b, 14).' This, he called the 'principle of poverty' — 'asceticism ... in service of enrichment of human life in the world (Steinberg 1952, 332).'

Finally, Steinberg asserts that Kropotkin does not adequately address the 'countless relations among people in which they are connected to one another in vertical lines such that one stands higher and the next lower.' Power, he continued, 'expresses itself in all human relations.' Representatives of the state are simply the most glaring examples:

> Their primary, subterranean roots extend into the life ways and intimate relations of human beings ... This power is neither physical nor juridical; it is but a spiritual mastery that rules with the greatest force over the deepest recesses of the human soul ... [There,] the super-social, or better put preso-cial, roots of all political and economic power are found. (Steinberg 1929a, 328)

It is 'already government,' Steinberg wrote, when one person in a relationship 'down from above and the other, up from below (Steinberg 1927a, 343).' Therefore, he insisted that 'revolutionary work must penetrate every cell of individual, intimate life: the family and the education of children, relations between men and women, between coworkers and between friends (Steinberg 1932).' In essence, Steinberg points to what is referred to as the 'tyranny of custom' — a problem that Emma Goldman, for instance, more famously raised in connection to Kropotkin's rather backward-gazing attitudes toward gender and sexuality (Woodcock 2004, 216; Hartung 1983; Haaland 1993, 1–24). As she argued, the revolution is not just about broad political structures. It is about the most intimate relations too; if these remain non-egalitarian, then the revolution as a whole has failed.*

For these reasons, Steinberg called for a true transitional period, consisting not in an 'extension of the old broken world' after the Bolshevik model (Steinberg 1929a, 330), but in a critical struggle 'to break the bones of the old statism' while acknowledging that 'shattered power is *still power* (Steinberg 1952, 120)' and that without broad cultural changes designed to extract the '*chinovnik and the gendarme* [bureaucrat and policeman] in the soul of humanity (Steinberg 1925, 12),' any process of 'organizing human society … creates power (Steinberg 1927a, 341).' In this way, Steinberg adopted for *socialism*, or revolutionary folkism, the 'broader path of *anarchization* as a revolutionary principle (Steinberg 1929b)' — in place of the 'famous formula about "abolishing the state,"' in the strictly negative sense, Steinberg proposed another: 'creatively killing the state!' by positively displacing it (Steinberg 1929a, 332). Identifying Kropotkin — whom he claimed for

---

* Here I wish to make note of a section of the original manuscript of this chapter which, for lack of space, could not be included in this volume. In it, I discuss the fact that in his creative and biographical works Steinberg relied almost solely on female characters to depict the moral vision of the revolution. In *The Thorny Path* (1927), Maria, the wife of Alexander, the protagonist of the story, who descends from high-minded ideals into cold-blooded calculation as to the use of revolutionary violence, challenges Alexander's justifications, eventually driving him to admit that 'it can't go on like this … other ways must be found.' More active roles are played in *You Have Triumphed Makhnachov!* by Irena and Ryazanskaya, members of the Revolutionary Committee who resist the same cold-blooded violence as defended by Makhnachov (a literary representation of Lenin) and his followers. This is even articulated within the framework of the Jewish imaginary; when Zuckerman (a Makhnachov ally) claims the right of vengeance against the ruling class that abetted anti-Jewish violence, Ryazanskaya rejects 'balancing historical accounts' in the name of universal justice. *Spiridonova: Revolutionary Terrorist* (1935) traces the life of Maria Spiridonova, a leading member of the Left Socialist Revolutionary Party, likewise representing her as the embodiment of that group's values.

narodism — as 'the apostle of this path (Steinberg 1929b)' he concluded
that revolutionary folkism:

> Accepts anarchism into its ideological space as an inner guiding and living
> principle ... Anarchism is, for us, not a social limit, an isolated island to which
> one must swim and stand on two feet. Anarchism is a spiritual wind that fills
> the sails of the transitional period, a spiritual principle that rests on the material
> of socialism. In this sense, anarchism stands not before folkism but within it.
> (Steinberg 1929a, 332)

That is, revolutionary folkism is anarchist in spirit and as anarchistic as
possible in practice. As Steinberg described it, it recognized the necessity of
social and political organization, an admission he took to be non-anarchistic
despite the fact that the program he proceeded to describe — 'democratization
of the social order, the territorial decentralization of its functions' the distribution of these functions among 'anarchist pact-unions (Steinberg 1927a, 342)'
according to a model essentially identical, again, to the one described above
— would have been acceptable to many, if not most anarchists. In brief
then, we conclude that Steinberg was, in his thinking, a stricter anarchist
than the anarchists themselves and that his 'socialism' was simply anarchism
by a different name.

Anarchizing the Jewish world

In an article written just a few years before his death, Steinberg noted that
at some point during his youth a proposal was made to establish a central
authority responsible for hiring and firing communal rabbis in the Baltic
States, but that the famed R. Hayyim Berlin nixed the plan, reasoning as
follows:

> Everyone knows, he said, that a kerosene lamp smokes, is dirty, sheds little
> light, and is quite expensive on top of everything. Electric light, on the other
> hand, is clean, bright, and cheap. And yet, electricity has one drawback: it
> works with power from a central station. If anything goes wrong in that center,
> darkness descends into all Jewish homes. But when a kerosene lamp goes out,
> there is darkness only in one house and the rest of the Jewish houses remain
> as bright as they had been.

'I recall this story,' Steinberg continued, 'whenever I read about the highly
organized, centralized activities of American and world-Jewish institutions,
and whenever I hear of discussions in less organized communities' as to
whether they ought to be 'decentralized, voluntary and cooperative' or organized around 'strict centralism and discipline.' Jewish history, he continued,
evolved under the sign of the former; Jews survived because Jewish life

was 'distributed among many different centers, each of which lived its own individual life.' Yet, he lamented, the lesson was not taken to heart and modern Jewish communities gravitated in the opposite direction, producing a 'bureaucratic structure that weakens or even destroys all activity on the part of the individual' and 'swallows ... [his] creative capacities (Steinberg 1954).' It is necessary, he therefore concluded elsewhere, to 'anarchize Jewish society (Thorin 1966).'

In part, this involved a redistribution of power within Jewish communities. To revolutionize Jewish life, he wrote, 'individual prophets are unnecessary' because 'the masses themselves can be their own collective prophet,' drawing strength and inspiration from 'the heroic past of the people,' the 'undying ideal' it stands for, and its sense of 'historical mission' for humanity as a whole (Steinberg 1952, 267).

More than that, however, it involved a socio-economic transformation. On this subject, Steinberg's proposals are thoroughly suffused with Kropotkinian and Tolstoyan elements. Mankind, he wrote in an unpublished essay, 'groans beneath the weight of ... modern civilization;' under the dehumanizing conditions of urban life, 'the spirit and soul of the individual is crippled.' For this reason, 'religious people' who, with the 'still, small voice' of 'purity, simplicity, [and] human wholeness,' have always 'proceeded in the name of the eternal treasuries of nature and spirit' must 'judge the powerful mechanical system of the present' and 'negate it when that is called for (Steinberg, undated B).' Accordingly, he proclaimed that the:

> New [Jewish] people cannot make peace with the foundations of human injustice. In their eyes, life must be separated from the evil and filth of their surroundings (Jewish or otherwise). They may not strive for wealth or power in society. They must be cold to the wonder of civilization. They must throw away the tools of the legal agents of destruction ... A religious idea world is maximalistic in essence and uncompromising in its demands. The new Jew must live such a life that the masses recognize that 'the name of God is called upon' him — then he will be able to influence the masses. The masses will then be illumined by the spark of holiness that has [recently] disappeared from its life.

The pious, he continued, must 'make an exit to a new mode of life (Steinberg 1935c).' But so long as they are 'taken with the treasures of modern civilization' they remain 'chained to the old world (Steinberg 1932).'

Therefore, Steinberg maintained, the 'first task of Jewish socialism' is separation from the 'petit-bourgeois, old-European householding, patriarchal merchant world' — this must become 'repulsive to Jewish folks-mensch.' Thus, he called for the rustification of the Jewish people. They must, he exhorted, 'come back to nature ... returning to agriculture' and living 'in a condition of reduced comfort and convenience' in order to acquire the 'sort of spiritual depth' that this way of life offers. 'Physical labor,' he held 'must become a national virtue, a Jewish honor;' it must be regarded as 'the beginning of a new Jewish life-epoch' capable of creating 'a whole new spiritual atmosphere' from which 'a new generation that is spiritually separated from the old world will bloom (Steinberg 1925, 57).' Anything less, any participation in the cultural and economic institutions 'where human injustice is born or established (Steinberg 1952, 333),' Steinberg considered akin to 'Jonah's *kikayon*,' serving merely to divert dangers cultural and material 'without bringing 'the redemption any closer (Steinberg 1925, 30).' Concretely, he praised the work of 'free associations of pioneering Jews' who built cooperative settlements in Palestine and lamented that these trailblazing projects were ultimately integrated 'into the narrow framework of statist discipline' such that 'their onetime libertarian spirit' began to recede (Steinberg 1954).'

Steinberg's Tolstoyan emphasis on Jewish rustification had much to do with the particular historical conditions of Eastern European Jewry — a population that had been (as indicated earlier) gradually herded into dense urban areas and driven to the economic margins. Ultimately, he believed in a program of economic integration like that proposed by Kropotkin in *Factories, Fields, and Workshops*. 'By connecting city and village,' he wrote, 'the creative capacity of working people becomes multifaceted.' At 'home in more areas of creative labor' their personalities will develop in a liberated manner, rendering them sensitive to 'the introduction of a new established order of state (*memshala*)' and better prepared to resist it. For this reason, Steinberg argued also that a Jewish socialist 'must heartily apply all his powers of intellect and imagination to establish productive cooperatives in the cities (Steinberg 1925, 63).

Complementing these economic and cultural changes, Steinberg's program of Jewish anarchization included political and organizational elements as well. In this, he was informed by the same diaspora autonomism that inspired Zalkind. While he believed that the 'Jewish masses' should 'pour themselves into the all-human universal in a brotherly manner,' striving to build up 'socialism in any land together with the people of that land,' he also defended their right to 'live intimately and deeply in their own national family.' After leaving Russia he therefore aspired to form a cross-class and international 'folks-movement' for an anomalous 'people that breathes as one' and yet 'defies political and geographical borders' — indeed, a people that is nourished by its 'geographical dispersion,' that shares 'social achievements and conflicts, artistic and spiritual consequences, folk customs and elevated dreams (Steinberg 1925, 65).'

Cultural and religious solidarity, Steinberg maintained, would serve as the foundation for economic solidarity. 'The rivers of Jewish life' — be they spiritual, economic, or political — he wrote, 'must flow together' to form 'a new Jewish synthesis. As he explained, the Jewish people have always lived in accord with the verse 'the Israelites set out ... and encamped (Numbers 33).' Therefore, 'their dispersal constitutes no obstruction to their unity;' on the contrary, 'immigration is the dynamic unity of the people.' In keeping with the model represented above by the distinction between kerosene and electric lighting, he proposed that 'when an economic crisis strikes' a certain country or field of industry, Jews elsewhere, or in other fields, 'can take it upon themselves to help those who suffer from the crisis.' For Steinberg, this was not to be treated as an incidental act of charity; 'charity, no matter how generous,' he believed 'does not change social life but 'on the contrary, it refines, supports, and strengthens the inhuman capitalist order (Steinberg 1935c).' Rather, he saw it as a system of mutual support on a 'folk-wide scale,' a transnational non-statist socialist society organized around a revolutionary 'congress of Jewish working people (Steinberg 1925, 44).'

This program never got off the ground. However, Steinberg's Freeland League was, at least until 1948, a serious alternative to Zionism and, therefore, a significant force in Jewish political life. Existing studies of this movement mainly highlight this aspect of Steinberg's work (Miler 2008; Sinclair 2009; Muraskin 2013). Fewer have identified it as a natural outgrowth of Steinberg's efforts to anarchize Jewish life (Birkenmaier 2014; Almagor 2017). Here, I aim to elaborate on this thesis by bracketing the specific projects he worked on, none of which succeeded — ironically, Stalin's Birobidzhan was the only Territorialist plan that did, and Steinberg opposed it (Steinberg 1934) — and attending to his vision for them, how he understood what they were about.

Following once again his customary dialectical approach, Steinberg distinguished between two ancient Jewish cities, Yavneh and Jerusalem — the former rising to prominence only after the destruction of the latter in 70 C. E. According to talmudic legend, Vespassian spared it at the behest of R. Yohanon b. Zakka (Gittin 56a–b). This geographical move represented a profound cultural shift: the capital city of the ancient Hebrew Republic, its centralized religion, priesthood, and its monarchy was traded for a center of rabbinic learning. The Torah — or Jewish civilization in the abstract — came to stand in for the state and, as time went on, also became what Heine would call a 'portable homeland (Boyarin 2015).' Steinberg transformed this change into an organizing principle: a vision of an anti-political, stateless, diaspora-people occupying a constellation of cultural homelands.

According to Steinberg, R. Yohanon acted *not* as a private individual, but 'was driven to it as if by an unspoken command of the people itself;' as an agent of its collective will. So he explained: they were 'disillusioned with their statehood, its errors, crimes, and sins.' Thus, 'to assure their spiritual survival and their innermost national-religious substance,' they rejected it. The 'streets of an embattled Jerusalem were strewn' not only with the shattered remnants of 'a fallen political order,' but the discarded shreds of a whole 'national-political ideology (Steinberg 1955, 235).' R. Yohanon merely gave popular sentiment a concrete expression.

As Steinberg proceeded to explain, he aimed not to save the homeland, but to 'transform the very concept of a Jewish homeland (Steinberg 1955, 235–236).' From then on, 'the life principle of the Jewish people' would not be organized around the idea of 'my land,' but around 'the power and sanctity of the spiritual-religious idea' that 'his presence fills all the earth (Isaiah 6:3; Steinberg 1952, 379–380).' It would not coalesce within the 'proud walls of Jerusalem,' but within the 'humble but indestructible walls of the *beyt midrash*, the house of study (Steinberg 1955, 236).'

This fundamental change in the relationship of Jewish identity to Jewish places and power produced a new conception of collective life: the tabernacle of the Torah 'always travelled with *Keneset Yisrael*,' the congregation of Israel writ large, that established 'countless Jerusalems in the diaspora (Steinberg 1955, 236).' As each community took root and situated itself in a new 'cultural environment (Steinberg 1948, 118),' it brought 'forth nothing but Jewishness' though in ever varying forms (Steinberg 1948, 120). As each such center fell, its inhabitants carried with them this accumulated cultural wealth to the next Jerusalem and increased it still further (Steinberg 1950). Thus, Judaism thrived not in spite of, but because of its dispersion — dispersion enriched it.

As Steinberg went on to explain, Jewish cultural vitality was ensured not only by dispersion itself, but also due to the fact that Jews did not waste 'their national energies on upholding states and the other institutions that belong to them (Simha 1966).' Rather, in response to the imperative 'you shall be to me a kingdom of priests and a holy nation (Exodus 19:6),' Judaism 'never concealed its rebellious nature,' its exclusive devotion to the 'King of Kings (Steinberg 1955, 241)' to whom alone sovereignty belongs (Steinberg 1952, 379).' This meant that 'in the midst of the Jewish people stood not the majestic throne of royalty, but the invisible glory of Mount Sinai (Steinberg 1955, 242).' Relying explicitly on Rocker's claim in *Nationalism and Culture* to the effect that Germany was a center of European culture until it became obsessed with national unification, Steinberg argued that the more a people grows 'in political, technical, and economic power, the less they supply themselves with the inner spiritual and moral power that builds and supports a lively people (Steinberg 1952, 379).' Thus, because the Jews upheld a 'concept of *peoplehood* nurtured on religious and moral demands' over and against 'the concept of statehood that continually swept the nations around them,' they 'felt stronger and even more sure (Steinberg 1955, 237).'

This way of thinking about Jewish collective identity — as organized around 'moral maximalism (Steinberg 1955)' and devotion to God as opposed to states and homelands — gave Steinberg the tools to articulate an anti-nationalist conception of peoplehood. The Jews of 'Yavneh,' he wrote, understand that 'fences and frontiers have always been the source of mis-understandings and conflicts,' and that 'the fewer frontiers, the greater the community (Steinberg 1948, 116).' They see that 'humanity is moving toward a world community … a new web of human liberation' and embrace it (Steinberg 1952, 438). In service of a 'higher idea,' they are not misled by power but strive 'for the complete redemption of the Jew, the human being, and the world (Steinberg 1956a). In this way, their 'nationalism' is 'simultaneously universalism' — the more he delves into his national culture,' the more a Jew of 'Yavneh' feels 'himself in harmony with humanity (Steinberg 1950).

In a similar vein, Steinberg contended that diaspora Jewish experience militates, so to speak, against militarism. 'In the course of their wandering throughout the world,' he wrote, 'the Jews have more than once seen how states and statist civilizations come to be, grow, reach a peak of power and influence' and then crumble as a result of 'sin and crime … [and] evil tyranny (Steinberg 1952, 379);' we 'who have seen what the gentiles do with their states cannot easily accept undertaking the same (Steinberg 1952, 424). Rather, 'the warning of the prophet Samuel against the institution of kings and rulers' remained valid:

> Concentration on *my* State, on '*my* country, right or wrong,' is responsible for that indifference and hostility to neighboring States, which must sooner or later lead to war. Thousands of injustices and stupidities which the average person condemns in his private life are transformed into just and wise actions the moment they are bedecked with state patriotism … [which even permits leaders] to violate the rights of their own peoples and to stifle the natural solidarity of mankind. (Steinberg 1946, 115)

Thus, if 'military-political power, diplomatic swindles, national patriotism, and propaganda disrupt humanity (Steinberg 1952, 437),' Yavneh fortifies the Jews against it and cultivates in them an appreciation for the fact that 'weapons are not objects of beauty and decoration, but things of dishonor (Steinberg 1955, 240; Shabbat 63a).'

We see, then, that interpreted in the light of his conception of Yavneh, the Freeland League appears as an extension of Steinberg's case for the anarchization of Jewish life. That is, it is not just a matter of decentralizing power and influence within any one community, but challenging state power, nationalism, and military might as Jewish objectives in general. It means embracing a principled diasporism that rejects even aspirations toward a fixed homeland, rejecting the 'fiction of an ingathering of exiles (Steinberg 1952, 416).'

The Jews as a revolution-people and Jewish socialism

We have repeatedly observed Steinberg's conviction that socialism is a moral project and that it stands, as such, against determinism. As he put it, 'moral consciousness rises above the surface of the prevailing society;' in issuing its absolute demands, it stands in 'proud opposition' and does 'not allow itself to be drawn into the elemental flow of history (Steinberg 1932).' Accordingly, 'socialism means throwing off the burden of the past ... seeking not continuity, but a break' with it (Steinberg 1952, 113). Steinberg saw the Jews as uniquely prepared for this apocalypse.

Echoing a certain Rosenzweigian ahistoricism, he contended that the Jews give 'a purely living meaning' to the principle of '*behira hofshit*, freedom of choice.' That is, they are not simply abnormal, but exist as a 'supra-historical' entity always in '*violation* of all historical laws' and outside of 'every historical tradition (Steinberg 1925, 29).' Having long resisted the supposedly inexorable laws of history, Steinberg saw the Jews as ripe for a revolution set to abolish them.

The idea of a historical break also implies difference; therefore, Steinberg identifies 'being-different' as a core organizing principle of socialism. In a world where 'there is opposition against every strange person and every thought,' Jews stood against the tide (Steinberg 1952, 250) in 'eternal opposition to every danger.' Therefore, 'anti-historical *hutspa* (Steinberg 1925, 32)' and 'spiritual rebellion (Steinberg 1927b)' come as second nature. Thus, Steinberg argued, they are singularly positioned to represent this value for others (Steinberg 1952, 250).

Among the features of the 'spiritual culture that constituted an armor against the persecutions (Steinberg 1925, 40)' was Israel's 'hope in a messiah,' however late in coming. As Steinberg understood it, this demonstrated that the people learned how to 'connect its prosaic concerns with a revolutionary ideal (Steinberg 1927b, 16)' rather than becoming mired in them. As he understood it, the messianic idea readied them for revolutionary action: to 'leave its super-historical position by super-historical means (Steinberg 1925, 31)' and thus bring about the new world that 'can be won only against the flowing waters of the laws of history (Steinberg 1926, 13).' Primed by suffering, Jews above all are 'interested in effecting the deepest change in people and institutions;' thus 'material for revolutionary explosiveness, lays in the very being of the Jewish condition (Steinberg 1925, 31).'

Perhaps most importantly, Steinberg saw the Torah as 'a revolutionary ideology ... hardened over centuries (Steinberg 1935b, 257)' essentially marked by a socialist ethic. There is, he wrote, 'no abyss between true socialism and true messianism ... the Jew who carries the messiah idea in his heart recognizes the ancient, undying dream in the modern words (Steinberg 1935c).' While he denied any direct correspondence between socialism and biblical or rabbinic law, he maintained that 'every law is the temporal form of a transhistorical social-historical spirit (Steinberg 1951a, 241)' and that these laws embody a certain spirit of preparedness for social revolution. For instance, the general imperative to sacrifice 'material goods for the sake of ethical religion,' the idea that 'all the earth is mine (Exodus 19:5)' that Steinberg understood to expresses disrespect for 'institutions of human property,' or the prophetic call to 'unlock fetters of wickedness (Isaiah 58:6; Steinberg, undated B). On this basis, he claimed an 'organic unity of Judaism and socialism (Steinberg 1951a, 241),' the modern movement simply representing an effort 'to realize — as practical *halacha* — the messianic dream for his people and for humanity as a whole (Steinberg 1935c).' Therefore, Steinberg claimed, it is 'easier for socialism to emerge among them than among others' as 'a *freely formed* ideal (Steinberg 1925, 32).'

Now, as we observed in the preceding section, Steinberg understood Jewish particularism as being intimately linked to a universal humanism. This is extremely clear in his reflections on the Jewish historical mission. On the one hand, he maintained that 'Jewish socialism means not the mechanical coloring of a general and national question (a Socialism for Jews),' but an entity unto itself suffused with 'Jewish spirit and substance, not 'a heavenly ideal' but the actual 'result of a folk history (Steinberg 1925, 31).' On the other hand, he held that there is 'no need for a Jew to leave the ranks of his own people in order to serve the cause of humanity (Steinberg 1948, 107)' because 'the Jewish socialist sees in his destructive power' — his ability to effect a 'radical reconstruction of the present world order' — the '*unification* of humanity and the Jewish people (Steinberg 1926, 11).' It is his way of taking 'responsibility for the whole of suffering humanity (Steinberg 1925, 24–25).'

Thus, Steinberg contended, the Jewish notion of chosenness has nothing at all to do with the 'German formula.' The latter is an expression of lust for privilege and power: 'I want to master the world because I am a German (Steinberg 1948, 107).' In contrast, when some group declares that it bears 'a historical revolutionary mission' it expresses not arrogance, but a sense of responsibility for their own and for the world's historical life (Steinberg 1952, 258)' Thus, the former says 'I want to serve the world because I am a Jew (Steinberg 1948, 107).' This sentiment is perhaps best expressed in

Steinberg's play, *You Have Triumphed Makhnachov*. There, Ryazanskaya, a Jewish revolutionary, remarks as follows:

> Today, where are all the Caesars, church fathers, and generals who have tread us underfoot? Where did they go? Where? They have disappeared into the *molekh* of their own hate. But we homeless vagabonds who have survived the darkness of hate and power, we live, and live actively. Is that not justice? ... I have also suffered pain and bitterness from my childhood on. It is for that precise reason that I am not one who takes vengeance, but a revolutionary ... We Jews take part in every revolution. Wherever there are people who want to throw off the last of their pain ... there are Jews there, and they fight, sacrifice themselves, and die. This is our 'vengeance' — that we who, more than any other, have sipped from the cup of sorrow will, with *our* feet, tread upon that cup for the sake of humanity.

For Ryazanskaya, the Jews are chosen through their suffering to take their rightful place among the revolutionary vanguard (Steinberg 1960). Jewish chosenness represents a struggle 'not in order to rule over other people,' but to fight with them and for them. Thus, Steinberg wrote, if 'we want to be the ... first to open the door to a new enlightened world ... we do not begrudge the efforts of others' to do the same. They too 'should be 'chosen (*atah bahartanu*)' peoples (Steinberg 1925, 31).'

Reflections on Zionism

Steinberg's negative position on statism as a viable moral option for Jewish political expression clearly indicates the tendency of his thinking on Zionism. His critique of violence and his conviction as to the revolutionary mission of the Jewish people also played a key role. However, as his collaboration with Natan Hofshi (they corresponded, he translated Hofshi's essays into Yiddish, and Hofshi composed for him a deeply sympathetic eulogy) proves, he — like Zalkind — objected, not to Zionism in all its forms, but to the specific direction which the movement took in the years leading up to 1948 and certainly following it. That is to say, he objected to the Jewish statism, militarism, and (sometimes) chauvinistic nationalism that it came to embody.

In keeping with his diasporic-internationalist conception of the relationship between peoples and lands, he equated the idea of exclusive territorial claims with a capitalist psychology of private property and contended that a 'socialist does not recognize state boundaries,' the whole earth being 'free for the whole human race' to settle and to work on the condition that the worker does not 'destroy his working brother.' Moreover, he denied that 'every incoming Jewish immigrant pushes out from his life-position ... Arab workers and farmers (Steinberg 1952, 266–267).' This may have occurred, but it did not *have* to; there was a legitimate question of implementation, but not of principle.

For several reasons, the land of Israel was an especially appealing destination. For one, he pointed out that 'it is the land in which Jewish creation … [first] sprouted' and therefore linked to 'many of the spiritual traditions and roots' which the continuity of this creation demands. More importantly he saw it as a virgin land, a place 'where the sun casts its youthful light, where the earth is still fertile.' For Steinberg, this 'fertility' was less an agricultural concern than a cultural one. As the 'least developed place in the 'developed" world, he saw Palestine as a vast field of 'wild grasses … free of the weeds of the present civilization' and, for this reason saw in it the potential for a 'socialist newland' where life could be 'built on new economic and cultural foundations.' Echoing Ahad Ha'am, he saw Palestine as a potential 'platform for the free revolutionary formation of the Jewish people' and therefore as a 'center of worldwide Jewish creativity.' Like Zalkind, however, Steinberg held that a place 'is the means and not the content of human life.' The 'geographical Palestine' was, in this sense, of secondary importance. As he expressed it, 'Palestine is *everywhere that the Jewish spirit burns* (Steinberg 1925, 59).' He praised the *haluzim* (Zionist pioneers) for their accomplishments in Palestine but did not share their conviction that Palestine alone could or should serve as the only site for such accomplishments.

In any case, Steinberg's understanding as to the potential of Palestine led him to place great hope in the early *haluzim*. Comparing them to the narodniks, who descended 'to the depth of the people,' he praised their 'yearning for radical transformation,' the fact that they not only took the task of salvation into their own hands, but 'shed the modern garments of worldwide civilization' and 'returned to the bare conditions of the wilderness' without turning back 'for the "melons" (Numbers 11:5) of Egypt that lie behind them.' Thus forging 'new paths in relations among people, between the individual and the collective, between the folk and humanity (Steinberg, undated D),' the *haluzim* represented for Steinberg 'not merely the youth of the people, but the making-youthful of its spirit (Steinberg 1925, 60).' Steinberg's respect for the *haluzim* did not extend to the Zionist movement as a whole. While he credited it with 'straightening the bent back of the people (Steinberg 1925, 17),' his praise stopped there. As we observed earlier, many of Steinberg's contemporaries opposed Zionism on the grounds of its utopianism, Palestine being supposed too resource-poor to support mass migration. Steinberg countered that it was '*not utopian enough* (Steinberg 1952, 200),' raising many of the same concerns that Zalkind had.

If among the *haluzim* Zionism represented a 'principled rebellion,' over time it came to look 'only toward the forms of life already proposed by the other nations, its ideal goes no farther than to be like the other peoples.' Thus, it became 'thickly overgrown with the European order (Steinberg 1925, 17)' it once rejected, its ideology being reduced to 'a copy of the presently ruling capitalist-statist ideology.' Its utopian vision degraded into 'a simple translation of reality (Steinberg 1952, 201–202)' into Hebrew. Intimately aware that 'modern states are built on diplomatic lies, democratic swindles, national violence-politics, military yokes, and economic exploitation,' he insisted the Jewish people must not 'build a copy of the surrounding world (Steinberg 1952, 289).'

Noteworthy is the way Steinberg extended his critique to the social-Zionist groups like *Poaley Zion*. 'Neither an iron centralized apparatus, nor a sovereign bureaucracy, he wrote in expression of his anarchist sympathies, 'can be the ideal for a socialist settlement.' Rather, he argued the 'functions of society' should be organized on 'freely willed, federative, loosely connected foundations' and divided among social organs. In this way, the land of Israel would develop from within, without the 'principle of dominion (Steinberg 1925, 61).' Social-Zionists, in contrast, expected to realize 'a utopian goal' by resorting to 'present-day, statist-European, technical-American means (Steinberg 1952, 200).' They accepted the state model and thereby stilled 'the yearning for revolutionary action with the calm waters of a coalition cabinet (Steinberg 1925, 18).'

Steinberg therefore regarded Zionist statism as a spiritual threat to Judaism. He felt that its 'realistic, all too realistic, notions' served to 'dry out and empty' the utopian substance from a people that thrives only on its utopian hopes. The state, he explained, is not just an 'empty mold' into which 'molten life-metal (Steinberg 1929c)' can later be poured. It has interests of its own that do not necessarily coincide with those of the people. Accordingly, Zionist efforts to take control of the land and to build a government 'became more important than building up the people, Jewish individuals themselves (Steinberg, undated D),' or tending to the 'individual Jewish soul (Steinberg 1952, 330).'

Nowhere was he more vehement in expressing this concern than when it came to the question of violence and its moral impact on Jewish communities in the holy land. Clearly, Steinberg operated within the colonialist imaginary (Almagor 2018; 2019) that saw the land as supremely open and thus free for development. However, he was not misled by the fiction that Palestine was literally a 'land without a people,' regarding inter-communal violence as an outgrowth of Zionist statism and, therefore, as evidence of its moral untenability. A truly 'socialist land of Israel,' Steinberg believed, 'cannot be built in the middle of an Arab Palestine that stands outside of it (Steinberg 1925, 62).' It must therefore be built, 'without the supporting superstructure of a state, upon foundations of voluntary collaboration …

peace, work, and mutual assistance (Steinberg 1956a).' That is, as a trans-national anarchist 'kibbutz of kibbutzim (Steinberg 1952, 389)' dedicated to *joint* anti-colonial, anti-imperialist struggle against 'exploiting states like England (Steinberg 1952, 207).' Only from refusal of 'any ambition to an exclusive statist dominion in the land ... can come the deepest brother-hood (Steinberg 1925, 61).' While it would be natural to expect this of a people returning 'to the land where its own prophets had asked mankind years ago for peace (Steinberg 1956a),' Steinberg remarked, it was not the reality.

'Blinded by political passions,' the Political Zionist mainstream treated the local population as an 'unimportant topographical feature' until they realized that a purely Jewish state could not be established in the middle of a 'boiling sea of Arab peoples,' Then, in spite of the fact that 'spilling human blood has always been eschewed' or accepted 'with trepidation' they concluded that 'Jewish redemption entails a bloody war (Steinberg 1947, 8)' against them. This divide between a traditional Jewish ethos and the path taken by modern Zionism constituted, for Steinberg, the crux of the problem. 'I am not afraid,' he wrote shortly before the Israeli War of Independence, of the fight to establish the state, but 'of the consequences of the fight (Steinberg 1946).' A tiny state founded against the will of its neighbors and therefore constantly under threat would become one in which 'Jewish life will stand in the service of military self-defence.' This, he feared, would cripple its moral and cultural development (Steinberg 1952, 383).'

After the war, Steinberg identified precisely this change, charging that 'a spirit of militarism and chauvinism is enveloping the population (Steinberg 1951b).' Instead of the ancient prophet proclamation of 'not by power, but by my spirit (Zechariah 4:6),' the principle of force took center stage. Ancient longing 'for the land of the prophets' became an 'aspiration for a kingdom, for political power (Steinberg 1953b);' the Jewish idea of redemption was reduced to 'the creation of a political nation like all other nations (Steinberg 1948, 115).' In this way, 'the whole program of Jewish life, its moral foundations, was basically altered (Steinberg 1953b). The central 'Jewish concept,' Steinberg explained, had always 'been the quest for harmony between thought and deed, the desire that politics and morals ought not to be two different worlds, but rather one and the same (Steinberg 1956a).' It had been about 'striving for peace, for justice, for the brotherhood of nations (Steinberg 1951b).' That is why, 'Jewish spiritual tradition has not allowed itself to be misled by states and rulers, by political and financial power, by physical force and armed might.' Turning aside from this tradition, Steinberg warned, the Jewish people risked losing 'its own historic face,' becoming 'like the rest of them, like the ruling nations of the West (Steinberg 1956a).'

This was not a threat Steinberg limited to the Jewish community of Israel. Rather, he saw it as a worldwide Jewish problem. This accusation is most pronounced in his response to the Qibya massacre (Steinberg 1953a). The fact, he wrote, 'that Jews ... could, in cold calculation, murder dozens of innocent men, women, and children ... is in itself a hair-raising crime,' but worse 'is the indifferent or satisfied reaction to this event (Steinberg 1953b)' in Jewish communities everywhere. 'Fatal proof of the moral upheaval taking place in the Jewish world' was ignored. Contrary to the example set by King David, who cried 'I stand guilty before the Lord (2 Samuel 12:13)' when confronted with his crime (Steinberg, undated E), they prevaricated: 'speeches began with: "of course we are sorry," and ended with: "but others are guilty too."' In the abyss between 'of course' and 'but,' Steinberg claimed 'was lost all the Jewish moral sensitivity which has guided our people throughout its history (Steinberg 1953b).'

Thus, Steinberg asked, how long can 'a wise and discerning people (Deuteronomy 4:6)' be stricken with 'uncritical enthusiasm' and 'struck blind (Steinberg, undated E)' concerning its own national projects? 'We dare not wait until nations ... come preaching morality to our sorely tried people, and tell it that it has not acted honestly, that it has spilled innocent blood,' he urged. The real criticism must 'come from the Jewish people itself, from the very depth of the Jewish soul ... We will permit no one to take from us this right and this privilege which we have accepted ourselves (Steinberg 1956b).' In this way, he suggested, the Jewish people must answer an existential question: 'do we wish simply to live, or do we wish to give life the meaning ascribed to it by the prophets (Steinberg 1935b, 289)?' — to truly be an '*atah bahartanu* (chosen)' people or just to pretend?

Conclusion

Through an idiosyncratic mix of prophetism, rabbinic legalism, Kantian idealism, socialist populism, anarchism, and syndicalism Steinberg sought to articulate a revolutionary vision capable of responding to the eternal call of justice in a timely manner. As he put it:

> The messiah-idea may not remain in the misty heights of a superhuman abstraction. A living messiah-idea and vision looks not only to coming genera-tions, to a future humanity; its fiery language is addressed to each generation. Each generation dresses this abstraction in the living garments of concrete history. Its eternal character consists in its being eternally concretized. To discover the concrete historical garment of the eternal messiah-idea — this is a task for every generation, and certainly for ours. (Steinberg, undated D)

In this manner, Steinberg was a radical messianist in the best possible sense. An 'honest gardener' of 'the times to come (Steinberg 1925, 15),' he spent his career planting the seeds of the universal in the fertile earth of the particular, striving for the 'moral maximum' without losing sight of the real people tasked with realizing it.

In closing this section on Zalkind and Steinberg, two individuals who played active roles in real popular movements, it is worthwhile briefly to consider them together. Though Steinberg was never affiliated with Valozyn, he was very much part of the synthesis of Jewish nationalism and narodism that Valozyn students participated in. Their anarchist tendencies therefore arise from the same source. Both were also part of the westward migration of Jewish students during the last years of the Russian Empire; only Zalkind became a Zionist and continued westward into the UK while Steinberg returned to Russia to participate in the revolution there. Here, their ideological paths could easily have split permanently and profoundly. However, their mutual disappointments — Steinberg's in the course of the Russian Revolution, Zalkind's in the direction taken by mainstream Zionism — set them once again along parallel paths. For reasons essentially identical, both embraced the cultural and practical pioneering vision of Hibbat Zion but, for political and moral reasons, believed territorialism to be a more appropriate response to threats against Jewish security and rejected mainstream Zionism. In this they both differed from the Jewish Labor Bund which pressed for *cultural*, but not territorial, autonomy (Almagor 2017). Promoting the former without the latter, they maintained, would mean neglecting concrete threats to Jewish life and limb in Europe. In spite of their separatism, both situated Jewish liberation within the context of an international struggle — Zalkind in the process of Judaizing anarchism, Steinberg in the process of anarchizing the Jewish Territorial Movement, which he aspired to integrate into a worldwide libertarian-socialist network. Thus, while they moved in different circles, they followed parallel trajectories, both as thinkers and as activists.

Notes

1 Unless otherwise noted, biographical information about Steinberg is derived from the memorial book published a few years after his death (Ravitch 1960). As of yet, there is no comprehensive intellectual biography of Steinberg in English. Eynav (1967) published a Hebrew-language text intended for the popular audience. German-language studies have also more recently appeared (Wallat 2013, 2014; Birkenmaier 2014; Grill 2014, 2015). Steinberg is also discussed in *In the Shadow of Zion* (Rovner 2014).

2 The Musar movement was an educational and cultural movement that developed in the nineteenth century among non-hasidic Jews in the Baltic States, especially Lithuania.

3 Telz was the seat of a prestigious Yeshiva, which Gordon headed.

4 Later, a significant influence on several twentieth-century Jewish thinkers, notably Erich Fromm, very little is known about Rabinkow. A master of oratory, he published but one essay (Rabinkow 1929). Recollections about him appear in *Sages and Saints* (Jung 1987), and scholarly work on his influence is limited in the extreme (Honigmann 1992).

5 The 1882 May Laws intensified the already crushing effects of restricting Jews to the Pale.

6 A full history of the Freeland League has yet to be written. The closest approximation is the two-volume Yiddish-language tome *Geshichte fun der Frayland Lige on fun Teritoriyalistishen Gedank* (Astor 1967). However, this text does not cover the final years of the movement. Several historical studies on particular projects have appeared; these are cited in Laura Almagor's more comprehensive research (Almagor 2015, 2017, 2018). See also Gur Alroey's (2016) work on the International Territorialist Organization.

7 This follows the inscription appearing on Steinberg's headstone.

The mystics

5

Shmuel Alexandrov (1865–1941)

3 Rabbi Shmuel Alexandrov, date unknown.

Shmuel Alexandrov (1865–1941) was born in the Belarusian city of Barysaw to a Habad-hasidic family that traced its origins to the famed R. Judah Loew, the Maharal of Prague (Belinson 1893; Bat-Yehuda 1987). Physically disabled (Slutsky 1967), the youth was gifted with a photographic memory (Maslanski 1929, 107). Tutored privately until his teens by the head of the local *beyt din* (Eisenstadt 1895, 10), he joined the student body of the Ets Hayyim yeshiva in Valozyn in 1884. There, like several other figures appearing in this book, he became involved with the Hibbat Zion movement and befriended Abraham Isaac Kook,[1] the future Ashkenazic chief rabbi of British Mandate Palestine.

Alexandrov's practical involvement with the movement was minimal. Like Ahad Ha'am (with whom he corresponded) he was concerned primarily with Jewish spiritual renaissance and less with politics.[2] His career as a public intellectual began with the publication of *Masekhet Nega'im* (1886), in which he combined modern Jewish theology and erudite, even pedantic, literary criticism. Throughout the late 1880s and 1890s he contributed many articles on rabbinics and *midrash* to early Hebrew-language periodicals like *ha-Magid* and *ha-Meylits* among others. Displaying in these publications both galling arrogance and considerable genius, he evoked both frustration and admiration.[3]

Maverick that he was, Alexandrov's career was abruptly interrupted when he intervened in what became an international scandal concerning the historicity of certain talmudic legends — most notably, the Hannukka miracle of lights (Likht 2016). Insisting on a strictly metaphorical reading in *Agadat Pah ha-Shemen* (1892), *Divrei Shmuel* (1892) and *Agadat Esh min ha-Shamayim* (1894), he antagonized his orthodox community sufficiently to ruin any chance of obtaining a rabbinic post. While continuing to teach privately (Bat-Yehuda and Rafael 1965, 115), he took up work as a bank clerk (Alexandrov 1907, 20)

After 1917, Alexandrov played a role in efforts to keep Judaism alive under Soviet rule by organizing clandestine educational initiatives and, perhaps more importantly, by offering his often despondent correspondents hope and encouragement (Teller 1954, 212–217, 382–384; Teller 1957, 39–51; Gershuni 1961, 126–128; Blau 2007) — efforts for which he was arrested on multiple occasions (Slutsky 1967; Gerasimova 2007). Prioritizing mind over matter (as per his wont), Alexandrov opted to use funds intended to secure his escape in order to finance the publication of his final book. Consequently, he was trapped behind the Iron Curtain at the outbreak of World War II and killed, together with the rest of Jewish Babruysk during the Nazi massacres there in August of 1941.

Alexandrov took the idea that 'all things' are in the Torah (M. Avot 5:25) as a robust programmatic statement validating the incorporation of secular literature, modern science, and Western philosophy into his interpretation of Jewish texts. In reading his work, one finds references ranging from Fichte and Schelling to Vladimir Solovyov, Darwin, Richard Avenarius, and Marx among many others. These sources, which inform an idiosyncratic interpretation of Judaism combining cosmopolitan nationalism and libertarian socialism with Jewish mysticism as embodied in the Habad-hasidic tradition (Luz 1981) appear in works like '*Esh-Da'at we-Ruah Le'umi* (1891), *Tel Tehiyah* (1896), *Resisei Tal* (1900), and especially his three-volume *Mikhtavei Mehkar u-Bikoret* (1907–31). This chapter draws on these texts and others to examine the continuity between Alexandrov's Schellingian ontology, his account of the historical dialectic of the empirical and Absolute I, his cosmopolitan nationalism, and his anarchism. We shall then conclude by reflecting on how all of this impacted his Zionism.

Three frames for interpreting the abolition of the law in Alexandrov's writings

The most important frame for interpreting Alexandrov's approach to Jewish law is found in the antinomian tradition outlined in the introduction to this volume. In brief, there exists a form of messianic speculation that stretches from talmudic through modern eras among rationalists and mystics alike, according to which the law will change, or even disappear altogether. I refer the reader to the discussion there.

A second frame has been discussed at length by Isaac Slater (2016): the influence of Russian sophiology as embodied in the writings of Vladimir Solovyov and especially the religious interpretation of the Nietzschean *ubermensch* that he and his circle, the 'God Seekers,' developed. According to Slater, the God Seekers rejected Nietzsche's atheism, but accepted his critique of Christianity and saw in his notion of the *ubermensch* heavenly yearning for divine humanity and earthly yearning for human divinity, both of which would culminate in a final reconciliation of good and bad, spirit and flesh. As Slater explains, Alexandrov adapted this notion by representing the prophet or sage as the *creator* of law, not just its *receiver* and *transmitter*. In this way, Alexandrov prefigures — albeit in a far more radical manner — Joseph Ber Soloveitchik's celebration of the Nietzschean powers of the 'halakhic man' who 'creates worlds,' by superimposing on this one legal categories determined through his interpretation of the Torah (Hartman 1989).

A third and related frame is found in the writings of F. W. J. Schelling, whose work exercised tremendous influence on Russian philosophy, especially Solovyov and his circle (Bielfeldt 2019; Rezvykh 2003). Here, I wish to emphasize the centrality of Schelling's romantic reflections on the story of

Empedocles, whose legendary suicide Holderlin famously interpreted as a rejection of 'one-sided existence,' an effort to overcome the subject–object divide by uniting completely with Nature (Foti 2006).

The young Schelling translated this striving into a relation between the 'empirical-I' and the 'Absolute-I.' In *Of the I as the Principle of Philosophy*, he wrote that the reality of the former depends on and therefore yearns for the latter, which encompasses the whole of being. However, because the Absolute-I is total, it has no object and therefore no self — selfhood being predicated on other-consciousness. This is taken to imply that the empirical-I yearns for its own destruction *qua* conscious subject — a yearning that, as Schelling pointed out in his *Philosophical Letters on Dogmatism and Criticism*, it cannot satisfy because this would mean surviving its own annihilation (Schelling 1980).

In his later writings, Schelling addressed this difficulty through the idea of 'transitive being.' In brief: the classical Parmendiean opposition between the one (the human individual included) and the many is overcome by asserting their essential co-implication; essence posits its unity as the multiplicity, and vice versa (Bowie 2016).

For Schelling, the union of the one (the Absolute-I) and the many (the empirical-I) had profound utopian implications. In the totality of the former, possibility and necessity coincide. Translated into moral terms: what may be done is what must be done, and vice versa; right and duty overlap. Represented as the subordination of the former to the latter, the rule of law presupposes their difference. Therefore, the interinclusion of Absolute-I and empirical-I comes to mean the dissolution of law. This zenith of moral progress, regarding all things *sub species aeternitatis* as Spinoza would put it, therefore entails the 'harmony of morality and bliss (Schelling 1980).' Alexandrov incorporated Schelling's model into his mystical-messianic vision of a 'religious revolution (Alexandrov 1910b)' consisting in the abrogation of the *halakha*.

Alexandrov's epistemology

Like Schelling, Alexandrov held Spinoza in high regard, representing his own conception of Judaism as the ultimate realization of the spinozian system (Alexandrov 1886a, 76). Nowhere is this relationship more evident than in his epistemology. It is well known that Spinoza distinguished between three types of knowledge. The first involved sensation and imagination, the second reason (Ethics II40S2). Alexandrov referred to the former as 'animal consciousness' and the latter as 'human consciousness,' the consciousness of the empirical-I. He also understood the connection between these forms of knowledge in roughly spinozist terms. According to Spinoza, our ideas about external bodies are defined in terms of our own body's experience of them (Ethics II.P16.C2); reason is the process of sorting these passive ideas (Ethics II.P29S) retained in memory (Ethics II.P18.S). Alexandrov likewise held that 'all knowledge is self-knowledge' and distinguished the human mind by the 'power of memory' by dint of which accumulates images, thus generating 'internal comprehension' from sensation (Alexandrov 1886a, 68–70). The third type of knowledge involves intuitive apprehension as to the situatedness of all things (Ethics II.P40.S2), including the human mind (E.V.P30), in the necessity of substance (Ethics V.P14). Alexandrov likewise spoke of the soul as an 'internal consciousness' that 'recognizes its essence' and 'extends to the universal essence' such that 'the form is united with its Former.' Thus, he interpreted 'I am the first and I am the last (Isaiah 44:6)' as a reference to the transitive unity of the Absolute and empirical-I (Alexandrov 1886a, 72). Crucially, Alexandrov expanded on Spinoza in two intersecting respects. Collapsing the distinction between 'psychology and sociology,' he ascribed to human collectives 'soul and essence.' Therefore, he extended to whole nations a calling 'to distinguish external from internal consciousness' and thus to commune with the Absolute-I — the same call ultimately applying to 'the mind of universal man (*ha-adam ha-klali*),' that is, to humanity as a whole (Alexandrov 1886a, 68–70).

Eden and the fall of man: external unity and its fragility

Like other Romantics (Beiser 2003, 146), Alexandrov integrated this human striving into a universal progression from the many to the one. In resonance with Schelling's *System of Transcendental Philosophy*, he spoke of Nature achieving consciousness in Adam and likewise of the process by which the veil of finitude is gradually drawn back to reveal the Absolute. This process is represented by the drama of mankind's departure from and final return to Eden.

Alexandrov wrote of a time 'before self-consciousness,' when 'the self was concealed in universal nature (Alexandrov 1886a, 68–70).' This 'animal-I' was immersed in the flood of experience and lacked reflexive self-consciousness, the ability to think about itself '*as if it were apart from itself* (Alexandrov 1905);' that is, it was 'unaware of its awareness.' Much less was it aware of God: 'immersed in the universal creator by way of an *external* connection … it knows nothing of it (Alexandrov 1886a, 72).' Therefore, Alexandrov asserted, these were 'days of shame and disgrace (Alexandrov 1886a, 68–70)' — not only for mankind, but for the earth entire. The 'creation' of Adam on the sixth day is taken to represent the end of this shame, the achievement of self-awareness robustly construed. If previously 'the world was without a mouth,' its muteness ceased when one of its limbs 'came and opened his mouth (Alexandrov 1899a).' Through Adam, who was 'formed from the dust of the earth (*adama*) (Alexandrov 1914a)' and remained in intimate contact with it, 'creation began to express all of those feelings that had been hidden within and could not be articulated, which had to be repressed until their potentiality was made actual (Alexandrov 1899a).'

Again reflecting his Schellingian influences (Schelling 1993, 6; McGrath 2010), Alexandrov drew on anthropomorphic language found throughout biblical and rabbinic texts to claim that the 'essential will and individuality (*ishutam*) (Alexandrov 1914a)' of each thing is part of a '*pattern* engraved on the throne of glory of the central, universal will' of God that 'coils' through 'different concatenations and different vestments (Alexandrov, undated).' Primitive humanity thus 'existed in a world that was all life and will (Alexandrov 1914a);' through his conscious service of the divine, he voiced the eagerness of all things 'to do,' or realize, 'the will of their Maker.' Foreshadowing the messianic abrogation of the law, Alexandrov describes this utopian condition of harmony in which mankind discerned in all things 'the radiance of the divine presence' as a *perpetual* Sabbath that rendered superfluous the actual observance of a Sabbath day (Alexandrov 1899a).

Yet, this Eden contained the seeds of its own undoing. To explain how, Alexandrov appealed to Avenarius' notion of 'introjection' according to which infants experience pure sensation until, observing in others an inner world, they infer the same concerning themselves (Krauss 2019, 13–40) and thus enter a world in which body and soul, mind and matter, stand apart from one another. Like Anton Pannekoek (1948), Alexandrov represented this shift as the 'philosophical fall of man.' Translating this idea into the language of Habad hasidism, he associated the tree of knowledge with the idea of '*klipat noga* (*Tanya*, I:1).' Here is not the place to fully elaborate as to the meaning of this term. In brief, however, it may be explained that the kabbalistic universe is subject to a quasi-Manichean battle between forces of holiness and forces of evil or impurity. The latter are called '*klipot*,' mere 'husks' without divine substance. Between these factions lies a special 'husk' that 'glows (*nogah*)' — it is illuminated with divine light, but *dimly*. Therefore, it is not thoroughly evil and can be redeemed. In Habad hasidic lore, it is transformed into a psychological category: the human ego, which is not intrinsically divine but can be made so (Margalith 1958; Block 1963; Schneider and Berke 2000). For Alexandrov's purposes, the notion of *klipat noga* refers to the fact of being (or seeming) otherwise than God, or 'universal unity.' Thus, he concluded, to have eaten from the tree means that Adam 'began to feel the "I" within himself' he became a distinct and self-aware subject (Alexandrov 1914b) apart from Nature and its God. As it were, he lost track of the place where 'heaven and earth kiss (Alexandrov 1914a).'

This had profound moral consequences. 'The source of the good inclination is the universal will,' Alexandrov wrote, while that of the bad inclination is the 'partial will' — that is, *individual* will (Alexandrov, undated; *Tanya* I:36). The extent to which one is estranged from God is the same extent to which his or her will is bad — that is, *ego driven* (Tanya I.6). Adam thus 'began to worry about himself (Alexandrov 1886a, 68–70)' and to forget 'the God who made him (Alexandrov 1899a).' In principle, the achievement of subjectivity entails recognizing and respecting it in others. That, however, depends on whether one is aware of him or herself '*as a creation* (Alexandrov 1905).' *Then*, the other is a brother or sister likewise 'created in the image of God (Alexandrov 1910b).' If, however, self-consciousness means *forgetting* the divine, then this moral bond with other people also diminishes. Applying this insight to the story of Cain and Abel, a man estranged from heaven and earth is not 'his brother's keeper (Alexandrov 1899a)' — solidarity is lost. Crucially, Alexandrov emphasized that this is true also on the collective scale. Citing an ancient midrash according to which Adam was originally as large as the earth, but shrank after the Fall (Sanhedrin 38a–b), he explained that because 'Adam felt within himself the God who created him' he was free of the 'borders that separate one people from the next (Alexandrov 1905).' Remarkably, Alexandrov even referenced New Testament sources: apprehending God's unity through his unity with God, Adam was 'neither Jew nor Greek (Galatians 3:28)' but human (Alexandrov 1931, 72). After the Fall, however, mankind fell prey to ego-driven national particularism as exemplified by the story of the Tower of Babylon. Having 'journeyed from the East (*kedem*) (Genesis 11:2)' — that is, 'from the One who preceded (*kadmono*) the world (GR 38:7)' — humanity was divided into seventy nations (Genesis 10:1–31), each 'producing its own spirit (Alexandrov 1886a, 43).' Thus, was the 'universal human (Alexandrov 1900a, 4)' reduced to a 'national human, humanity as divided among different nations, each in possession of its own land and its own language (Alexandrov 1905, 16),' all operating in a world 'governed by a war for survival' in which 'peoples are pitted against one another (Alexandrov 1900a, 9–10).'

Thus, Alexandrov interpreted the Fall of Man as a decline on the part of the empirical-I from its identity with the Absolute-I, from (good) universal will to (bad) particular will — this operating on both individual and collective scales — and, finally, from the unity of right with duty to their separation and, by extension, the necessity of law. What is more important, however, is the fact that he determined the original identity as an *external* one. In classical Schellingian fashion, he therefore regarded the rupture of human consciousness as a necessary one. As he put it: it was 'God's intention from the beginning' that mankind should eat the fruit of knowledge (Alexandrov 1902; Shabbat 77b) so that a truer unity could ultimately be achieved. In part, Alexandrov saw this as accomplished by the revelation of the Torah, which is called the 'tree of life (Proverbs 3:18),' and which rabbinic legend credits with extracting 'the snake's venom (Shabbat 157b)' from the Israelites — that is, with purifying them from the spiritual damage caused by Adam and Eve when they heeded the serpent's advice and ate from the tree of knowledge. According to Alexandrov, this was no cause for chauvinistic pride; it merely tasked them with a grander messianic mission: 'rectifying the world with the sovereignty of God and purifying mankind' as a whole (Alexandrov 1931, 72).

Nationalism and cosmopolitanism: the mission of Israel

In my earlier discussion of Zalkind's thought, I indicated Fichte's impact on Jewish nationalism. There, focus was placed on the corporate analogy. There is, however, another important aspect to Fichtean nationalism that is crucial for understanding Alexandrov: its cosmopolitanism. To begin with, let us briefly clarify what we mean by the term. When asked where he came from, Diogenes the Cynic is said to have replied 'I am a citizen of the world,' a claim the stoics later modified, arguing that each of us dwells in two communities, the community of our birth and the community of mankind as a whole, in which all human beings are 'our fellow citizens and neighbors.' As Martha Nussbaum (1994) has explained, this does not mean that people ought to think of themselves as *devoid* of the smaller-scale affiliations that enrich human life, but rather as 'surrounded by concentric circles' beginning with the family and concluding with humanity as a whole. Over the course of the eighteenth and nineteenth centuries, the idea of a nation or people sharing common origins, language, culture, or 'folk-spirit' broadly construed came to be included among these circles. This is to say that if the nation is often construed as a group of people united not only by a 'mistaken,' or mythic, 'view about the past,' but also by 'a common dislike of their neighbors (Deutsch 1969, 3),' it was also understood in cosmopolitan terms. Fichte championed this interpretation. He regarded cosmopolitan consciousness as the goal of human existence and believed that, in the course of reaching it, traditional government would gradually wither away so that the rule of one person over another would *simply and clearly disappear.* Crucially, however, he positioned the *Germans* as the apostles of this goal, representing German nationalism as universal in character and contrasting it with the narrow and egoistic nationalism of other peoples

(Kohn 1949b). Alexandrov, who was familiar with Fichte's work (Alexandrov 1910b), Judaized it, replacing the Germans with the Jews.

Alexandrov began with a critique of the Enlightenment. Scientific advances revealed a world governed by universal natural laws, and technological progress brought people closer together than they had ever been before (Alexandrov 1905). These, paired with parallel developments in the humanities, woke 'mankind from its dream-filled sleep, teaching them humanism.' Yet, this cosmopolitan awakening dissolved into racism and coarse nationalism so that, within the span of a century, they returned to sleep. This occurred, contended Alexandrov, because the Enlightenment came by way of an impure source (Alexandrov 1892b): not 'pure feelings' of human brotherhood, but cold intellect (Alexandrov 1900a) — that is, the tree of knowledge. Referencing Darwin and Spencer, he explained that human beings were said to share a common nature, but an *animal* one. In this way, they were tossed into a beastial 'struggle for survival' in which the 'great swallow the small' — albeit in a more technologically refined manner (Alexandrov 1905). Thus, he argued, each nation shut itself into its own 'ark' to protect itself (Alexandrov 1891a) against the others and a fractured ideal to be 'written with fire and blood' upon every collective undertaking (Alexandrov 1905).

Evidently drawing on hasidic sources, according to which people are divided from one another by dint of their bodies and united by dint of their souls (Tanya I:32), he argued that the solution is a 'pure and holy cosmopolitanism produced by the living God' who 'peeks through the latticework (Song of Songs 2:9)' of the Torah. By representing the common nature of humanity as its 'divine image,' the Torah lifts people *above* their animal instincts (Alexandrov 1905), extracting them from mutual struggle and heralding the day when 'the glory of the Lord will be revealed to mankind and all nations will be guided by this universal light (Alexandrov 1892b).'[4] Asking themselves, 'have we not all one father? Did not one God create us? Why do we break faith with one another? (Malachi 2:10)' they will be restored to the edenic consciousness according to which 'one universal God created one universal world and there were no borders between one nation and the next (Alexandrov 1901).

To elaborate, let us consider Alexandrov's account as to the essential character of Judaism. In the mishnaic tractate of *Pirkei Avot* (2:9) we find a dispute as to what the 'good path' consists in: to be a good friend, a good neighbor, or a good *heart*. In the introduction to this volume, I raised the question of neighborly love and its boundaries; namely that some rabbis extended it only to Israel, while others included humanity in its entirety. According to Alexandrov, this apparent dichotomy is expressed in the distinction between friend and neighbor, one representing national exclusivity, the other a 'cosmopolitan ideal' according to which 'one must love everyone

created in the image of God without distinguishing between one's own
people and those of another (Alexandrov 1896, 19).' In the end a 'good
heart' is favored over both — presumably to communicate that they are
not in contradiction but actually one and the same thing. This is because
the Torah *of Israel* 'has the form of the universal,' making it fitting for
mankind entire (Alexandrov 1931, 22). Thus, it is 'by the light of Judaism'
that 'we see the universal light that shines throughout the world (Alexandrov
1886a, 73).'

This claim about the nature of the Torah positioned Alexandrov to define
Jewish national identity in Fichtean terms. In some rabbinic sources, the
biblical verse 'you, my flock, flock that I tend, are men (Ezekiel 34:31)' is
interpreted as an exclusion, denying humanity of others (Yebamot 61a;
Ma'amare Admur ha-Zaken 5569, 207) — it is interpreted as if to say that
you, the children of Israel, are men but others are not. Alexandrov took a
different approach. Having, he believed, 'achieved perfect unity of form
and Former,' and therefore achieved 'the highest degree of self-consciousness'
— namely, *internal* union with the 'universal essence (Alexandrov 1886a,
76)' — Israel functions as 'the soul of all humanity (Alexandrov 1886a,
76),' bearing 'the likeness of the human collective (Alexandrov 1900a, 19).'
In other words, Israel's nationalism is 'a universal nationalism that forever
conveys light to humanity as a whole (Alexandrov 1900a, 5).' In this sense
the flock of Israel are 'men,' not to exclude but to include: Israel embodies
the whole and is therefore responsible for sharing this consciousness with
others.

This convergence of cosmopolitanism and nationalism is exemplified in
Alexandrov's interpretation of the difference between Exodus 20:8–11, where
the Sabbath commemorates creation, and Deuteronomy 5:12–15, where it
commemorates the exodus from Egypt. The one story applies to mankind
as a whole, the other to Israel alone. Yet, both are subject to a single
commemorative act. As he explained, the latter is for the sake of the former:
as a cosmopolitan nation, Israel observes the Sabbath in order to convey
its universal message to the rest of the world (Alexandrov 1905). It serves
as a 'universal kingdom of priests' conveying to humanity Malachi's lesson,
that 'the earth was created for everyone equally, that every person is a
citizen (Alexandrov 1896, 50)' thereof, thus erasing 'particular national
borders (Alexandrov 1905)' and realizing the kingdom of God.

In this way, the Jewish people are tasked with reversing the effects of
'the sin of the Tree of knowledge' and thus bringing about 'the day that is
entirely Sabbath (Alexandrov 1902),' when 'mankind will be filled with
knowledge and the glory of God will be revealed to all flesh as it was at
first (Alexandrov 1899a),' when the fractured unity of mankind will be
repaired and the cosmopolitan ideal restored. If Adam's consumption of

the forbidden fruit marked a process of descent from 'universal' to 'national' humanity, the sinaitic revelation that Israel brings to the world marks the reverse process (Alexandrov 1902). Paradoxically then, Israel must preserve its distinctiveness in order to operate as a solvent, breaking down divisions erected after the Fall (Alexandrov 1896, 52).

The process is said to culminate in the reunion of heaven and earth: 'the Lord will be one and his name' — that is, 'his creation, which is the name of God' — will be one (Zechariah 14:9; Alexandrov 1905).' More than that, the 'final era will have the advantage over the first,' mankind will join the trees of knowledge and life (Alexandrov 1902, 267). For Alexandrov, this fusion had multiple valences. In part, it involved knowledge of the aforementioned second type: synthesis of Torah and science; no longer would knowledge goes hand in hand with neglect of the divine and therefore the divine in man. We shall bracket this aspect of his thought so as to focus on the *intuitive* reintegration of the empirical-I with the Absolute-I and the Nietzschean, law-abrogating powers this is understood to confer. In this third type of knowledge, we truly speak of *transcending* Eden.

Intuition and the transitive-being-of-God: the messianic beyond of Eden

In *Esh-Da'at we-Ruah Le'umi* ('The fire of religion and national spirit') Alexandrov discusses the nature of universal nationalism in a way that serves to frame his conception of intuition as the *transitive* unity of the empirical-I and the Absolute-I. He described the Jewish soul as having been 'hewn from the throne of glory, from the universal supernal light (Alexandrov 1891b).' Considered on its own, this is not a terribly original claim; the idea has roots in an ancient midrashic tradition and a long history of esoteric interpretation (Wolfson 1992). In light of Habad hasidic thought, however, it takes on a specific meaning which was certainly not lost on Alexandrov. According to R. Schneur Zalman of Liadi, a distinction is to be made between writing and engraving: the written letter is attached to the surface on which it appears, but the engraved letter is of its very substance (*Likutei Torah, Behukotai* 45d–46a) — it is both *distinct* and at the same time undifferentiated. This, I think, gets to the essence of what Alexandrov wished to convey in his description of intuition.

Drawing further on Habad terminology (Foxbrunner 1993), Alexandrov rejects both traditional theists who believe in a God that 'surrounds all worlds' and pantheists who believe the divine to 'fill all worlds.' Rather, he averred, pure monotheism involves cleaving unto the 'God who surrounds all worlds and *also* fills all worlds (Alexandrov 1931, 70–71).' To explain what he had in mind, let us consider Genesis 1:5, 'and there was evening and there was morning, one day (*yom ehad*).' From the fact that the verse reads 'and there was' rather than 'let there be, R. Simon inferred that time already existed; R. Abahu added that God had spent his time building and destroying worlds (GR 3:7).' Maimonides rejected this claim without equivocation (Guide II:30). As he saw it, time is inseparable from matter (Guide II: Introduction, P5–7) and cannot be predicated of God without contradicting the doctrine of divine unity (Guide II:1). Alexandrov appealed to Schelling in order to convey an altogether different conception of the divine based on 'I am He—I am the first, And I am the last as well (Isaiah 48:12–13).' The Absolute, he wrote, 'is a oneness in which all oppositions are united: being and nothingness, finite and infinite, necessity and negation, form and Former, matter and force.' In this sense, it includes time. He interpreted R. Abahu accordingly: insofar as the finite world is 'united completely with the infinite, it is not created' — as it were, it is 'destroyed in itself.' In this sense, it is 'both created and destroyed' at once; 'heaven and earth kiss' in the Absolute (Alexandrov 1931, 38–39).

Alexandrov developed his conception of intuition from this claim about the nature of God. In kabbalistic sources, the spiritual universe is divided up into four hierarchically organized 'worlds;' from highest to lowest, these are: Emanation (*Azilut*), Creation (*Beriyah*), Formation (*Yezirah*), and Making (*Asiyah*). Here is not the place to elaborate at length, but the highest and the lowest constitute a realm 'substantially identical with the divinity' and a 'spiritual archetype of the material world of the senses' respectively (Scholem 1995b, 272). Relying again on Habad sources, he argued that these four worlds are actually one world regarded from different perspectives. From an unrefined perspective, it will seem like *Asiya*, like a 'material and limited' place. From a more elevated perspective, it will seem like *Astilut*, the realm of the divine; one will achieve intuition: 'the divine union of the one who rises above to the infinite Absolute' and thus come 'to know and to feel himself in the universal aspect of the world,' cleaving 'unto the divine and infinite' and becoming 'a part of divinity (Alexandrov 1931, 39–40).' From this point of vantage, material and finite things — including the self — appear under the aspect of infinity.

By thus uniting 'form with its Former (Alexandrov 1886a, 70),' the Fall of Man — 'the filth of *klipat noga*' or 'introjection (Alexandrov 1914b)' — is overcome, not simply by returning to Eden, but by transcending it. In Eden, Adam was originally submerged in the Absolute, but in an external manner because he had not yet achieved subjectivity. That came by way of the tree of knowledge, *klipat noga*, which also alienated him from God, from nature, and from other people. Thereafter, 'the whole task of humanity' was '*uprooting subjectivism* and the [empirical]-I, solipsism, at its root

(Alexandrov 1914c).' Alexandrov believed that this would happen, but gradually over the course of history. Ultimately, however, mankind would achieve an '*internal* awareness' of its 'essence, which extends to the universal essence (Alexandrov 1886a, 72) — without disappearing, individual consciousness would be regarded under the aspect of infinity.

Just as Schelling articulated his vision of this paradoxical union by interpreting the legend of Empedocles, Alexandrov appealed to Habad traditions of ideational self-annihilation (*bitul*).[5] The imperative to martyrdom, he wrote:

> Is addressed to the heart, for it is the seat of consciousness. Why should it not sacrifice itself in the sanctification of God? For the essence of the soul hands itself over and, wherever it is, it remains itself. Thus did the ancient sage Euripides say it well: 'the lover lives in the body of another' … When one sanctifies the name of God, his soul does not dwell or reside any longer in a separate, human body … This is the Torah of the I and its development: to express the I outwardly and to unite it with the universal essence. According to Lessing, this universal essence conceives itself … in eternity, perpetually actualizing itself. In this way, the form and its Former actualize themselves together; they kiss one another and unite in perfect unity. (Alexandrov 1931, 73)

In intuition, then, the dialectical relation between the empirical-I and the Absolute-I reaches its final synthesis. What is equally important, this very synthesis is also a union of wills. If, '*insofar as it is divided from the universal will,*' the former disappears (Alexandrov 1914b) that is not because it has no will, but because there is no difference. As we shall observe in the following section, this has profound antinomian implications.

Intuition and the messsianic abrogation of the law

There is a principle in rabbinic law according to which the study of Torah overrides the observance of the precepts of law when the two conflict (Mo'ed Katan 9b). Alexandrov expanded this notion to convey the idea that the spirit of the law overrides its letter. This notion, he infers from an ancient legend described the primordial Torah as 'white fire engraved with black fire (J. Shekalim 25b).' Comparing it to the sun's 'sheath (Psalms 84:12),' Alexandrov represented the latter as the *concealment* of the former. Just as the sun will one day be 'removed from its sheath (B, Nedarim 8b),' so too will the exoteric dimension of the Torah give way to its esoteric dimension: 'the messiah will remove this mask with his spirit and all flesh shall then see that the mouth of God speaks (Isaiah 40:5; Alexandrov 1891b). Drawing an analogy from the divine 'filling' and 'surrounding' of worlds, Alexandrov spoke of the filling and surrounding of the Torah: it is necessary to study the letters (Alexandrov 1909), but without forgetting that they are merely 'chambers into which the infinite light shines (Alexandrov 1931, 69).'

Alexandrov indexed the dichotomy between exoteric and esoteric dimensions of the Torah to two further distinctions: eternity versus time, and simplicity versus complexity. Throughout the third part of his *Guide*, Maimonides defended Jewish law by explaining it historically. In doing so, he subordinating it to eternal truths, the contemplation of which constitutes true perfection (Guide III:27). Alexandrov likewise argued that the law is 'rooted in the world of experiences that occurred to our ancestors (Alexandrov 1931, 41).' Maimonides, however, considered time an *objective* reality (Guide I:73) from which human beings cannot be extricated; limited in perspective and therefore morally flawed (*Guide* I:2), mankind *requires* law.

Appealing to Kant, Alexandrov stressed the *subjectivity* of time and maintained that mankind can intuit, or 'imagine pure eternity (Alexandrov 1891c).' The implication, Alexandrov explained in interpreting 'the commandment is a lamp, the Torah is a light (Proverbs 6:23),' he therefore wrote that:

> Just as a lamp provides *temporary* illumination, so too do the precepts provide but temporary illumination. Scripture compares the Torah to a light to teach that just as sunlight shines *forever*, so too the Torah. Therefore, the source of the light of the precepts is not the infinite and eternal light; were their source eternal, they would shine forever. The nature of the precepts dictates the conclusion that they will be abolished in the future; their illumination is temporary. Yet, the Torah, Israel, and the Holy One, blessed be He are one. (Alexandrov 1939)

Viewed *sub species aeternitatis*, 'basking in the rays of the divine presence (Alexandrov 1891c),' the law — letters, the body, the lamp of the Torah — give way to its light.

The same consequence arises from Alexandrov's distinction between simple and composite intellects. In the *Mishneh Torah*, Maimonides distinguished between divine and human intellects. The latter is 'composite' in the sense that it 'knows with a knowledge that is external to itself, while the former is 'simple' because God and God's knowledge are one. That is, God knows of his creations through himself as their cause whereas we know of things insofar as they are apart from us (Foundations of the Torah 2:10). Referencing mystical, especially Habad, traditions according to which the Torah is identified with the mind of God (*Tanya* I:4), Alexandrov drew a parallel distinction. On the one hand, it is an intellect 'so simple that no limit defines it (Alexandrov 1931, 32–33)' and therefore 'has nothing to do with impurity and purity, prohibition and permission (Alexandrov 1931, 37).' On the other hand, it contains practical precepts. These, he explained, are 'merely an analogy to divine wisdom' that 'precedes the world of particulars

(Alexandrov 1910a, 5–7).' Just like analogies are discarded when the analogue is comprehended, so too is the law abrogated when 'the divine idea will be engraved and deeply impressed upon the tablets of everyone's heart.' The 'spiritual idea' of the Torah will stand on its own and shed the precepts, which 'are merely adornments and garments (Alexandrov 1939)' of provisional significance. Convinced as to the *real* possibility of intuitively knowing God — as it were, living in the world of Emanation — it became possible for him to contemplate transcending not only the temporal and spatial limits to be found in the world of Action, but also the moral and legal categories attending to a person operating within them. On the basis of these conclusions, Alexandrov called for a 'transcendent Judaism (*yahadut elyona*)' that 'surrounds and fills the worlds of Torah,' one that does not 'rely on text alone,' but rises above it (Alexandrov 1909), recognizing that 'the writing was God's writing, engraved (*harut*) upon the tablets (Exodus 32:16)' — that is, the freedom (*herut*) to interpret and even to abrogate the decrees of the Holy One, blessed be he, issues a decree and the righteous person nullifies it (Moed Katan 16b; Alexandrov 1931, 29).'

This transcendent Judaism reaches a truly radical extreme. Appealing to Schelling's *Philosophy of Art*, Alexandrov wrote that 'beauty is the union of the infinity of spirit and the finitude of matter (Schelling 1989, 85).' The one who relates to the world from the standpoint of *Azilut*, uniting finite and infinite in the Absolute, 'becomes the partner of God in the work of creation.' Exercising 'absolute freedom' of will in creatively dictating the law, he or she defines the contours of divine will and in this sense *makes God*. Drawing on a zoharic teaching usually understood as a reference to the theurgic power of the precepts of Jewish law — 'you shall do them (*va'asitem otam*) (Leviticus 19:37),' the precepts, means 'you shall make Him (*va'asitem oto*) (Zohar 3:113a)' — Alexandrov offered a shocking reversal of Exodus 32:33, instructing his reader to 'make for yourself a God to go before you (Alexandrov 1931, 50–51).'

All of this being said, it would be incorrect to suppose that Alexandrov advocated the simple abandonment of traditional practice. Where 'practical precepts are concerned,' he wrote, 'everything depends on the spirit of the person, the time, and the place (Alexandrov 1931, 64).' As species evolve, so too do law and custom. Comparing the law to the anointing oil in which spices were steeped until their fragrance was absorbed (Exodus 30:22–23; Alexandrov 1900a, 10), Alexandrov argued that people are 'unable to contemplate the universal luminary in the Torah without first having considered each of the six hundred and thirteen rays of light (Alexandrov 1891c),' the precepts, emanating from it. Though the aim may be 'wisdom,' it is achieved through 'fear of the Lord (Proverbs 9:10).' The law, he contended, cleanses human desires (Alexandrov 1896, 7). In this way, 'the spirit of purity is internalized by mankind' and its 'evil inclination' progressively diminishes; as it does, imperceptible changes in communal practice will take place, culminating in the abrogation of the law. A beautiful analogy is used to communicate the idea: 'when a child is learning to read, he must sound out every letter; an adult, in contrast, can make sense of an entire page in a single glance' and also comprehend it in a more mature manner; likewise 'he who studies the universal Torah' need not bother with the details of practice (Alexandrov 1931, 15). This is not to say that children need not sound out their letters but, rather, that they eventually grow out of it; the same goes for practical precepts of the Torah. For this reason, Alexandrov anticipated the dissolution of 'practical Judaism (Alexandrov 1910a, 7)' but insisted that this come about through the natural evolution of Jewish culture (Alexandrov 1939; 1931, 25; 1910, 10). In this sense, Alexandrov's theory of law can be understood as a radical appropriation of Rabban Gamliel's teaching: 'do His will as though it were your will, so that He will do your will as though it were His (M. Avot 2:4)' — Alexandrov simply deleted the 'as though.'[6]

Anarchism, pacifism, diasporism

Alexandrov's engagement with anarchism arises from a number of sources. For one, his cosmopolitanism and his faith in moral progress committed him to an egalitarian vision of universal justice and freedom. Based on the prophetic challenge, 'have we not all one father? Did not one God create us? Why do we break faith with one another? (Malachi 2:10)' he argued that the Torah is 'filled with feeling for humanity as a whole,' implying an 'obligation to assist the poor and oppressed so that all members of society enjoy an equal degree of honor' and 'equal rights.' If it 'despises slavery' — Israel being 'my servants, and not the servants of servants (Kiddushin 22b)' — then it extends the same sentiment to others, seeking 'freedom for the land and for all of the inhabitants thereof without distinguishing between one people and the next (Alexandrov 1905, 234).' For this reason, Alexandrov identified as a libertarian socialist, 'libertarianism and eternal justice' being 'precisely the ethic of Judaism (Alexandrov, undated).'

Another source of Alexandrov's anarchism lies in the faith he placed in the power of moral progress and the basic goodness of mankind. 'The various forms of libertarianism rooted in *love and feeling*,' he wrote, have 'an ancient source in Judaism,' which means that loyalty to the one does not contradict loyalty to the other (Alexandrov 1907, 23). Citing in one place the authority of Bruno Wille (1860–1928), a prominent German anarchist affiliated with Gustav Landauer, Alexandrov robustly affirmed the human capacity to 'learn through experience and correct errors (Alexandrov 1910a, 4).' Adam, he explained, was created by God 'in the most perfect manner;' if a 'snake came to wrap itself around his ankle (Alexandrov 1910a, 9),' God will 'slaughter' it as mankind progresses toward the messianic horizon (Sukkah 52a). Then, the law 'will become superfluous.' Restored to its pristine moral origins, and governed by 'moral feelings' mankind 'does not require a master to issue commands; one simply rejoices in doing good in itself.' As Zechariah taught, God makes the 'unclean spirit vanish from the land' he removes the prophets as well (Zechariah 13:2–3) — a people with healthy 'moral intuitions needs no prophet to teach morals and to inspire them to act justly (Alexandrov 1910a, 8–9).'

Distinguishing his libertarian socialism from the libertinism of historical figures like Joséphin Péladan (Ziegler 1988) and fictional characters like Heinrich in Gerhart Hauptmann's *Sunken Bell*, Alexandrov associated this conviction with 'moderate anarchists' — Kropotkin, Proudhon, Godwin, and Tolstoy for instance — 'who reject all discipline' and insist that 'a person must be free in his actions.' To them, he said, 'it is human nature to do only that which is good and upright.' By 'his own free will,' one naturally acts 'not only in his own interests, but in those of his fellow too.' Therefore 'moral intuitions are strong enough' to dispense with 'external force.' Indeed, force causes 'inclinations to become evil' and the restoration of humanity's 'first nature' depends on freeing people from it (Alexandrov 1910a, 8–9). The belief that 'a morally and intellectually superior person, not a strongman' is the product of freedom, Alexandrov, too, took to be among the 'foundations of anarchism' that are found in Judaism (Alexandrov 1910a, 9).

He developed this idea by returning again to the principle of neighborly love — the very 'banner of libertarian doctrine' — and pairing it with another of Hillel's remarks:' if I am here everything is here, and if I am not here who is here (Sukkah 53a).' The one expresses 'social-feeling,' but the other appears to contradict it by championing radical individualism. Hillel's phrasing of the golden rule — 'what is hateful to you, do not do to others (Shabbat 31a) is, in two respects understood as the hermeneutic key to reconciling this difficulty. One, it implies that when the individual is undefined, so too his or her duty:

> So long as my 'I' has yet to develop and I do not know myself with any precision, I also know not what to do for my neighbor. Thus, it is only when 'I am here' that 'everything is here,' *then* 'ethics may teach us that 'what is hateful to you, do not do to your neighbour. (Alexandrov 1910b)

An individual must 'develop freely, in his particular essence (Alexandrov 1910a, 9)' if he or she is to become a moral agent. Two, it speaks to a question of motivation. Without self-love, 'whence love for others?' Only when the I becomes 'an object of my concern' can that concern be extended to 'every other I,' all of which are 'hewn from the same source.' Therefore, Alexandrov concluded, 'social feeling does not reduce the status of the individual (Alexandrov 1910b).' On the contrary, it is predicated on 'the mutual happiness of individual and society;' thus, 'moral Judaism' and 'moral anarchism … kiss (Alexandrov 1910a, 9).'

The superordination of spirit over matter serves as another basis for Alexandrov's anarchism. In the Jerusalem talmud it is taught that 'we do not anoint priests as kings (Horayot 3:2).' Alexandrov understood this as a reference to the 'nation of priests' that — alluding to the difference between the anointing of priests and kings (Horayot 11b) — 'needs only the holy and divine oil (Alexandrov 1896, 54)' of eternal spirit and not 'the oil of state' that, because 'the true king of the people is the divine lawgiver,' was 'sanctified for its time only,' when the people had yet to absorb the 'universal spirit' of the 'Living God (1900a, 13).' Like Steinberg and others, Alexandrov drew inspiration from the way that R. Johanan b. Zakkai traded Jerusalem for Yavneh in order to 'preserve the culture of Israel' within which 'the scroll stands above the sword of state.' For this reason, he explained, the shofar — that 'represents freedom and liberty … salvation and of the redemption of our souls' — was blown in Yavneh on the Sabbath (in spite of earlier rabbinic restrictions on doing so outside of Jerusalem) but not in the surrounding countryside (*medinah*) (Rosh Hashanah 29b). Reading the word '*medinah*' according to its modern usage, in reference to the state, he explained that Israel has 'no statist aims in their [shofar] sounding; they know that it is not 'not by might, nor by power, but by my spirit (Zechariah 4:6)" that human liberty is achieved (1898b–c). Relying 'on no state but Yavneh,' Israel undertakes instead to rectify 'the world with the sovereignty of God (Alexandrov 1898a).'

Appealing to Kropotkin, Alexandrov maintained that because 'there is no abyss between thought and action,' the 'religious revolution' he championed would naturally extend beyond the realm of ideas and transform the world order (Alexandrov 1910b). This brings us to the question of method — how would it do so? Like most other figures discussed in this volume, Alexandrov upheld the pacifist principle of ends-means correspondence. This, he articulated by expounding laws related to the Jubilee — the biblical year of liberation and equality that over time took on a profound messianic valence (Scholem 1990, 460–496). 'It is only in sanctity that freedom can be received,' he explained, only by thoroughly absorbing 'the idea that the whole earth belongs to God' by releasing our hold over it during the cycle of Sabbatical years that precede the Jubilee. Likewise, it cannot come 'via the source of destruction, the battle for survival which leaves innumerable corpses.'

Therefore, it is announced on the Day of Atonement, a sacred fast during which this struggle, which has its origins in the first sin, is renounced. When these conditions are met, 'holy liberty' is achieved (Alexandrov 1905).

Fundamentally, however, Alexandrov's pacifism is grounded in his cosmopolitan theology. According to rabbinic legend, Alexander of Macedon once asked an assembly of rabbis 'who is called mighty?' Wryly, they replied 'he who conquers his inclination (Tamid 32a).' Alexandrov glossed this response as follows: 'strength means strength of will and a powerful heart that fears nothing;' he who achieves this is truly mighty, 'not one who imagines himself able to dominate the world (Alexandrov 1896, 37).' The ability to conquer 'the inclinations of the human heart' arises from 'feelings of universal love for everything created in the image of God.' These feelings extract one 'from his particular national borders,' therefore eliminating the ideological foundation of 'war between nations' and 'conflicts between neighbors (Alexandrov 1905).' In other words, revolution involves a transformation of the heart.

This revolution, Alexandrov believed, takes place through a process of spiritualization best expressed through his interpretation of the rabbinic aphorism: 'the sword and the scroll descend from heaven bound together (LR 35:6),' which he paired with the biblical story of Jacob and Esau — the former, a 'dweller in tents' of learning, the latter a hunter — who entered the world via a single womb (Genesis 25:23–27). Rashi explained their relationship as follows: 'when one rises, the other falls (Genesis 25:23).' Alexandrov interpreted this relationship of sword versus scroll, Jacob versus Esau, as a twofold dialectic. On the one hand, he understood it to imply a process of spiritualization — after the fall of the ancient Hebrew Republic, Jewish 'feeling for statecraft and for the sword was forgotten; to destroy and damage was regarded as shameful;' in this way, the 'sword of state' is 'transformed into the scroll,' into spirit. The strength of Israel came to lies 'in the fact that it was a people of the book.' Doing so, they serve in their function as a kingdom of priests, teaching humanity to 'live by the book such that "nation shall not lift up sword against nation (Isaiah 2:4; Alexandrov 1896, 67–70)."' That is, the spiritual force of the children of Jacob undermines the material force represented by Esau.

In making this claim, Alexandrov celebrated the paradoxical power of weakness in a striking letter to R. Aaron Shmuel Tamaret (later to be discussed). Against Nietzsche, who ascribed to the Jews a pernicious slave mentality (Duffy and Mittelman 1988), he drew a metaphysical analogy:

> All progress in the world is due to the weakness and the necessity of primordial matter. How can the progress of morals operate on a different principle? Therefore, it does not reduce the status of morals at all that they are the

product of weak people who require justice for survival ... Likewise, the status
of our Torah is not reduced by the fact that it is based on morals and sympathy,
that Israel is the weakest nation. This is a natural law, all intellectual and
moral progress comes from the suffering of matter and the overwhelming
force of energy released by this softening.

Therefore, Alexandrov challenged contemporaries, Israel ought not exchange
the 'morals in our Torah' for the sword; the former is in fact the stronger
(Alexandrov 1910a, 34–35).

There are numerous examples of Alexandrov's efforts to interpret, or
reinterpret, martial elements in Jewish tradition and, therefore, to advance
this process of transition from sword to scroll. A good example is his read
on the significance of Hanukkah. From the decision to emphasize the
rededication of the Temple rather than the victory over the Greeks he inferred
that the rabbis intended to teach that 'we ought to forget about the state
and stop sending our best and brightest to slaughter,' set aside sovereignty
and 'take refuge with God (Alexandrov 1892a, 8–9).' He interpreted the
message of Purim — a holiday that celebrates the conclusion of the Book
of Esther, in which the Jews, who were threatened with destruction due to
the wicked machinations of a government minister and the foolishness of
an inept Persian emperor, achieve not only salvation, but a crushing military
victory over their enemies — similarly: as a spiritual victory over the inclination 'to kill and annihilate (Esther 3:13; Alexandrov 1891c).' In other words,
the simple meaning of scripture, in which a concrete battle is fought and
won, gives way to its allegorical meaning and becomes a victory over victory
and the violence by means of which it is obtained.

Likewise, Alexandrov highlighted the way in which the rabbis systematically
reinterpreted scriptural record of the ancient Hebrew warrior culture. For
instance, a scriptural verse like 'mighty one, gird your sword upon your
thigh (Psalms 45:4)' becomes a reference to the study of Torah (Shabbat
63b). 'With my sword and with my bow (*ba-kashti*) (Genesis 48:22)' becomes
a reference to Torah study and prayer (*bakashati*) (Mekhilta 14:10). Similarly,
David's descent to slay 'a lion in the midst of a pit in time of snow (2
Samuel 23:20),' is taken to imply that he studied the whole *Sifra of the
School of Rab* (a midrashic commentary on Leviticus) on a short winter's
day (Shabbat 18b). For Alexandrov, each such example demonstrates that
'sword and bow are transformed into a scroll, into ethics and the outpouring
of the soul,' so that just as weevil fells mighty cedars with its mouth alone,
so too the 'worm of Jacob (Isaiah 41:14; Alexandrov 1896, 67–70)' — study
and prayer, holy language — replace weaponry and the field of battle shifts
to hearts and minds. As Alexandrov understood it, Israel fights not to
conquer the world but to transform it for the better.

This same process, Alexandrov pointed out, is applied to the land. Phrases like 'your days will be prolonged in the land (Deuteronomy 5:16)' and 'they will inherit the land forever (Isaiah 60:21)' are interpreted as references to the messianic era (Hullin 142a) and the world to come (Sanhedrin 90a). From such examples, Alexandrov inferred that 'once they were dispersed, this land became a land of the spirit (Alexandrov 1896, 69). This brings us to the subject of Alexandrov's diasporism. For Alexandrov, the cosmopolitan dissolution of national *identities* went hand in hand with erasure of national *borders*. Elaborating the story of the Tower of Babylon, he explained that the people there had faith, but it was primarily motivated by fear of dispersion, being scattered all over the world (Genesis 11:4);' coming second to ephemeral things like state and soil, theirs was the sort of 'gathering not for the sake of heaven' which, the rabbis taught, cannot endure (M. Avot 4:7). For all nations that came to be 'in their own land (Alexandrov 1896, 43),' the same order of priorities is said to apply.

In contrast, Israel 'was formed in a land not its own,' in Egypt and then in the wilderness. It gathered at Sinai 'for the sake of heaven (Alexandrov 1896, 43);' the divine idea became Israel's 'allotment (Deuteronomy 32:9).' Thus, they came to share the 'characteristics of the Holy One, blessed be he.' As he is 'the place of the world, though the world is not his place,' so too Israel is 'found in place, but that place is not their place (Alexandrov 1896, 64).' Arguably inspired by Bakunin's representation of slavic statelessness as a national attribute predisposing them to anarchism, where statelessness and powerlessness become anti-statism and resistance to power (Shatz 1990, 38–41, 46), or by Landauer's application of the same idea to the Jewish diaspora (Grauer 1994), Alexandrov essentialized Jewish placelessness.

Israelite placelessness was expressed even after entering Canaan via the Jubilee, when land ownership was suspended, thus demonstrating that it 'belongs to God' and conveying 'the cosmopolitanism of feeling, that a nation ought not be bound to its land (Alexandrov 1905).' Building on scriptural associations between the Jubilee and exile (2 Chronicles 36:21), Alexandrov explained further that the latter is not so much a punishment for neglect of the former, but its most profound expression: Israel became 'a citizen of the earth (Alexandrov 1902),' thus testifying to 'the unity of the Creator and his creation' — just as the former is one and undivided, so too the latter (Alexandrov 1905). If, therefore, the rabbis taught that 'on the day the temple was destroyed, the messiah was born (J. Berakhot 2:4),' Alexandrov took it to mean that exile *is* redemption insofar as it represents the 'universal messianic spirit' of the divine presence (Alexandrov 1900a, 15). For Alexandrov, the diaspora was not only the embodiment of *Israelite* cosmopolitanism, but the means by which Israel fulfills its cosmopolitan mission to the nations. In 'their own land, they could only rectify themselves,' he wrote, but 'being dispersed throughout the earth, they were able to rectify the whole world (Alexandrov 1902),' causing 'the spirit of God' to hover over the surface of the 'raging waters' of Babylon, Media, Greece, and Rome (Alexandrov 1900a, 15)' so as to 'overturn the order of things and impart unto the peoples 'pure of speech, so that they all invoke the Lord by name and serve him with one accord (Zephaniah 3:9; Alexandrov 1896, 43).'

Thus, we find that Alexandrov's vision as to the reunion of the empirical-I and the Absolute-I via mystical intuition has three implications. One, a thoroughly cosmopolitan conception of Jewish identity. Two, a messianic antinomianism articulated in anarchist terms. Three, a pacifism roughly parallel to Tolstoy's and his Jewish disciples. Finally, a conception of the Jewish diaspora according to which it coincides with redemption.

Implications for Zionism

From the foregoing, Alexandrov's position on Zionism becomes quite clear: he strongly supported a religious version of Ahad Ha'am's Cultural Zionism, but rejected Political Zionism without equivocation. This conclusion is perhaps best exemplified via his presentation of the spiritual profiles of Moses and R. Akiva — two figures paired against one another in a famous rabbinic legend in which the former is transported to the study hall of the latter and cannot even recognize Torah teachings reported by the latter in his name (Menahot 29b).

In that legend, Akiva is described as one who 'expounds on each and every crown' traditionally embellishing the *letters* of the Torah 'piles and piles of laws.' As Alexandrov explained it, R. Akiva's spiritual horizon was limited to the proverbial 'four cubits of the law,' having engaged the Torah in a 'manner that merely filled all worlds' — 'piling up additional boundaries and fences' — without reaching the level of 'surrounding all worlds.' This approach to Jewish tradition which, as it were, ignores the divine voice and attends only to its echo, is considered 'a sort of imprecation of the Torah (Alexandrov 1931, 27).' Not only that, but it is described as a spiritually alienated, way of thinking associated both with exile and with false messianism. On the one hand, Alexandrov appealed to a story in which the rabbis disqualified an offering sent to the Temple in Jerusalem by the Roman emperor because it did not meet ritual specifications; treated as rebellion, their refusal precipitated the war in which Jerusalem fell and Israel was dispersed among the nations (Taanit 19b). Here, excessive scrupulousness concerning fine details of the law is blamed for precipitating exile. On the other hand, Alexandrov appealed to the messianic pretensions of Shimon Bar Kokhba, who led a failed revolt against Rome during 132–135 CE. Other rabbis dismissed these pretensions because Bar Kokhba fell short of the 'he shall smell (*reho*) the truth' neither with his eyes, nor with his ears, but 'by his reverence for the Lord (Isaiah 11:3);' like Nietzscheans (Le Guerer 2002) before the fact, the ancient rabbis ascribed messianic significance to the attainment of knowledge via olfaction. As Alexandrov interpreted them: faithful to the law, but lacking a spirit (*ruah*) — in this context, lacking a messianic sense of smell (*reyah*) — R. Akiva supported Bar Kokhba (Sanhedrin 93b; Alexandrov 1909). I would argue that, for Alexandrov, R. Akiva's textual materialism and his superficial messianism represented the Political Zionists who sought to hasten a secular redemption.

'When a people yearns for redemption,' Alexandrov believed, 'it is impossible to rely on text alone.' The people require 'spiritual giants who rise above the Torah (Alexandrov 1909)' — Moses, the archetypal savior, is the exemplar of the antinomian, cosmopolitan-nationalism behind this claim. The 'source of Moses' soul was the universal world,' he wrote, 'for he is the giver of the Torah and the one who studies Torah need not observe the particular precepts (Alexandrov 1931, 19).' Thus he read the famous legend according to which the ministering angels sought to convince God not to bestow the Torah to Israel (Shabbat 88b) as expressing Moses' *own reluctance*; his 'angelic' character 'disallowed him from bringing the spirituality of the Torah down below and covering it with the thick cloud of practical precepts.' If he did so nonetheless, Alexandrov interpreted his eagerness to enter the land so that the law 'could be fulfilled through him (Sota 14b)' against the grain of traditional interpretation: not as a desire to obey the law, but 'to introduce the universal into the land of Israel,' allowing the people observe it under his influence and gradually rise above it (Alexandrov 1931, 47). In the same way, he sought to ensure that the people would 'not be raised with a feeling for their birthplace,' for a particular land, but set their sights on the messianic kingdom of God (Alexandrov 1931, 19). I would argue that, for Alexandrov, Moses' universalism represented the sort of spiritual renaissance, or redemption, that Cultural Zionists like Ahad Ha'am sought to hasten.

Accordingly, Alexandrov distinguished between 'excellent children of Zion' who aim to revive the 'religious culture of our people' and 'new Zionists who want only to establish a Jewish state' — the doctrine of the latter being 'the farthest thing from our religion.' This distinction is articulated by way of an analogy to a debate as to whether the precept of preparing a Hannuka lamp is primarily fulfilled by kindling the lights or by setting them in place (Shabbat 22b) — the former representing spiritual awakening, the latter establishing a Jewish State. True 'Lovers of Zion' — a reference to Hibbat Zion; its name connoting the same — adhere to the first view, Political Zionists to the second (Alexandrov 1899c). As he saw it, this distinction was less an either-or than a matter of degree and emphasis. Contending that cosmopolitan Torah will go 'out from Zion (Isaiah 2:3)' to the world at large, he insisted on the meaningfulness and validity of Jewish settlement in the ancestral homeland and condemned those who denied it (Alexandrov 1899b). Like Ahad Ha'am and most figures considered in this volume, he considered the establishment of a 'spiritual center' there, a place for the renaissance of national spirit, to be crucial for Israel's universal mission (Alexandrov 1891d). As Zalkind also suggested, this center would be populated by a cultural elite free from the proverbial 'forty-nine gates of impurity' — the idolatrous taint of enslavement, whether to sovereign texts or sovereign people (Alexandrov 1900b). In other words, the lamp must be placed, but its placement must serve the light it is to shed and not the converse.

For this reason, Alexandrov also denied this center should have served as the first step for a general ingathering of exiles. In consonance with his vision as to the mission of Israel, he argued that 'when Israel is dispersed throughout the world, it will be easier for them to collect the universal feelings embedded in creation so that they can be refined in Jerusalem.' Drawing here on the kabbalistic notion of gathering and reuniting the luminous shards of a broken god (Fine 1989), Alexandrov suggested that because the spiritual center is intended to serve as a focal point not just for Jewish revival, but for reconstituting 'the image of God' in humanity, a general ingathering would actually hinder progress. As the cosmopolitan nation, Israel must penetrate the world entire so as to channel the universal to and from the proverbial 'gateway to heaven (Genesis 28:17),' establishing everywhere the kingdom of God (Alexandrov 1892b).

Conclusion

In a letter to Micha Joseph Berdichevsky, with whom he studied in Valozyn and shared a great deal intellectually, Alexandrov wrote that, just as there is no place empty of God, so too his Torah, which therefore 'encompasses all the spirits in the world (Alexandrov 1907, 45).' Alexandrov was a medium most skilled in channeling these spirits in articulation of a modern Judaism loyal to tradition but not mired in it. His mystical and messianic vision of a higher Eden in which the I, empirical and Absolute, is translated into a conception of Jewish identity spanning the divide between particular and universal, a cosmopolitan nationalism by virtue of which 'Jew' and 'Greek' cohere in the divine. This convergence of identities translated into the abrogation of physical borders and, therefore, conflict over them — hence Alexandrov's diasporism and pacifism. The same union framed Alexandrov's anarchism: a mystical overcoming of the external practice through which the individual becomes, as it were, his own God and lawgiver. In this way, he fashioned a strikingly idiosyncratic form of Cultural Zionism, which stood far apart from the various Political forms that came to predominate after his death.

Notes

1 For more on their relationship, see Ish-Shalom and Rosenberg (1991, 59–60 127, 409); Ish-Shalom (1993, 49, 116, 236); Shneor (2002); Brill (2012, 240–242).

2 For more on Alexandrov's Zionism, see Schwartz (2002, 13, 50, 63, 114–115, 217); Slater (2014).

3 See, for instance, Berdichevsky's (1888) remarks in *Ha-Zefira*. Recognizing Alexandrov's genius in talmud and philosophy, he complained that the young scholar was wasting his talents on critical notes when he should be putting his own ideas into writing.

4 Here, it is worth noting that Alexandrov aggressively reinterprets the Habad account of this relationship between divided bodies and united souls. In the original source, there is a fundamental distinction between (divine) Israelite souls and (evil) gentile souls (Tanya I:1) — the former alone being capable of unity through transcendence. Alexandrov eliminated this distinction; in Habad hasidic terms, he extended the category 'Israel' to include humanity as a whole, thus rendering 'gentile' a null set. For more on this issue, see Wolfson (2010).

5 See, for instance, the essay on Hanukkah in Dovber Shneuri's *Shaarei Orah*, a book that influenced Alexandrov's controversial reading of the Hanukkah story.

6 Alternatively, there are instances in which Alexandrov toyed with the notion of what might be called an 'uncommanded command.' Interpreting along Rousseauian lines a rabbinic legend according to which Israel was initially forced to *accept* the Torah, but later *fulfilled* it willingly (B. Shabbat 88a), he argued that progress is initially imposed but eventually embraced freely (Alexandrov 1900c).' This freedom is described in Kantian terms. 'When we negate the heteronymous force (*koah zar*) that affects us,' Alexandrov wrote, we do not necessarily reject the *action*, but the heteronomy of the command; it can be, or come to be, an autonomous (*atsma'i*) impulse (Alexandrov 1914d). This is a way that Alexandrov explained the tradition that the commandments of the Torah will be abolished in the messianic era: when 'the master who commands is found in the inner recesses of our own hearts … the commandments will be abolished (Alexandrov 1891e).' That is to say, they simply cease to function *as commands*. The uncommanded command falls into the traditional category of divine 'service for its own sake (Pesahim 50b).'

In explicitly Schellingian terms, the *mizwot* are described as 'material limbs' of a 'spiritual Torah' and, in that sense, as 'the limit found in the limitless' or the infinite 'revealed in the likeness of time and place (Alexandrov 1931, 41).' The individual relates to the totality of precepts as a single decree representing 'six hundred and thirteen forms of cleavage (Alexandrov 1931, 43–44)' to the divine will of which it is itself a part (Alexandrov 1908). On this model, it is possible to imagine a messianic abrogation of the law that is much more conservative: a shift in attitude rather than a practical change.

6

Yehudah Ashlag (1885–1954)

4 Rabbi Yehudah Ashlag, date unknown.

The brightness that shines from above!
There, behind the dividing curtain,
the secret of the righteous radiates;
light and darkness shine as one
(Ashlag, 1956)

According to legend, the Baal Shem Tov, the founder of the hasidic movement, rose up to heaven in a vision and asked the messiah when he would arrive. The messiah answered: 'when your wellsprings overflow.' Bracketing the messianic element of this anecdote, it exemplifies a scholarly truism: that from its inception hasidism aimed to bring kabbalism to the people (Scholem 1995b, 329). While twentieth-century neo-hasidic revivals drawing on the hasidism to creatively reformulate Jewish spirituality for the Westernized Jewish masses (Persico 2014; Biale 2017, 556–574) demonstrated the same tendency, it was most radically exemplified by followers of R. Yehudah Ashlag (1885–1954). Starting in the early 1940s with figures like Levi Yitshak Krakovsky (Meir 2013), but gathering momentum during the 1960s and 1970s with the founding of the Kabbalah Center under the leadership of R. Phillip Berg, a modified and simplified version of Ashlagian teachings was brought to the general public (Myers 2007). This trend peaked around the turn of the twenty-first century, when celebrity influencers — Madonna, most prominently — turned pop-kabbalah into a fad (Huss 2005a; Myers 2008).

It is thus in his role as a modern expositor of popular kabbalism that a Warsaw-born rabbi educated among the hasidim of Gur, Parysow, and Belz (Huss 2004) has come to be known in the world. Believing himself to be a reincarnation of Isaac Luria and therefore authorizing himself to determine the true meaning of Lurianic doctrine, Ashlag undertook a massive project of exposition (Zagoria-Moffet 2017). His primary works include a lengthy commentary on Hayyim Vital's *Ez Hayyim* (1926–30), a systematic presenta-tion of kabbalistic theology entitled *Talmud Eser Sefirot* (1937), a commentary on Hayyim Vital's *Sha'ar ha-Kavanot* (1940), and finally his monumental commentary on the Zohar, the *Sulam* (1948–1955), for which he is best known.

Ashlagian kabbalah — and its offshoots — has proven extremely polarizing in its own right. It has been dismissed as vulgar and inauthentic, not only by many traditionalists, but also and especially by scholars of Jewish mysticism going back to Gershom Scholem himself (Huss 2005b, 2007, 2015). As Boaz Huss has explained, the discourse of authenticity has its roots in the eighteenth-century romantic longing to 'escape the perils of modernity.' It depends on a sense of cultural distance that is arguably inseparable from a certain orientalism (Anidjar and Funkenstein 1996). Modern and postmodern interpretations of kabbalah, especially when proffered by urbane professionals, bring it all too close and threaten this whole enterprise (Huss 2005b, 2007, 2015). As a pure and unadulterated transmission from antiquity, kabbalah has never been 'authentic;' this is undisputed in the scholarly literature. Indeed, its intersection with philosophy (among other influences) accompanied its twelfth-century emergence and persisted through the modern period (Tirosh-Samuelson 2003). I do not recognize a fundamental distinction between efforts to structure kabbalistic lore on the basis of neoplatonic categories (as attempted in the seventeenth century, for instance, by Abraham Cohen de Herrera) and parallel efforts appealing to post-Kantian philosophy and psychology along lines indicated by Ashlag and his disciples. For this reason, recent scholarly attention to their work is most welcome[1] — not least because it has begun to draw attention to the radical manner in which Ashlag translated his approach to kabbalah into a political theology (Huss 2004; Ravid 2013; Shapira 2013; Zagoria-Moffet 2017).

Like Alexandrov, Ashlag's intellectual horizon extended beyond his immediate social and religious milieu. His external studies included Spinoza, Locke, Hegel, Marx, Nietzsche, James, Rawls, and Schopenhauer (Huss 2004). His commentaries reflect some of these influences, but they become most pronounced in a series of essays written around 1933 that were later gathered into collections *Matan Torah*, *Pri Hakham*, and *Kitvey ha-Dor ha-Aharon*. These are the texts that primarily concern us here because it is in them that Ashlag — who took part in anarchist demonstrations in Warsaw during the 1905 Russian Revolution[2] and also welcomed the 1917 Revolution with excitement (Huss 2004) — explicated his social thought most clearly. It is contended that while Ashlag did not appeal directly to the anarchist tradition in articulating his views, his critique of Soviet state-communism and the alternative that he championed, 'altruistic communism,' place him within the libertarian socialist tradition. It is contended likewise that while his view as to the special capacity of Jewish people to realize 'altruistic communism' draws on certain apparently racialized tropes that have threaded their way through the kabbalistic tradition (Wolfson 2006), his tendency and inclination is actually to de-essentialize cultural difference and to interpret it in social-constructionist terms. While in doing so, he continues to ascribe to the Jews a unique and central role in bringing about world revolution, he is ultimately committed to a universalist vision wherein the religious, cultural, economic, and political transformation he recommends ultimately applies to everyone because the internal, spiritual, shift this requires can be accomplished *by* everyone.

Beginning with a brief exposition of Schopenhauer's moral philosophy — which I take to be far more crucial to an understanding of Ashlag than Marxist communism — it is my intention to explicate his moral interpretation of the kabbalistic doctrine of *zimzum*, its relation to the will-to-give and the will-to-receive — or altruism and egoism — and the way these character traits frame both his critique of state-communism and his embrace of anarcho-communism.

Schopenhauer: will, representation, pessimism, and morality

Schopenhauer's thought is based on a twofold critique of Kant. In *The Fourfold Root of the Principle of Sufficient Reason* (PSR), he argued that the PSR (that everything must have a reason or cause) is predicated on the real difference between subjects who explain and objects to be explained (16). Kant's distinction between phenomenal (the world as it appears to us) and noumenal (the world as it is in itself) is interpreted accordingly: its theoretical basis is the PSR and, by extension, the subject–object relation. He also argued as an *a priori* intuition grounding the orderly experience of *subjective* phenomena, the law of causality is misapplied when extended to mind-independent noumenal *objects* (21–24), which is to negate and subjectify both the subject–object relation and the PSR.

In his *The World as Will and as Representation*, Schopenhauer posited instead that the world exists as will and its representation, which are *one and the same thing* regarded from two different perspectives. Having concluded that the subject–object relation is merely a product of phenomenal experience, he contended that the noumenal will is an undifferentiated whole without any particular object, a state of meaningless and indefinite striving that is subjectively individuated. By analogy to the Australian bulldog-ant that consumes its own tail when cut in half, he argued that thus individuated, the blind striving of will turns against itself, yielding a Hobbsian 'war of all against all.' Hence, his pessimism: as individuals, we are condemned to egoism, to desire more than we can ever have, to struggle with others to get it, and thus to suffer (Wicks 2019).

Schopenhauer's solution is to lift the proverbial 'veil of maya (*World as Will and as Representation* 51),' to transcend individuation. Ultimately, this is the promise of death; it 'abolishes this person' so that the difference between I and not-I ceases (Schopenhauer 1958, 507). If a degree of egoism is inescapable while this blessing has yet to occur, Schopenhauer recommended compassion, which he defined as 'one individual's again recognizing in another his own self, his own true inner nature (Schopenhauer 1998, 209),' this constituting the metaphysical foundation of ethics. In other words, moral practice serves an escape from the shackles of being oneself. Crucially, another important escape is ascetic discipline and, through it, the mystical experience of giving up all private willing by union with the divine or by spiritual extinction (Schopenhauer 1958, 610–613).

Schopenhauer himself condemned Jews for their 'pernicious optimism (Schopenhauer 1958, 623)' in clinging to life and refusing to assimilate or die. Accordingly, he accused them of constitutional egoism and parasitism (Schopenhauer 1971; 1893). As Alexandrov Judaized Fichte, however, so Ashlag did with Schopenhauer. He did so by departing from the philosopher in a few crucial ways. One, he distinguished between altruistic and egoistic *desires*, which is to say, contra Schopenhauer, that the former is not a negation of will, but *another type* of will — a divine will. Two, he treated will as a form predicated of being rather than as an essence constituting it (Ashlag 2015, 78–79); this means it is subject to change. That is, he implied, one can transform his or her will; this being, in his view, the whole purpose of human existence.

Moral and political ontology: the will to give, the will to receive, devekut, and hishtavut

Biblical authors almost never wrote propositionally, relying instead on narrative and law to express their ideas (Levinson 2008, 48). If, therefore, a systematically developed moral psychology is absent from these texts, certain basic assumptions about human nature are readily discernible. For instance, that human beings are knowers of good and evil (Genesis 3:5), that desire often drives them to behave badly (Genesis 6:5), and that they are nonetheless capable of heeding a higher moral calling (Genesis 4:7). In rabbinic literature, this basic schema was developed into a relationship between competing inclinations: an inclination for evil with which each person is born, and an inclination for good that develops over time through proper training (Avot d'Rabbi Natan 16:2). Over the course of time, and largely in response to kabbalistic influence, this psychological distinction took on ontological hues. On the one hand, moral distinctions between good and evil were reduced to an underlying metaphysical divide between the 'side of holiness' and the 'other side (Scholem 1991).' On the other hand, private impulses became instantiations of these forces and the individual was transformed into their battleground (*Likutey Amarim Tanya* 1:9).

Ashlag placed his stamp on this model, contending there are two fundamental tendencies at work in the world and in the individual. The 'side of holiness' and the inclination for good became a 'will-to-give,' while the 'other side' and the evil inclination became 'a will-to-receive.' The relationship between the will-to-give and the will-to-receive is articulated via a novel interpretation of the Lurianic doctrine of *zimzum*, according to which infinite divine light regressed into itself, leaving an 'empty space' within which finite things, the universe, can come to be. In the wake of this *zimzum*, this self-contraction, the divine light reveals itself again, only in a limited fashion, as a fine ray of divine light radiating into the empty space and constituting a creative force that gives life to worlds (Scholem 1976).

In keeping with the hasidic tendency to psychologize kabbalistic theosophy (Scholem 1995b, 340–341), Ashlag understood this myth as an interplay of wills. As he explained it, the infinite divine light represents a will-to-give, a desire to bestow good. The desire to give, however, can be good only if there is a corresponding desire to receive what is being given; otherwise it is simply violence. In this respect, the will-to-give necessarily implies a corresponding will-to-receive — an emptiness that naturally wishes to be filled (Ashlag 1956, 17–18). Against the Manichean grain of some kabbalistic models, Ashlag thus suggests that the will-to-give and the will-to-receive are not, in essence, two distinct wills but one will with two aspects.

It is because the will-to-give bears in itself the will-to-receive that it is radiated forth *from* the divine essence in the first place. Incorporeal things, Ashlag explained, are distinguished from one another by virtue of their defining qualities, their forms (Ashlag 1956, 15). Obliquely appealing to the Platonic notion, he means to suggest that such things differ by virtue of the fact that they are constituted by defining features that differ. The divine essence is absolutely sufficient in being and unable to receive — that is its form or definition. The will-to-receive is the very principle of reception and therefore constitutes an opposing form. Therefore the two are ontologically distinct. Because it is possessed of an implicit will-to-receive, the will-to-give therefore emanates from but is not identical to the divine essence (Ashlag 1956, 23).

To explain why Ashlag understood this to be the case, it is necessary to elaborate on his doctrine of equivalence of form (*hishtavut zura*). In his *Petiha le-Hokhmat ha-Kabbalah*, the introduction to his commentary on the Zohar, he explained that physical things are, first and foremost, distinguished from one another spatially; one thing is different from another at least insofar as they do not occupy the same place. Incorporeal things, in contrast, are distinguished from one another by their 'form.' To explain this, he drew an analogy to two people: when they feel or think similarly, they are 'close' to one another; when they differ, they are 'far' from each other (Ashlag, 1961, 4). If their thoughts and feelings were *exactly* alike, then they would be one person and not two — this is what Ashlag meant by *hishtavut zura* or the lack thereof. In essence, two ideas that are differently defined are not the same and therefore stand at a conceptual distance from one another. Represented as polar opposites, the will-to-give and the will-to-receive naturally fit this description. Insofar as the radiance of the divine essence, the will-to-give, contains within itself an implicit will-to-receive, the former is not the same as the essence of God. This is why it radiates *outward*.

Zimzum, according to Ashlag's interpretation, represents an effort on the part of the will-to-receive implicit in the will-to-give to achieve *hishtavut zura* with the latter and thereby to perfectly join itself to the divine essence: it transformed itself into a pouring-vessel, a thing that receives *in order to give* and, therefore, into a type of giving thing. In doing so, however, it left an 'empty space' — that is to say, the will-to-receive considered in itself, *apart from* the will-to-give (Ashlag 1956, 18–19). It is within this space, and as expressions of this space, that particular things — individual souls especially — ultimately came to be.

Like Schopenhauer, who identified the principle of individuation with an indefinite egoistic drive, Ashlag therefore identified the essence of creation (that is, the fact of being otherwise than God) with the will-to-receive (Ashlag 1956, 23). Indeed, he claimed that created matter itself is nothing other than the will-to-receive (Ashlag 1956, 26). Thus, he wrote that:

> If we wish to discern the individual and unique aspect of each thing ... it is nothing other than the will to receive, which is the whole particular form of a thing ... limiting it both quantitatively and qualitatively in terms of what it draws toward itself and what it pushes away from itself. (Ashlag 1995, 123)

The human soul considered as a *distinct* thing is the most significant example because it represents the true and final object of God's magnanimous will-to-give (Ashlag 1956, 18); it above all things is defined by its desires. As Ashlag wrote in his *Petiha*, 'our being is nothing less than the will to take (Ashlag, 1961, 8).'

Unlike Schopenhauer, however, Ashlag believed that the individuating will-to-receive contains within itself an internal contradiction by dint of which it is turned inside out. Building on the rabbinic belief that handouts are the 'bread of shame (J. Orla 1:3)' that people naturally avoid whenever possible, he inferred that just as the will-to-give implies a will-to-receive, so too does the will-to-receive imply a will-to-give (Ashlag 1956, 20). Since 'there is no force in spirituality,' and the will-to-receive must *want* what it receives, its realization is predicated on a will-to-give; a soul must give in order to be willing to receive (Ashlag 1956, 18).

In part, this is accomplished by the study of Torah and the observance of its *mizwot* (Ashlag 1956, 19). As Ashlag understood them, they represent different ways of 'giving back' to God and therefore 'earning' the good that God bestows (Ashlag 1956, 16, 21). As he wrote in the *Petiha*, it is through the study of Torah and the observance of its precepts that the 'form of the will to receive is transformed into a will to give (Ashlag 1961, 5). Like the will-to-receive encompassed in the will-to-give, the human soul then achieves *hishtavut zura*; having become a giving thing, it shares the form of the divine (Ashlag 1956, 15) from which it is therefore indistinguishable. Following quite literally a talmudic model according to which cleavage (*devekut*) to God is accomplished via *imitatio dei* (Kiddushin 111b), Ashlag contended that the soul returns 'to its prior connection with God's essence ... like an organ which was once severed from the body but was subsequently reattached and came once again to know the thoughts of the body as a whole as it did before it was detached therefrom (Ashlag 1995, 149).' Naturally, this mechanism is not limited to the performance of ritual commandments but, as the ancient rabbis themselves indicated (Shabbat 133b), it extends also to human generosity, compassion, and mercy — which are, after all, imperatives unto themselves.

From his moral ontology, Ashlag derived a political typology. On the one hand, there are 'narrow egoists.' These are people deficient in neighborly love (Ashlag 2015, 174) who succumb to the will-to-receive and act only for themselves even when seeming to act for others (Ashlag 2015, 17) and who therefore 'acquire a nature of hatred and exploitation (Ashlag 2015, 174).' This state of mind, Ashlag identifies with the destructive spirit of capitalism (Ashlag 2015, 20–21). On the other hand, there are altruists who 'sacrifice all their days for the well-being of others without any reward,' neglecting 'their own needs to help others (Ashlag 2015, 17).'[3] These folk, who embody the will-to-give and represent 'society's constructive force (Ashlag 2015, 174),' are the 'communists, who fight for the benefit of oppressed among all the nations of the world' and 'are willing to pay for it with their very lives (Ashlag 2015, 17).'

Just as *hishtavut* and *devekut* constitute the salvation of the individual human soul, reuniting it with its divine source, so too did communism represent, for Ashlag, 'the law of the messiah (Ashlag 2015, 16)' — the social and political equivalent of the same spiritual process.

Critique of state-communism

Ashlag's embrace of communism as the socio-political expression of altruistic *hishtavut* must be distinguished from the state-communism ultimately established in Russia. On the one hand, he reported elation in response to the 1917 revolutionary victory:

> How happy we were when communism came to practical experimentation in a nation as big as Russia! It was clear to us that after a few years the regime of justice and happiness would appear before the entire world, and thus the capitalist regime would vanish from the world in the wink of an eye. (Ashlag 2015, 57)

Yet, Ashlag's messianic expectations, however, were quickly disappointed. The question is why.

Engels' (1892, 6, 42) basic critique of utopian socialism was that it endeavored to realize an ideal kingdom of justice without taking into account the real historical struggle between oppressed and oppressor. Ashlag channeled the same fundamental critique, crediting the Marxists with actually incorporating 'the oppressed themselves in the war of communism.' Yet, he unequivocally rejected what he took to be the egoistic grounds on which this was done. The masses, he wrote, were drawn into the struggle *not* by evoking their higher moral sense, but by exciting 'hatred of the opposing class (Ashlag 2015, 176)' and appealing to their egoistic *interests* (Ashlag 2015, 18). Pace the many modern commentators who have associated communism with the ethos of 'what is mine is yours, what is yours is mine' that the sages dismissed as foolish fancy, he claimed that they relied on the ethos of 'what is mine is mine, what is yours is yours (M. Avot 5:10; Ashlag 2015, 30)' that is often associated with rampant capitalism (Hellinger 2012). I understand this to imply that in Ashlag's view, there is little substantial moral difference between the materialism of Marxist communism and the capitalism it opposed — proletarian selfishness being no better than bourgeois selfishness.

Bracketing religious objections, Ashlag believed this way of organizing the struggle served merely to rally the people against its perceived enemies without cultivating the moral conditions necessary for creating and maintaining a communist society. Without altruistic foundations, Ashlag contended, motivation will decline when earnings are not indexed to the amount or quality of their labor (Ashlag 2015, 18–19). If resistance is not overcome via some internal transformation, it is neutralized coercively, through a system of rewards and punishments (Ashlag 2015, 20). To manage this system, supervisors must be appointed and either paid according to the additional burden of overseeing others or managed in turn. 'Without sufficient supervision, the rewards and punishments are certain to be inadequate,' he wrote. But insofar as 'there is no harder work than standing over people and agonizing them,' managers themselves will have to be supervised unless they are paid in keeping with the added tribulation they endure. Thus, together with the wage relation comes a wage differential in itself inconsistent with communist ideals (Ashlag 2015, 23–24). The end result, Ashlag contended, is a reproduction of the same old exploitative social division of labor (Ashlag 2015, 25). If in 'bourgeois regimes, the capitalists and the middle class' dominate, 'managers' do the same in egoistic communist regimes; either way, 'the strong will exploit the laboring weak as far as they are able and show no mercy,' taking for themselves 'the butter and the cream, leaving

the workers with only the meager whey (Ashlag 2015, 22).' Without direct
control — as opposed to 'ownership' as mediated by the state — over the
means of production coupled with the spiritual maturity to manage them
altruistically, workers 'have no greater foothold or benefit' and remain under
the thumb of 'managers who will control them (Ashlag 2015, 43, 60).' The
relation between those who exploit and those who are exploited will persist,
only in a different form and, as Ashlag saw it, 'it is inconsequential whether'
the former are 'capitalists and merchants,' as in the bourgeois regime, or
'managers, supervisors, intellectuals, and distributors,' as in the state-
communist regime (Ashlag 2015, 22)

According to Ashlag, not only will a regime based on egoistic communism
simply reproduce capitalist relations of production, it will do so in a still
more brutal fashion (Ashlag 2015, 25). Thus, he explains how coercion
and subordination naturally led the way to a totalitarian state. Egoism, he
argued, is not in short supply and 'ideals are not hereditary.' Inheritors of
power are apt to succumb to natural human self-centeredness and either to
dismantle the communist regime outright or to preserve its outer form while
using it to their own advantage, thus creating 'a nation of lords (Ashlag
2015, 20–21). Mitigating its capacity to destroy the communist regime
meant conducting an unceasing war against the public (Ashlag 2015, 40)
and thus handing the government over to 'autocratic executives in absolute
dictatorship.' With sword in hand 'for killing, incarceration' and arbitrary
punishment, they reduced civil rights (Ashlag 2015, 44–45, 61) and democratic
processes to a symbolic minimum in order to suppress the counter-revolution.
Yet, he averred, 'a bayonet-dependent government cannot persist' indefinitely
(Ashlag 2015, 20–21, 40).' In other words, a communist revolution based
on force rather than moral transformation is inherently fragile.

Possibly referring to the collapse of the Second Socialist International
during World War I, which dissolved along national lines, he contended
further that a communism established on egoistic foundations falls short
of the internationalist vision that characterizes all truly revolutionary movements. 'If one is forbidden to exploit one's friend,' no nation should 'be
allowed to exploit its fellow nations; therefore, 'international communism
must be instituted (Ashlag 2015, 33).' Yet, he argued, even supposing that
a communist regime was established in each individual country, a 'communism
based on [what is] mine is mine' does 'nothing to remove the mutual envy
among nations (Ashlag 2015, 38).' This is because there is then no 'compelling
reason for nations rich in means of production, raw materials, and civilization
to share ... equally with the poor nations. Therefore, 'a just division within
each nation for itself' — if indeed this is actually achieved — 'will not assist
just division among the nations whatsoever (Ashlag 2015, 29, 63).' In this
way, communism grounded in egoistic interests fails also to 'ensure the

minimal existence of people in the world' by preventing wars (Ashlag 2015, 27–28). Therefore, even if the internal fragility of the egoistic regime is overcome, it will be unable to mitigate enmity among neighboring states; therefore it stands under perpetual threat.

In sum, Ashlag rejected Marxist materialism because, grounded in egoistic interests rather than altruistic magnanimity, he considered it inconsistent with his moral ontology. He believed, furthermore, that it was directly responsible for the betrayal of the revolution, leading to the reintroduction of class hierarchy and undermining socialist internationalism. As he saw it, the alternative between capitalist and state-communist regimes is negligible.

Transformation: religion versus character education

Ashlag's critique of state-communism left him not disillusioned, but in anticipation of a 'pure' or 'corrected' form built on altruistic foundations (Ashlag 2015, 19, 30). Before elaborating on his vision of what this would entail, let us first consider his understanding of the path to its accomplishment. In essence, he believed that 'a society cannot be good unless its majority is good (Ashlag 2015, 61).' What this meant, for him, is that progress cannot be forced; it must be willed by the people and may, therefore, come about only by way of their inner transformation.

Ashlag's reflections on the question of educating for altruism appear contradictory. In several places, he contended that 'no training in the world will reverse human nature from egoism to altruism' and from this concluded that coercive state-communism cannot be justified on the grounds that it paves the way to a more 'perfect communism (Ashlag 2015, 20).' Elsewhere, however, he appealed to the rabbinic notion that observing precepts 'not for their own sake' leads to observing them 'for their own sake (Sanhedrin 105b)' and indicated that 'egoistic communism is but a step on the way to justice' — but a *step* nonetheless. Indeed, he went so far as to suggest that due to natural human 'craving for possessions, it is *impossible* to build altruistic communism unless egoistic communism comes first (Ashlag 2015, 33–35).'

I believe that the gap between these opposing claims is bridged by appealing to his understanding of the power of public opinion and the various ways in which it can be cultivated. Like other religious anarchists considered in this volume, Ashlag relied — though, in his case, not explicitly — on Kropotkin's faith in the power of custom to regulate social behavior. The public, he wrote, is possessed of a 'collective imagination where all the acts related to the general public are imprinted.' Judging on the basis of generally recognized notions as to what is good and what is bad, the members of any community 'praise and glorify the doers of the beneficial acts' so as to motivate their repetition, and 'vehemently condemn the doers of detrimental actions' so as to ward off their repetition (Ashlag 2015, 83–84). In this way, public opinion serves to shape the opinions of its constituents: avoiding shame and seeking respect, they are habituated into socially acceptable patterns of conduct.

The problem with this approach, so Ashlag contended, is twofold. For one, he doubted the ability of a secular educational system to establish a lasting state of public opinion conducive to communism. The force of instruction, he contended, 'tends to weaken' over time due to the pressure of natural human instincts so that the idealists of one generation have 'no assurance that their sons will continue' along the same path. Even supposing that the right values were taught, they would not endure. The more funda-mental problem is that mere public opinion 'cannot *exceed* the viewpoint of the public (Ashlag, undated);' if the public is in error, then it will encourage corrupt patterns of behavior. The ethics of a secular communist regime, Ashlag indicated, are essentially utilitarian; it is a 'morality based on public benefit' — that is, the needs of the public so far as the public understands them. Most likely with Kropotkin's *Mutual Aid* in mind, he went on to explain that this type of moral 'reasoning' is not uniquely human, but 'exists also in social animals' and from this fact deduced that it is sufficient only for maintaining an animal-like way of life. Public interest is 'evaluated only according to the specific state of that public (Ashlag 2015, 45–47)' and the public is naturally fickle. Thus, a 'great murderer' can be considered 'patriotic and well mannered (Ashlag 2015, 108)' if only 'an experienced and competent speaker' stands up to convince them of it. Then, 'several hundred years of education vanish like a [popping] soap bubble (Ashlag 2015, 25).' Common sense morality, in short, is only as reliable as common sense.

According to Ashlag, religion alone has the power to elevate public opinion beyond mere common sense, to embrace altruistic patterns of thinking and acting — 'working according to the ability and receiving according to the need (Ashlag 2015, 29) — irrespective of their apparent rationality. Therefore, he called upon his readers to 'take religion from the possessors' and turn it 'into an instrument in the hands of the workers (Ashlag 2015, 122).' There are several ways in which he held religion to contribute to revolutionary progress, some more profound than others. In the most external sense, it supplies moral convictions with a solid and authoritative foundation. The difference, between secular and religious idealists, he wrote, is that the former 'cannot convince anyone of his preference for justice or who so necessitates it' and has no adequate reply to Nietzsche's challenge: perhaps moral sense 'is but faintness of heart.' In contrast, the latter can 'boldly counter that it is so commanded by the Lord' and confidently 'give his life for it (Ashlag 2015, 50)' because, oriented toward the Highest Good, it is imbued with eternal meaning and purpose and these are 'imperative for any mindful being (Ashlag 2015, 94).' In this way, religion supplies an existential ground for altruistic behavior. For Ashlag, God serves not only as a source of moral authority, but also as a final executor of justice. If nothing else, the *fear* of God, or belief in spiritual reward and punishment (Ashlag 2015, 29), bolsters compliance; thus religion and idealism 'complement one another; where the ideal cannot be in the majority, religion *forcefully* rules the primitive majority incapable of ideals due to its possessiveness and its desire to work less and receive more (Ashlag 2015, 67).'

Building on rabbinic interpretation of 'all that the Lord has spoken we will faithfully do (Exodus 24:7)' according to which 'doing (*na'aseh*)' implies mere obedience, while 'faithfully (*nishmah*)' implies understanding and choice (Shabbat 88a), Ashlag held that spiritual force becomes freedom: it 'begins coercively, it ends voluntarily (Ashlag 2015, 67).' This is where his approach reaches deeper and religion actually comes to function as pedagogy. People cannot simply be 'stunned' into obedience to a moral code (Ashlag 2015, 48); they must be convinced and transformed. On the one hand, religion offers a *reason* for altruistic behavior. 'We must understand,' he explained, that 'if it is not worthwhile to live for myself, is it worthwhile to live for a thousand others like me, or a billion (Ashlag 2015, 106)?' Faith, he contended, supplies this reason: in *every* person there is a 'spark that demands unification with God ... If someone generates the satisfaction of this desire in that person, he will agree to anything (Ashlag 2015, 73).' This includes, of course, altruistic deeds undertaken 'to benefit the Creator, whether for oneself, or for the entire world (Ashlag 2015, 106).' Supposing that *devekut* is the innermost desire of a human being, that it is achieved through *hishtavut*, and that *hishtavut* is produced through altruistic behavior, the latter becomes desirable; it is not coerced.

More concretely, Ashlag developed a notion of personal transformation via *habitus*, which he called 'psychophysical parallelism (Ashlag 2015, 91, 93, 111).' We have already seen that Ashlag regarded the practical observance of the precepts as a means for creations to achieve *hishtavut*, equivalence of form, vis-a-vis the Creator. Concretely, however, what this means is that they serve to habituate people to altruistic ways of thinking, feeling, and acting. This process, Ashlag expressed in the idea of 'psychophysical parallelism (Ashlag 2015, 91)' — a principle he explicitly derived from Spinoza's ideas about the relation between divine attributes of thought and extension. There is, he wrote:

> Nothing in the senses that is not present in actions first. Thus, the acts beget senses, and senses beget understanding. For example, it is impossible for the

senses to take pleasure in bestowal before they actually bestow. Moreover, it is impossible to understand and perceive the great importance of bestowal before it is tasted in the senses. Likewise, it is impossible to taste pleasure in *devekut* before one performs many good deeds that can affect it, meaning by strict observance of this condition to bring Him contentment, or in other words, delight in the contentment given to the Creator by performing the commandment. After one feels the great pleasure in the acts, it is possible to understand Him, to the extent of that pleasure. (Ashlag 2015, 96–97)

This is how Ashlag interpreted the rabbinic notion that by observing the precepts 'not for their own sake (*lishmah*),' one comes to do so 'for their own sake (Sanhedrin 105b)' — the appropriate mental state comes as a consequence of correct action. Observing religious precepts trains the faithful to act out of unselfish motives and to enjoy doing so. In this respect, Ashlag drew little distinction between ritual precepts and moral precepts. Both, he indicated, serve one and the same function: to achieve service *lishmah*; striving oneself to please one's Creator instead of oneself through study and ritual leads to 'giving to others in a natural manner' so that the creation 'continually progresses, eventually reaching the level of utterly destroying within himself the aspect of self-love and receiving for himself so that his moral attributes are entirely devoted to giving, or receiving in order to give.' In other words, religious practice serves to 'purify' the soul (GR. 44:1; Ashlag 1999).

We find, then, that while Ashlag ascribes tremendous importance to public opinion as a mechanism for maintaining the social order, he is deeply sceptical as to the efficacy of secular means for fostering altruistic attitudes. He believed instead that these moral characteristics can only be cultivated via habits undergirded by faith in their meaningfulness. Habitual altruism, he maintained, ultimately has a transformative effect; communism then need not be imposed by force from above, but arises naturally and voluntarily from below.

On the nature of altruistic or libertarian communism

With an understanding of Ashlag's moral ontology, his critique as to the egoistic foundations of state-communism, and his understanding as to the necessarily religious foundations of an altruistic libertarian communism, it is possible to elaborate on the nature of the latter. Here, I shall examine his propositions for a universal religion capable of fulfilling this function, then proceed to examine its implications for the status of property and the place of the individual in a communist society.

We have already observed that, in Ashlag's view, the major error of egoistic state-communism was the notion that it could be imposed from above by a minority. The first rule of altruistic communism, is therefore 'to establish the moral level of the majority of the public on a basis that will necessitate and guarantee that the corrected communism will never be corrupted (Ashlag 2015, 30, 36).' That is, a religious basis, a 'collective religion of all the nations' though not necessarily a particular confession — its essence being the obligation of each member of society to give to others 'to the extent that the life of one's friend will come before one's own life Ashlag 2015, 70.' As Ashlag understood it, this faith is embodied in the biblical formula 'love your fellow as yourself (Ashlag 2015, 70).

Echoing his account as to the purpose of human life generally, Ashlag maintained that 'the aim of the service entailed in the Torah and its commandments is *devekut* to God' via *devekut* to his attributes.' Just as 'God acts only to give to and to help others,' he wrote, 'so too must your deeds be solely for the sake of giving to and helping others;' then, he assures his reader, 'your *devekut* to God will be complete (Ashlag 1995, 145).' Addressing a specifically Jewish audience, he expressed this imperative as follows:

> One must love one's fellow in the same measure that one loves oneself ... This means that you are obligated to stand on guard to satisfy the needs of every member of the Jewish people ... just as you stand on guard to satisfy your own needs ... If that is not enough, the simple meaning of the obligation regarding love of the other is that we are obligated to put the needs of our neighbor before our own ... If one has but a single chair and his fellow has none, the law is that if he sits on it and does not give it to his fellow he violates the commandment to love one's fellow as himself, for in this case he does not satisfy the needs of his fellow as he satisfies his own needs. Likewise, if he neither sits on it nor allow his fellow to do so ... he is obligated to allow his fellow to sit on it while he himself sits on the floor or stands. It is self-understood that the same applies to everything that one has but which one's fellow lacks. (Ashlag 1995, 18–20)

Although in this passage, Ashlag speaks of mutual obligation within the Jewish community, from the fact that he explicitly extended the doctrine of neighborly love to all human beings, it is clear that the same imperative is ultimately addressed to everyone. Thus, he asked:

> What prerogative and ownership over raw materials in the soil has one nation over others? Who legislated this proprietary law? All the more so when they have acquired it by means of swords and bayonets! Also, why should one nation exploit another if it is unjust to every individual? In a word: as abolition of property is just for the individual, so it is just for every nation ... If proprietary laws and rules of inheritance do not permit possession rights to individuals,

why would they permit an entire nation? As just division is applied among individuals within the nation, there should also be internationally just division in raw materials, productive means, and accumulated properties for all the nations equally ... There should be no division whatsoever among individuals, a single nation, or all the nations in the world. (Ashlag 2015, 64)

An international mutualism according to which the 'corporeal basis of each nation should be abolished (Ashlag 2015, 132),' he believed, could only be accomplished via altruistic communism, one built on the religion of fraternal love rather than egoistic interest. Otherwise, wealthy and powerful nations would have no reason to sacrifice their own happiness for their weak and impoverished neighbors. Ashlag thus recommended radical altruism for each individual and for all nations, this being the material meaning of the imperative to 'love the Lord your God with all your heart and with all your soul and with all your might (Deuteronomy 6:5),' where 'your might' is understood to imply 'your wealth (M. Berakhot 9:5).' One must, he demanded, labor 'behalf of his fellow' in 'order to find grace in the eyes of the Blessed Creator, who spoke and whom we obey (Ashlag 1995, 90).'

Concretely, Ashlag understood the principle of neighborly love to require 'a just distribution of wealth' as expressed in the classical formula 'from each according to his ability and to each according to his need.' This, he understood according to a roughly mutualistic model. Mutualists like Proudhon, for instance, upheld a distinction between possession and ownership — possession involving the right of use, ownership the right to profits in excess of use. He maintained that a society based on altruistic communism is one in which people retain the right to the former but not the latter (Guerin 1970, 48; Proudhon 2011, 100). Along similar lines, Ashlag wrote that 'there is property, but its owner cannot receive profit in excess of his needs,' these being 'profits made by the communal life' and therefore 'public property belonging to the members of that collective (Ashlag 2015, 101–102).'

As Ashlag understood it, the right to possess extends not only to items of personal use, but also to the means of production. That is to say, he expressed considerable skepticism as to their collectivization. Although members of a collective corporation receive 'their daily bread,' he argued, 'only the handful of managers has the entire ownership, and they do with the national property as they see fit.' Their theoretical co-owners, the workers, have no agency and therefore derive 'no delight' from 'the executives and the functionaries' that 'humiliate them as the dust of the earth' by dictating *to them* the terms of their subsistence (Ashlag 2015, 26–27).

Ashlag's mutualist internationalism framed not only his economic views, but more generally his views on the relationship between individual and society on the one hand, and national identity on the other. The former, we shall address here, the latter in the section that follows According to Ashlag, a special form of individual initiative and expression is crucial to the health of a society built on altruistic-communist foundations (Ashlag 2015, 38, 59). On the one hand, he envisioned a moral equivalent to the capitalist war of all against all: competition in the bestowal of good and in the cultivation of altruistic moral traits (Ashlag 2015, 117, 132). On the other hand, it is expressed through self-determination in the satisfaction of communal labor needs. Distinguishing, with Marx, between labor-time devoted to the basic reproduction of the labor force in general and surplus labor-time that can be devoted to the 'full development of the individual, which in turn reacts back upon the productive power of labour as itself the greatest productive power (Marx 1973, 631),' Ashlag envisioned a system in which individuals determine both the extent of their ability vis-a-vis necessary labor — social pressure and religious conviction being deemed sufficient to ensure honesty — and also the forms of their creative contributions outside of that (Ashlag 2015, 117–119).

Beyond defending economic initiative, Ashlag had a robust notion as to the centrality of freedom and individuality. Against Maimonides, he insisted on a radically anthropocentric conception of the universe. In keeping with the talmudic teaching, according to which each individual must say of himself 'the world was created for me (Sanhedrin 37a), he contended that 'the end of every inclination of true individuality is to become an exalted concept of immeasurable importance' that 'will never again arise in the world.' While these inclinations are yet maturing into 'true concepts' they may appear bad, but 'to destroy or suppress' them is to deprive 'the world of the exalted and wondrous notion that will take shape at the conclusion of its development.' Care must instead be taken to assist them in the 'ripening' process (Ashlag 1995, 122).

This, Ashlag maintained, is especially important in an anarcho-communist society wherein many external markers of difference (wealth, power, and so on) are eliminated. When humanity achieves 'perfection in loving others,' he wrote, 'all bodies will be gathered together as one body with one heart.' Because 'love among bodies naturally leads to shared views,' steps will have to be taken to protect 'individual freedom' of thought; 'disputes and debate' being the foundation of 'all intellectual progress (Ashlag 1995, 133).' As I understand him, Ashlag drew a distinction in forms of *hishtavut*: it is of tremendous moral and spiritual value when oriented 'vertically,' when it governs the relationship between man and God, but a mortal threat in all respects when oriented 'horizontally,' when it governs the relationship between people. As we shall observe in the section that follows, he extended the same reasoning to national-cultural groups as well.

Ashlag's individualism helps us to better understand his conception of public opinion as a governing force in a libertarian socialist society. On the one hand, he wrote that, by force of necessity (Ashlag 1995, 88),' human beings are '*obliged* to live in society' and responsible, therefore, 'for ensuring that society endures and thrives.' This, he maintained, justifies the 'right of the majority to expropriate the freedom of the individual contrary to his will, and to *compel him*,' to act in the public interest (Ashlag 1995, 123–131). On the other hand, he wrote, 'nothing more humiliating and degrading for a person than being governed by brute-force (Ashlag 2015, 34)' and therefore deemed it 'absolutely forbidden ... to appeal to any of the judicial establishments ... or any forms existing in the brute-force regime (Ashlag 2015, 32).' In the altruistic society he envisioned, 'judgment relying on force will be completely revoked' and 'all conflicts among members of society shall be resolved among the concerned parties (Ashlag 2015, 72).'

This apparent contradiction can be resolved by appeal to the modified court system Ashlag proposed. As he had it, 'courts' should have two functions. One, *positively* managing public opinion by 'awarding accolades' to outstanding altruists. Two, by assisting in the process of determining the boundaries of 'each according to his ability.' For instance, by lowering expectations when they legitimately cannot be met (Ashlag 2015, 118–119), or by organizing the education of those who truly fall short of otherwise reasonable ones — assigning 'special pedagogues ... to turn that person around through ... gentle persuasion ... argumentation and explanation of the benefit of society (Ashlag 2015, 34, 72)' — and then afterward facilitating their social rehabilitation (Ashlag 2015, 118). That being said, he denied these courts the power to compel cooperation, relying instead on the force of public opinion: 'one who rejects the court's decision will be condemned by public opinion, and that is all (Ashlag 2015, 72).' In other words, compulsion, or the expropriation of freedom, is ultimately carried out in an informal manner through the relationships that are either strengthened or weakened by the choices that individuals make. Supposing that nobody wishes to be held in contempt, he believed that communities possess sufficient social power to impose their will without overt force.

It is in *this* way that 'altruistic communism will finally completely annul the brute-force regime' so that 'every man will do that which is right in his own eyes (Ashlag 2015, 34).' Each individual will have the right to behave as they deem fit. However, this freedom will not shield him or her from public opinion, which is simply the sum of judgments that others are entitled to form. Nor, for that matter, will it shield him or her from the ultimate consequences of egoism; namely 'war, famine, and what follows from them

(Ashlag 1995, 88). Ultimately, the 'reward' for altruism is an altruistic society; the 'punishment' for egoism is an egoistic society.

Nationalism and the Jewish role in realizing altruistic communism

As Ashlag understood it, the imperative to particularity indicated in the preceding section applies not only to individuals, but also to individual cultural groups. While all such groups must, in his view, accept the universal religion of neighborly love, he also believed that 'each may follow its own religion and tradition, and one must not interfere in the other (Ashlag 2015, 70).' More than that, he considered collective cultural rights to be the foundation of individual rights. Appealing to something like Jung's collective unconscious, he wrote that our inclinations and customs come to us by way of a great chain of human creativity:

> The subconscious of each individual bears the whole spiritual inheritance of his ancestors ... This whole inheritance is accounted to the individual. He is obliged to protect its sense and spirit so that it is not blurred ... [and] so that every individual may remain with the whole of his inheritance. Then the opposition among them will stand forever and ensure perpetually the inquiry and intellectual progress that constitutes the whole advantage of humanity. (Ashlag 1995, 134)

Just as the loss of individual difference is like 'severing a limb' from 'creation as a whole,' each soul constituting a unique revelation of divine being, so too cultural difference — both forms being conceived as essential to the progress. Accordingly, he condemned the Soviets for suppressing minority cultures and 'preventing them from living their lives according to inclinations they have inherited from their ancestors (Ashlag 1995, 123–124).

Ashlag's defense of cultural individuation constitutes the basis of his understanding as to the global revolution. He maintained that 'the entire world is one family' and that 'the framework of communism should ultimately encircle the entire world.' However, he saw this as a gradual process. 'Each nation the majority of whose public has been educated to bestowal upon one another will enter the international communist framework' one by one, he wrote. Clearly adopting Ahad Ha'am's notion of a 'spiritual center' for the Jewish people while at the same time universalizing it, he contended that these isolated pockets of altruistic communism will serve as 'focal points' for human progress as a whole (Ashlag 2015, 31–32, 69).

For several reasons, the Jewish people is understood as the exemplar in this respect. Drawing on the idea of its chosenness and its obligation to serve as a 'light of nations (Isaiah 49:6),' he wrote that the 'nobler nation must take upon itself to set an example for the entire world (Ashlag 2015, 41)' and school the rest in 'religion, justice, and peace (Ashlag 2015, 75).' Less paternalistically, he also argued like Alexandrov that the Jews are not 'more idealistic' than others, but having 'suffered from tyranny more than all other nations' they are also more 'prepared to seek counsel' as to its abolition (Ashlag 2015, 42).' In this respect, he compared Israel to 'the heart that takes shape before the other organs' but evokes in them similar passion.

Most of all, however, Ashlag simply believed that the Torah which organizes Jewish life embodies the universal, even 'cosmopolitan,' doctrine on which the society of the future must be based (Ashlag 2015, 65). In large part, this is based on his interpretation of the imperative to neighborly love, which is understood to represent the Torah's sum and substance — 'the whole essence of which is nothing other than love of the other which, practically speaking ... means benefiting others (Ashlag 1995, 83),' *all* others, without boundaries.

What distinguishes the Jews, in this respect, is the fact that they have already received this doctrine as *Torah*. That is, as an obligation that must be fulfilled for its own sake (*lishmah*). It is natural to resist dedicating 'even a minor deed to the benefit of others,' and, even when doing so, to expect some form of recompense. For this reason, he explained, the sages taught that all 'kindness a gentile does, he does for his own purposes (Bava Batra 10b).' It is not that Jews are intrinsically 'more idealistic' than others (Ashlag 2015, 42); 'heaven forfend!' he exclaimed, that any fool should interpret this statement as an expression of nationalism or racism (Ashlag 1995, 19). Rather, it is a matter of the social structure which Jewish religion imparts on the Jewish community. Without the Torah and its precepts, which the Jews observe 'for their own sake,' he maintained 'there would be no scheme in the world that could transform our nature (Ashlag 1995, 146–149).' Through the habit engendered by this practice 'one slowly parts from the laws of nature and acquires a second nature, which is love of the other (Ashlag 1995, 24).'

But this begs the question: *why* do the Jews have this Torah? Ashlag responded by posing it in a different form: why was the Torah not offered to the forefathers? His answer constitutes a close foil to Alexandrov's. For Alexandrov, the form in which Israel received the Torah at Sinai was of a lesser order than the transcendent and anomian Torah observed by the forefathers. Ashlag is less concerned with any difference in form or content than the fact that it was *given* to the children of Israel and not to their progenitors.

His explanation involves a radical interpretation of the principle of *arevut*, according to which all Jews are considered responsible for or guarantors for one another (Shevu'ot 39a) — literally, 'mixed together.' The forefathers, in contrast, were 'just isolated individuals.' In this distinction he found an important key. Individuals, or a small number of people, he explained, cannot uphold 'the standard indicated by the commandment to love one's fellow as one loves oneself' in the fullest sense; therefore, the Torah remains beyond them. It was offered only once *mutual responsibility* and mutual aid, *arevut*, could be ensured throughout an *entire community*:

> The Torah was not given to them before each and every Jew was asked whether or not he accepts the commandment of loving the others ... as himself in the fullest sense. That is, that each Jew *accepts the responsibility* to be concerned with and work for every other member of the people, to satisfy all of his needs in a measure not inferior to the concern a man naturally show for his own needs. Once everyone agreed ... each became responsible for ensuring that no member of the people lacks anything. *Only then* were they ready to receive the Torah, for this general responsibility exempted every individual of the people from concern for his own well-being and enabled him to fulfill the commandment to love one's fellow as one loves oneself in the fullest sense, to give everything one owns to whoever needs it, without worrying about maintaining oneself — he knows and trusts that he is surrounded by six hundred thousand reliable friends who can do the worrying for him. It is for this reason that the Torah could not be received ... until [after] the Exodus from Egypt, at which point they became a people unto themselves. (Ashlag 1995, 31–32)

Becoming a people, as Ashlag understood it, means radical solidarity — a 'bond with the collective' that makes for the formation of a 'single body (Ashlag 2015, 148).' It is possible, he argued, to set aside self interest when, and only when, one trusts that others have done the same. In this state of universal selflessness, one is paradoxically self-assured because he or she can comfortably rely on others. A shared oath of allegiance unites them.

If this oath, Ashlag insisted furthermore, unites the Jewish people, it does not separate them from humanity as a whole or the ultimate vision for a universal regime of altruistic love. On the contrary, appealing to the teaching of R. Elazar, son of Shimon b. Yohai (the legendary author of the Zohar), that one who performs a single commandment tips the 'scales' of merit not only for himself, but *for the whole world* (Kiddushin 40b) — that is, he or she pushes the world toward its messianic apex — he argued that Jewish solidarity implies universal solidarity:

> That Jews are responsible for one another is not enough; according to him, everyone in the world is responsible for one another. It is not that this view contradicts the other; everyone acknowledges that to begin with it is enough

for one people to fulfill the Torah. But this is just the beginning of the rectification of the world ...

The ultimate rectification of the world will take place when all its denizens have been initiated into the secret of divine service, as it is written 'the Lord shall be king over all the earth; in that day there shall be one Lord with one name (Zechariah 14:9)' ... [Until then,] it is upon the Jewish people, by engaging the Torah and its commandments for their own sake, to prepare themselves and all humankind, developing in the acceptance of this exalted task of loving the other, which is the ladder that leads to the purpose of creation: *devekut* to God.

This is what R. Elazar b. Shimon b. Yohai meant when he said that the whole world is judged according to the majority. If the scale of merit — which refers to the exalted character of love for another — outweighs the filthy scale of guilt, then the people of the world are able to submit and say, like Israel, 'we will do and we will obey (Exodus 24:7).' Not so beforehand, before they attain to a majority of merits; then, self-love prevents them from accepting God's yolk. (Ashlag 1995, 34–35)

So, on Ashlag's account, the Jewish community is unique because — as embodied in the exclamation 'we will do and we will obey' — its members accepted the Torah (that is, love and mutual responsibility for one another) unconditionally. In principle, this prepared them to transition directly into a regime of altruistic communism. They united with one another to form a single body, but not an isolated one.

Rather, the 'entire world is one family' that must ultimately (if gradually) be 'encircled within the 'framework of communism (Ashlag 2015, 31).' It is, Ashlag argued, 'incumbent upon Israel to accept internationalist communism first of all nations, and to be a symbol of the good and beautiful appearance of this regime (Ashlag, undated)' and — like one who 'measures out sesame seeds, adding them one by one until the scales tip (Ashlag 1995, 35)' — work toward the 'rectification of the world,' toward a messianic condition of universal solidarity and mutual aid in which '*all* members of human society will be gathered together as a single body with one heart filled with knowledge of God (Ashlag 1995, 101).

In sum, Ashlag regarded the Jews as a sort of revolutionary vanguard, not due to any intrinsic quality, but due to the fact that Jewish life is governed by the Torah and its precepts, which enjoin them to achieve *devekut* by imitating God's attributes of mercy and kindness. As he saw it, other nations can and will do the same, but the ability to concretely realize this ideal depends on solidarity, *arevut*. Having pledged to obey the Torah, this is why the Jews are prepared to live in keeping with the altruistic libertarian socialist ideal. Other nations have yet to do so. Spreading this universal human solidarity therefore becomes the messianic task of the Jewish people.[4]

Conclusion

In opening my discussion of Ashlag's mystical libertarian communism, I quoted the poem with which he introduced his *Talmud Eser ha-Sefirot*:

> The brightness that shines from above!
> There, behind the dividing curtain,
> the secret of the righteous radiates;
> light and darkness shine as one.

In closing, we may perhaps offer an interpretation. Ashlag wrote of a supernal light; this refers to the infinite light that preceded creation, the will-to-give. The dividing curtain represents the *zimzum* during which this light contracted into itself. The secret of the light is the fact that in it, light and darkness shine as one. I would venture to suggest that this refers to the idea of *hishtavut*. That is, the transformation by dint of which the will-to-receive becomes akin, and therefore achieves *devekut*, to the will-to-give by receiving *in order to give*. The whole of Ashlag's socio-political doctrine is contained in this passage.

Like Schopenhauer, he reduced all of reality to an interplay of wills. But contrary to Schopenhauer, he believed that one's ego does not condemn him to existential misery. It is possible to transform the ego into an altruistic drive because people want to believe that they *deserve* what they get, and this feeling comes from giving it to others. The highest form of giving, as Ashlag understood it, is to give *everything*, which he takes to imply a form of libertarian communism. Unlike state-communism, it is based on intrinsic altruistic motives and need not be coerced. Within this utopian scheme, Ashlag saw the Jews as playing a central role because they achieved *arevut*, solidarity: able to rely on the good-will of others, each member of the community could relinquish his selfish concerns and focus solely on others. Like Alexandrov, he believed that the very nature of Jewish national solidarity lent itself to international solidarity because its essence is neighborly love, which has no borders. As these borders spread so too does the universal messianic horizon in which all human beings figure.

To conclude this section on mystical approaches to anarcho-Judaism, let us briefly consider Alexandrov together with Ashlag. Both evidently believed that a meaningful parallel can be drawn between post-Kantian continental philosophy and Jewish mysticism; Alexandrov attended mainly to Schelling and his readers, Ashlag to Schopenhauer. In spite of Schopenhauer's vehement objections, the sympathy between his system and that of Schelling was recognized upon the publication of *World as Will and Representation*: both are metaphysics of will; Alexandrov and Ashlag can be described in similar terms, as kabbalists of will. The differences between them — most notably, their attitudes toward Jewish law — can be accounted for in terms of the philosophers that inspired them. In essence, the difference between Schelling and Schopenhauer is this. Schelling sustained a distinct hope that the will manifested in histories both natural and human strives towards and can achieve a harmonious, just, and in this sense meaningful end. At least in his early work, the fundamental source of human anxiety consists in the dissonance between the private will of the individual and this universal and essentially benevolent will; naturally, salvation consists in reducing or eliminating the distance between them. Adopting this basic model, Alexandrov could anticipate a time in which definite articulations of benevolence historically solidified in the law give way to more fluid expression reflective of the consonance between the individual and the Absolute-I. For Schopenhauer will is ultimately a meaningless and directionless striving and salvation (if any is to be had) consists in transcending it; that is, in transcending the self. Ashlag avoided this pessimistic conclusion by introducing a dynamic interplay between different types of wills: altruistic and egoistic ones. Because individuation depends on the latter, pure altruism implies self-annihilation and is therefore beyond the capacities of human beings (for the most part). However, because the will-to-receive is ultimately implied by and contained in the divine will-to-give, a degree of salvation is achievable through *hishtavut*: when an individual becomes like God by behaving altruistically (as embodied by adherence to Jewish law) he or she achieves equivalence of form or definition with the divine. Because this equivalence is not given, but must be constantly performed, the law cannot be abrogated. Thus, while they share a metaphysics of will, Alexandrov and Ashlag reach fundamentally different conclusions regarding the salience of practical Judaism as a libertarian tradition.

Notes

1 Scholarly literature dealing with Ashlag directly will be indicated in the course of this chapter. For studies focused on the Kabbalah Center from a theological perspective: Myers (2007, 2008, 2010), Garb (2009), Skartveit (2010), Feinstein (2012), Meir (2013), Bauer (2019), Carr (2020), Margolin (2020). There are several other studies of a more sociological nature examining the global spread of the Center or its impact in specific countries.

2 Huss (2004) and others before him describe these as 'communist' demonstrations. I suspect that, given the strength of the Jewish anarchist movement in Warsaw, these were anarchist uprisings. Jewish anarchists also organized strikes throughout the city during the Polish uprising of 1905 (Nagorski 1977); I consider it likely that Ashlag took part in these.

3 For more on the distinction between altruism and egoism in Ashlag, see Garb (2009, 52–59).
4 It would be an exaggeration to describe Ashlag as a Zionist. However, he saw in the kibbutz movement a sign of the sort of development he anticipated. In keeping with his gradualist approach, he believed that the 'crown of the regime of the fist will be negated' as a network of small and autonomous altruistic communes are founded to serve as 'world center toward which nations and countries turn.' If this were to remain the model of Zionist development in the holy land, he argued, then the movement might thrive. On the other hand, he held that 'all Zionism will be abolished if, heaven forbid, *this* return is canceled' — that is, a return not simply to the land, but to the spiritual revolution to which Judaism is called (Ashlag, undated).

The pacifists

7

Yehudah-Leyb Don-Yahiya (1869–1941)

5 Rabbi Yehudah-Leyb Don-Yahiya.

Yehudah-Leyb Don-Yahiya (1869–1941) was born in the Belarusian city of Drahichy where his father — a Habad hasid whose family traced its origins to the Babylonian Exiliarchs and thence (by tradition) to the House of David — served as community rabbi. Don-Yahiya was raised among the rabbinic elite of his day.[1] Like other figures discussed in this book, he also attended the Ets Hayyim Yeshiva in Valozyn and, there, became involved in Hibbat Zion (Ungerfeld 1954). After its closure, he assumed several rabbinic positions throughout Belarus and Russia (Don-Yahiya 1914; Maimon 1999, 50; 2006, 103), ultimately landing in the Ukrainian city of Chernihiv (Rabinovitch 1937). As an active clergyman, he suffered when the country was absorbed by the USSR in 1922. By 1929, circumstances became unbearable (Rabinovitch 1937; Schneersohn 1983, 420; 1993, 209–210) and he abruptly fled,[2] emigrating first to London, where he assumed a brief rabbinic post (Kloyzner 1959) before departing to Palestine in 1930. Settling in Tel Aviv, Don-Yahiya opened a synagogue and led a Habad community there (Shabbatay 1938; Bukiet 2008, 70) until his death in 1941.

Don-Yahiya was not especially prolific. He took part in the halachic discourse of his day, publishing several responses other than those included in his primary work, the two volumes of *Bikure Yehudah* (1930–39). He was also instrumental in the formation of the Mizrahi (religious Zionist) party,[3] for which he composed *Tsiyonut me-Nekudat Hashkafat ha-Da'at* (1902). In this work, Don-Yahiya contended that the holy land is 'especially suited for the service of God and for praying to him for the general, complete, and eternal redemption (Don-Yahiya 1902, 7),' by which he intended a spiritual revolution involving kindness, mercy, and justice for all (Don-Yahiya 1902, 20–21). The exiles are gathered to pray, not to fight. Like Ahad Ha'am, Don-Yahiya also wrote of cultural autonomy, the ability of Jewish communities 'to live in their own way and after their own spirit (Don-Yahiya 1902, 14)' without impediments posed by a gentile environment (Don-Yahiya 1902, 18–19), of cultural-religious renaissance under the influence of a 'new heaven and a new earth,' and of moral rehabilitation of the people of Israel, degraded by persecution. Perhaps most significant from a historical perspective, Don-Yahiya insisted that all of this be done with the cooperation of the Ottoman government (Don-Yahiya 1902, 20), which is to say that, like other Cultural Zionists, Don-Yahiya sought to establish a spiritual center for Jewish life, but not a Jewish state. Don-Yahiya's anti-statism appeared in his later writings within the framework of his Tolstoy-inspired discussions of faith, justice, and non-violence.

In the first volume of *Bikure Yehudah*, he commented on a famous midrashic legend, according to which God initially offered his Torah to all of the other nations; Israel accepted it, while the rest balked at prohibitions supposedly in contradiction to their national character (Sifre, Deuteronomy

343). Don-Yahiya focused on the Roman refusal. For reasons not relevant here, the ancient rabbis associated Rome with the biblical figure of Esau (J. Ta'anit 4:8; Hadas-Lebel 1984), who lived by the sword (Genesis 27:40). In other words, they saw it as a civilization constituted by violence — this being the reason, according to the midrash in question, that they could not accept a code prohibiting murder. Pairing the Torah against the core of Roman society in this context, Don-Yahiya inferred that non-violence constitutes the very essence of the Torah and of Israel (Don-Yahiya 1930, 6), which is 'entirely one (Zohar Hadash 73a)' with it.

According to Don-Yahiya, this essence is expressed in the biblical notion of Israel as a priestly kingdom and 'holy nation (Exodus 19:6; Don-Yahiya 1930, 6n).' Israel, he explained, is defined by its faith in God as creator (Kiddushin 40a; Megillah 13a) which, in turn, is the basis of a revolutionary vision of justice and peace. As the prophet asked: 'have we not all one father? Has not one God created us? Why do we break faith with one another (Malachi 2:10; Don-Yahiya 1930, 11)?' Don-Yahiya paraphrased as follows: 'since we are all children of a single God, how can anyone cheat his brother? If man is created in the image of God, how could anyone be so bold as to kill, to humiliate, or to degrade the very image of God? (Don-Yahiya 1930, 14).' This is the meaning of Israelite holiness: a selfless commitment to human fraternity grounded in faith. Selfishness, even in the formal service of justice, is considered idolatrous (Don-Yahiya 1930, 18).

For Don-Yahiya, it is not that justice is inconceivable without faith, but that it is *infirm*. Everyone, he acknowledged, pays lip service to the 'love of all mankind' and the centrality of justice (Don-Yahiya 1930, 19, 29), but yet they fall short of their ideals. Without faith, he argued, people observe the laws of justice in a perfunctory manner while seeking ways to surreptitiously circumvent them (Don-Yahiya 1930, 17). As he understood it, there are two reasons for this. First, they are based on a utilitarian ethic: justice is not good in itself, but because it is *beneficial*; thus it is reduced to the law of self-preservation. As Don-Yahia saw it, a world governed by mere self-preservation is ultimately a 'bitter war for survival in which each' individual 'lives by the death and destruction' of his neighbor and 'the stronger succeeds (Don-Yahiya 1930, 13).' Second, because 'social ordinances' are operative only within the community that institutes them. Therefore, when one community is confronted with another that has otherwise 'determined its mode of self-preservation,' its members will permit themselves 'to dispense with the life of the other (Don-Yahiya 1930, 17–18).' As that 'excellent man, Leo Tolstoy' said, it is impossible to extirpate evil 'until the people of the world ... achieve spiritual wholeness by understanding, by feeling and deeply recognizing that the victory of justice and its truth flows from faith in God and not from the fist (Don-Yahiya 1930, 32).'

Accordingly, Don-Yahiya lamented the gushing 'tears of the exploited at the hands of their exploiters (Don-Yahiya 1930, 31–32)' and praised the revolutionary ethic of 'mercy and love of man,' its 'enthusiasm for justice and for the equality of all men, that the mighty not dominate the weak, the capitalist the worker.' This, he insisted, is also the sentiment of 'true believers' who 'yearn daily for the day that justice is the rule of the land.' For them, however, it is a sentiment with 'sanctity to it,' whereas enthusiasm without the backing of faith may one day extend to Marx and the next to Nietzsche, 'who admires violence (*takifut*) and advocates the perfection of the strongest and most violent animal ... who annihilates utterly the weaker (Don-Yahiya 1930, 14–15).' Appealing to Ivan Kriloff's (1883, 178–179) fable concerning the boar who digs at the roots of an oak while devouring acorns, thus destroying his own source of sustenance, Don-Yahiya avers that the 'fruits of love for mankind and mercy for poor tired workers grows from the tree of faith in the one God' who created all men (Don Yahiya 1930, 32–33). A heart 'transformed by true and living faith (Don-Yahiya 1930, 17)' is the basis of real change; therefore revolutionaries who destroy the foundations of faith undermine their entire project.

Beyond the issue of permanence, Don-Yahiya also drew on Tolstoy to address the question of existential foundations. Referencing Tolstoy's *Confessions* and the crisis that drove him to faith, Don-Yahiya argued that material wealth is no guarantee of happiness. Thus, he contended, 'even when human equality is realized so that there obtains neither capitalist nor worker, neither strong nor weak, but all men live together, drawing from the same purse and sharing the same sum of wealth' — that is, even after the external goals of the revolution are achieved — people will resist the conclusion that human beings are 'born only to eat and drink for seventy or eighty years and then to die like an animal.' Therefore, they will seek out a sense of ultimate purpose — the sort that faith supplies (Don Yahiya 1930, 22; 33). In this respect, faith functions as the ground of revolution and also its ultimate fulfillment.

Perhaps the most interesting feature of Don-Yahiya's thought is the way that he adapted Tolstoy's doctrine of passive resistance.[4] He referenced an obscure rabbinic legend asserting that there are some instances in which 'the weak cast fear upon the strong.' Two of these are: the lion's fear of the *mafgiyah*, and the Leviathan's fear of the *kilbit* (Shabbat 77b). Rashi comments that a *mafgiyah* is a small creature with a loud voice such that the lion mistakes it for something larger and flees, while a *kilbit* is a small worm found in the ears of large fish. Don-Yahiya interpreted as follows. While it is natural that 'the strong swallow the weak and that the stronger is victorious,' the weak also have 'advantages over the strong,' another sort of strength 'that the powerful lack.' This, he wrote, is not a 'quantity of force (*gevurah*),' but a qualitative power arising from 'the special attributes' of the weak, which 'give them courage and confidence against the mighty, the great, the strong, and the terrible.' The special attribute of the weak is their moral voice:

> The lion is the king of the beasts, a powerful tyrant (*ariz*)! Why does it fear a small animal? With but one of his great fingernails can he not end its life? I do not fear its force, answers the lion, but its voice. When it raises its awful voice, it seems to me that it protests the fact that I am the king of beasts and that I sustain myself by the death of my servants, that my faithful servants are the food for my hungry soul. I am moved to reproach myself when I hear the awful voice of the *mafgiyah*! But what good is it to kill this *mafgiyah* or some other? I cannot annihilate the whole species!

Thus, says the *mafgiyah*:

> We know and understand well that it is not our strength that you fear, but our voice; when we cry out 'the Lord is one!' — that makes your shattered heart tremble. Deep in your heart, you realize ... that 'the Lord is one' nullifies your very essence, that you succeed insofar as other men, men just like you, fail. You will feel ashamed so long as there are Jews who cry out 'the Lord is one' [and conclude from this] that since we all have one father, brothers should not betray one another. The yellow beast among you will tremble and be seized with horror before the Jew.

The same follows for the *kilbit* and the Leviathan:

> A small *kilbit*, what inspires it to battle the mighty Leviathan? If the latter opens its mouth will not the former find therein its grave? If it strikes with its tail, will not the many waters overwhelm? The *kilbit* discovered a unique stratagem: it enters the ear of the fish. The Leviathan may become enraged ... it may stir up mighty waves in the great ocean so that the rest of the sea creatures tremble ... but for nought; the *kilbit* has found a safe place in the depths of the Leviathan's ear. (Don-Yahiya 1930, 10–12)

Paraphrasing Tolstoy, he wrote elsewhere that 'evil cannot be removed with evil but merely leads to an endless cycle of violence. If, he asked, 'there is no justice other than force,' then even supposing that the oppressor is overwhelmed by the sheer mass of the oppressed in revolt, what stops them from utilizing any advantage, 'some advanced knowledge or technical subterfuge concealed from the people' and responding in kind when the opportunity arises (Don-Yahiya 1930, 32)? Rather, Don-Yahiya concludes, strength 'is not quantitative, but qualitative.' In the end, 'the voice of Israel, the truth, will penetrate the ear of the Leviathan,' the state and its representatives, so that 'no man will rise up against his brother to murder him, nor will they send the best of their children and their brothers to fight in wars and to be slaughtered (Don-Yahiya 1930, 10–12).' It is through the power of moral truth embodied in passive resistance, through just means, that a just cause is brought to fruition.

Don-Yahiya thus endeavored to communicate a universal message of human solidarity in authentically Jewish language. Building on explicitly Tolstoyan foundations, he argued that the essential message of Judaism is faith in God the creator, which is taken to imply the irreducible sanctity of human life. Like Tolstoy, Don-Yahiya condemned revolutionary violence while upholding the revolutionary ideal of universal justice and equality. He insisted that faith provides both the existential ground for revolutionary change and a moral framework for bringing it about: its means must correspond to its ends. When the oppressed rise up, their power consists in the qualitative force of moral truth, not the quantitative force of military might and domination. Thus, Don-Yahiya advocated a revolution of the heart via passive resistance and saw this as a way for the tiny *mafgiyah* to drive away the mighty lion, the miniscule *kilbit* to defeat the great Leviathan, the modern state and the violence it carries with it. Presumably, he applied the same non-violent ideal to his Zionist vision. These themes, which appear in embryonic form in Don-Yahiya's writings, were further developed in the work of his younger contemporaries: Avraham Yehudah Heyn and Natan Hofshi.

Notes

1 Don-Yahiya was tutored by his renowned uncle, Eliezer Don-Yahiya (Don-Yahiya 2004), an open supporter of the movement who also mentored the young Avraham Isaac Kook, who would later become the first Chief Ashkenazic rabbi of British Mandate Palestine (Don-Yahiya 1932, 23–25). After the closure of Ets Hayyim in 1892, he joined the famed Hayyim Soloveitchik in Brest (Don-Yahiya 1939, 297). Thereafter, he was trained in practical rabbinics by R. Shlomo ha-Kohen of Vilnius (Don Yahiya 1939, 297; Shmuel 1994, 216), who edited the Vilna edition of the talmud, and whose glosses appear in the margins thereof under the title *Heshek Shlomo*. Arguably, Don-Yahiya was by far the most advanced rabbinic scholar of the 'anarchist *minyan*.'
2 The first volume of his *Bikure Yehudah* was rushed to print before being completed and ends abruptly; the final page of the 1933 edition explains that Don-Yahiya was forced to flee the USSR before completing revisions.
3 Don-Yahiya appears among the signatories to a letter sent out in order to gather activists for the conference that lead to the formation of the Mizrahi (Multiple Authors 1903).
4 Here, Don-Yahiya cites, in Russian transliterated into Hebrew, an essay entitled 'Resist Not,' which he ascribes to Tolstoy. So far as I am aware, there is no such title and Don-Yahiya merely intends to reference the Tolstoyan principle of non-resistance. However, the citation suggests that he read Tolstoy in Russian.

8

Avraham Yehudah Heyn (1880–1957)

6 Rabbi Avraham Yehudah Heyn, date unknown.

Avraham Yehudah Heyn (1880–1957) was born in Chernihiv to the renowned Habad hasid David Tsvi Heyn (Gotlieb 1912, 126), who then served as its chief rabbi (he later emigrated to Palestine, at which point Don-Yahiya assumed the post). Not only did he hail from the same community as Don-Yahiya, but also traced his ancestry to the same family lineage (Heyn 1931, 70–71; Laine 2013, 259–319). Heyn was too young to have attended Valozyn before its closure, but his anarcho-pacifism and his Cultural Zionism (Klarmen 1931; Anonymous 1932b) clearly reflect Don-Yahiya's influence and, by extension, the trace of that institution. As he would later argue: 'we do not need a Jewish State like the Political Zionists say,' but 'a state of Jewishness (Anonymous 1932a).'

After obtaining private ordination, Heyn assumed several rabbinic posts throughout Eastern Europe (Gotlieb 1912, 126; Viernik 1921). Like Don-Yahiya and Alexandrov, he worked to support Jewish religious life after the 1917 Revolution and was therefore forced to flee two years later. Serving as a communal rabbi in several different communities, he eventually migrated to France (Yeyushson 1932; Goldshlag 1956), but was once again dislocated by the rising Nazi threat, at which point he left for Palestine. Arriving in 1935 and settling first in Tel Aviv, Heyn continued his rabbinic career, playing a central role in Habad hasidic life in that city and elsewhere (Soker 1937; A. H. A. 1957; Heyn 1958, 8). Eventually he relocated to Jerusalem, where he assumed leadership, both of the Beyt ha-Midrash Ha-Rambam and of the division of the Jewish Agency that would eventually become the Israeli Ministry of Culture (Anonymous 1945, 1946, 1949; Zohar 2003, 132). While fulfilling these roles, Heyn lectured frequently on Jewish philosophy and hasidic thought for the remaining twenty years of his life. While delivering a sermon on the subject of Abraham's defense of the people of Sodom, he fell ill on the Sabbath of Penitence in 1957 and passed away just a few days later, on the morning of the Day of Atonement (Zevin 1957).

While Heyn published several essays in Hebrew-language journals of the day, his teachings are mainly found in his three-volume *opus*, *be-Malkhut ha-Yahadut* (In the Kingdom of Judaism), which was mostly edited during his lifetime but only published after his death (1958–70). Intended to evoke Tolstoy's *Kingdom of God*, the work reflects the influence of Don-Yahiya and in many ways constituted Heyn's theological response to the violence of his times. His earliest essays were written in response to the Beilis trials of 1913 (Zeitlin 1913); rather than demonstrating the absurdity of the blood libel from a strictly *halakhic* standpoint, he made the much bolder move of defining Judaism itself in terms of its abhorrence for 'blood' and its unmitigated respect for human life. These essays served to shape a systematic account of Jewish non-violence and anarcho-pacifism that governed the remainder of his work. This chapter observes how Heyn's belief — that the

absolute sanctity of the individual constitutes the essential message of Judaism
— frames his pacifism, his socialism, and his anarchism while complicating
his relationship with Zionism.

The absolute sanctity of human life as the essence of Judaism

If Don-Yahiya began with the idea of God as Creator, Heyn's thought began
with the sixth commandment. Against the grain of rabbinic consensus, Heyn
interpreted it as a prohibition against taking human life in *any* form, not
just murder. In an essay entitled, like one of Tolstoy's lesser-read texts, 'Thou
Shalt Not Kill,' he explains that the prohibition has three senses: the Roman,
the anarcho-individualist, and that of the Torah (Heyn 1958, 73).

According to the Roman, or the statist sense — that elsewhere Heyn
ascribes to 'European civilization' as a whole (Heyn 1958, 96–97) — the
individual is regarded as nothing 'but a tool of the community ... a small
nail in the structure of the great universal' for the sake of which he can be
sacrificed (Heyn 1970, 335). Accordingly, murder is sanctified when it serves
the collective and condemned only when the collective is threatened. Murder
is considered sinful not because 'someone has been killed' but because 'this
constitutes a threat to the whole (Heyn 1958, 74–76).' By this logic, killing
is warranted when it serves the public good:

> Where the whole discerns that it requires someone's blood, or blood in general,
> his blood is shed like that of an ox or a goat. Moreover, this slaughter is
> sanctified. The life and the being of the one is nothing more than a footstool
> for the life and prosperity of the many. (Heyn 1958, 77)

In brief, the value of an individual life is subordinated to the public interest;
the sixth commandment loses its radical moral sense and becomes a function
of public order.

In stark contrast, the anarcho-individualist[1] denies the very existence of
the collective and contends that the individual is a world unto himself. In
this sense, the logic of self-sacrifice becomes absurd: 'if the individual is
everything and his destruction is the destruction of everything, for the sake
of what could he be sacrificed (Heyn 1958, 77)?' However, this absurdity
also spills over into license: if 'there is nothing in the world to which the
particular is subordinated' he 'is free in his actions without any external
restraint to his soul's desires.' Not even the prohibition of murder restrains
him (Heyn 1958, 77–78). Praising Kropotkin as 'the righteous man of the
new world' and as 'a pure and crystalline soul' Heyn acknowledged his
response to this difficulty: the prohibition is wise counsel because the neighbor
will permit your blood if you permit his (Heyn 1958, 78–79).[2] Nonetheless,

he found it lacking in one crucial respect: the choice between slaying or being slain. Heyn contended that in this case, the anarcho-individualist puts his own life first, so that the prohibition of murder is not unqualified (Heyn 1958, 80). In contrast, he argued, the Torah asks 'who says your blood is redder?' and obligates self-sacrifice (Sanhedrin 74a). This implies, so he continued, that human life is *sacred* and that uprooting it for *any* reason is sinful; the prohibition of murder is '*without conditions* (Heyn 1970, 201),' there being no fundamental difference 'between the slaughter of the innocent and the slaughter of the guilty (Heyn 1958, 117).' This, he taught, is not something 'inscribed on the tablets' of the law, 'but the tablets themselves (Heyn 1958, 81),' 'the essence of Jewish religion ... its starting point, the fundamental foundation of its soul (Heyn 1970, 187).' To deny it, Heyn averred, is not simply to deny the foundations of the Torah, but to become a murderer *in potentia* (Heyn 1958, 81). This is the 'thou shalt not kill' of the Torah.

Drawing on a theological tradition with roots in Maimonides (*Guide* 1:57), Heyn grounded this sanctity in a distinction between notions of 'oneness' and 'uniqueness.' According to Maimonides, 'one' means 'one among many,' whereas the 'unique' is the *only* one. Maimonides restricted this notion to God. Representing this distinction as an opposition between quantitative (extrinsic, or relative) and qualitative (intrinsic, or absolute) value, Heyn extended it to human beings. In Israel, he wrote:

> The attribute of being has always been raised to the highest cultic status, [it is regarded as] a noble and absolute concept, a singular and unique joy. [Being] appears as the central point of its inner substance, its essence and source ... This is the secret reason as to why the unique and explicit name (*shem ha-meyuhad we-ha-meforash*) of this people, of its God, is Being (*Havayeh*) ... This is the Jewish doctrine of life. (Heyn 1958, 96–97)

Thinking along roughly Kantian lines, he argued that objects are utile, potential means to other ends. This means that their value is relative to the ends they serve, for which they may be destroyed. Appealing to the census-taboo found in biblical and rabbinic literature alike (Berakhot 62b; Neufeld 1994), which he abstracted into a prohibition against quantifying people, Heyn contended that a person 'is not a means, but an end' unto himself. Neither an object nor property, the individual is not 'one,' but *qualitatively unique* — an 'absolute essence (Heyn 1958, 7, 5).' Expressing the same notion in distinctly liturgical language, Heyn wrote that each individual 'bears the aspect of Being such that there is nothing other than him (*efes zulato*, a phrase appearing the *Aleynu* prayer),' then 'the whole world exists for him and he does not exist for the sake of the world (Heyn 1958, 159).' As the rabbis expressed it: when a single life is destroyed, it is as if a whole world was destroyed (Sanhedrin 37a; Heyn 1958, 9, 39–42, 213–214).'

From the uniqueness and sanctity of the individual human life, Heyn derived two intersecting principles. First, that ends never justify means. Judaism, he wrote, condemns 'good deeds' performed by way of transgressions (Sukkot 30a–32b; Heyn 1970, 318), holding effects to be impure if they come about by impure means (Heyn 1970, 193). This is directly implied by the uniqueness of human life. If each life is an end unto itself, if it is sinful to treat human life as quantitative value and thus to objectify it; it follows that means and ends must always correspond (at least where people are concerned); redemption, the ultimate revelation of human sanctity, must be realized in the process of achieving it (Heyn 1958, 159). Second, that the individual is irreducible to the collective, the latter being nothing more than an aggregate viewed from without: 'the whole world is nothing more than a collective of individuals in which men live one by one ... the distinction between individual and collective obtains only from the perspective of those who regard the former from without (Heyn 1958, 69);' indeed, he continued elsewhere, there is no 'majority, no congregation, no collective, no society, no higher purpose considered in itself; there is no *real* existence but the unique individual (Heyn 1958, 77).' Thus, he wrote, people 'are not like drops of water that can be stirred together so that, in the end, they become a single entity (Heyn 1970, 143).'

Thus we find that Heyn transformed a prohibition against *murder* first into an 'absolute and unconditional prohibition of killing (Heyn 1970, 201),' and then into universal prohibition against *violence*, which he defined as any act of objectification.[3] From this prohibition, he inferred the moral necessity of ends-means correspondence and the irreducibility of the individual vis-a-vis the group — both of these notions being crucial features of anarchist discourse (Franks 2018; Gordon 2018a).

Sanctity of life as the ground of pacifism

Like Alexandrov, Heyn was deeply offended by Nietzsche's account of Judaism in the *Genealogy of Morals*. Also like Alexandrov, he undertook to 'transvalue' it. It is true, he admitted, Judaism 'consists entirely in a screed against the right of force (*zekhut shel ha-koah*).' Yet, he argued, that is not to say that weakness is raised to cult status; rather, Judaism 'wrestles against the strong arm' of the oppressor in order 'to make everyone strong, to uproot weakness' and in *this* way elevates the poor and oppressed (Heyn 1958, 46). In this section we shall examine this screed in relation to Heyn's opposition to military violence and economic violence.

'Wicked and criminal visions like war,' Heyn asserted, are inconceivable without denying that each person 'is absolutely holy, having no substitution, accounting, or replacement in another (Heyn 1958, 155).' They are predicated on precisely the utilitarian logic to which Judaism is, on Heyn's account, the antithesis. Only if individual life is subordinated to the interest of the collective — if the ends thereof justify the destructive means to achieve them — can a lost human life be met with the same indifference as a 'shattered tool' for which there are many replacements (Heyn 1958, 9–10). It is this way of thinking that allows 'wretched little Cains,' the 'warriors, the statesmen and nationalists, the idealists and redeemers' in every generation 'to transform the whole world into a gigantic slaughterhouse (Heyn 1958, 216).' In contrast, Judaism 'is a religion of justice' grounded on the golden mean which, in this case means: 'if you would not wish to be a sacrifice against your will, for whatever end, for some other god or principle ... do it not to your neighbor (Heyn 1958, 45).'

As such, Heyn is necessarily committed to principled and uncompromising pacifism. As he points out, theological revulsion for war and violence extends, in Jewish sources, even to its implements. Based on a rabbinic ruling prohibiting the carrying of weapons on the Sabbath in which it is contended that they are not adornments but objects of shame (M. Shabbat 6:4), Heyn remarks that this:

> Represents an absolute restructuring of the system ... the sword — a tool and symbol of might in battle, courage, victory, and dominion — is not an adornment, but a disgrace ... So long as weapons serve as adornments for their bearers, there is no room for peace. Not only is there no room for its ultimate victory, but even for declaration as to the moral and legal truth thereof. Removing the crown of glory from weapons, calling them a disgrace, constitutes a significant blow to the ethical foundation of the Molekh of blood. (Heyn 1958, 23; 1970, 190)

As it were, the path to 'nation shall not take up sword against nation' leads through 'they shall beat their swords into plowshares (Isaiah 2:4).' By reviling even the implements of war, the culture that produces them is transformed. As Heyn went on to explain, the fact that such convictions are expressed not directly, but incidentally, in the course of a minor legal discussion, attests that it is not disputed in the slightest, but simply taken for granted. It constitutes the core and universal value of Judaism that needs no further elaboration.

For Heyn, the same standard applies to revolutions, however necessary (Heyn 1970, 318). As he saw it, radical change demands personal insight and self-awareness. Appealing to the idiom of Lurianic kabbalah according to which shards of a broken God are concealed within 'shells' or 'husks' and must be released (Scholem 1976), he asserted that to question the proverbial 'nakedness of the King,' which is the violence and injustice of the rule of one man over another, one must 'break every barrier, breach every veil of concealment, every covering and hard shell that has clung to his soul from without (Heyn 1963, 246–247).' Having achieved clarity of self, the heart must be 'shaken to its core' and kindled with a 'new fire that burns away every strange fire, a powerful fire that incinerates hell entirely (Heyn 1958, 202–203).' Following longstanding hasidic precedent in interpreting the mythic 'husks' along psychological lines, as indifference or coldness, Heyn envisions a process of breaking the broken vessels and releasing divine lights of human warmth.

This 'revolution of the heart' is not carried out with 'swords and spears, with bombs and mines (Heyn 1958, 202–203)' but with fraternal feeling which, following Tolstoy, Heyn regarded as 'the secret of redemption (Heyn 1958, 271).' Whereas Tolstoy attributed this message to Jesus, however, Heyn attributed it to Abraham, the 'father of the multitude of nations (Genesis 48:19)' who rendered brethren 'all the inhabitants of the world' and posed to them the same prophetic question posed throughout this volume: 'why do we break faith with one another (Malachi 2:10; Heyn 1958, 274)?'

Although Heyn was soft on details, he believed in the strength of personal connections, that words which come from the heart enter the heart (Berakhot 6b). 'It is the nature of the good to do good,' is an aphorism that appears frequently in Habad hasidic texts; it is often used to explain God's motivation in creating the world. Heyn interpreted it as a 'desire for others' that permeates, albeit in a concealed way, all things that God made. The more a person uncovers the divinity in him or herself, the 'supernal attribute of uniqueness' that comes from 'the absolute individual, the absolutely unique,' the more he or she discovers 'the attribute of being good and doing good.' In 'thirsting' for others, he or she evokes the same yearning in them and, in this way takes part in the Abrahamic mission of 'making souls (Genesis 12:5; Heyn 1970, 46–48).' That is, transforming people and with them the world as a whole.

Sanctity of life as the ground of socialism

Heyn applied a similar line of reasoning to economic inequality, which he also regarded as a form of violence. Based on a rabbinic anecdote to the effect that man was created alone 'so that one might not say to his friend: my father is greater than your father (Sanhedrin 37a),' Heyn contended that Judaism 'demolishes every barrier' and 'denies the differentiation of men,' establishing the 'principle of equality not as a mere right, but as an absolute condition that cannot be contested (Heyn 1958, 28).' If human being is unique, he explained:

> Class divisions are inconceivable. Neither distinctions of quantity nor of quality are conscionable. The final ideal of such a worldview necessarily involves absolute equality for everyone in everything ... The poverty of one cannot be justified by the wealth of others. Since the individual is the absolute master of his own 'I,' the destruction of one 'I' for the sake of another cannot be legitimated. One man cannot be sacrificed for another no matter the reason. (Heyn 1970, 39)

Here, we see that for Heyn the notion of 'sacrifice' is not limited to the body, but also to wealth. One person's well-being cannot come at the expense of another's.

Heyn articulates this prohibition in a radical manner. The Torah as 'absolute justice,' he argues, determines 'absolute rights,' which are 'all one thing: the uniqueness of existence.' Any other right, he asserted, is essentially conventional; this includes property rights. Thus, he wrote: that when 'an object belonging to one person, comes to belong to another,' the transfer is 'is nothing more than an order of things devised by human beings.' Heyn held this to be self evident concerning 'external means of acquisition,' through purchase and exchange. More profoundly, he also extended it to 'essential and internal' acquisitions, to those made through direct labor. No product of labor, he argued, is 'without a drop of foreign causation.' All things come to be through a multiplicity of causes. 'The material of labor, the tools, and land, together with its yield' he argued, are essential to the process but not intrinsic to the worker; they bear the labor of others and are acquired by mere convention. The same line of reasoning extends even products of the spirit: 'the eye sees and the ear hears' while the artist or thinker is scarcely aware 'that his mind and his heart are being sown' with ideas that later sprout during the creative process. Thus, his work is not 'without external causes;' it too comes 'via the domain of another.' Drawing an analogy to the rabbinic principle that partners to a single deed share liability for damages (Bava Kama 51a), Heyn indicated that partnership in the production process implies shared claims to the results (Heyn 1970, 202–203). In this way, society as a whole 'has proprietary status where wealth is concerned insofar as wealth is produced within and passes through it (Heyn 1958, 264).' To claim it for oneself is to steal it; thus, echoing Proudhon, he contended that property is 'obtained *via theft* (Heyn 1970, 202).'

Radicalizing an argument appearing in the collected letters of the Shneur Zalman of Liadi, the founder of the Habad hasidic movement (*Igeret ha-Kodesh*: 16), Heyn cited 'if your kinsman is in dire straits ... let him live *with you* (Leviticus 25:35),' from which the talmudic sages inferred that 'your life takes precedence (Baba Mezi'a 62a).' The right to self-preservation might be extended to the sphere of economics but, as Heyn explained, this applies 'only when needs are equal.' Otherwise, greater need connotes greater right. 'It is forbidden,' he continues, 'for someone to provide raiment for himself when his neighbor needs bread, to furnish his home when his friend lacks what to cover his skin with (Heyn 1958, 32–33).' Nobody has a right to accumulate while others live in poverty; suffering is the limit of property. If each human being is *unique*, he explained, 'class divisions are inconceivable.' Just as Judaism prohibits 'the destruction of one man, even for the sake of saving another,' so too the 'poverty of one cannot be justified by the wealth of others.' Therefore, Judaism upholds as a moral obligation 'equality for everyone in everything.' No man is entitled to wealth if 'the smallest of men' does not enjoy its fullness as well (Heyn 1958, 39).

Finally, Heyn appeals to what David Graeber (2011, 98) calls 'baseline communism.' Consider, he instructs, the case of 'one benefits and the other loses nothing.' In such a case, Jewish tradition obliges one to avoid the 'characteristic of Sodom (Avot 5:10)'[4] and refuse; 'if you lose nothing [in doing so] you are obligated to grant to the other use of everything that is yours (Heyne 1970, 288).' Here, we see that it is not only a matter of need that dissolves proprietary rights, but also human decency; nobody is entitled to insist on what he takes to be his when sharing causes no harm. In sum, while Heyn does not deny individuals the right to *possess* goods, he denies the right to hold *property*. Broadly speaking, he maintains 'from each according to his ability and to each according to his need.' That is what justice demands; to fall short of this ideal is to do violence to the unique essence of the human individual.

Sanctity of life as the ground of anarchism

In distinguishing between the one and the unique, we saw that a subject is valued qualitatively, while an object, property, is valued quantitatively — the latter serving as a means to an end, the former existing only for itself as an absolute value. The term Heyn used to denote ownership was *ba'alut*, which also suggests *dominion*. This implies that the sanctity of human life also means that people cannot be ruled. Hence the foundation of Heyn's anarchism:

> Human blood is the universal currency with which everything is purchased: islands, colonies, markets … and so on. On this foundation, there is no difference between one government and the next. Government means compulsion and compulsion means blood; it lives on blood. (Heyn 1958, 81–82)

It is along these lines that Heyn interpreted 'if you make for Me an altar of stones, do not build it of hewn stones; for by wielding your tool upon them you have profaned them (Exodus 20:22). As explained in the mishnah (Midot 3:4), iron was created to shorten human life and the altar to extend it; the two are incompatible. So Heyn elaborated: 'state institutions, and states themselves, are built primarily on blood and by the sword ... That which is fashioned from blood and drips with it, above all, cannot become an altar (Heyn 1958, 22).' They are essentially profane, standing in violent contradiction to the Jewish ethos.

Thus, Heyn contended, 'sacrificing the individual for the sake of the collective originates from a prior doctrine: that of dividing the inhabitants of the world into masters and slaves (Heyn 1958, 69–70).' Appealing to an incident recorded in Kropotkin's memoirs — in which the author recounts how his grandfather earned a medal of courage for saving someone from a fire by sending his serf to do it (Heyn 1958, 69–70; Kropotkin 1999, 10–11) — he noted that for the master, his 'men were nothing more than objects ... not humans but carriers of determinate value' that may be shattered at will like any other tool. In the course of generations, Heyn went on to explain,

> There has been subordination to kings, to flags, parties, states, and so on. There has even been a forgery of man himself whereby he sends himself to death, to destruction, via members of parliament he has chosen from among his own ... Thus, the form of slavery has changed, but the foundation remains: an external authority hovers above ... There is always someone who climbs the mountain and sends those who stand at its base. Whether he climbs in purity or impurity, he sends ... he sends because he is the master. They are sent because they are under his authority and not their own, because they are slaves. (Heyn 1970, 209–210)

According to Heyn, this insight constitutes the cornerstone of 'the great city of ideal anarchism (Heyn 1970, 209).' Namely, 'total negation of servitude and authority of one man over another' that in turn negates at its source 'the idea of sacrificing the one for the many (Heyn 1958, 69–70).' That is how he understood the rabbinic adage that 'whoever destroys a single life is as if he destroyed an entire world (*Sanhedrin* 37a)' to imply that absolute sanctity of the individual and, therefore, that 'there are no two lives which belong to one of them;' each being 'the sole master of himself (Heyn 1958, 42–43).'

Thus far, however, we have considered only the negative element of Heyn's anarchism and also neglected its relation to the Torah as a source of law, or obligation, in Jewish tradition. On the one hand, he held that 'man is naturally a social animal' such that 'the life of the individual cannot be complete, healthy, and full without the life of the community.' This is true in both material and spiritual senses. 'From the bread that he eats to the garment that he wears' a plurality of hands are involved; similarly, 'from the thought born in the heart of a man until the bound book' there are 'many souls at work.' Perhaps more importantly, 'life itself is not felt without other people,' when it is without 'brotherhood and connection.' In this sense, 'a soul lives only gathered together' with others. Nonetheless, like the air that they live by but not for, people exist for themselves (Heyn 1958, 86–87) and community 'has no claim over the sovereign authority of the individual (Heyn 1958, 43).' This is how Heyn envisions redemption:

> 'No longer will a man teach his neighbor, or a man his brother, to say know the Lord, for they will all know me (Jeremiah 31:34)' and 'They will neither harm nor destroy ... for the earth will be filled with the knowledge of the Lord as the waters cover the sea (Isaiah 11:9).' It is not just that one man will no longer enjoy a material advantage over another, that advantage which is essentially the result of violence. Even the *spiritual* advantage of one man over another will be negated. [The distinction between] great and small, strong and weak, shall not be, not just materially, but also in spirit, for it is advantage that constitutes the foundation for the rule of one man over another ... Each individual is the absolute and sole master of his 'I.' No 'I' bends to the authority of another 'I'... every individual is his own master. (Heyn 1958, 38–39)

Ignoring the tense of the biblical verse, Heyn speaks of the present: government, which mitigates the sovereign authority of the individual, is therefore inherently bound up in the destruction of human life in its fullest sense. This is the central lesson he took from the story of the exodus. The exodus teaches that God intended to liberate Israel from 'fear of men' and from 'fear of governments,' thus indicating that Judaism is 'fundamentally hostile to all the ropes and chains of the state (Heyn 1958, 87).'

However, this hostility is coupled with a sense of responsibility and belonging. This aspect of Heyn's thought appears in his reflections on the revelation at Sinai as described in rabbinic interpretation of '[the people] took their places at the foot (*be-tahtit*) of the mountain (Exodus 19:17).' The word *tahtit* can also imply 'beneath.' Based on this ambiguity, one rabbi suggested that the mountain was suspended overhead and that the people were to be crushed beneath it unless they accepted the Torah. Another countered that this would constitute a 'substantial objection' to the legitimacy of the Torah (Shabbat 88a).' In this retort, Heyn discerned a radical formulation of the principle of freedom of choice (*behira hofshit*). Judaism, he wrote, 'is literally inconceivable without the principle of free choice,' which is an 'an outgrowth of the right of existence' and so, 'the immediate consequence of absolute justice' that Judaism demands. Since, he continued, it 'is not a gift or kindness,' but 'comes only from itself,' no 'stipulation, no

limit, no boundary can be imposed on it from without.' The measure of
freedom in the Torah of Israel, he explained, is therefore truly unlimited:

> No authority external to the individual can compel him and rule over his
> freedom. Only he himself may compel himself ... If you erase this point, the
> point of being, its holiness and its right, from our faith ... then you render
> its substance a forgery ... our special substance is the idea of 'beating' swords
> [into plowshares], the pulverization of the gods of power, compulsion, and
> the altars of man. (Heyn 1970, 261–272).

The principle of *behira hofshit* is typically paired against determinism in
discussions tackling the threat that ideas about divine providence pose to
the moral framework of the Torah — people are enjoined to act or refrain
from acting; without the freedom to obey or disobey, the attending rewards
and punishments would be both meaningless and unjust (Maimonides,
Mishneh Torah. Hilkhot Teshuva 5). If *behira hofshit* traditionally functioned
as a presupposition for judgement, Heyn transformed it into a moral and
political obligation unto itself: people must be treated as free agents and
never compelled, not by God and not by man, this being the very essence
of the Torah.

Heyn interpreted the suspension of Mt. Sinai in the aforementioned
anecdote accordingly. Gesturing toward a midrash according to which the
patriarchs and matriarchs are called 'mountains and hills (*Sifre* 353, on
Deuteronomy 33:15)' and the legend according to which both observed the
Torah prior to Sinai (Yoma 28b), he argued that the image of the hovering
mountain signifies *not* external compulsion, but 'a different sort of authority;'
namely, an 'inward sense of responsibility to ancestral tradition.' It is only
that such loyalty must come from within and cannot be compelled (Heyn
1970, 272). In other words, he does not dismiss obligation and responsibility;
rather, he maintains that these must come from within.

This balance between freedom and responsibility extended to Heyn's
approach to Jewish law and its interpretation. He relied on three basic
principles to supply him with the flexibility he needed. The first and most
important was a rabbinic claim to the effect that basic principles of the
Torah are like 'mountains hanging by hairs (Hagigah 10a),' that is, without
firm or definite scriptural ground. So he explained:

> There are no general principles or signs to recognize the inner substance. It
> is something sensed by the one who feels it. It is a matter of intuition, the
> intuition of the heart. There is being and essence in a book. There is that
> which is written and that which is not written, the point and substance, time
> and eternity ... Only a special sense, a unique palette, a definite intuition, is
> able to divine the true aspect of the matter. (Heyn 1970, 200)

The people who cultivate their palette by immersing themselves in the Torah, thereby gaining an intimate and intuitive sense of its true meaning, 'become Sinai,' as it were:

> There are such that immerse themselves in the wells of creation and who become so saturated with them that they become one with them. 'The Torah of the Lord is his desire, and in his Torah he meditates (Psalms 1:2)' — at first it is the Torah of the Lord, afterwards it becomes his own. Thus do we find even with respect to Rabbi Eliezer the Great — whose distinctive quality was that 'he never said anything which he heard not from the mouth of his teacher (Sukkah 28a)' and who said of himself that he resembles a reservoir from which can be extracted only what was put into it — that his teacher, R. Yohanon b. Zakkay had said to him '*you are able to say words of Torah in excess of what was received at Sina*i (Pirkei d'Rabi Eliezer 2:3),' and of him that he 'resembles a well which flows with more water than it receives. (M. Avot 2:8; Heyn 1970, 93)

As Heyn understood it, 'becoming Sinai' gives license to innovate, to create new Torah. It also frees him to eliminate or to circumnavigate aspects of the Torah such as it is received which come to contradict its spirit: 'One who is able to 'tie crowns for every letter of the Torah (Menahot 29b)' like R. Akiva is also able to uproot its mountains.' That is, a person like Rabbi Akiva, who is said to have interpreted the Torah so finely as to make meaning of its scribal embellishments (and who, it may be noted, Heyn judges quite differently than Alexandrov), is also a person who can transcend its word in the name of something higher. Here, we see that the tension between freedom and responsibility is mediated by the right to interpret. Crucially, this right is not ultimately restricted to the elite. Rather, it extends to the people as a whole:

> It is upon us to understand the book in the heart of the people, not the book that sits in the ark [in the synagogue]. This book, which is filled with contradictions and oppositions, resides in a single heart, where — in spite of all its tears — it finds rest. It is upon us to divine and to teach this wondrous unity. Truly, this is the main point of the whole book. The true meaning of the book is the way it is read, not the way it is written, that which is absorbed by the tablet of the heart and not that which is cast like a golden statue or [hewn like] a marble idol.

In this sense, Heyn distinguished between the Torah as *given* at Sinai and as *taken from* Sinai (Heyn 1970, 197), insisting that 'the kingdom of Judaism is *within us* (Heyn 1958, 241).' The recipient of the given Torah is subject to it and lacks authority over it, but also responsibility for it. The one who *takes* the Torah from Sinai bears both authority and also responsibility.

The other two principles are essentially hermeneutic tools Heyn used to model taking the Torah from Sinai and assuming responsibility for it. The second principle relies on the rabbinic practice of circumventing biblical law by creating legal fictions. The classical example of this is the *prozbul*, which allowed lenders, who would otherwise be reluctant to offer credit, to transfer private loans to the courts so that they could be collected during the Sabbatical year when they would otherwise be cancelled. Heyn expanded this notion in response to Torah laws mandating the death penalty for certain offences. Pointing to exceedingly restrictive procedural requirements for reaching a guilty verdict in capital cases, he concluded, contra Maimonides (*Mishneh Torah. Sanhedrin* 14:10), that 'the death penalties in the Torah are, from within the law itself, not subject to materialization ... they were not written in order to be realized. The law-giver saw to it that this would be impossible. There could never actually be an execution carried out by a court governed by Jewish law (Heyn 1958, 262).' These punishments, he argued, were 'strictly theoretical, not practical (Heyn 1958, 106),' meant '*only to serve as a threat* (Heyn 1958, 22).'

The third principle involves the rabbinic notion that certain biblical laws were not promulgated as ideals, but as concessions to flawed people who should not be emulated, the infamous case of the war bride (Deuteronomy 21:11) being the classical example: acknowledging in theory the legality of capturing brides in the heat of battle, they condemned the practice in no uncertain terms (Kiddushin 21b). Explicitly adopting Abravanel's position on the matter, Heyn used this hermeneutic tactic to neutralize biblical and rabbinic laws surrounding the legitimate monarchy:

> Some things were said lovingly and gracefully, supernal beauty and truth desire them. Other things, even commandments, were said in anger to begin with so that it is the will of heaven that they never come to pass. The chapter dealing with the monarchy constitutes a whole chapter in the Torah containing explicit and detailed laws and rules. Yet, the first prophet, of whom it is said that he is to be measured against Moses and Aaron together, announced aloud 'you have done evil in the eyes of God in seeking a king (1 Samuel 8:6).' Thus did R. Nehorai ... say that all the laws pertaining to kings were commandments given in anger. The sages of homiletic teachings further elaborated as to the suffering, as it were, of the God of freedom and the destruction of slavery, where the chapter concerning kings is concerned. I said that you should be free of kings in the city and likewise in the wilderness, yet you seek a king?! (Heyn 1970, 200–201)

While the Hebrew monarchy fell long ago and no respectable rabbinic figure today imagines its pre-messianic reconstruction, the myth and memory of this institution carries enormous weight as an element of messianic expectation. Here, therefore, Heyn does not so much respond to or strive to neutralize a concrete reality as much as to shape the Jewish political imagination from within. That is to say, he excludes from it monarchic recidivism.

In sum, we find that Heyn sees in the uniqueness of the individual his or her exclusive authority over themselves. Dominion, he contends, is just another form of ownership and therefore degrades the divine in man. Consequently, he rejects the form of the state in which one person rules over another. Yet, he embraces the internal sense of responsibility that motivates individuals to adhere to beneficial communal norms. This, he explores within the framework of the revelation at Sinai in which freedom and responsibility are mediated through a process of interpretation that continues on through generations. The interpreter heeds tradition but is not beholden to or mired in it.

A revolution of the heart: Heyn's approach to radical change

As we saw earlier in our analysis of Steinberg, morally necessary radical change constitutes a central question confronting pacifists. How may it be accomplished without violence? Heyn invites revolution as a necessary response to violence and injustice but holds, like Tolstoy, that it must be conducted in a manner consistent with its goals.

Heyn believed that revolution calls, above all, for a sort of youthful innocence. One whose 'soul has not yet been seduced' by 'society and its false doctrines,'are able to question and be astonished' at the proverbial 'nakedness of the King (Heyn 1963, 246–247).' Clarity of vision makes way for a process of inner transformation that Heyn called a 'revolution of the heart.' This revolution is not made 'with swords and spears, with bombs and mines, nor with any secret weapon.' These, he averred, 'are not our tools;' like Alexandrov and Don-Yahiya, he held that these 'are the tools of Esau and not of Jacob.' More importantly, he held that such tools are 'already rusty,' for 'swords have never brought salvation;' rather, 'the sword is a thing that naturally swings around,' in the end striking the one who wields it (Heyn 1958, 202–203).

Appealing to Tolstoyan faith in the brotherhood of humanity, Heyn suggested that 'the secret of redemption' is replacing the old 'me or you' with 'a new and revolutionary 'me *and* you (Heyn 1958, 271).' All having 'one Father' who 'created us,' we naturally ask 'why do we deal treacherously every man against his brother (Malachi 2:10)?' Accordingly, he wrote:

> On Rosh HaShanah and Yom Kippur, the days of days, we pray 'make all of them [the nations] a single bundle (*agudah ahat*).' Likewise it is written 'I will pour a pure language upon the nations (Zephania 3:9)' — that is our mission

and the teaching of our mission. Real Judaism announces the revolution of the heart; that is, the notion that the world is built up with kindness and not with brutality. Judaism sees the secret of redemption in absolute equality. (Heyn 1958, 274)

The revolution of the heart meant, for Heyn, cultivating a sense of universal human solidarity which, he believed, would overcome violence and oppression without force.

Revolutions require revolutionaries. As he did for Alexandrov, Abraham, the 'father of the multitude of nations (Genesis 48:19)' who 'made all the inhabitants of the world into brothers (Midrash Tanhuma, Lekh Lekha 2:1),' serves as the model (Heyn 1958, 274). Abraham's revolution, Heyn wrote, was 'not conducted with blood and fire. The revolutionaries were led neither via punishments nor signs, neither by tyrant nor prince;' rather, he proclaimed that 'the world is not without its king (BR 42:5).' In the first place, we see that the Abrahamic revolution meant proclaiming the kingdom of heaven, the sovereignty of God. For Heyn, however, Abraham's method was as important as his message: Abraham reached out to others in a 'paternal' — that is, an intimate and loving — manner, aiming less to direct than to cultivate moral insight. He did not plant seeds of change through rational proofs, but by drawing out the good in others:

'It is the nature of the good to do good' — this is the fundamental and existential character of the absolute individual, the absolutely unique. There is, in that nature, the unique key to the hidden wonder of the first inclination to create the worlds and to form man. The desire to do good that is in the nature of the good is what encouraged that One who is alone to create others, that which is other than himself. The desire to do good is, in essence, a desire for others. This is what penetrates others from the very beginning. The same goes for man. The more something has the supernal attribute of uniqueness … from the absolutely unique, the more it has the attribute of being good and doing good, the more it feels a thirst for others, a capacity to 'make souls.' (Heyn 1970, 46–48)

Carrying forward Rashi's reading of 'the souls that they [Abraham and Sarah] made in Haran (Genesis 12:5),' according to which the teacher is compared to a creator of people, Heyn draws the parallel between God's act of creation, which arose from his uniqueness and his goodness, to human acts. Eschewing 'spiritual mastery' over others, a disciple of Abraham does not try to convince people of anything, but reaches out to them from the point of his or her uniqueness and, in a spirit of kindness, evokes in them the same, igniting fellow-feeling already there by demonstrating its origin in the source of all good.

As Heyn proceeded to explain, the altruistic idea that it is 'the nature of the good to do good' is a function of the uniqueness of the individual — it arises not in spite of his absoluteness, but because of it.

> The one who needs nobody is the one who everyone needs and who refines them. The perfect giver is the one who receives nothing by dint of his nature. The true benefactor is the one who needs good from nobody else in the world. This is the principle and substance of love which is not dependent on something (M. Avot 5:16). Specifically this love, where one receives nothing from the beloved, is true love. The unique one who is never negated, which is not created on condition, has no condition of cessation. In other words … he who benefits not from that which is of others enjoys the others themselves; he is pleased by their pleasure — or, what is more, from their essential existence. (Heyn 1970, 46–48)

Indirectly articulating in Jewish terms Nietzsche's notion of generosity, according to which the sovereign individual bestows upon others from the fullness and plenitude of his own being (Schoeman 2007), Heyn argues that the divine absoluteness and unconditionality in man is the existential foundation for the altruistic practice of 'making souls.' Reaching out to others without expectation or need for reciprocity is infectious; it puts them in touch with the same quality and makes for the sort of moral transformation that renders superfluous the organized violence of the state.

This process constitutes a revolutionary program consistent with a prohibition against killing that is without conditions (Heyn 1970, 201) because its means cohere with its ends. It is non-violent, but not passive. On the contrary, if it involves solidarity with the weak, it is by no means an 'ethic of weaklings and slaves.' Rather, it is a declaration of 'holy war against the prime cause of weakness and the weak: the force of war and aggression.' It is ultimately founded on 'the principle that what is hateful to you, you should not do not to another,' the meaning of which is 'love thy neighbor as thyself (*Sifra* 2:12)' — that is, strength through solidarity.

Implications for Zionism

Like most other members of the 'anarchist *minyan*,' Heyn adopted a twofold approach to the national question. On the one hand, he rejected political nationalism in no uncertain terms:

> Every human sacrifice, every martyrdom … is the work of nationalism. Even Symon Petliura and his generals do what they do in the name of nationalism. Nationalism is used to justify the governmental abuse and the sacrifice of

human life. They engrave one word on the staff of rage that you take in your hands and, with its black magic transform the world into a chaotic ruin. This name has two letters: *dalet-mem* [*dam*, blood]! Human blood! ... The knife with which men are slaughtered, the spear with which men are stabbed, destroy it! (Heyn 1958, 60–61)

Comparing mainstream Zionist leadership to antisemitic murderers like the Ukrainian general, Symon Petliura, Heyn enjoins them to 'place the slaughtered, the suffering, and those buried alive before their eyes' and thus to dispense with political nationalism. On the other hand, he heartily endorsed cultural nationalism. Comparing nations to craftsmen who compete with practitioners of the same craft but not with craftsmen in other fields, he wrote that true liberties do not contradict one another:

On the contrary, they fulfill one another ... The extent to which the independence of each people is enhanced, the extent to which there is in them nothing of others, is the same extent to which they do not impinge on others and are not impinged upon ... Each nation comes to the world to sing its song, to play its unique melody [so that] ... the relation among nations is like that among members of an orchestra. (Heyn 1970, 312)

Voicing a sentiment shared by Zalkind, he essentially argues that national individuation is not an impediment to peace but its presupposition. The problem, he indicates, is not national difference but national chauvinism; this spoils international harmony just as an orchestra would be ruined were it dominated by players of one instrument to the exclusion of others.

Yet, Heyn also veered from this pluralistic vision, ascribing to Israel a 'yearning for the day that its freedom will penetrate the world, when everyone will do as she does.' This yearning, he claimed, is 'much deeper than its equivalents' among other nations who yearn likewise both because it resorts neither to 'compulsion nor force in any form,' and also because it is not about 'decrees' or 'customs.' This 'humble and innocent intention does not rest on a Jewish government, on state and territorial sovereignty.' Rather, 'Israel's dominion in the world' refers to an 'outpouring of influence,' to the way the people serve as 'channels for the idea of God and bearers of the kingdom of heaven.' As he explained, 'the earthly Jerusalem is considered a ruler in the world only to the extent that it corresponds to the heavenly Jerusalem (Heyn 1970, 318).' For this reason, Heyn saw in Jewish cultural nationalism a universal humanistic character (Heyn 1958, 274) that he would likely have regarded as chauvinistic in other circumstances.

As I see it, this ambiguity as to the nature of Jewish nationalism — the way it is made to stand apart from other nationalisms — is the basis of Heyn's less than consistent response to the foundation of the State of Israel in 1948. A response consistent with his general train of thought would presumably involve questioning the shift from the pioneering ideals shared by early Zionists who labored to build up the land, to the statism that ultimately won the day — much like Zalkind did. That is not what occurred. In some early instances he adopted a roughly diasporic position, arguing that 'the nations of the world, they are nations of the land, state, and ground' while contending in contrast that 'the book is our territory, the spring and source of our national identity,' the ground to which our national 'umbilical cord is attached (Heyn 1963, 198–199).' Later on, however, he would argue not only that 'the eternal people requires its own portion in the world, its own private domain, its own borders' but also that the 'strictest justice' dictates that 'our rights to this land,' rooted in the bible itself 'are far greater than the rights of any other nation to its own (Heyn 1970, 171).' From insisting on the right to land, he proceeded to defend the formation of a Jewish state to which he ascribed moral qualities he denied every other sort of state. 'When the Jewish State is founded,' he wrote, it will be the 'opposite of the form of non-Jewish states;' it will function as 'the service vessel of man, the individual' so that 'no man has dominion over another' and none will be sacrificed for the interests of the collective (Heyn 1958, 101–102). Accordingly, he continued elsewhere:

> A state of the Torah ... *this is our desire and soul's hope toward which we ought direct all of our labor* ... Political life constitutes a whole chapter of life which must be impressed with the seal of Sinai and with the mark of Israel. 'Make him [God] king in heaven and on earth and in all four directions' — this is not simply a metaphysical notion ... It teaches the purification of the secular and the sanctification of the holy. (Heyn 1958, 279)

Whereas in other contexts Heyn posed the kingdom of God against the state, here they overlap. God's sacred dominion, the anti-authoritarian 'seal of Sinai,' becomes synonymous with a profane political institution and Heyn found himself defending a paradoxical sort of 'anarcho-statism,' a state without sovereignty corresponding to a 'non-chauvinistic' form of national chauvinism.

In spite of its theoretical inconsistencies, Heyn's readiness to embrace Zionist statism contained an important critical component. 'Not even the building of Zion purifies spilling blood, not even the building of Jerusalem (Heyn 1958, 71),' he wrote, because 'a kingdom of Israel without a kingdom of Judaism is a mere skeleton,' and the latter is built on the 'explicit name' of God; that is, on the sanctity of human-being (Heyn 1958, 120–121).' Thus, he argued, if 'it has been decreed for our generation to build the state of Judaism after thousands of years of earthly and heavenly ruins, the structure must be eternally built without tools of destruction;' it must be built with 'the hands of Jacob, the hands of Moses,' and not 'the hands of

Esau, bloody hands (Heyn 1958, 145).' Accordingly, he denounced the rising tide of Jewish militarism, those come 'to build the sanctuary of Judaism on blood and on the power of iron (Heyn 1970, 189)' or who 'await the day that Israel will also be able to step over corpses.' Such people, he contended may 'descend from the body of Israel, but certainly not from its soul (Heyn 1963, 107).' Perhaps more importantly, he claimed that they undermine Israel's 'right to a private domain unto itself, to a special dwelling place in the world' and that whatever they do manage to build either 'has nothing to do with Judaism' or contradicts it entirely: in the name of 'building a sanctuary for the living God,' they actually construct 'an altar for Satan, for the spirit of destruction, a structure for human sacrifice (Heyn 1970, 1889).'

Thus, if Heyn's later writings depart from the ideological purity of his earlier contributions, falling short of a clear-cut rejection of nationalism and statism in all forms, we do find a record of a struggle meaningful in its own right. While defending the basic legitimacy of Israel's existence, he remained acutely sensitive to the moral challenge it involved. He understood all too well that resorting to violence in order to achieve national goals, that dominating others, undermines the moral foundations of the enterprise from within, irrespective of how such things are judged by others. While he may be faulted for hubris in hoping that one state-building project among countless others could avoid these pitfalls simply because it was conducted by Jews, his hope may also serve to frame sympathetic critique moving forward.

Conclusion

To conclude, then, we found that Heyn interprets the prohibition of killing as an affirmation of the absolute sanctity of life. He took this to imply that human life is unique and irreducible, an inviolable end unto itself. Hence the foundation of Heyn's philosophy of non-violence. As we addressed it, this philosophy renders Heyn a pacifist libertarian socialist or anarchist; he opposes war, economic inequality, and dominion as inconsistent with the sanctity of man. Like Tolstoy, he endorsed revolution but insisted that its means must correspond to its ends and therefore maintained that it must come about via moral transformation. Finally, we found that in spite of his individualism, Heyn upheld a form of cultural nationalism. While he understood this in pluralistic and non-chauvinistic terms, he made a certain exception for the Jews: their values, he considered universal. This led him to a sort of Zionist exceptionalism according to which a Jewish State might escape the moral and political pitfalls into which other states stumble.

Nonetheless, this hope served a critical function, allowing us to ask with him how to respond when his expectations were not met.

Notes

1 I translate Heyn's term, *ba'aley ha-anokhiyut*, as 'anarcho-individualism' as opposed simply to 'individualism' for several reasons. First of all, he addresses Kropotkin (not an anarcho-individualist, but certainly an anarchist) and not a liberal individualist. More importantly, he supposes that *ba'aley ha-anokhiyut* rejects all moral constraints to individual liberty, a position closer to Stirner's than to any other (Stirner 2005, 179, 291).

2 See Kropotkin's *Anarchist Morality* (1898). There he writes that the ultimate moral principle is 'do to others what you would have them do to you in the same circumstances,' adding that this is 'merely a piece of advice' — but very good advice born of much experience. Ironically, Kropotkin bases his morality on a principle many took to constitute the essence of the Torah and yet Heyn disputes it.

3 The Kantian background of this claim is palpable. For more on the link between Kantianism and Anarchism, see May (1990, 2011); Wolff (1970).

4 See Ketubot 103a; Bava Kama 20a–21a, Tosafot to Bava Batra 12b *divrey ha-maskil* '*k'gon*.'

9

Natan Hofshi (1890–1980)

7 Natan Hofshi, date unknown.

Unlike other figures examined in this volume, Natan Hofshi (1890–1980) was not the scion of any line of scholars or saints. Born to a family Gur hasidim from the Polish town of Wolbrom (Hofshi 1964a, 5, 9), Hofshi was raised on the farm they owned and operated. He attended the local *heder* and reported having memorized the bible, but his formal education ended there (Hofshi 1964a, 11). Although the Gur sect is notoriously anti-modern and, like most other hasidic groups, staunchly anti-Zionist, Hofshi's family was engaged with the broader world (Hofshi 1964a, 22–23). They were loosely affiliated with Hibbat Zion (Hofshi 1964a, 9–11) and, after 1897, supported the nascent Zionist movement (Hofshi 1964a, 9). Under these influences, Hofshi surreptitiously assumed leadership roles in a variety of Zionist youth groups (Hofshi 1964a, 12) before finally departing for Palestine in 1909.

In Palestine, he initially worked as an itinerant agricultural laborer (Hofshi 1964a, 13–20). In the course of his travels, he made the acquaintance of A. D. Gordon (Hofshi 1964a, 32), an important theoretician of Practical Zionism and a founder of ha-Po'el ha-Za'ir, a pacifist and non-Marxist Zionist labor movement (Rose 1964). Under Gordon's influence, Hofshi adopted the Tolstoyan ideals of vegetarianism, manual labor, simplicity of living, and practical anarchism (Hofshi 1964a, 29; Epstein 1998; Feldman 2004, 306; Ratzabi 2011). This connection is essential to understanding the ideological parity between Hofshi and other members of the anarchist *minyan*, some thirty years his senior. Hofshi came of age in a different time, but his mentor belonged to the intellectual world of Hibbat Zion and carried anarcho-narodnik and Tolstoyan influences to a new generation. While 'Gordon's subversive ideas' would be largely forgotten in the 'process of Zionist myth-making' that reduced him to an example of 'dedication to agricultural labour and Jewish renewal (Horrox 2009, 31),' and many former members of ha-Poel ha-Za'ir would go on to play important roles in Mapai — a Labor Zionist pary formed from its merger with Ahdut Haavodah under the leadership of David Ben-Gurion — Hofshi remained true to his mentor's original vision.

Rising tensions between Jewish returnees and the local Arab population caused Hofshi to question the feasibility of living 'year after year in an atmosphere of hatred, anxiety, the clash of weapons, endless gunfire and nightly strikes (Hofshi 1964a, 35).' Caught in the famous Battle of Tel Hai (Zerubavel 1991), these doubts came to a head in 1920. Describing his experiences holding watch in Metula during the conflict that led to a famous battle in the nearby village of Tel Hai (near the volatile border between the English and French Mandates), he wrote:

One of my friends made a joke that brought me back to myself and enabled me to understand what was happening. '[Look!] the vegetarian with the instruments of death in his hand like a murderer!' When he said this, he burst into laughter; his was the victory and mine was the humiliation. But no, good friend, the shame is both of ours, all of ours. Let us lower our heads and cry in disgrace ... At the very beginning of our revival, the initial budding of our spring ... it was sealed in blood, a stain that cannot be cleansed ... It was our dream to rebuild our ruined bodies and souls in peace, but then satan came with his cruel laughter and mocked our dreams! Cry not over the dead! Cry over the light that has faded, to the feelings of love that have withered before their time, over the weeds of hatred that have taken their place. Can salted land sprout? Can a nation grow from a land polluted with fire and brimstone, hated and vengeance? (Hofshi 1964a, 44; 1920)

Contra Trumpeldor, who fell in that battle and whose dying words, 'it is good to die for our country,' became a patriotic mantra repeated until today, Hofshi concluded from the violence that violence is inimical to national renaissance. On the basis of this conclusion, Hofshi joined better-known figures like Martin Buber in the founding of Brit Shalom (Hofshi 1930), a small and short-lived effort to promote Jewish-Arab coexistence through the formation of a binational state (Hattis 1970; Lavsky 1996). More importantly, he founded the Palestinian (later, the Israeli) branch of the War Resisters' International (Hofshi 1964a, 60).[1] It was in this role that Hofshi earned his notoriety, consistently maintaining a pacifist stance throughout World War II (Hofshi 1939; Hofshi 1943a–b) and later opposing Eichmann's execution (Hofshi 1962) — positions for which he was denounced as a traitor (Mar 1942; Guy 1949; Shoro 1967). After 1948, he earned the distinction of being the first Israeli to be imprisoned for draft evasion (Anonymous 1948)[2] and headed early efforts to secure draft exemptions for conscientious objectors (Anonymous 1950; Anonymous 1954a–g; Eshel 1954; Keren 2002). Equally important, he publicly and explicitly addressed the problem of minority rights and Israeli state violence (Hofshi 1935; Anonymous 1952; AMK 1953; Hofshi 1964b; Hofshi 1965a–b), even going so far as to propose a halt to Jewish *aliyah* (Zevuloni 1962). Thus was he branded a 'moral parasite (Ben-Gurion 1950; Anonymous 1954e; Anonymous 1954f)' and accused of feeding 'poisonous snakes (Sholom 1932)' while ignoring their danger (Anonymous 1961).

Hofshi, more than Don-Yahiya or Heyn, fully embodied Tolstoyan anarcho-pacifism — not only as a matter of ideology, but in his daily life. He embraced veganism long before it was fashionable (LeBlanc 2001) and eschewed the city, tending an organic farm until his retirement in the 1970s. Hofshi's letters and essays appeared in several Hebrew-language newspapers. An edited collection under the title *Ba-Lev u-ba-Nefesh: Be-Ma'avak al Am we-Adam* was published in 1964 by his friends and students. Celebrated by Jewish anarchists like Hirschauge and Steinberg (Anonymous 1954f;

Anonymous 1954h), his work was widely dismissed by the Zionist mainstream (Anonymous 1965; Asaf 1965a–b). What is most striking and most significant, however, is that Hofshi shook the moral foundations of modern Zionism *not* from the outside, but from deep within. His work resonates both with the idealistic pioneering spirit of the so-called Second Aliya and also with a profound sense of humanity and justice. It challenges what Zionism became in the name of what it was — or at least what Hofshi took it to be. This chapter examines Hofshi's account of 'religious feeling' as the basis for pacifism and libertarian socialism while attending to the ways that his reflections on both shaped his response to Zionist statism and the Arab-Israeli conflict that, in his view, it created.

Religious feeling: human sanctity and fraternity

Many, Hofshi lamented, yearn for a golden age of universal peace and brotherhood, but in the meantime maintain that in the name of security it is necessary to be realistic, to 'uproot our profane softness of heart' and dirty our hands with blood while waiting for an 'infinitely distant day' when the 'kingdom of heaven' will, without 'deep penitence, without concerted preparation,' miraculously arrive 'while people are still immersed in blood, when human hands are still filthied with the blood of their fellow man.' This 'criminal delusion,' Hoshi explained, constitutes an evasion of the mission expressed in the 'thin still voice (1 Kings 19:2)' that 'incessantly whispers: return you mortals (Psalms 90:3; Hofshi 1964a, 190)!' The golden age can, Hofshi insisted, only be attained by actively striving to realize it in the here and now.

Hofshi took this to imply a moral imperative to means-ends correspondence, which he articulated by comparing Tomás de Torquemada, the Iberian grand inquisitor, and Mahatma Gandhi. Both were 'religious fanatics,' he wrote, but their fanaticism led them in opposing directions:

> For Torquemada, all means were legitimate — coercion, force, pressure, violence, even killing the one who refuses to submit ... Gandhi disdains means which are inappropriate for good purposes. He is a fanatic for the Torah that teaches us to love other people because they are people, a love not dependent on anything else, a love the whole being of which is opposition to force and violence. (Hofshi 1964a, 255)

Establishing truth and justice, peace and brotherhood, demands fanatical devotion; but only such as expressed in accord with the goal. People, he contended, are not 'means to some distant end;' no end is holy when attaining it means that 'life may be treated as profane.' Rather, man is the measure of holiness — 'we are, ourselves, the end (Hofshi 1964a, 60).' *This* conception of holiness, he insisted, must 'serve as the fundamental principle of human community,' which 'exists for the sake of the individual' and not the reverse (Hofshi 1964a, 53). The alternative viewpoint, Torquemada's implicit assertion that ends justify means, is a 'false Torah,' a 'doctrine of violence and of course power' which justifies the idea that 'the stronger prevails, that the majority rules over the minority' and leads to 'dictatorship, to war by any means' in order to assert control (Hofshi 1964a, 55).

This notion constitutes the core of what Hofshi identified as the 'religious feeling' that forms the basis of true life. 'Recognize and feel that there is a God, that we all have the same father,' he recommended, and thus heed:

> The true religion, the religion taught by the prophets of Israel and pursued by the sages of the nations, which does not permit exploitation or hatred, robbery, murder, or any other evils. In light of this faith in the holiness of life, that people we were created in the image of God, in light of this religion which burns unceasingly in the heart against wickedness and evil, in light of *this* faith, the unending striving for the good, for the divine truth ... passes from the degraded status of laws and provisions ... to the more reliable and certain status of strong and heartfelt faith. (Hofshi 1964a, 67)

A person of faith, he continued, 'ought to be one who cares, one for whom pain and suffering — every affront to the body of his fellow human being, son of one and the same father in heaven — matter.' He will 'neither rest nor take enjoyment' so long as they are afflicted either materially or spiritually (Hofshi 1964a, 200). This faith, together with the 'pure humanism,' the 'feeling of human brotherhood and disdain for violence' of the 'Hillelian principle' that he took it to imply — what is hateful to you, do not to another (Shabbat 31a) — represent the theological foundation his thought (Hofshi 1964a, 284). As he put it:

> The prophets all endeavored toward this one thing: to open the eyes of the blind so that they see we are all brothers, the children of one father, family-peoples branching from the one great father-tree of humanity, of all being, so that they see and finally recognize the terrible tragedy, the abysmal sin, of reciprocal and ongoing murder. Concerning this central point, Judaism first established a position with the announcement of the eternal command 'do not kill (Exodus 20:12)' and then concluded the idea [with the claim that] 'nations shall not raise the sword against one another and they shall no longer teach war (Isaiah 2:4)' and with the idea of universal peace: 'and the wolf shall lie down with the lamb (Isaiah 11:6).' In the practical language of day-to-day life, this central point is expressed in Hillel's wonderful instruction: 'what is hateful to you, do not to your neighbor (Shabbat 31a),' which, according to him, sums up the Jewish teaching. (Hofshi 1964a, 84)

Here, we observe in Hofshi's train of thought a pattern equivalent to the one traced by his elders, Heyn and Don-Yahiya. The prohibition of murder is rooted in the notion that mankind is created in the image of God, or that all people are God's children and therefore siblings. This then serves as the basis for a comprehensive pacifist theology. 'Religious feeling,' a deep sense of shared humanity, dissolves the ideological infrastructure for justified violence. They are reduced to their common denominator and interpreted as a blasphemous affront to the image of God in mankind.

Religious pacifism

In an essay titled, like those of Tolstoy and Heyn before him, 'Thou Shalt not Kill,' Hofshi argues that 'religious feeling' entails a moral objection not only to offensive, but also defensive violence. Acknowledging the distinction between 'war in defense of the state,' which is often conflated with the homeland to the natural love of which it appeals, 'war in defense of social order,' and 'war for the protection and liberation of the oppressed,' he nonetheless contended that 'war is a crime against humanity insofar as it is a crime against human life,' and thus concluded that 'out of a tremendous love of mankind, we decided to support no war of any kind be it offensive or defensive (Hofshi 1964a, 50–53).' As he explained:

> Everyone is terrified of the horrible wars that threatens us … we are afraid of all the suffering and the troubles that are likely to come with the war. We are concerned for our bodies, our well-being, our property, and so on; our minds are busy thinking about how to avoid this, how to dodge the tragedy … but we focus not enough, or not at all, on a more penetrating question: how can we rise up against our brothers, who like us were created in the image of God, and kill them? How can we become murderers and shedders of blood? How will be able to bear the stain of blood, the mark of Cain, that cannot be cleansed? (Hofshi 1938; 1964, 77)

Besides the fact that defence is an inherently blurry notion often exploited to make mere violence appear more acceptable, Hofshi rejected it on moral and also pragmatic grounds 'immorality cannot preserve order, protect our homeland, or free the proletariat;' it coarsens peoples, leads to atrocities, and ultimately brings 'an end to every freedom so that the apparent victory of the persecuted only increases their burden (Hofshi 1964a, 50–53).'

More so than Heyn and Don-Yahiya, Hofshi made explicit his objection, not simply to direct participation in, but also to indirect contributions to, any war effort. 'What is a state and what power does it have,' he asked 'without millions and tens of millions of people doing its work?' Every day, he continued:

> Millions of people wake up and part from the loving gaze of their families, kiss their dear children and their wives, and travel to their workplace, to the holy task of producing extremely sophisticated implements for killing, slaughter, and destruction ... to support their beloved families. This horrific labor on which depends the destruction and annihilation of other beloved families together with the families under consideration is a definite preparation for assured mutual destruction. [But people] do not see anything wrong with it. (Hofshi 1964a, 212)

Hofshi did. He opposed not only direct military service, but also 'manufacturing weapons, making loans' or even 'dedicating our labor to war so that others can conduct it.' It is necessary, he held, to 'recognize the deep causes of war and to struggle in order to nullify those causes.' Thus, he contended:

> There is great value in concretizing the principle of non-participation in violence — e.g. refusal to manufacture weapons, the material of war, and everything that is helpful and useful to armies and the conducting war. Members of the movement accept upon themselves as a living responsibility everything that is involved in realizing non-participation in violence.

This, Hofshi held, is ultimately the only way to uproot war from the world so that 'love, fraternity, and equality govern relations between people.' Under no circumstances may we devote 'our labor to war so that others can conduct it (Hofshi 1964a, 50–53)' — this would mean acquiescing to the 'annihilation of other beloved families' in the name of supporting our own (Hofshi 1964a, 212).

Appealing directly to Tolstoy, Hofshi denied passive resistance means non-resistance to evil. Rather, he insisted, 'human life in its entirety is a war against evil, an opposition to evil with the assistance of love and understanding.' It is simply that 'from among all the means of opposing evil' he chose 'those which entail no justification for violence, no war against evil using evil means (Hofshi 1964a, 84).' To resist evil in an absolute sense is to uproot it from its sources in the heart rather than addressing only its external manifestations in hatred, violence, and 'the rule of brother over brother.' One must recognize that salvation lies within:

> Distance yourselves from evil and do not participate in it. Refrain from submitting to evil, from supporting it, from serving it, and it will immediately fall; for without you it is nothing. Abandon the path of hatred and climb the path of love for every creature. The path of life is not in heaven or across the sea, it is very close to us. The day that people begin to think about their world and responsibility for each of their actions in light of the command, 'what is

hateful to you, do not to another,' then hope for true life will sprout. (Hofshi 1964a, 58–59)

Attending to this 'thin still voice of love for every creation,' Hofshi maintained, removes from evil its agency. Without people willing to perpetuate an evil it cannot be realized. Thus it disappears into nothingness.

Hofshi agreed that the law of 'kill or be killed' is superficially convincing because threats to our safety are real and security must be ensured. Yet, drawing on Hillel's teaching, he explained that:

> The eternal law of 'you were killed insofar as you killed (M. Avot 2:6)' ... is a truth that has been proven in every land and by the history of every people. All of the famous tyrants who conquered peoples and destroyed lands, thus meriting, by their atrocities, the title of 'greatness' according to fawning historians — what was their end? What was the end of their heroic accomplishments? Before them went death and slaughter, behind them chaos and confusion ... Concerning all of these and everything like them, the true education says 'let not my person be included in their council, Let not my being be counted in their assembly. For when angry they slay men.' (Genesis 49:6).

In contrast, an ostensibly powerless people like Israel somehow survived. In this sense violence is not only morally untenable, it is self defeating (Hofshi 1964a, 101).

The special problem of Jewish militarism

According to Hofshi, it is the 'mission of Abraham and all of his descendents' to serve as exemplars of 'justice and fairness (Genesis 18:17–19; Hofshi 1972)' — this, and not 'national pride or chauvinist-egoist racial superiority' is what he took 'chosenness' to mean. Thus, 'from Israel, more responsibility for truth, justice, uprightness, and love is demanded (Hofshi 1964a, 336). It is an insult to the 'Jewish-religious universal (Hofshi 1964a, 296)' when a Jew shakes himself 'from his faith that mankind is created in the image of God, from following the path paved by the prophets of Israel, "not by might, nor by power, but by my spirit (Zechariah 4:6)"' and transforms 'instruction shall come forth from Zion (Isaiah 2:3)' into 'the tools of destruction, murder, and ruin go out from Zion (Hofshi 1964a, 159).' The insult, he averred, is all the more bitter when proponents of 'blood and fire' don an 'external religious husk,' when even 'those who lay tefillin' combine the 'laws of the *Shulkhan Arukh* (the Code of Jewish Law)' with 'the teachings of Clausewitz and Moltke' and 'bow to Mars' in lieu of 'our father in heaven who created all men as brothers (Hofshi 1964a, 156).'

Hofshi did not deny that Judaism arose from a biblical warrior culture. Rather, like Heyn and Alexandrov, he believed that the spirit of the Torah progressively overcomes its letter. The prophets and their disciples, the talmud sages, he contended 'absolutely nullified what was nullified,' that is, what atrophied over time 'as Judaism developed and the moral condition of the people rose from 'let no soul live (Deuteronomy 20:16)' to 'what is hateful to you, do not to others (Shabbat 31a).' Thus, he asserted, 'Jeremiah and the other prophets absolutely nullified the warpath' for all time and that the rabbis, in opposing ancient Hebrew uprisings against the Romans, rejected 'the obligatory wars in the Torah and the place of war in the bible as a whole (Hofshi 1964a, 305).' From that time forward, the elders of Israel throughout the generations chose, over the path of the sword, that of 'not by might, nor by power, but by my spirit (Zechariah 4:6).' To 'deviate from this path,' he claimed, 'was regarded as a deviation from Judaism itself' — it meant that 'Esau-Constantine dwells in the Tents of Jacob (Hofshi 1964a, 156)' and defiles them.

Thus, Hofshi regarded the rise of Zionist militancy beginning in the 1920s as a regressive tendency. There are, he wrote, those who 'endeavor to breathe new life, to ignite the sleeping coals, of Jewish militarism. They try to instill us with the faith that we shall achieve our national goals with blood and with weapons, by killing and destruction.' They believe that 'we must build the land of Israel even if it is necessary to make a deal with the devil.' Borrowing the language of biblical condemnation of worshippers of the golden calf, Hofshi denounced them accordingly:

> Satan! He is the faithful partner whom they have found to bring us to this point of internal and external crisis ... 'This is your god Israel (Exodus 32:8)!' Not a new human spirit, not freedom from groundlessness ... only by partnering with Satan, will Judah rise ... Will this create for us a new, free community or a new people of mankind? Will being caught up in Cain's trade revive us ?' (Hofshi 1964a, 39–40)

Contending, like Jabotinsky, that 'with blood and fire Judah fell and with blood and fire it will rise again (Luz 1987),' they taught that 'a nation's glory lies in conquering its enemies in the killing field, that the land is acquired using the satanic tools and methods that horrified earlier generations of Jews' and thus the 'tents of Jacob (Numbers 24:5)' were replaced by 'pagan temples in the Roman style (Hofshi 1964a, 182).' Drawing on the midrashic themes similar to those used by Heyn, Hofshi likewise associates violence with Esau and then to Rome, only he pushes the link to the extreme by appealing to related traditions, placing both under the angelic guardianship of Samael, or Satan (Midrash Tanhuma, Genesis 32:35). In his judgement, the direction taken by the Zionist mainstream situated the movement similarly.

Hofshi's bitter struggle against the moral direction adopted by his peers should not be interpreted as a repudiation of Zionism. Rather, he should be understood as someone striving to restore the movement to its original direction as he understood it after the 'national disaster' and 'the tremendous human regression' represented by the changes it underwent in the decades preceding the establishment of the State of Israel. 'It is our duty,' he announced that:

> To loudly proclaim that this is not the way ... Anyone in whose heart the flame of God and humanity has yet to be extinguished ... whoever has the prohibition 'do not kill' engraved in his soul with letters of fire, *whoever believes that Zion will be redeemed* with justice and not with 'blood and fire' must rise up ... against the propaganda spread by the cult of militarism. (Hofshi 1964a, 40)

It is not, he insisted, necessary to realize Zionism in this blood-soaked manner (Hofshi 1964a, 252).' On the contrary, citing the so-called 'three oaths (Ketubot 111a)' earlier adopted by ultra-orthodox anti-Zionists to support *their* position, he contended that the promise 'not to go up [to the land] with an army' means not that they should not go, but that 'redemption does not come via the strength of the arm (Hofshi 1964a, 87).' Rather, he argued:

> Isaiah opposes oppression and, like Moses at the Sea of Reeds, promises Hezekiah and the people that *the Lord will fight for you*. No army defeated Sennacherib; rather, it was an angel of God that struck the Assyrian army ... or God himself. It was not like the invasion of Canaan and the wars waged by David; then, armies fought the enemy. This path was rejected completely beginning with the later prophets.

Their message was, instead, that God 'will come to the assistance of his people (Hofshi 1964a, 308–309).' Thus, Hofshi concluded, we must rely 'on our father in heaven who warned us against following the erroneous path' of blood and fire, of trust in armies, that constitutes a 'distortion, forgery, and misrepresentation of the path of true Judaism (Hofshi 1964a, 316).' As he continued elsewhere: 'only labor, actual work by hand, gives a people the merit to live a national life, a free life ... Better to die and not dirty our hands with blood,' a point that he finally drives in by citing Hayyim Bialik's poem *On the Threshold of the Study Hall*: 'than be a lion among lions, with lambs I'd rather perish (Hofshi 1964a, 40). Here we see that Hofshi's ire is not directed against the project of renewing Jewish life in the ancestral homeland, but against the idea that this can (or even should) be accomplished in a way that runs against the grain of fundamental Jewish values.

Zionism and the Palestinian Arabs

While Zalkind, Don-Yahiya, and Heyn all lived — for at least some period of time — in Palestine or Israel, Hofshi was the only one of the four to sustain any real contact with Palestinian Arabs. He spoke Arabic and offered numerous testimonies as to his dealings with his neighbors while working in the agricultural settlements he called home. While it is not difficult to infer from their writings the form that their responses could or should have taken, the Jewish-Arab relationship was something that touched Hofshi far more viscerally. Therefore, he addressed it at length and with great passion.

Hofshi firmly believed that 'it was our right to come here not simply because it is a human right to settle' wherever refuge can be found and livelihood gained, but 'because this is the land of *Israel*' and 'we have been connected to it for thousands of years (Hofshi 1964a, 239).' We came 'with a clean conscience, with pure intentions and clean hands, as brother men and exiled, homeless, sons returning to their birthplace' in order to realize the universal Jewish mission that was originally proclaimed from Zion (Hofshi 1964a, 329).

But since the people of Israel were exiled due to the 'bloodshed and baseless hatred (Yoma 9b)' that 'Jewish tradition has since trained us to abominate,' returning only to 'take hold of Esau's weapons so as to kill their neighbors,' would constitute a destructive regression. Should Israel 'forget its religion ... the eternal divine command "do not murder!" and dirty its hands with innocent blood,' its claim to redemption becomes void (Hofshi 1964a, 79). Hofshi endorsed the Zionist vision, but only on the condition that it be actualized in 'a just and upright manner' without the 'spirit of hostility and alienation (Hofshi 1964a, 324).' That is not what happened. Reminding his audience that conflicts are not necessary, but arise from *choices*, Hofshi therefore called for reflection as to why Israel found itself at war 'with all of our neighbors (Hofshi 1964a, 282).

As he told it, the problem began with an ideological decision: the 'Zionist leadership' turned to 'the implements of the angel of death' and 'assigned to the junkyard' Jewish traditions of non-violence when it resolved to 'found a sovereign Jewish State' despite Arab protests and the consequent threat of war (Hofshi 1964a, 282). Indeed, he stated frankly, most 'looked at the presence of Arabs as something temporary and passing, something that would eventually fade away as our power grew (Hofshi 1964a, 282).' From that moment on, he claimed, 'the attributes which mark Jewish identity ...

humility, mercy, and kindness' were forcefully excised and 'a tacit seal of approval was given to Deir Yassin, Qibya, Kafr Qasim, and the like (Hofshi 1964a, 191–192).'

The war came, and Arab inhabitants of the land were dispossessed (Hofshi 1964a, 170) 'or ghettoized, humiliated, and forced to live under military rule (Hofshi 1964a, 282).' Thus, 'human beings like us who only yesterday dwelt securely on the land they inherited from their fathers' came to suffer a precarious and dependent existence (Hofshi 1964a, 249). In spite of all this human suffering, he lamented, many Jews considered it a 'miracle from heaven' and looked 'forward to further miracles (Hofshi 1964a, 134)' or 'like an ostrich' stuck 'their heads in the sand' and sought to relegate a still-simmering problem to the past (Hofshi 1964a, 249).

As he saw it, a more adequate response would be multivalent. For one, contrition. We 'consider the relation between the Jewish government and the [Arab] refugees' to be:

> Sinful, a betrayal of Judaism, a degrading stain on the prophetic vision of the return to Zion with justice, peace, fairness, and as a true example for other nations. We stand in bitter struggle with the evil spirit that prevails in the Zionist movement and, throughout this struggle, never lose sight of what brought this evil spirit to bear … We consider it a shameful disaster that Jacob abandoned the perfect and peaceful path for the path of Esau, the way of 'you shall live by the sword.' The eternally oppressed learned the teaching of the eternal oppressor.

Therefore, he concluded, 'we call our people to penitence, to straighten what is crooked on our own behalf, and also on behalf of our brother-enemies together as one in our shared homeland (Hofshi 1964a, 340).' In part, this would take the form of a 'spiritual-religious revolution (Hofshi 1964a, 134)' involving the renunciation of 'chauvinist nationalism (Hofshi 1964a, 172).' This would mean reversing both the 'emphatic refusal to admit that two peoples share historical rights to a common homeland' and the consequent 'rule of the one as master over the majority of the population of the other (Hofshi 1964a, 189).' More concretely, it would mean reparations: 'if Jews do not release their homes and their property, which were appropriated by the Nazis in Germany, if they insist now on reparations, appealing to the law, to justice, and to what is moral,' he wrote, 'all the more so those who inhabited this land for generations;' therefore, 'return what was stolen, cease oppression, compensate the deprived, the expelled, and the dispossessed (Hofshi 1964a, 249).'

Hofshi also enjoined his readers to reflect on the moral cost of perpetual conflict. 'One sin leads to another,' he wrote. The results of the first war created a 'need to protect what was stolen by way of a total militarization of the entire congregation of Israel in the land of Israel (Hofshi 1964a, 170)' that could only be sustained by poisoning youth 'during the spring of their lives' by educating them 'to hate, to [conduct] murderous battle, to fight with bayonets, to have hardened hearts (Hofshi 1964a, 289).' The soul-made-soldier must quash 'the deep inner voice that attests to the holiness of human life, created in the image of God' and thus become 'an obedient tool (Hofshi 1964a, 189).' The Jewish soul, Hofshi indicated, is the cost of the Jewish state. Therefore, he begged his audience to think 'like children of Israel, and not like Esau and Moltke,' to honor the 'image of God' and not he 'who kills much' and therefore 'has more badges of honor-shame on his chest (Hofshi 1964a, 289).

Beyond penitence, restitution, and appreciation as to moral costs, Hofshi demanded that responsibility be taken for forging positive and productive relationships. On scriptural authority, — 'as face answers to face in water, So does one man's heart to another (Proverbs 27:19)' — he insisted that 'our dealings with the Arabs must be as with brothers (Hofshi 1964a, 53).' Israelis, he explained, must strive with all our ability, to unite the hearts of two peoples, the Arabs and the Jews, which live here 'through the economic, social, cultural, and communal ties that strengthen mutual feelings of 'human brotherhood (Hofshi 1964a, 129).' After all, he maintained, there is 'plenty of room in the land for two peoples (Hofshi 1964a, 53)' together to 'express their unique national qualities (Hofshi 1964a, 130).'

Pacifism and anti-statism

In spite of Hofshi's hopes, statism flourished during the decade prior to 1948 and exultantly eliminated other streams of Zionist thought thereafter (Hofshi 1964a, 340, 1974). The movement then became thoroughly 'hypnotized by the idea of the state, by the idea of the sovereign government of Israel (Hofshi 1964a, 98, 244).' This 'distorted and falsified' the 'prophetic vision of ... moral and social regeneration (Hofshi 1964a, 272).' 'Emphatic refusal to admit' shared claims to 'a common homeland' and passionate insistence as to the right of one to rule 'as master' over the other became the rule of the day (Hofshi 1964a, 189). Thus held captive by 'radical fanatics for Jewish statehood, a Jewish military (Hofshi 1964a, 96), for 'armed Jewish power (Hofshi 1964a, 98),' the Zionist movement, abandoned 'the perfect and peaceful path for the path of Esau,' betraying Judaism and leaving 'a degrading stain on the prophetic vision' of its return to Zion (Hofshi 1964a, 340), a vision that was already being realized 'before the establishment of the state, without force and government compulsion (Hofshi 1964a, 322).' Accordingly, Hofshi claimed that 'Ben-Gurion brought a great tragedy on Israel, it is called the State' — without it, he says, there would be no war and both peoples would live together' in peace (Hofshi 1950).

This brings us to his direct critique of Zionist statism and, indeed, of statism in general. Echoing Ahad Ha'am, Hofshi argues that in the Jewish prophetic vision, 'there would be no question of war with neighboring peoples, no rule of a new nation over those who had inhabited the land for generations' but rather, simply the creation of a 'center for Jewish set-tlement based on the purest principles of Jewish-humanism as is fitting and appropriate for Israel, which carries the prophetic message of peace, human brotherhood, and universal justice (Hofshi 1964a, 181)' — a justice that is incompatible with statecraft, for 'statecraft and justice … are things which contradict one another (Hofshi 1922).' Thus, he wrote, did the state of Israel destroy and 'continues to destroy the true *land* of Israel of our prophets and sages.' The fruit of wars, its origins 'testify as to its nature.' In contrast, the land of Israel 'was being revived before the establishment of the state, without force and government compulsion (Hofshi 1964a, 322).' Only that movement was taken captive by 'radical fanatics for Jewish statehood, a Jewish military (Hofshi 1964a, 96),' for 'armed Jewish power (Hofshi 1964a, 98).' For Hofshi, then, the problem is not Zionism as such, but the direction it took.

He rejected the path of 'state and military-diplomatic Zionism' but expresses faith in the prospect of 'realizing a Zionism in the spirit of the prophets and sages (Hofshi 1964a, 243)' — a Zionism that has 'no particular admira-tion for' armies, for 'regimes, [or for] the authority of the state (Hofshi 1964a, 98).' Like the prophet Samuel, Hofshi regards the establishment of human kingdoms as a rejection of divine sovereignty; 'none of the kings, good or bad, even the best of them, were what God wanted' — all displeased him. Even faith in the Davidic messiah, Hofshi contends, appeals *not* to David insofar as he served as king, but, 'to the David who was a simple shepherd (Hofshi 1964a, 268).'

'The struggle between good and evil is in human hands,' in the hands of each individual (Hofshi 1964a, 296), he wrote. The first step is not to 'cultivate the State by our own efforts' by 'doing its work and protecting it.' Who is 'a Herod, a Caligula, a Czar Nikolai, a Hitler' he asked 'without the foolishness, stupidity, and dumbness of the masses called to conduct a holy war against the chains which they themselves forge on a daily basis (Hofshi 1964a, 212)?' This begins, he argued, with self-transformation. Society, he wrote:

Will not become good before people themselves change. More than against the capitalist regime, we must struggle against the spirit of capitalism within us. Then the regime will fall on its own. It is not by the brutal force which we exert against the brutal force of fascism that we are liberated from horrors, but by tearing up the roots of fascism from our souls, from the souls of our youth, by liberating ourselves from national, class, and political chauvinism. (Hofshi 1964a, 55)

Appealing directly to the work of the famous anarchist Gustav Landauer, whom he called 'bone of our bone and the flesh of our flesh,' Hofshi wrote that 'the renewal of humanity depends on the renewal of the individual, that the labor of revitalizing life is essentially the labor of rectifying mankind from the bottom up.' Small changes, 'in the individual's daily life,' he continues, 'are what produces [large-scale] change in the people and in humanity,' when people 'take account of their inner world,' and liberate themselves from 'inner slavery (Hofshi 1964a, 81).' 'Redemption and salvation (Hofshi 1964a, 212)' come when a 'spiritual storm' from within blows away 'the desire for rule (Hofshi 1964a, 45),' clearing the air and inspiring 'mutual faith (Hofshi 1964a, 84).'

In one respect, this is a matter of education. 'Traditional education,' he wrote, 'regards the world as an arena of mutual war' and 'instills faith in the fatal necessity of this war and prepares students to take part in the task (Hofshi 1964a, 101).' We require instead, he argued, a new educational model:

> Power, strategy, factionalism, the desire for sovereignty and, above all, faith in the idea that the ends justify the means must become objects of disgust. A new relation vigorously negating raw power in all its forms, military and civil must be taught. It must be an education that encourages collective action after the manner taught by Tolstoy and concretized by Gandhi. A human relation even toward the opponent and the enemy ... a relation like that between brothers, even if one of them is in error. (Hofshi 1964a, 56)

Schools that 'teach neighborly love and the sanctity of human life,' Hofshi believed, would transform the world. Their students:

> Will not serve as pliable material for rogues and schemers, they will not be quick to spill blood on command from above, to respond to the external discipline of rulers, commanders, or political parties; they will listen to their inner voice. They will learn ... to despise Esau's blessing 'you shall live by the sword.' (Hofshi 1964a, 101)

Inspired by Tolstoy and Gandhi, Hofshi maintained that educational reform designed to uproot complacency and imbue students with an unshakable sensitivity to the holiness of human life would prepare students to abolish evil by refusing to participate in it. For him, this included resistance to the institutions through which organized violence is made both possible and necessary.

In another respect, it is a matter of constructing the social, political, and economic structures capable of replacing the state. For him, this involved 'religious communism (Hofshi 1964a, 45)' generally and formulating an authentically Jewish, form of 'libertarian socialism' in particular. On the whole, he wrote:

> Socialism deals only with removing the shackles of economy and state from the worker; it strives toward a government that is better and more just — one without classes. But it is pleased to accept the 'pleasures' of civilization that have transformed labor from a living act of creation into a mechanical process, dead and hateful and lacking in any meaning. Socialism promises the working man all the pleasures of this world that only wealthy people enjoy at present. But it doesn't bother considering the tragedy of degeneration, destruction, and dissolution that progressively threatens the persistence of body and soul alike after the revolutionization of labor. It doesn't oppose the concentration of great masses of people into the cities and their complete alienation from God's world [together with all the social ills this produces], which is the result of a lack of faith in the existence of a Godly spark, the image of God in mankind. (Hofshi 1964a, 246–247)

The prophets of Israel, he contended 'were much more than socialists; their dream encompassed more and was far deeper (Hofshi 1964a, 246–247).' They evoked 'a spirit that clears the air and inspires mutual faith (Hofshi 1964a, 840' and by faith moved people to liberate themselves from 'small mindedness, from stinginess, from the egoism of stiff-neckedness' and, above all, 'from the desire for rule (Hofshi 1964a, 45).'

Concretely, as the lengthy passage in the preceding paragraph suggests, Hofshi linked this shift in human spirit inspired by the prophets to fundamental changes in the way that people live their day-to-day lives. Modern materialism and consumerism, he felt, leave no room for spiritual transformation. Therefore he advocated the agrarian anarchism promoted by Tolstoy and after him by A. D. Gordon (Tsirkin-Sadan, 2012). The state, he explained, has many 'poisonous and destructive fruits;' these include 'mechanization, the herd instinct, stupidity and enslavement (Hofshi 1964a, 97–98)' as well as (here paraphrasing Steinberg) 'police, armies, censors, blind patriotism, hatred and jealousy, war among brothers, exploitation, theft, and the spilling of innocent blood (Hofshi 1964a, 181)' — the Jewish state is no different. Therefore, it must be dismantled. Hofshi recalled a time when Zionism was truly revolutionary, when its aim was:

> Creating a life-existence that was Jewish-human, a new ethic, a living example in the life of the individual and of the people [that involved] working the land by hand, the simple life, making do with little, caution regarding exploiting others, aversion to anything which smacked of enjoying money or property not earned by the sweat of one's brow. (Hofshi 1964a, 18)

Then, 'centralization of the flocks ... a mass of followers below organized from above by a few leaders,' he says, was not the objective (Hofshi 1964a, 81). Rather, people were motivated by 'the pure desire to reformulate the moral foundations of human life on the basis of freedom and brotherhood (Hofshi 1964a, 45),' on 'the negation of the rule of one person over another person (Hofshi 1964a, 150),' on eliminating 'differences of position and separating boundaries (Hofshi 1964a, 53),' and on eliminating 'exploiters and exploited (Hofshi 1964a, 72).' 'Free and equal people (Hofshi 1964a, 136),' he says, sought to form 'free congregations that willingly unite (Hofshi 1964a, 81)' in the spirit 'of mutual aid (Hofshi 1964a, 53)' in order 'to live in peace, love, and mutual understanding' without 'compulsion of any form (Hofshi 1964a, 45).'

Concretely, this 'spiritual and social revolutionization' of 'our daily life (Hofshi 1964a, 72)' was to be a 'human congregation constructed of cells (Hofshi 1964a, 81)' taking the form of cooperative (Hofshi 1964a, 72) 'free working villages' governed on anarchist principles.[3] Evoking Tolstoy, he argues that:

> If redemption comes to the world, it will not come about via revolutions and uprisings; it will not come about via external changes in the government or in the ownership of property but from a return to village life and agricultural labor. Distance from the earth, from the source of nourishment and vitality, is the cause of all the suffering and tragedy that has struck mankind from time immemorial. This is the cause of poverty and hunger on the one hand and, on the other, wealth and luxury which, in turn, has led to revolutions and counter-revolutions, wars, and all the horrors connected with them. If the day comes when people come to understand, know, and recognize their place in the world, casting from themselves the yoke of subjugation and tyranny that they laid upon themselves, then the world will be composed of a network of villages which shall create for themselves the necessary local industries in cooperation with other villages according to their needs. The city will be a sad memory from the days of human barbarity and ignorance.

Not the State, but the free working village, Hofshi thus contended, is the true answer to the modern social and political questions, especially to 'the dream of national revival (Hofshi 1964a, 63).'[4]

In sum, Hofshi's vision involved four basic principles. One, personalism and familiarity. By widening and deepening the life of the individual, the life of the community follows suite. Then, its members live as a family whose lives and property are intertwined, in social and economic equality. Two, labor; Hofshi believed that the sort of familial mutuality he anticipated could only be achieved through the mutual task of creatively sustaining human life. Three, spiritual development; because Hofshi believed — like other religious anarcho-pacifists considered here — that the revolution of the heart is the foundation of world-revolution, cultivating the former becomes an imperative. Finally, and perhaps most importantly, a commitment to applying the same ideals to others; if, he says, 'our external relations are not founded on the same principles as our life within the settlement, nothing new, or nothing at all will have been innovated (Hofshi 1964a, 60).' In other words, the utopian vision of agrarian anarchism must be extended beyond the Jewish community to include the other ethnic and national groups in the land. These represent the basic structure of Hofshi's vision for communal life in the anarchic form which he held was the only true solution to the violent and oppressive effects of the centralized state.

Conclusion

It may be that Zionism's 'center of gravity was transferred' from 'concrete labor and a simple, modest, way of life' to the altar of statecraft and the endeavor to normalize Jewish experience by making 'us like the rest of the nations (Hofshi 1964a, 256)' — a coinage that, like Heyn, Hofshi borrowed from the prophet Samuel as an expression of contempt for the ideal of human sovereignty. It may be that Hofshi's vision seems improbable and, given all that has transpired since 1948, even impossible. But 'fans of compulsion and central government' have always defamed such ideas, ambitions for a 'higher way of life (Hofshi 1964a, 136).' They are therefore neither more nor less present for us than they ever were; Hofshi's is a vision that ever awaits its visionaries. It is especially important, moreover, as a vision formulated not at the periphery of the Zionist movement, but (despite his vehement criticisms) very much at its center. Hofshi was part of a movement that played a major role in the development of modern Zionism. Having remained true (in his mind at least) to its original principles long after the tides turned and his comrades embraced more conventional notions of Jewish liberation involving state sovereignty and military strength, Hofshi held open the possibility of a Zionist alternative grounded in humanistic ideas of peaceful coexistence, loving mutual aide, and shared sovereignty. Arguably, in the wake of a history, that cannot simply be put in reverse, this is of far greater significance than any alternative to Zionism.

Notes

1 Strangely, a book-length study of the movement makes no mention of Hofshi's role (Bar-On 1996).

2 Prevailing scholarship ascribes this distinction to Joseph Abileah (Bing 1990; Epstein 1998). Abileah's trial was better publicized, but the article I have cited indicates that Hofshi was imprisoned in May 1948. Abileah was not sentenced until August of that year.

3 He wrote, for example, that he 'refused to join the regulations committee in Nahalal for my own reasons. What were they? I deny that human beings are able to make general laws and regulations for every plague, every mishap, every damage to the life of the community ... For those who know what is going on, is more needed? ... It is not the proposal of laws that leads to the end, but the end which generates the laws that it requires (Hofshi 1964a, 115).'

4 See Tolstoy's positive response to the idea of Jewish agricultural settlements in Palestine (Krauskopf 1911, 14, 19); cf. the comparison of modern Jewish and Gandhian-Tolstoyan views of redemptive labor (Chatterjee, 1997).

10

Aaron Shmuel Tamaret (1869–1931)

8 Rabbi Aaron Shmuel Tamaret, date unknown.

This is the touchstone distinguishing the true from the false prophet: when the true prophet stands up to share rebuke with his congregation, his teeth are on edge; he fears lest they toss him from the stage in their fury, for his rebuke is directed against them, against his own congregation. In contrast, the false prophet stands surely on his platform and lightheartedly glances about, basking in the appreciation of his congregation while he furiously rebukes others. (Tamaret 1992, 51–52)

The author of these lines, Aaron Shmuel Tamaret (1869–1931), was undoubtedly one of the true prophets, a twentieth-century Elijah who stood, as it were, on a Mt. Carmel all his own to castigate both the modern priests of Baal and also his own wavering congregation — the faithless and the men of faith alike. Interpreting *pure* faith as a valorization of individuality, and false or idolatrous faith as its destruction, he posed his unique understanding of Judaism against what he regarded as latter-day idolatries: nationalism, patriotism, statism, and militarism.

Born in a small village near the Belarusian city of Malecz into a rabbinic family of some repute, Tamaret was deeply shaped, not only by the bucolic atmosphere of village life, but also by the violence that disturbed it — both from within and from without. Struck by the inhumanity of his antisemitic neighbors and also by the cruelty and loss they themselves suffered — for instance, as conscripts during the Russo-Turkish War — this sensitive youth effectively became a pacifist of conscience even before he knew the word (Tamaret 1993, 162–163).

Having shown scholarly aptitude, Tamaret left home at an early age to study among the members of the *kollel* in Malecz itself (Tamaret 1993, 163), earning there his reputation as an *ilui*, a talmudic genius (Ben-Ezra 1978, 66–70). Married in 1886 into a rabbinic family from Milejczyce, a town near the Polish city of Bialystok, he studied under his father-in-law for two years before 'exiling himself to a place of Torah (M. Avot 4:7)' — in this case, to the Kollel ha-Perushim of Kovno. Founded by Israel Salanter, father of the Musar Movement, which placed great emphasis on ethical education, the Kollel would seem to have been an ideal destination for someone like Tamaret. By then, however, his horizons had expanded beyond the institutional capacities of the ultra-orthodox community. So he claimed, his peers spoke of nothing but obtaining *semikha* (rabbinic ordination), while he was concerned with 'struggle against ... wicked governments and negating war' by penetrating 'the human heart' with 'reason, understanding, and a sense of justice' — violent means being 'forms of murder forbidden by the Torah (Tamaret 1993, 164).'

Tamaret therefore left for the Valozyn Yeshiva (Ben-Ezra, 1978), which ignored practical rabbinics and focused on the study of Torah for its own sake. There, he became a close student of the famed R. Hayyim Soloveitchik

(Anonymous 1931a; Slodki 1938), and like many of his fellow students joined Hibbat Zion. After Valozyn's 1892 collapse, Tamaret returned home to Milejczyce, where he assumed rabbinic leadership after the death of his father in-law (Ben-Ezra, 1978). In spite of more prestigious opportunities — he was offered a teaching position in Chaim Tchernowitz's yeshiva in Odessa, declining it in spite of encouragement from none other than Hayyim Nahman Bialik (Ungerfeld 1954), and also a prominent rabbinic post in Warsaw (Ben-Ezra 1978) — he would remain in Milejczyce for the rest of his life.

Adopting the pseudonym '*Ehad ha-Rabanim ha-Margishim* (A Sensitive Rabbi),' Tamaret began publishing his (initially) pro-Zionist views after resettling in Milejczyce (Tamaret 1900a–l). He attended the 1900 WZO congress in London, but this proved profoundly disappointing. Put off by the way discussions about the relationship between Jewish national and religious identities were handled (he felt that the secularist elite behaved in a patronizing manner and had no real interest in sharing power with religious factions), he left alienated from the movement and determined to articulate against it 'a religious-ethical position based on the Torah, the prophets, and the traditional Jewish ethicists, one which has no part in statecraft or class politics, but attends to the purification of the human heart (Tamaret 1993, 167).' That being said, he — like several other religious Jewish anarchists — expressed sympathy throughout his life for the 'Zionism of R. Judah ha-Levi (Tamaret 1929, 76).' That is, one that embodies yearning not for the land where 'our fathers fought wars,' but the one where the prophets 'cast fire and brimstone on wars (Tamaret 1993, 173).'

Tamaret went on to develop these controversial ideas through six book-length publications and a handful of shorter editorial articles. His works include: *Judaism and Freedom* (1904), *The Ethics of the Torah and of Judaism* (1912), *The Pure Faith and the Religion of the Masses* (1912), *The Congregation of Israel and the Wars of the Gentiles* (1920), *The Hand of Aaron* (1923), and *Three Improper Couplings* (1930). With 'holy arrogance and great power (Anonymous 1930; Zeitlin 1930a),' Tamaret endeavored throughout these works to reframe the diaspora — not a tragedy, but a moral and political accomplishment (Weinstein 1978; Wokenfield 2007; Gendler 2010) — and to defend diaspora Judaism and Jewry (Tamaret 1908, 1911, 1913a-c; Anonymous 1931b), especially during and after the 1914 Russian Revolution as communities in the Pale of Settlement suffered under an increasingly antisemitic government (Tamaret 1993, 171–173; Ben-Ezra 1978; Tamaret 1920b–c).

Having devoted himself to his community and to his ideals for a lifetime, Tamaret fell ill sometime in the late spring or early summer of 1931 (Anonymous 1931a) and was taken to Warsaw for emergency treatment. With expressions of concern for the oppressed poor for whom 'nobody is concerned (Lipshitz 1991, 226)' on his lips, he died in the arms of Hillel Zeitlin of neo-hasidic fame — his, then, longtime friend and intellectual adversary.[1] Eulogized widely, though not always tenderly, Tamaret subsequently fell into relative obscurity. Untimely as they were, his ideas have only recently begun to attract the attention they richly deserve.

This chapter examines first Tamaret's typology of religious phenomena, in which he develops a dichotomy between idolatry and pure faith and describes religion as a middling phenomenon between them. It then considers the way he interprets nationalism, patriotism, statism, and militarism as modern forms of idolatry. The remainder of the chapter is devoted to elaborating Tamaret's response to these idolatries as a religiously committed Jew. This includes his revaluation of the diaspora, his account as to the anarchist structure of the diasporic Jewish community, and his understanding both as to the correct revolutionary path and the role that Jews ought to plan in seeing it through.

Idolatry, religion, and pure faith: Tamaret's typology of religious phenomena

As discussed in the introduction to this volume, critique of religion was among the central features of classical anarchist discourse. Anarchist thinkers objected to the hierarchical and authoritarian structure of religious institutions, equated religious faith with ignorance and subservience, and regarded both as impediments to human liberation. Mikhail Bakunin was among the most vehement, and also the most influential, of these anarchist critics of religion. In brief, he held that the relationship between God and humanity is mirrored within human relationships. As he understood it: mankind is nothing relative to God, therefore people are nothing relative to one another. He therefore concluded that atheism is a prerequisite of liberty and equality (Bakunin 1970, 34, 69, 78; 1971, 138, 142). Tamaret drew the same parallel but reached another conclusion.

Tamaret's analysis begins with a classical question: 'how did faith come to entail opposing elements: violence and murder on the one hand, and the soul's delight on the other (Tamaret 1912, 19)?' His answer began with the contention that religion is 'the expression of [human] self-recognition;' it reflects 'the way man understands himself and his place in the world.' As this standing changes, so too its religious manifestation. As it were, religious ideas are humanity's 'citizenship papers in the kingdom of creation (Tamaret 1992, 58–59).' In a surprisingly materialistic manner, Tamaret maintained that this depends on the degree of human control over natural forces; in other words, religious ideas are indexed to technological progress. 'When human self-consciousness first bloomed it brought nothing but sorrow,' he wrote. 'Surrounded by hordes of terrifying natural enemies,' forces of nature over which they had no control, primitive people saw themselves as negated 'before the order of heaven (Tamaret 1992, 59–60).' Therefore, they submitted passively to deities personifying what they could not control. For Tamaret, ancient paganism (*datot ha'aliliyot*) was grounded in lack of technological development, which meant lack of agency that was then translated into fatalism. As people gained the ability to 'conquer nature and extract from it [thir] needs,' they came to regard themselves, in contrast, as '*free citizens*' of creation. Then, the 'buds of true *faith* began to sprout (Tamaret 1992, 60)' — the character of faith being expressed through the Hebrew word for it, *emunah*, which suggests 'endurance and strength (Tamaret 1992, 116).' In contrast to paganism, faith was grounded in technological advancement, which created agency that was then translated into individuality and freedom.

To the parallel between technology and theology and the consequent dichotomy between paganism and faith, fatalism and freedom, corresponded, for Tamaret, to a political dichotomy; just as the 'kingdom of creation' assumes pagan and divine forms, so too human kingdoms. There are, Tamaret averred, 'two forms of earthly governance, of political citizenship: autocracy and democracy.' Under the first, people are 'bound and subjugated, formed only to administer to' others; under the second, they are 'free to wander the earth in its entirety, to suck at the breast of nature' as they see fit (Tamaret 1992, 61). Tyranny is pagan, liberty is the parallel of faith.

As Tamaret explained, the conquest of nature demanded organization. He contended that *technical* divisions of labor naturally ossified into *social* divisions of labor and that this created a conundrum. Progress demanded both a spirit emboldened by *emunah* and also one prepared to 'become the tool of another.' The solution: a hybrid called 'religion' that is 'infused with traces of divinity,' of faith, but nonetheless idolatrous in essence. Religion, he wrote:

> Strokes the cheek of the common man while whispering into his ear pleasant stories … that mankind is raised from angels, that he is a spark of God, that he can himself become a God if he so desires. The masses listen intently to this pleasant whispering; it drives them to ecstasy. All the while … religion infects him with paganism. For, after whispering to him about the importance of mankind, it tends to conclude as follows: mankind's importance, his prominence, obtains because he was chosen for and sanctified to the service of the Creator such that he ought do nothing more in life than kneel and bow to the God in heaven and to his holy ones, his representatives on earth. (Tamaret 1992, 62–63)

Religion ennobles mankind just enough to participate in the conquest of nature, but not enough to deliver them from their earthly masters. In this way, it divides humanity into two camps: masters, who 'enjoy divine freedom,' and slaves who, intoxicated by its appearance 'dance in a ring, so to speak, at someone else's wedding (Tamaret 1992, 74).' That is to say, it transforms this conquest from a mechanism of liberation into a mechanism of enslavement.

In essence, Tamaret concurred with Bakunin's judgment on *religion* and on *religious* conceptions of God, but blamed the problem on residual idolatry and proposed to resolve it through the restoration of pure faith. Tamaret's conception of religion — more so than pure idolatry — constitutes the theoretical ground of his treatment of nationalism, patriotism, statism, and militarism which, in his view, likewise offer the impression of liberation while in fact undermining it.

Modern idols and their worship: nationalism, patriotism, statism, and militarism

Tamaret was neither the first nor the last to draw the distinction between Jewish and pagan faiths; it is as old as the bible, in which the 'living God' of Israel, an active being that is attentive to human concern and that animates people, readying them for action (Deuteronomy 4:4), is contrasted with the 'idols of the nations' which, like untamed forces of nature, are depicted as blind and deaf, dead to all things human and deadening for 'those who fashion them (Psalms 135:15–18).' Nor was he the first to link the notion of *emunah* and individualism, or positive self-esteem; Maimonides, for instance, claimed long before him that the forty-year desert sojourn of the Israelites (the period during which Jewish faith was revealed) was mainly intended to purge them of their former docility (Guide 3:32). The novelty of Tamaret's contribution lies not only in its explicitness, but also in the radicalism with which he applies the analogy between idolatry (or its religious incarnations) and modern phenomena like nationalism, statism, militarism, and patriotism — the last of which I define, following Orwell (1968, 362), as an identification not with people or political entities, but *places*.

As we saw earlier, Tamaret treated religion as a sort of ruse. There is another ruse which must be understood in order to frame his reflections on nationalism, patriotism, statism, and militarism; it involves his estimation of human nature. Tamaret interpreted the scriptural verse 'God made man upright; but they have sought out many contrivances (Ecclesiastes 7:29).' In a line of reasoning resonant with, though not necessarily influenced by, Rousseau's *Discourse on Inequality* (1755) and Diderot's *Supplement to the Voyage of Bougainville* (1796), Tamaret contended that there are two types of evil. People have an animal nature and are often overcome by violent passions; crimes arising from them are neither systematic nor justified. The criminal 'recognizes that he perpetrates evil' and does not persuade 'others to abandon their own values.' Subject, however, to the corrupting forces of civilization, the human mind can be perverted so that evil comes to be regarded as *good*. As it were, it 'walks upright in the streets of the city and struts about without meeting any opposition (Tamaret 1968)' — indeed, it is applauded. Like Rousseau, he regarded the process of organizing human society as a corrupting force on moral sensibility. Like Diderot, he believed that suppressing natural and ephemeral outbursts of violence via the process of systematization only leads to system-wide outbursts of greater intensity and severity. This civilized barbarism, combined with the idolatrous force of religion, framed Tamaret's reflections on nationalism, patriotism, statism, and militarism. We shall examine each phenomenon separately.

Arguably influenced by the same Fichtean sources as Zalkind (see above), Tamaret appealed to a corporate analogy in his account of nationalism. A healthy body is characterized by mutualism: the vitality of the whole depends on the vitality of its parts. Therefore, each part 'both feeds and is fed (Tamaret 1905, 83),' taking what it needs and leaving the rest. The same goes for a healthy society: recognizing each individual as the work of God, people 'treat each other like brothers (Tamaret 1905, 86),' benefitting from one another in a way that exhausts none such that 'there are neither oppressors nor oppressed, consumers nor consumed (Tamaret 1905, 83).' Just as the healthy body does not sacrifice one of its parts for the sake of another, so too a healthy society (Tamaret 1905, 84). Continuing this corporate analogy, he described nationalism as a sort of 'anti-vaccine.' If a vaccine is a pathogen in reduced form that immunizes the body *against disease*, nationalism functions the same way but in reverse. It is a sort of 'euthogen' in reduced form — *care*, but only for one's own — that immunizes the body politic against the 'plague' of humane feeling. Corrupt people 'utilize the power of generosity for cruelty, the power of love and brotherhood for enmity, the power of connection for separation (Tamaret 1905, 82).

From this nationalist 'euthogen,' the body politic contracts a sort of autoimmune disorder and turns against itself. Directing the flow of hatred outward, to eliminate 'foreign' bodies, strong cells gather around themselves 'piles and piles of weaker cells (Tamaret 1905, 86)' by appealing to the 'closeness of brotherhood' they supposedly share. The latter then 'become food, to be chewed and digested for the benefit' of the strong, who are themselves ultimately 'swallowed by those still stronger (Tamaret 1905, 84).' Thus:

> All of the despicable inclinations of individual members of the nation are
> focused in a single direction, constituting a flooding river of national egoism

that is embodied in the magistrates of the parliament who sit and devise statist schemes in the name of the good of the people as a whole, something which really means: I am, and there is nothing other than me. (Tamaret 1905, 24; Isaiah 47:8; Zephania 2:15)

Tamaret shows that nationalism is grounded in an 'alimentary' or 'sacrificial' logic whereby, for the sake of a supposedly common good, some individuals and individual groups are consumed and absorbed, *used* by others — nationalism is like a tumor which consolidates the vital force of the body politic that it simultaneously destroys. As he dramatizes the situation, it is as if leader-tumors declare 'individual people do not have the right to live and endure! Long live the nation! Long live the state! Let humanity go to hell (Tamaret 1905, 87)!'

While Tamaret described nationalism as 'coarse egoism (Tamaret 1905, 90),' it is crucial to understand that it is a *group* egoism in which the individual, identifying him or herself with the whole, disappears. Hence its idolatrous hue. There is no difference, he contended, between nationalist faith and:

Pagan faiths, which conclude that mankind was created for the sake of some god or another. On the basis of such faiths, we have no guarantee against the elite becoming agents of the angel of silence [death], concluding their debates with a resolution to destroy individual human lives, to offer, on the altar of the law, real human life, flesh and blood, for the sake of the figurative life which priests of one god or another speak of. (Tamaret 1905, 85)

In this respect, modern nationalism is very much a 'religious' phenomenon in Tamaret's sense of the word: a dangerous hybrid of paganism and pure faith. Its constitutive egoism gives the impression of liberty while actually destroying it, annihilating the self and subjugating it to the whims of other people by way of its fictive aggrandizement.

Tamaret rejected patriotism and statism on similar grounds. Ancient paganism, he wrote, was not merely a passive reaction to inadequate agency; it was also existential: deficiency was experienced as an active need to serve something greater. Likewise was 'the god known as Birthplace' created to fill an existential abyss. In a manner reminiscent of Weber and the Frankfurt School theorists that followed him (Adorno and Horkheimer 2002, 94–136), Tamaret wrote of a world disenchanted by enlightenment rationalism and of souls 'progressively emptied out (Tamaret 1920a, 16–17)' by its egoism yet unsatisfied by distracting entertainments. Rather than addressing the problem, however, its symptoms are superficially assuaged.

In essence, Tamaret argued that the spiritual desolation of the modern egoist is alleviated by extending himself over others by force. Extracting recognition from without, his own frail sense of being is confirmed; conversely, 'he who expresses his somethingness by waving around a sword expresses nothing more than his nothingness and his degradation.' Ability alone becomes the measure of existence. Yet, ability is optimized when pooled. So construed, individual being is paradoxically solidified when it disappears into the collective. Thus are modern people:

> Prepared to transfer his particular glory, his particular self-inflation, into a collective store of arrogance called the state, which enables them to join all their individual swords into one large sword that extends over a territory ... to hang this sword on the thigh of the giant idol called the birthplace.

'Hewn from the collective,' children of the motherland, citizens of the state, welcome abasement at 'the feet of their god in order to' partake of its conceit; when its mighty sword flashes, each 'experiences this as if he himself had lifted his sword (Tamaret 1920a, 19).' Being is experienced vicariously through the power of state over an expanding homeland. Appealing to a strikingly scatological image, Tamaret explains it elsewhere as follows. The world of today, he says:

> is like a tall ladder that is built of rungs: one on top of the other, one below the other. The head of each citizen is tucked under the tail of another who is above him, while the tail of each is nestled on the head of one below him. Thus, is each person in one respect a lord and in another respect a slave. Before the one above him, each squirms along like a worm crawling through garbage while at the same time trampling someone else like a bear.

The disgraced souls that are party to it are 'half prideful and half ashamed,' but 'none are free (Tamaret 1920a, 47).' In this way, 'spiritual plagues like patriotism (Tamaret 1923, 6)' and statism, as 'racist, statist, nationalism (Tamaret 1920a, 82),' constitute 'religious' phenomena from a structural standpoint. All respond to the existential component of an agency deficit. All fraudulently proffer the liberty of pure faith while liquidating it in fact by subordinating the individual to the collective.

Let us now consider the question of militarism. As we have already seen, nation, state, and homeland function according to an alimentary logic. The weak allow themselves to be consumed by the strong, the particular by the collective, so as to partake in its strength and thus be confirmed in being. This strength is expressed through conquest of the foreigner: the foreigner within, who is excluded from the nascent body politic, and the foreign enemy without. This fraudulent self-by-other-means is organized around the 'collective sword' and asserted through conquest; militarism serves as its binding force. As Tamaret put it, war is the worship that the modern gods of nationalism, patriotism, and statism demand (Tamaret 1920a, 16).' In this way, war permeates 'the knot of politics: either war in the simple sense, blood and fire and the shooting of real bullets ... or, at least, a war of words, of mutual jealousy and rancor (Tamaret 1905, 26).'

To elaborate further, we may briefly consider Tamaret's account as to the origin of war. People, he explained, have long regarded war as an inevitability. The ancients saw it as an earthly manifestation of heavenly conflicts. Having killed the gods, modern people saw it as the result of natural hostilities — among nations and races, or between classes. Yet, he insisted, it 'doesn't matter whether the mask they wear is made of heavenly decrees or the decrees of nature;' nationalist, racist, or classist, these explanations reduce agency to perceived necessity and in this way repeat the same old idolatrous error.

Operating on the sacrificial logic that ends sanctify means (Tamaret 1993, 167), men are sent 'onto the fields of slaughter (Tamaret 1929, 6)' in the name of some presumed common good relative to which the value of their own lives is subordinated. If before neither the forces of nature nor the forces of heaven, modern man negates himself before the forces of nationalism, statism, and patriotism through militarism.

Ultra-orthodoxy versus Zionism: two sides of the same coin

Although they disagree on how to heal it, ultra-orthodox communities and the Zionist movement agree that *galut*, exile, is ultimately a 'festering wound (Tamaret 1992, 87)' in need of salve. Tamaret took the orthodox position to be embodied in an exchange recorded in the talmud. It is reported that many Jews reacted to the destruction of the temple by renouncing meat and wine. They deemed it improper to enjoy what was once part of the Temple service. R. Yehoshua discerned nihilistic undertones in their asceticism and rejected the proposal, reminding them that by the same logic fruit, bread, and even water should be eschewed — these also had ritual functions (Bava Batra 60b).

According to Tamaret, this exchange arose from a basic disagreement as to the nature of religion. R. Yehoshua believed that 'you who held fast to the Lord your God are all alive today (Deuteronomy 4:4)' — that is, 'connection to the living God, to pure faith, provides support, strength, and power to those who hold tight to it (Tamaret 1992, 81).' It is meant to affirm and empower human life. In contrast, the ascetics held that 'man was created for his religion, to be enslaved by it (Tamaret 1992, 76).' It alone being 'your life and the length of your days (Deuteronomy 30:20),' they concluded that without the land of Israel or the Temple, without the ability to observe the whole Torah, the days of Israel had come to an end. Thus, they resolved to 'gradually liquidate (Tamaret 1992, 78)' the people through a program of extreme renunciation Tamaret calls 'neurotic piety (Tamaret 1992, 76–78),'[2] which extinguishes 'every spark of self-awareness (Tamaret 1992, 82)' and ensures 'the negation of humanity and its submission to hidden powers (Tamaret 1992, 76)' — supernatural and otherwise.

As Tamaret told the story, R. Yehoshua's position initially held sway. Yet, because in exile 'divine phenomena did not appear anew' and 'persecution and suffering' became the norm, 'the echo of pure faith progressively weakened, while the crushing and oppressive spirit' took its place and 'came to govern Jewish life (Tamaret 1992, 83).' The 'shoots of paganism took root (Tamaret 1992, 76).' Judaism ceased to be a *faith* and came to emit the 'scent of nihilism (Tamaret 1992, 74)' like any other *religion*. Concerning this shift, Tamaret proclaimed:

> Away 'religion' together with its cathedrals and bell towers which she rings and announces 'honor thy tyrants!' ... Away neurotic piety, which curls itself up like a worm and quietly inserts itself behind the stove in the study hall in Radin and which ... prays for the well being of the 'whip' which ensures that its fastidiousness survives. Away the plague ... called 'a totally pious Jew (*a gants frumer id*)'. (Tamaret 1992, 116)

This is an interesting passage for several reasons. One, Tamaret implicitly personified the nihilism of neurotic piety. Like Alexandrov (1907, 3–4), he saw R. Yisrael Meir Kagan — who headed the Yeshiva in Radin and is still revered by Lithuanian Jews, especially for his work on laws governing speech, in which he takes so extreme a position as to render free exchange impossible — as its embodiment. Two, he explicitly associated *Jewish* neurotic piety with the church, as if to say that Jewish hyper-legalism is a mirror image of Christianity and, therefore, a paradoxical reflection of Christianization. Three, he referenced the 'prayer for the government' which — despite its biblical roots (Jeremiah 29:7) — he interpreted as an expression of idolatrous submission to power. In short, ultra-orthodoxy is cast as a pagan regression from the pure and rebellious *faith* of Israel consisting in a resolution to negate the people using its *religion*. Political Zionism, which stood instead for the negation of *exile*, represents the foil to this approach (Ratzabi 1995).

Tamaret characterized Zionist embrace of nationalism, patriotism, statism, and militarism as 'ape-like imitation of Western customs' or, echoing the prophet Samuel, of seeking the dubious 'distinction of being *like the rest of the nations* (Tamaret 1905, 33–34).' Appealing to midrashic accounts attesting to the Abrahamic destruction of patrilineal idols (GR38:13), Tamaret wrote of a 'Jewish vocation of swimming against the tide' — especially *this* tide. He interpreted the verse 'go out from your land, from your birthplace, and from your father's house (Genesis 12:1)' as a divine imperative to part even from intangible idols like nationalism, patriotism, statism, and militarism

(Tamaret 1920a, 73–74). Zionists, in contrast, court this 'poisonous god (Tamaret 1905, 60),' thus constituting 'a plague on the Jewish people' threatening a 'liquidation of Judaism (Tamaret 1926c).'

One element of this liquidation is Zionist acquiescence to the supposed pagan viewpoint that the individual is subordinate to the collective and that people are therefore expendable. The Torah, he said, 'despises separation among people' and cannot abide by the conclusion that nationalist monstrosities are inevitable and that Jews may therefore partake in 'racial division and *exploitation* (Tamaret 1905, 90).' Neither does it cohere with the 'despicable doctrine of patriotism' that 'sows death and hatred into the relation between peoples (Tamaret 1992, 51–52).' Similarly, Tamaret rejected Zionist adoption of the abominable 'way of the state (Tamaret 1929, 51),' which treats human blood as 'a form of transferable property with which its owner can, without impediment, do with as he pleases (Tamaret 1905, 12).' Finally, Tamaret considered Zionist militarism a 'betrayal of our national ethic' as expressed in the prophetic utterance 'not by force, not by strength, but by my spirit (Zechariah 4:6)' — that is, he explained, 'not with armies and not with raw power (Tamaret 1926a).' To behave otherwise is to disgrace 'the image of God that is in man (Tamaret 1920a, 22)' and, in this way, an act of idolatry.

Another element of this liquidation is the related issue of centralization, which has both geographical and political aspects. Jewish identity, Tamaret maintains, is fundamentally grounded in Torah, which 'cannot be confined to a single land,' for scripture teaches that it is 'longer than the earth's circumference (Job 11:9; Tamaret 1923, 71).' True 'Judaism has its center fixed in the heart (Tamaret 1985, 60);' it cannot 'be confined to or materialized in a definite territory (Tamaret 1929, 71).' The idea of a national home or a spiritual center constitutes a 'spirituality of the center,' which Tamaret considers to be fundamentally pagan in character and describes in terms evocative of the Mosaic response to the ancient sin of the golden calf (Tamaret 1985, 60–61).

The problem of centralization also arises in relation to the question of political power. The anti-authoritarian bent of Tamaret's thought can be traced back to his earliest writings, in which his hostility to secular authority quickly extended itself to human authority in general. Whenever someone takes the lead, he says, 'always, the question will be raised: who made you head? On what basis do you take it upon yourself to respond to the lack of a center? You want me to obey you? Why not the opposite?' The Torah, he says, already serves an organizing function, and 'its authority over the people comes from God who alone has the right to rule over us (Tamaret 1901a).' As for its practical application, Tamaret maintained that as they 'have always done,' the people will 'produce groupings without organization and administration ... without police and taskmasters (Tamaret 1901b).' In short, a factional power struggle became a *struggle against power*. Contra Zionist vanguardism (Tamaret 1905, 3), which divided the 'people into two camps, those who lead and those who are led (Tamaret 1905, 53),' Tamaret contended that Israel must 'purify and cleanse itself from within of ... the Leviathan (Tamaret 1920a, 73)' because 'Jewish identity is not constructed around a state; its spirit and form is preserved without the coarse sheath of sovereignty (Jeremiah 35:7; Tamaret 1920a, 74).'

A final element of this liquidation has to do with the idea of Jewish chosenness as a real moral vocation and responsibility. When Zionists 'take refuge in the shade of the new *ashera* called Hebrew Nationalism (Tamaret 1905, 95),' or embrace the sodomite ethos of 'what is mine is mine, what is yours is yours (Avot 5:13; Tamaret 1929, 71)' underlying patriotism, it discredits the very idea of justice. Not only did Israel introduce the world to notions like the 'image of God' that *all* people share, and that the earth was given to *all* 'the children of men (Psalms 115:16; Tamaret 1905, 37),' but Israel has suffered the most from neglect of these principles. To then affirm the correctness of opposing principles is to support transgressors (Tamaret 1929, 72). Likewise, when the only 'people that has until now rejected the sword (Tamaret 1926b),' relying 'solely on its moral strength (Tamaret 1929, 39)' and dreaming that 'in the end' humanity will turn from its errors (Tamaret 1926b), suddenly behaves like 'a pack of wolves (Tamaret 1926a),' it is 'a death blow to Isaiah's ideal of 'nation shall not raise a sword against nation (Isaiah 2:4; Tamaret 1926a)' — especially when that same people suffered from the sword most.

All this being said, Tamaret — like other figures studied in this volume — expressed sympathy for a certain type of Zionism. 'Statist Zionists, he explained, 'yearn for the land on which our *kings* walked, the kings of Israel, while the people have always yearned for the land on which the *prophets*, the prophets of Israel, walked (Tamaret 1920a, 77).' Therefore, he wrote:

> I sympathize with Jewish pioneers who establish themselves in the land of Israel ... but on the condition that the land of Israel which a Jew yearns to revive and to settle upon is ... not the place on which our fathers fought wars, but the land [on which the prophets] cast fire and brimstone on wars. (Tamaret 1993, 173)

'In keeping with the spirit of its salvation,' he concluded elsewhere, the people of Israel 'should revive the work of the old Hibbat Zion (Tamaret 1905, 37)' in the spirit of Judah ha-Levi, not of Trumpeldor (Tamaret 1929, 76).

A vision of pure faith: anarcho-diasporic transvaluation of *galut*

As noted in earlier chapters, efforts to challenge strictly negative conceptions of *galut* like those described in the preceding section and to cast it in a more positive light are not unheard of in the history of Jewish thought. Indeed, the idea goes back at least to the talmud, where it is suggested that Israel was exiled in order to attract converts (Pesahim 87b). Such efforts, however, neither contradict nor exclude messianic notions about the ultimate restoration of sovereignty and the ingathering of exiles. Tamaret stands out because his conception of *emunah* consists in a *total* transvaluation of the *galut*: it is understood neither as an evil, nor as a means to some final end, but as an end unto itself. Exile becomes redemption.

This shift is indicated by the verse 'I have put off my coat; how shall I put it on? I have washed my feet; how shall I defile them (Song of Songs 5:3)?' According to Tamaret, it expresses a radical reversal of traditional Jewish attitudes toward the diaspora. State and homeland become forms of defilement from which the congregation of Israel has been cleansed. In other words, Tamaret called for what Anna Elena Torres has called 'Anarchist diasporism' — 'the anti-statism of stateless peoples (Torres 2016: xiii–xv).' Interpreting the phrases 'I have put off my coat' and 'I have washed my feet,' Tamaret asked: which coat has been removed? Which filth has been cleansed? He answered as follows:

> The bow of our strength was broken together with our arm of state two thousand years ago. Since then, we have organized ourselves so as to live without a Jewish government. Having tasted once the death of a state, *we merited to undress our national soul from that ugly body, from state machinations, from dealing with kings and princes, which are like a body and a sheath for the soul of the people.* (Tamaret 1905, 98)

The coat that has been removed, the filth that has been cleansed, is state and homeland. Accordingly, he interpreted the questions 'how shall I put it on?' and 'how shall I defile them?' as follows. How can a people thus liberated 'wish to go back and to be embodied in the ugly material of the state (Tamaret 1905, 100)?' Here, we see that against the grain of tradition as expressed among Zionists and the orthodox alike, Tamaret regards exile as a manifestly positive transition from moral contamination to moral purity (Weinstein 1978).

To fully appreciate just how radical a shift this is, it is necessary to observe the way in which Tamaret retold Jewish history from Egyptian servitude through the fall of the Second Hebrew Commonwealth. Building on his distinction between natural and artificial violence, Tamaret contended that slavery is an example of the latter and that this is indicated by the verse 'let us deal shrewdly with them … otherwise in the event of war they may join our enemies in fighting against us and rise from the ground (Exodus 1:10).' Pretending 'that they were threatened by the Israelites,' the Egyptians 'bent their bodies to the ground (Tamaret 1968).' Theirs was a calculated crime for which rational justification was sought; not a sudden crime of passion. Thus, it embodied the idolatrous tendency to subordinate individual lives to some higher good or greater force.

The 'idolatrous' character of this shift is most evident in Tamaret's striking interpretation of its theological ground. In Jewish tradition (Rashi, Genesis 1:1), the divine attributes of creation and judgement is represented by the name 'Elohim (God),' while the attribute of mercifully sustaining creation is represented by the name 'Yahweh (Lord).' He held that while Abraham undertook to imitate God in both respects (Tamaret 1912, 81–82; 87–89), 'by my name, the Lord, I did not make myself *fully* known to them (Exodus 6:3)' — that is, Abraham did not understand it sufficiently to communicate its meaning to others. His students therefore neglected the quality of mercy and concluded that 'just as might makes right in the conquest of nature,' so too among men. In this way the Abrahamic *emunah* (which, as we saw above, goes hand in hand with human agency vis-a-vis the forces of nature) became Abrahamic *religion*; corrupted with idolatrous element that seemed to permit 'conquering the conquerors and forcing them to labor on one's behalf (Tamaret 1912, 87).'

As Tamaret told the story, Abrahamic religion reached its zenith in Egypt, where Pharaoh — in the belief that he had divine sanction (Tamaret 1912, 86) — systematically pressed people into servitude to 'conquer nature on his behalf (Tamaret 1912, 84).' Thus did he interpret the verse 'who is the Lord that I should heed him (Exodus 5:2)?' as a rejection of the 'beggar (*shnorer*) god' who proclaims liberty to enslaved folk and thus hinders the sacred task of labor, of conquering nature, in the name of Elohim. This perversion of Abraham's legacy also accounted, Tamaret contended, for Israelite acquiescence. Interpreting rabbinic traditions as to their unworthiness for redemption (ER 13:28), he wrote that over time the people 'came to respect the power of the fist which their masters used (Tamaret 1912, 40).' That is, they considered violence and domination to be theologically justified — apathy regarding the beaten Hebrew slave (Exodus 2:11) being taken for a case in point.

On Tamaret's reading, therefore, the ten plagues served a threefold function. One, they demonstrated the divine attribute of mercy (Exodus 6:5; Tamaret 1912, 88). Accordingly, they demonstrated how utterly God loathes 'that most vile falsehood, the domination of one person by another (Tamaret 1968).' Most importantly, they served to interrupt the cycle of violence and make way for a new vision. Anticipating themes later developed in Benjamin's

Critique of Violence (1968, 277–300), he interpreted rabbinic traditions about the 'angel of destruction' that knows no boundaries once it is released (Mekhilta 13:17) as follows. While it would have been possible for Moses to incite a slave revolt and thus to achieve freedom via natural causes, God intervened miraculously:

> In order not to give permission to the destroyer *within them*, for once having permission there will be no distinguishing between righteous and wicked, and from 'defender' one becomes in the end 'aggressor' ... [Thus,] your abstention from any participation in the vengeance upon Egypt will prevent the plague of vengeance from stirring the power of the destroyer which is in you yourselves (Tamaret 1968).

This is Tamaret's understanding as to the meaning of '*I* will go through the land of Egypt (Exodus 12:12)' — God brought Israel out of Egypt with a 'mighty hand' so that Israelite hands could relinquish might. As it were, so that Egypt could be brought out of Israel.

Sinaic revelation constituted the apex of God's rebuttal to Egypt. For one, it took place in the middle of a desolate wilderness, 'without a state and without an organized army,' thus communicating the 'negation and the absolute nothingness of material power (Tamaret 1920a, 28).' In this condition, Israel was prepared to receive a Torah existing to instill the heart with a 'love of justice' and a 'hatred of evil (Amos 5:15; Tamaret 1912, 89).' Tamaret interpreted the first of the ten commandments — 'I the Lord am your God who brought you out of the land of Egypt, the house of bondage (Exodus 20:2)' — as a manifesto of *emunah*. Building on a longstanding theme in biblical hermeneutics (Exodus 34:6), Tamaret emphasized that the *Lord* spoke, announcing himself as a merciful redeemer and not simply as the creator-God of a natural order in which the strong swallow the weak. His take cut through centuries of debate over whether the first of the ten commandments is mainly about what God *is*, or what God *does*.[3] Foreshadowing thinkers like Levinas (1987, 153–173), for whom God signifies an ethical relation and not a being, Tamaret followed a quasi-Sabbatean line of reasoning, distinguishing between the inscrutable God and the 'God of Israel' disclosed at Sinai.[4] The latter, he explained, is identical to its moral attributes as expressed in having extracted Israel from the 'house of bondage;' namely: 'justice and uprightness and, above all, *hatred of the coarse power of the fist ... of the raw power of violence, hatred of man's rule over man to his detriment* (Tamaret 1920a, 126).'

R. Joshua b. Levi once punned 'incised (*harut*) upon the tablets (Exodus 32:16)' to suggest that there is freedom (*herut*) only found through Torah (Avot 6:3). Tamaret understood this freedom in *positive* terms; he considered it irreducible to *mere* liberation (Tamaret 1912, 33). If, he explained, freedom is treated as something 'held by others, from whom it must be taken,' then it has no foundation other than ability;' that is, the ability to seize it. In other words, reducing freedom to liberty implies an ethic of 'might makes right' — not repudiation of a perverse ethos, but simply its reversal. Mere liberation, he continued, does not guarantee that the former slave 'will not himself become an oppressor' — especially if he or she came by it by violent means. Because he who stands with a 'sword hanging from his thigh indicates that' he himself 'is hanging from his sword,' that his sense of self is bound up in it. This means that he is subject to the same inner desolation, the same idolatry of vicarious-being that plagues adherents of nationalism, statism, patriotism, and militarism (Tamaret 1920a, 42–44).

Tamaret defined the freedom of the Torah as the work of a 'people contracting ... to live intimately with the divine presence (Tamaret 1920a, 32, 35).' That is, as a form of freedom determined from within, 'needing no external confirmation.' It need not be seized from others and, therefore, operates outside of the ethic of 'might makes right.' In this way it represented a guarantee that liberated people would 'not themselves become oppressors' and could *therefore* be said to constitute 'an emphatic curse upon the despotic kings and princes (Tamaret 1920a, 45–46)' — it was not a reversal of roles but a rejection of the system itself. This is how Tamaret interpreted the biblical vision of a 'priestly kingdom (Exodus 19:6).' In the wilderness, 'without a state and without an organized army,' Israel undertook a 'complete withdrawal ... from the sheath of material nationalism,' from the state and from all its accompanying institutions. They lived by 'the Torah of exile ... the Torah as it is understood among the exiled (Tamaret 1920a, 42).'

Tamaret applied both his characterization of the Torah and his idealization of the period of desert wandering to a radical extreme. Contrary to rabbinic consensus, according to which the centralization of Israelite government was deemed obligatory (Sanhedrin 20b) — or, even idealized (Neusner 2007; Cohn 2008) — Tamaret followed Isaac Abravanel in adopting a literal reading of 1 Samuel chapter eight and therefore represented the establishment of the monarchy as a national failure, as a confirmation of the Mosaic prophecy that Israel would 'grow haughty and ... forget the Lord (Deuteronomy 8:14).' The divine presence, he said, was gradually 'repulsed and driven away from them by the coarse statist spirit that then took hold of them (Tamaret 1920a, 29).' Accordingly, he spoke of David's 'kingly, tyrannical soul' and ascribed the same characterization to Solomon (Tamaret 1920a, 31). A 'king of peace,' he wrote, 'remains a king;' Solomon merely expressed the 'sovereign disposition to extend [oneself] over others' in a more subtle form, by a 'magisterial pat on the back (Tamaret 1920a, 31)' that said everything without having to put his military on display. Perhaps most surprisingly, he represented their ambition to construct the Jerusalem Temple as 'better suited to the soul of a king than that of a pious man.' The Temple, he contended, 'supported the authority of the kings by serving as a charm, drawing the people to their side (Tamaret 1920a, 33).'

Therefore, far from lamenting the destruction of the first and second Hebrew Commonwealths, Tamaret celebrated it. On his account, Babylonian captivity disabused the people of 'their statist arrogance,' thus restoring 'the divine presence to its place in hearts that were isolated and numb (Tamaret 1920a, 33).' This shift, he explained, was embodied by the restoration of the Torah to its central role as the organizing factor in Jewish life (the mishnah was codified during this period). Indeed, he contended that after returning to the land, religious leaders of the day resisted the reestablishment of Synagogue and State alike, projects ultimately undertaken only in response to Persian pressure (Tamaret 1920a, 34). For this reason, they 'did not press for a war of liberation' when the Romans later took over, nor when they destroyed the Temple and carted away the sacred furniture. As he articulated it, 'we took the ... substance of those implements, the holy spirit;' their material container being of no significance at all. The same goes for exile: Israel was driven from 'the earthly foundation, the territory.' It was then that 'the people of Israel grew wings of liberation,' divesting itself of 'the remaining traces of the ugly husk, the tools of material nationalism (Tamaret 1920a, 36).'

As Tamaret saw it, redemption is not the *abrogation* of exile; *it is exile* in the sense that it represents a restoration of exodus from Egypt and the way of life that took shape in the wilderness. By 'annexing exile' Israel became a 'mobile civilization (Tamaret 1923, 8)'[5] dependent 'on no land, no king, and no prince (Tamaret 1920a, 67).' *Therefore*, it was freed to once again undertake its true mission: 'spreading justice and uprightness, hatred for the oppressor and mercy for the oppressed (Tamaret 1912, 127).' In short, the 'exile of the divine presence' means 'the divine presence of exile (Tamaret 1920a, 24)' — it means stateless anti-statism or, following Anna Elena Torres' (2016) coinage, anarcho-diasporism.[6]

Institutions of Jewish anarcho-diasporism

Having accounted for Tamaret's annexation of exile, and his unequivocal rejection of the Jewish statism both ancient and (by implication) modern, it is worth considering his ideal vision for diaspora life. This includes communal institutions, modalities of leadership, and public ritual.

Building on Hegel (1975, 692), Kropotkin and Landauer treated civic architecture as the embodiment of communal values. They identified the cathedral as a preeminent expression of the mutuality that characterized the medieval commune (Kropotkin 1902, 211; Landauer 2010, 127–133). Abba Gordin — a leading figure among Russian anarchists during and after the 1917 revolution who later emigrated to the United States, where he played a similar role, editing several anarchist journals and publishing a number of Yiddish-language books — applied the same idea to the Jewish *beyt midrash*, or study hall (Nedava 1974), where, he contended, an 'inter-individual' entity called the 'congregation of Israel' collectively articulated its norms independently of the state. As Gordin (1940, 40–41, 165–169) conceived it, this cooperative institution ought to serve as a model for others; thus he positioned the Jewish community at the cultural core of world revolution (Gordin 1940, 170–180).

Referencing the legendary meeting of R. Yohanon b. Zakkai and Vespasian, the Roman commander who sacked Jerusalem (Gittin 56b), during which the sage secured the rabbinic academy in Yavneh rather than attempting to save Jerusalem, Tamaret articulated a similar vision. As he interpreted it, R. Yohanon was not a collaborator but a rebel. In keeping with the vocation of a 'nation of priests,' he stood against everything Rome represented by rejecting the state, its capital city, and its temple in favor of the Torah and the *beyt midrash* in which it is studied. 'So long as the voice of Jacob is heard in the synagogues and houses of study,' he wrote, 'the hands of Esau have no authority (Pesikta Zuta, Genesis 27:22; Tamaret 1920a, 36).'

More than as a place of resistance, Tamaret saw the *beyt midrash* as an institution both reflective and productive of communal cohesion. 'When a Jew enters the *beyt midrash* to present himself before He who rests his name thereon, he feels that he has entered into society with his brothers (Tamaret 1912, 24).' Seeking intimacy with the divine presence in the proverbial 'four cubits of the law (Berakhot 8a; Tamaret 1920a, 37),' they spread it also to 'all the Jewish homes connected to it.' United in this way, Tamaret contended, Jews were able to resist the forces of assimilation and maintain themselves as a distinct community. This he held to be significant, not as an end unto itself, but because in doing so they kept alive the diaspora as a living ideal; had they assimilated, the diaspora would have come to an end (Tamaret 1920a, 38).

Beyond its institutional value, the *beyt midrash* is also norm-productive — as Gordin put it, it generates collectively determined 'social-ethical teachings.' Tamaret elaborated at greater length, articulating a vision of voluntary law organized around the notion that the 'man shall live (Leviticus 18:5)' by the law and not die by it (Sanhedrin 74a), which he took to imply that the law exists for mankind and not the reverse. Thus, he wrote:

> I recognize no duties (*hovot*) in the world; a person must be free of duty. Even the precepts of the Torah are called commands (*mizwot*), not duties. They are

called commands only in order to *sweeten* these actions, for a person is pleased to fulfill the will of God above ... How could it possibly be appropriate to speak of duties where people are concerned, the creation made in the image of God? Just as the Creator is free in all of his actions, so too people have no duties; not even duties involving good deeds. Rather, it is fitting for a person to *will* good deeds. Perhaps this is the idea of '[I adjure you, O daughters of Jerusalem, by the gazelles, and by the hinds of the field], that you awaken not, nor stir up love, until it please (Song of Songs 3:5)' — i.e. until you want to do it. (Tamaret 1986, 220)

Like Kropotkin, who in works like *Mutual Aid* highlighted the force of custom as an alternative to the laws of state from an anthropological perspective, Tamaret spoke as an insider to a particular folk, emphasizing the same: *halakha* (Jewish law) as a freely willed system of folk law that must be promulgated in a manner consistent with its essence, freedom (Tamaret 1992, 115). That means:

Sanctify God's name by refraining from stepping over the heads of the holy people like the barbaric Zionist intelligentsia. When they come to enact their reforms, they must endeavor to remove from their work the image of guardianship and rule over others. They must encourage free development by 'adorning themselves' in such a way that others are naturally moved to follow suite and to undertake beneficial actions. (Tamaret 1905, 37)

In short, leadership means serving as a living example (Tamaret 1992, 116). Above all, it means heeding the fourth commandment, which prohibits idolatry and which — in keeping with his understanding of thereof — Tamaret interpreted as a reminder not to behave like a 'cossack of religion (Tamaret 1992, 115–116),' forcing one's fellow 'to be responsible for commandments against his will (Tamaret 1968).'

That being said, Tamaret upheld the value of *halakhic* practice robustly construed. In reflecting on traditional distinctions between precepts regulating relations between people and precepts regulating relations with God (M. Yoma 8:9), he held that 'commandments governing the relations between man and God were given by the Creator in order to widen the human heart so that it loves and feels mercy for others (Tamaret 1912, 54).' Subject to command, mankind is 'regarded as substantial, as something which occupies a place;' naturally, he extends the same regard to others, empathizing with 'everything created in the image of God.' For this reason, Tamaret insisted on the integrity of the law as a whole, *including* its ritual elements: negating precepts regulating relations with God is to 'destroy the source of human dignity (Tamaret 1912, 57)' and would undermine the foundation of precepts regulating relations between people.

Moreover, Tamaret saw public ritual as a way of cultivating consensus around guiding principles. Several examples of his moral hermeneutic may be cited. For our purposes, however, we shall briefly focus on his interpretation of the Yom Kippur fast. Traditionally understood as a penitentiary practice (Maimonides, *Mishneh Torah: Laws of Fasts* 1:1–3), Tamaret saw it differently. Bodily needs, he wrote, are satisfied by 'annihilating and eradicating the objects of nourishment.' On the holy day, one 'ought not fill his body via the destruction of another' but rather exercise restraint such that he 'himself undergoes annihilation (Tamaret 1912, 17).' While the fast ends, the message remains. This, Tamaret stressed by pointing out the fact that the liberating Jubilee was historically proclaimed on Yom Kippur (Leviticus 25:9). Because, he wrote, only bodily drives 'muddy the relations among us, dividing us into those who subjugate and those who are subjugated (Tamaret 1912, 22)' these distinctions disappear when the corresponding drives are dampened or eliminated. In other words, the communal fast enacts the moral transformation of society at large: a universal renunciation of exploitation and oppression.

Through diasporic consciousness in combination with the libertarian institution of the *beyt midrash*, the laws of freedom it promulgates, and the public rituals of the Jewish community, true freedom thus becomes the 'inheritance of this exiled people of the Torah (Tamaret 1929, 48).' This inheritance, however, is one ultimately to be shared. Having 'abandoned the sword' together with the land and become a subversive spiritual 'kingdom within a kingdom (Tamaret 1920a, 68),' the Jewish community came to constitute, according to Tamaret, a 'messianic font,' bringing 'redemption to the earth' by planting 'the seeds of the prophetic mission, which is our exilic formation (Tamaret 1920a, 40).'

Revolution of the heart

Tamaret's conviction as to the 'uselessness and emptiness of responding with force' to force (Tamaret 1992, 111) will come as no surprise. Armed conflict would necessarily mean idolatrous reduction of human life to relative utilitarian value. In this way, it would simply repeat past sins and invite the 'blemish of despotism' to bloom anew (Tamaret 1912, 32). Instead, he called for a 'revolution of the heart' to neutralize 'wolf-like relations between people (Tamaret 1920a, 21).' To rectify the social order, he wrote:

> The evil inclination of the heart must be conquered. Social justice does not depend on politics, but on the purification of the human 'I' — opening one's eyes so that he reflects upon and recognizes who and what he is, and where he is going. *Then*, all of his aims will be transformed [and he will acknowledge that] communal life is based on mutual aid. (Tamaret 1993, 169)

This change, he explained, is one that every person can and must bring about in himself. It is not a task for vanguardist political parties, but permeates every day life.

Here, *emunah* — as opposed to religion — is said to play a central role. For one, the idea of God serves as an object of emulation. Absolute and sufficient unto itself, the divine has no impetus to fight with others. As creator and sustainer, it exemplifies care (Tamaret 1912, 12). The idea of God as the creator of mankind emphasizes, furthermore, that a person 'is not an ownerless object, but sanctified property' that 'cannot be infringed upon for any reason, good or bad (Tamaret 1992, 72).' More than that, it suggests that each person exists for a reason and that instead of competing for survival, people ought to 'assist one another in achieving victory over nature and so preparing from it sustenance for all (Tamaret 1912, 20).' Like Tolstoy, he appealed to the prophetic utterance 'have we not all one father? Has not one God created us? Why do we break faith with one another (Malachi 2:10; Tamaret 1905, 77)?' The idea of God as creator of mankind grounds the principle of human brotherhood. Finally, the idea of God supplies the existential foundation of moral progress. Without God as the answer, Tamaret believed, the question 'for whom and why do I labor?' will eat away one's thoughts like 'a burrowing moth,' thus impeding one's 'conquest of himself, his natural selfishness (*anokhiyut*) (Tamaret 1992, 68–69).'

Without explicitly citing Tolstoy, Tamaret recommends an equivalent model for resistance in the name of this revolution of the heart. Sovereignty, he argued, may be taken by force, but it cannot be maintained that way; 'to plant or to permanently uproot' a social or political order, one must address 'the human will to act.' Real change begins and ends with motivation and this is transformed by 'spiritual force' alone. This means that people with 'little power to affect the body,' may yet 'have much power over the soul, over the human spirit (Tamaret 1992, 113).'

Prefiguring R. Joseph Ber Soloveitchik's representation of '*halakhic* man' as a creator of *theoretical* worlds,[7] Tamaret saw him as endowed with God's created power and, so, capable of creating a new world order within the old. 'When one person raises his fist against another,' he therefore argued, the air around him is, as it were, 'filled with waving fists.' However, good deeds have the same ability to effect the sort of atmospheric change (Tamaret 1912, 39) that ultimately transforms a culture. That is, to change hearts and minds.

Interpreting a claim made in the *Tosefot* (a medieval commentary on the talmud) to Baba Kama 23a to the effect that a person must be more careful about harming others than avoiding harm himself, Tamaret recommended quietism in the face of violence and force. Comply, he wrote, 'if some violent man commands you to chop wood for him, to draw water for him, or to shine his shoes.' God implanted 'feelings of justice and mercy ... in the human heart' and the oppressor will naturally regret his trespass, 'be ashamed before the tortured and withdraw its hand (Tamaret 1905, 29).' In contrast, he insisted, 'when it comes to things which will tarnish your soul' — striking others, punishing them, or ordering them around — one must resist with all his strength, letting the oppressor know that 'you are already chained firmly in the service of the Just Master, who resides in your heart and that you are unable to be anybody's bruising cane.' This he contended, will impress upon him the realization that he, and not his victim, is the subhuman, for he agreed to the despicable task of persecution (Tamaret 1986, 219).'

Citing the authority of Isaiah — 'he shall strike down a land with the rod of his mouth and slay the wicked with the breath of his lips (Isaiah 11:4)' — Tamaret argued like Tolstoy that 'stubbornness is our primary weapon' because we fight for that which 'cannot be taken by means of a sword (Tamaret 1920a, 41–42).' Thus, he proposed to bring about the 'downfall of tyranny by throwing at the tyrant not bombs, *but a look of contempt*' conveying 'deep hatred and absolute disgust for murder and violence (Tamaret 1992, 112–113; Cohen 2015).' Supposing that God put 'feelings of justice and mercy ... in the human heart,' the torturer will naturally feel 'ashamed before the tortured and withdraw his hand (Tamaret 1905, 29).' Thus does the rebellious Jew kill 'the wicked with spirit,' forcing them to feel for 'the degradation of the oppressed.' The world is filled with violence, Tamaret maintained, *only* because this feeling is numbed (Tamaret 1992, 112–113); reviving it therefore enthrones 'the God of truth and righteousness in the world,' adding 'power to the kingdom of justice (Tamaret 1968).'

The Jewish diasporic mission

The people of Israel, Tamaret contended, were the first to introduce *emunah* into the world. Who then, he asked, is more 'qualified to continue the development of pure faith, the realization of the prophetic vision within life?' Thus, 'to he who began the deed, we say: continue (Tamaret 1992, 76).' In answering the question of *how*, we address not only the Jewish mission so far as Tamaret understood it, but also clarify an important ambiguity in his understanding as to the nature of *emunah*.

Many *maskilim* saw themselves as inheritors of Maimonides, not least because they conceived of the Jewish national mission in doctrinal terms: an obligation to teach the world about (ethical) monotheism. Tamaret maintained that 'this sort of belief can exist in the world without Israel

(Tamaret 1920a, 54).' More importantly, he rejected the pedagogical core of the mission itself. Were Israel tasked with *teaching*, it would be:

> Upon us to approach them and reflect upon them as much as possible. For it is a fundamental principle of pedagogy that the teacher must penetrate the spirits of his students and adapt to their worldview as much as possible such that the students understand him. In this way, our relation to the gentiles can turn into a case where one 'comes as a teacher but turns out to be a pupil (Hullin 28a).' This would destroy our uniqueness as a people and blur the form of our Torah that we came to teach them. (Tamaret 1920a, 53)

To insist on Jewish distinctness (as implied at least by the supposition of a distinctly *Jewish* mission) is to deny that the Jews were 'exiled from our land and dispersed among other nations in order to school them in the divine religion (Tamaret 1920a, 52).' Indeed, he continued:

> We are not even *suited* to be teachers, for *we have no religion* in the sense that this is understood by the people of the world — a concept that is abstract and strange, which stands outside the borders of life, the border of things human. (Tamaret 1920a, 56)

This latter claim leads us to Tamaret's conception of what Jewish *emunah* entails concretely and, also, what it has to do with the rest of the world.

The 'divine message (*da'at*) taught by the prophets,' Tamaret explained, 'comes from the word *mudeh*, which means familiarity, or closeness (Tamaret 1920a, 54).' As he defined it, this closeness or intimacy consists not in knowledge, but in the 'purification of the human soul,' elevating it to 'an ethical peak' and thus rendering it 'a soft, pure, and refined creature ... in communion with the divine presence (Tamaret 1920a, 54).' This intimacy is embodied in the:

> Torah, the Torah of life, which is integrated into the whole of Jewish life — it is in the people and the people are in it; they are inseparable ... The content of this Torah is the closeness of God, i.e. the magnanimity and refinement of character in which the exilic Jew is unique ... . It is not a religion like that of the other peoples. Nor is it essentially a philosophy or a theology. Rather, *it is a civilization, a unique civilization, a way of life that is unlike that of any other people.* (Tamaret 1920a, 56)

This idea of Judaism as a civilization — with which Tamaret anticipated Mordechai Kaplan by several decades — explains for him, both the legitimacy and also the importance of Jewish particularity.

In line with his approach to communal leadership, which emphasizes 'free development (Tamaret 1905, 37)' through guidance and modeling over 'guardianship (*apotroposut*) and rule over others (Tamaret 1920a, 53),' Tamaret contended that Israel is tasked with becoming first 'a light *unto itself* ... and *incidentally* becoming *a light unto the nations.*' Like the flames of the candelabrum in the ancient Temple, which were inclined inward but nonetheless radiated outward, so too Israel among the nations. Our 'influence on others,' he wrote, 'will happen of its own accord,' for:

> The task of being a light unto the nations does not imply that there obtains between us a relation of tutelage ... their enlightenment is something that depends upon them, not us ... It entails, for us, no particular action, nor any special intention regarding them. Rather, this light (as implied by the menorah in the temple, the flames of which inclined toward the lamp itself) must be inwardly directed. Then our light will, of itself, shine toward the gentiles when they see something noble in our world. Our 'tutelage' of the gentiles is indirect; it is not about theory, but practice; *we are to set an example.* (Tamaret 1920a, 52)

In this way, teaching indirectly and by example only, the people of Israel, says Tamaret, are 'fated to constitute the *luz* bone[8] of the spine from which a spiritual revival of the dead begins for humanity as a whole;' and 'even before that time' ensuring 'that at least a small corner of the world remains free of the contamination that fills the rest (Tamaret 1920a, 55).'

This brings us back to Tamaret's view as to the redemptive function of exile. While people tend intuitively to grant that one retains their humanity even when homeless, the same cannot be said of peoples without states. Jewish life in diaspora is the counterexample; it demonstrates not only that collective life is possible 'without a kingdom or a state' or territory, but that when identity is bound up in such things, 'it relies on a fragile reed (Tamaret 1920a, 59–61).' Thus, Tamaret declared:

> To maintain the existence of our people in exile, the existence of the 'national example,' is our universal obligation in exile. It is not to spread the diasporic doctrine of Israel that we went into exile among the nations. Rather, it was to raise and sustain before the nations a Jewish-diaspora people and a living example of the doctrine. (Tamaret 1920a, 75)

The task of dispersion, in other words, is to demonstrate the force of dispersion as a living ideal: collective identity sans territory and state.

By extension, he suggested that when the sages said that a home absent of Torah will be destroyed (Sanhedrin 92a) they spoke not only of 'an individual structure, but also peoples and whole countries (Tamaret 1920a, 17).' The prophetic vision of 'nation shall not take up Sword against nation (Micha 4:3),' he argued, is predicated neither on the establishment of an international court in the Hague, nor on the condition of a League of Nations, but 'the land shall be filled with devotion (*deya*) to the Lord (Isaiah 11:9.' Following Genesis 4:1, Tamaret interpreted '*deya* (lit. knowledge)' as 'intimacy' and therefore contended that Jewish anarcho-diasporism, the Torah broadly construed — which puts intimacy with the divine over nationalism, patriotism, statism, and militarism — is the prophylactic to collective destruction, to war. The proverbial 'disputes of Abaye and Rava,' he maintained, 'are a foundation for opposition against the bloody wars of the nations and of states (Tamaret 1923, 12).'

Tamaret believed that World War I — during which people were forced to dig 'in the ground like weasels and rats, rolling around in these trenches for days and years in moisture and filth, dirt and boils, plague and the stench of dead bodies' only to despoil and destroy the labor of others (Tamaret 1920a, 64) — 'revealed the nakedness of the earth (Tamaret 1920a, 66).' Therefore, he maintained, 'the time has come for the revival of Judaism (Tamaret 1992, 109).' The nations, he hoped, would 'flee from the waves of war like sheep wandering from field to field' and 'like true Jews' become exiles by amputating from themselves 'the arrogant wings of the citizenship (Tamaret 1920a, 64).' They too might then create a civilization organized around moral principles and in rejection of 'the ugliness of one person's rule over another, which is to his detriment (Tamaret 1912, 38).' Then, 'the era of sacrifices, when one swallows his fellow,' will be brought to an end (Tamaret 1912, 84) and 'the culture of Esau,' which 'lives by the sword and is likewise consumed by it' will be shattered so that 'the footsteps of the messiah ... will become audible (Tamaret 1920a, 22).' Through the people that experienced the 'exile of the Divine Presence,' the world at large will come to recognize 'the Divine Presence of Exile (Tamaret 1920a, 24).

Conclusion

R. Aaron Shmuel Tamaret's pacifist anarcho-diasporism shatters the religious, historical, social, and political categories that emerged from the ideological ferment of the late nineteenth century and ossified thereafter. He sided with Zionists — and likewise with the Modern Orthodoxy — in rejecting nihilistic pietism and demanding a material reconstruction of Jewish life. Yet, he rejected Zionism itself on moral grounds. Israel, he maintained, must stand firm in its commitment to Abraham's mission. It must resist the temptation of foreign gods and smash the idols of nation, land, and state. It must reject the hypnosis of the spinning sword. In holding his ground against the historical tides, in battling both camps — Zionists who saw no further than the horizon of the Jewish State (as opposed to members of Hibbat Zion who, in his view, escaped this pitfall) and also the ultra-orthodox who could see no further than the final page of the Code of Jewish Law — Tamaret proved himself a 'prophet' by his definition, and not a charlatan.

Concluding this chapter, let us briefly reflect on the anarcho-pacifists as a whole. All four of them drew on similar, if not identical, scriptural and rabbinic sources to articulate their constructions of Jewish political identity. All believed that Jewish tradition stands in diametric opposition to force and violence and that this implies equality, liberty, and fraternity. Like others considered in this volume, they upheld a conception of 'fraternity' that preserved Jewish particularity while at the same time making way for universal human solidarity. They aspired to radical social and political transformation but denied that this could be brought about by violent means, maintaining instead that moral insight is the key to revolution — a key held, as they understood it, by the Jews. All, even Tamaret, ultimately believed that these values could be translated into a movement like Hibbat Zion, but they were divided on the modern Zionist movement. Don-Yahiya, and especially Heyn, ultimately made their peace with it; Hofshi, and especially Tamaret, did not. As I shall discuss in the general conclusion to this volume, all offered us a nuanced and sensitive critique of Zionism and Jewish nationalism that remains relevant today.

Notes

1 The friendship and intellectual commonality between Tamaret and Zeitlin is noted in Daniel (1932) and Weinberg (1967). See also Zeitlin (1926a–b). Zeitlin deeply admired Tamaret, but also challenged his radicalism and his '*mitnagdic*' tendency to see things strictly in black and white without admitting any shades of grey (Zeitlin 1930b). See also Aaron Zeitlin's (1961) less generous reflections on Tamaret's thought, which he calls 'absurd,' 'false,' and 'one-sided.'

2 *Hithasdut hashashanit*; the word *hashash* connotes concern or worry. I have translated *hashashanit* as 'neurotic' in order to convey the sense of persistent anxiety or worry. Tamaret's terminological choice is also attuned to the rabbinic idea of *hashash*; if there is reason to worry that one may come to transgress some prohibition — if there is a *hashash* — the rabbis tend to rule stringently so as to allay that concern. In adopting this position, Tamaret explicitly rejects the position held by H. Graetz, who believed that the isolating force of talmudic piety had a preservative function vis-a-vis Jewish identity (Meyer 1987, 217–241; Glatzer 2009, 161).

3 Maimonides, for instance, read Exodus 20:2 as an imperative to believe in God and ultimately understood it to imply the necessity of distinguishing between the true being of the divine and the attributes *imaginatively* ascribed to it by dint of its actions (Guide 1:54). In contrast, Rashi interpreted it as an exhortation: because I am the merciful one who took you out of Egypt, you ought to submit to me.

4 Sabbatianism was a failed seventeenth-century messianic movement centered around the figure of Shabbatai Zevi. His followers formulated a complex and thoroughly heretical theology that cannot be addressed here; one of its elements, however, involved a firm distinction between the purely abstract *deus absconditus*

of the philosophers and the God of Israel who reveals himself in history (Scholem 1995a, 78–141; Maciejko 2017, 69).

5 This notion was innovated by I. M. Jost (Jost 1824, 103), reincarnated in the later work of Graetz (Meyer 1987, 229–244) and Dubnow (Dubnova-Erlich 1991; Dubnow 2011, 2012), given poetic expression in Heine (Schrøder-Simonsen 2016), and recently reprised by Daniel Boyarin (Boyarin 2015).

6 Following Torres (2016, 1), I use these terms interchangeably.

7 See the second part of *Halakhic Man*. This link raises interesting questions as to the provenance of the phrase. Tamaret was a student of Soloveitchik's grandfather; it is therefore possible that this notion began with Hayyim Brisker.

8 Jewish legend has it that there is a bone in the upper spine that never decays, and it is from this bone that the body will be reconstituted during the prophesied resurrection of the dead (Reichman and Rosner 1996).

Conclusion: contemporary relevance

> It is the monstrous temple of Baal
> that the worshippers solemnly penetrate ...
> One after another,
> generations enter its voracious mouth;
> for the fatality of sacrifice
> dominates all civilization
> and the same barbarous god demands
> the same worship
> (Eugen Relgis, 'El Nuevo Templo)

At the outset, I indicated the growing body of research in the field of Jewish anarchism. Paul Avrich's groundbreaking work placed Jews at the center of anarchist activity in Russia (Avrich 2015, 15–18, 44) and in the United States (Avrich 2005, 1990). Other historians followed, notably more recent book-length publications like Kenyon Zimmer's (2015) *Immigrants Against the State: Yiddish and Italian Anarchism in America*. These studies and others like them operate largely on the macro-scale, are historically oriented, and are mainly interested in the Jewish role in the labor movement. Others, like Cindy Milstein's (2020) *There is Nothing So Whole as a Broken Heart: Mending the World as Jewish Anarchists*, and Anna Elena Torres' (2016) *Any Minute Now the World's Overflowing Its Border: Anarchist Modernism and Yiddish Literature*, are more individually focused, attending to the convergence of anarchism and Judaism, but from a literary and poetic perspective. The major contribution of the present volume consists in the fact that it operates on the micro-scale, focusing on the lives and the thought of specific individuals, that it mainly attends to this convergence from a *theological* perspective, and that in doing so it departs from existing scholarly literature on this subject by addressing the work of Jewish traditionalists and thus challenges the prevailing dichotomy between cultural conservatism and leftward-facing political radicalism.

To do so, we initially wondered as to what might have transpired had Rabbi Singer not directly returned from the Radzyminer *shtibl* to his home on Krochmalna Street, but instead taken a short detour to the Judaica Library next to the Great Synagogue. We wondered as to the influence that Aaron Pinhas Gross and the anarchist youth he studied with might have had. Having examined the work of our 'anarchist *minyan*' we are better positioned to speculate on the topics they may have covered. Here, I shall consider several themes that appeared repeatedly throughout this study: Jewish collective identity, the mission of Israel, the question of organization (geographical, institutional, legal, and economic), and the place of violence. I shall then conclude with a separate section containing proposals as to contemporary relevance of anarcho-Jewish perspectives.

Anarcho-Judaism: major themes

As noted in previous chapters, anarchism has historically been cosmopolitan in tendency and, therefore, hostile to nationalism. According to Mina Grauer (1994), however, a predominantly Jewish minority saw the matter differently and situated national struggles within the broader fight for liberation. As Uri Gordon (2018b) has explained, a distinction was often made between 'nations,' which exist in relation to their respective states, and 'peoples' that exist apart from them, constituted on either 'naturalistic' grounds defined by ties of land, language, and kinship, or 'cultural' grounds defined by localized folk ways in flux. Our study both confirms and complicates these descriptions. Proponents of anarcho-Judaism shared with other anarchists a deep-seated revulsion for chauvinistic nationalism, especially when it took hold of the Jewish imagination. However, they embraced notions of Jewish peoplehood that do not easily fall into the categories Gordon proposes, both because they synthesized naturalistic and cultural elements and also because they integrated religious considerations.

Zalkind and Steinberg combined naturalist and culturalist approaches, emphasizing ties, not only of language and kinship, but also shared culture. However, by treating diaspora as an essential component of Jewish people-hood, they denied that a shared homeland or even a common locality is a central feature of national identity. Ashlag and Alexandrov held Jews to be united as a people on the basis of kinship ties, but understood these ties in spiritual not in biological terms. Alexandrov, moreover, synthesized national-ism and cosmopolitanism by representing the Jews as the vanguard of universal humanism. In a similar vein, Don-Yahiya, Heyn, and Hofshi defined Jewish peoplehood in terms of shared moral commitments and a common mission to humanity based on them. Tamaret stood alone in his uncompromising rejection of nationalism of any sort, insisting that faith, as he understood it — intimacy with the divine — is the only authentic expression of collective Jewish identity.

For members of the anarchist *minyan*, national identity was mostly bound up intimately with the idea of a national mission. Zalkind stood out in this respect by denying that Jewish collective identity and mutual solidarity contradicts anarchist internationalism without ascribing to it any special redemptive function. For Don-Yahiya, Heyn, Hofshi, and also Ashlag, the moral and spiritual core of Jewish collective identity — be it the sanctity of human life, the siblinghood of mankind, or the principle of neighborly love — laid out a clear mission: either through direct instruction or by serving as a living example to lead the way in a revolution of the heart that would produce universal peace, liberty, and social justice. Steinberg, Alexandrov, and especially Tamaret, transformed diaspora consciousness into a universal moral and political goal for which Jews, having both historical experience and a well-developed theology, should serve as a vanguard.

The notion of diaspora consciousness brings us to the question of geography as a principle of organization. For proponents of anarcho-Judaism, who largely positioned themselves in relation to Zionism, the place and meaning of the land of Israel was an important aspect of efforts to formulate decentralized structures of Jewish power and Jewish liberation. Many transformed the historical Jewish experience of alienation into a revolutionary lever that, they hoped, would overturn the gentile territorial-state. If nobody is at home, many reasoned, then everybody is at home; if exclusive claims to definite borders are abolished, then there are no borders to defend or to expand. Inspired by the exodus narrative, Tamaret took this line of reasoning to its ultimate extreme by representing the homeland as an idol to be smashed. Alexandrov's cosmopolitan vision had not only national, but also geographical significance and therefore took on global dimensions. Yet, just as his universal humanism was instantiated in the Jewish people, so too was the land of Israel treated as a staging ground for the spiritual revolution they would initiate. Steinberg and Zalkind likewise appealed to diasporic consciousness in their promotion of Jewish territorialism, which would concentrate Jews within well-defined borders but not necessarily, or not only, those of the holy land. This global horizon receded in the work of Don-Yahiya, Heyn, Hofshi, and Ashlag. While they certainly envisioned a universal revolution of the heart, they focused their efforts on the Jewish homeland, aiming to build it up and be built up thereby, not to assume dominion over it or over its other inhabitants.

This leads us to other forms of organization: political, legal, social, and economic. Anarcho-Judaism was initially framed within the history of persecution suffered by Russian Jewry. Whereas Political Zionists defined the *gentile* state serving gentile interests as the fundamental problem and therefore sought to create a Jewish equivalent, Jewish anarchists, or libertarian socialists, concluded that the problem was the state itself and sought ways to organize themselves otherwise, formulating a vision of political and economic egalitarianism. Proponents of anarcho-Judaism reached the same conclusion, but drew on their own religious texts, traditions, and institutions of local self-governance to articulate their vision. For instance, the municipal *beyt din* (court) and larger regional bodies like the 'council of the four lands' that coordinated Jewish communities in the Polish-Lithuanian Commonwealth between the sixteenth and eighteenth centuries were used to articulate federative models of anarchist governance in Jewish terms.

Jewish law represented both an opportunity and a challenge. On the one hand, it fit well into the model for communal self-regulation on the basis of 'folk-ways' supported by Kropotkin. It was also seen as a pedagogic mechanism for training people in the altruistic values on which libertarian society is based.

On the other hand, it was limited in the same ways as Kropotkin's model: in many respects historically petrified, it posed its own impediments to liberation. When this difficulty was addressed, an evolutionary approach was adopted. With varying degrees of radicalism, several members of the anarchist *minyan* believed that the Torah partakes of divine authority that is then transferred to human interpreters such that the law develops and changes (or even disappears) as moral ideas progress. Their emphasis on the open-ended character of talmudic and later rabbinic legal debate parallels anarchist notions of a polycentric law that takes shape organically through dialogue within a collective (Borovoj 1989).

This approach to Jewish law could very well have served as an answer to some of the difficulties raised in the introduction to this volume involving both the absence of women from the ranks of the anarchist *minyan* and also the general neglect of Jewish women's liberation. Though he celebrated the traditional (patriarchal) Jewish family (Alexandrov 1899d) and explicitly distinguished his anarchism from the libertine androgyny (Alexandrov 1907, 24) he associated with figures like Joséphin Péladan (an occultist and art-theorist who, albeit in his own misogynistic manner, promoted the subversion of gender roles) Alexandrov begrudgingly admitted the gradual dissolution of connubial regulations (Alexandrov 1931, 24–25). This was essentially to anticipate the abolition of marriage and, by implication, traditional gender roles. Other evolutionary approaches to traditional Jewish practice would naturally allow less extreme changes, and certainly the democratization of Jewish learning that would have enabled women to participate in the discourse of anarcho-Judaism.

If they fell short in the arena of women's liberation, proponents of anarcho-Judaism nonetheless welcomed, like other Jewish anarchists, other drastic political and social changes. Idealistic in intellectual tendency, they regarded historical materialism as a threat to the moral agency they deemed central to the making of revolution and to keeping revolutions on course toward their true goals. Either directly or indirectly, most were profoundly influenced by Kant, posing the second and third iterations of the categorical imperative — that human beings must always be treated as ends in themselves, or autonomous wills, and never compelled to function as means to other ends — as the very essence of Judaism. In keeping with the consensus that prevailed until recently, that Kant had no just war theory and that his ethics precluded it (Orend 1999), proponents of anarcho-Judaism generally reduced war to violence and treated it as anathema. Albeit with deep reservations, Steinberg stood out in his claim that pure hands cover guilty consciences when injustice is effectively tolerated due to lack of intervention. Zalkind, Don-Yahiya, Hofshi, and Tamaret shared Tolstoy's faith in the power of passive resistance, denying that it entails non-resistance to evil. Heyn, Alexandrov, Ashlag, and Hofshi emphasized the role of faith in generating human solidarity in opposition to violence — either by cultivating a sense of brotherhood, or by removing the impediment of the individual ego. As a rule then, they upheld the anarchist principle of ends-means correspondence, which they took to imply the moral necessity of pacifism and therefore rejected armed revolution in the same way that the rejected military action in any other circumstance. They stood for a revolution of the heart.

Had R. Singer made his way to Aaron Pinhas Gross' *minyan*, then, he would have observed debates drawing on the bible and talmud, rabbinic literature, the classics of Jewish philosophy, kabbalah, and hasidism, as well as modern European philosophy, science, and political theory. Had he been looking for a simple convergence of Judaism and anarchism without challenge to traditional conceptions of the former, he would not have found it. However, he would have discovered men of sincere faith striving to define for themselves what it means to be a Jew, how traditional practices and institutions should inform Jewish self-organization, how those same practices and institutions can change to meet fresh challenges without losing authenticity, the role that Jews should play in carrying out their messianic vocation for humanity, and the means by which to fulfill it.

Critical utopianism and anarcho-Judaism

Benjamin Franks (2006, 13) contends that prefiguration (the principle of ends-means correspondence) constitutes a 'core anarchist commitment.' According to Cindy Milstein (2010, 86), it is through this commitment that anarchism 'retains a utopian impulse.' In part, this means striving to directly realize ends as means, to ensure so far as possible that practice and principle coincide. More so, it means developing new critical discourses unrestrained by the prevailing order of things, and above all 'willingness to endure the impossibility of success as a condition of struggle (Kinna 2016b).' To understand how anarchist utopianism contributes to critical discourse and motivates struggle, it is necessary to better understand utopianism as a phenomenon.

The German sociologist Karl Mannheim distinguished between 'world-preserving' and 'world-destroying' tendencies; the former, ideology, the latter utopian (Mannheim 2013, 173). This is a useful heuristic, but one that requires further elaboration. According to Michael Gardiner, classical utopian literature in fact operates more like ideology, preserving rather than shattering worlds. As he explains, 'total utopias' that strive to superimpose harmonious systems on an otherwise recalcitrant reality do so by excluding difference, while 'nostalgic' utopias that evoke golden ages past compensate for their loss by promoting retrenchment in order to stave off further losses (Gardiner 1992). Ursula Le Guin's famous short story, *The Ones Who Walk Away from Omelas*, is perhaps the most eloquent representation of this problem. *Omelas* is depicted as a society perfect in every respect except for one: its existence hinges on the exclusion of someone unlike the rest, a 'defective' child. It demonstrates the way that classical utopias legitimate and also conceal authoritarian power structures.

Le Guin's text presents us with an alternative to classical utopianism, the 'critical utopia,' which conveys reflexive awareness as to the limits of the dominant utopian tradition and illuminates other ways of living without systematizing them or promoting authoritarianism by squeezing out autonomy. It rejects the utopian *blueprint* while retaining the utopian *dream* (Moylan 2014, 1–14). According to Ernst Bloch (1986, 623), critical utopianism is also 'mediated by process;' that is, it delivers 'forms and contents which have already developed in the womb of present society,' anticipating a better tomorrow already prefigured today.' Drawing on Walter Benjamin's *Theses on the Philosophy of History*, the same can be said of the past. He wrote that 'the past carries with it a temporal index by which it is referred to redemption.' Each generation, he continued, is endowed with a 'weak messianic power' that consists in its 'astrological' ability to discern the fragments of history that, in conjunction with the present, form a redemptive 'constellation' and thus illuminate the future (Benjamin 1968). This is to say that the past is also pregnant with form and content waiting to be delivered. If history often serves an *ideological* function because it is generally written by the victor (Benjamin 2003, 406), retelling it from another point of view serves a *utopian* function; expanding the horizons of political imagination, it becomes a subversive act.

I believe that recovering the canon of anarcho-Judaism is one such act of subversion because it puts prevailing narratives about Jewish political, religious, and national identities in question while at the same time organizing an unsystematic utopian dream that may not intersect with reality but beckons to it from above, tracing the contours of a new messianic 'constellation' and in this way responding to the challenges of the present. Chief among these, the question of Zionism, which has appeared as a constant theme throughout this volume and which has also become a deeply controversial topic both within the Jewish community and beyond it.

Zionism and anarcho-Judaism

Zionism began as a utopian vision. From Herzl's *Altneuland*, which Bloch (1986, 603) described as a bourgeois utopia of the 'immediately attainable' and Yitshak Conforti (2011b) more generously calls a 'realistic utopia,' to the more radical project of the kibbutz movement (Buber 1996, 139–150), it was at once nostalgic (Ohana and Shia 2019) and progressive, messianic and in its own way critical (Ohana 2012, 5–13). This utopian vision, however, made the crucial passage from dream to reality. For this reason, some have suggested that, having achieved its goals, Zionism became an *obsolete* ideology (Kaplan 2015). Based on Mannheim's dichotomy, I would argue the contrary: *it then became an ideology*, a 'world preserving' force bolstering a definite state of affairs ripe for utopian critique. Here, the 'weak messianic power' of the historical gaze plays a central role in two respects. Marginal figures excluded from historical narratives that explain and justify this state of affairs appear to us in a constellation of resistance, 'destroying worlds' by posing again the fundamental questions to which these narratives were an answer. At the same time, their stories took shape largely within the broader milieu of Zionism and Jewish nationalism such that a world destroyed is reconstructed, as it were, from its own vestigial organs — it becomes something *new* without becoming something *else*.

The importance of this distinction cannot be underestimated. As many figures discussed in this volume emphasized, the enduring power of Torah to consolidate Jewish collective identity consists in its character as a living tradition capable of bridging past and present, assuming fresh meaning without (to borrow a turn of phrase used to describe the apostasy of Elisha ben Abuya, who was mentioned in our introduction) 'severing its shoots (Hagigah 14b)' — without being uprooted from layers of meaning previously accumulated. I think that the same approach applies to other mechanisms for organizing collective identity; when reinterpretation prevails over cancellation, resistance to change is more easily circumnavigated. As

I see it, the question then shifts from 'whether Zionism' to how or in what sense. Anarcho-Judaism provides some tools for responding to these questions.

Returning briefly to ground covered in previous chapters, we note that during its inaugural congress in 1897, the World Zionist Organization ratified the so-called Basel Program, which entailed cultivating national consciousness, settling and building up Palestine, and establishing there a recognized Jewish 'national home.' In the ambiguity of this phrase, which could refer either to a state or to a 'spiritual center,' lay both the divide between Political and Cultural-Practical Zionism, and also an implicit distinction as to the shape of Jewish nationalism. A center for the renaissance of Jewish culture would naturally be grounded in an ethnic nationalism; the nationalism undergirding a state could be civic in character (Kohn 1946, 330–331). These distinctions eventually collapsed into one another, giving rise to the idea of a *Jewish* State. This elision was not merely ideological, but also manifested itself institutionally. The institutional network created to serve the Jewish community in British Mandate Palestine was not dismantled in 1948, but absorbed by the democratic State of Israel. The latter therefore took shape as a composite of ethnic and civic institutions that were never fully reconciled (Gordon 1997; Avishai 2008).

Here is not the place to elaborate, but this hybrid democracy has begun to tear at the seams between the two poles of its genesis. Questioning how democratic Israel *really is*, post-Zionists aim to transform it into a state that is truly for *all* of its citizens and to construct national identity along universalistic and civic lines (Kaplan 2005b). Questioning how democratic Israel *should be*, neo-Zionists promote a program of ethno-nationalism and territorial maximalism (Ram 2000) that is at best indifferent to Arab human rights (Magid 2019; Persico 2019). In this way, long-suppressed internal tensions come to a head. Jewish anarcho-utopian critique cuts unevenly along this divide. It challenges the simple dichotomy between universal and particular, questions the relationship between the people and the land, rejects *any* sort of human sovereignty as a *Jewish* ideal, and identifies violence as a *cultural* problem, not merely a political one.

Anarcho-Judaism challenges the simple dichotomy between universal and particular in at least two respects. Arguably, the distinction between ethnic and civic conceptions of national identity parallel the traditional dialectic between bonds of kinship and covenant (Elazar 1983) — Jews as the children of Israel, or as the people of the Torah. There is, however, another foundation of collective identity that rarely plays into such discussions. According to several talmudic sources, a Jew is one who is 'merciful, bashful, and benevolent (Yevamot 79a; Betsa 32b).' Identity is constructed neither on the basis of kinship nor of covenant, neither on ethnic nor on civic bonds, but on fundamental moral virtues. Ehud Luz has argued that so long as public debate revolves around a choice between 'Jewish culture and abstract universal culture,' there is little basis for moral or political discourse between the disputants (Luz 2008, 275). The moral construction of Jewish identity adopted by several proponents of anarcho-Judaism obviates this choice. Ideas about the sacredness of human life, human fraternity, or even diaspora may mark a particular national group but cannot be monopolized by one; they are (or can be) shared values. In this sense, they unite the universal and the particular. Alternatively, efforts like those of Zalkind and Steinberg to define Jewish national identity in terms of common folkways — so that the Jews become a *people-in-praxis* and Jewishness something one does rather than something one is — overcome the ethnic-civic divide and make for an open-ended political ontology. Mutual belonging can be created through shared patterns of behavior that naturally arise through daily exchange and interaction.

Anarcho-Judaism questions the relationship between the people and land. Most mainstream responses to competing Israeli and Palestinian claims to the land 'between the river and the sea' involve dividing it between them. Bracketing questions as to the feasibility or desirability of such a plan, it would ultimately come down to a question of drawing mutually acceptable borders. This is a fundamental error because borders have never been the central issue. The central issue has always been about the nature of the relationship between land and people, whether having or claiming a homeland implies the right to *political sovereignty* over it (Magid 2017). Reversing the order of priority and starting with the question of borders means either presupposing that it does or denying that there is a difference. Anarcho-Jewish perspectives disambiguate homeland and state — again, in a way that cuts unevenly across contemporary ideological divides.

The idea of a Jewish homeland was almost universally recognized by proponents of anarcho-Judaism, but this was neither an exclusive claim nor one that implied the right to political sovereignty (much less over any other people). Rather, they anticipated the creation of a spiritual center along the lines described by Ahad Ha'am and celebrated the back-to-the earth ethic of Hibbat Zion and the early Zionist pioneers. In sum, they put land before state. Contemporary neo-Zionist ethno-nationalists comport themselves similarly (Persico 2019) but their claims are exclusive; they deny or ignore Palestinian attachments to *their* homeland. Anarcho-Jewish perspectives make way for a certain synthesis of post-Zionism and neo-Zionism: they replace the 'state for all of its citizens' with a 'homeland for all of its inhabitants.' It is precisely such an approach that informs grassroots movements like Roots (Mollov and Lavie 2018) and A Land for All (Rappaport 2017) that strive to overcome the one-state/two-state impasse.

Anarcho-diasporic reservations about land-centric constructions of Jewish autonomy and Jewish identity further enrich this line of thinking. By establishing a sovereign Jewish state in the Jewish homeland, Zionists aspired to 'normalize' the Jewish people, transforming them into 'a nation like all the other nations (1 Samuel 8:20).' Paradoxically, by making them 'a people that dwells apart (Numbers 23:9)' in the literal sense, they mitigated moral, spiritual, political, and social aspects of Jewish difference; in this sense the movement was the 'legitimate heir to assimilation (Arendt 2009, 56).' The reduction of Jewish difference was compounded by the fact that Zionist historical consciousness, or Jewish identity as seen through Zionist eyes, was organized around the 'negation of exile.' Tracing a mythic continuum between the sovereign Hebrew nation of antiquity and its modern revival, Jewish existence during the intermediate period was represented as meaningless and deficient. If it arose from a yearning for liberation, it actually entailed suppressing entire cultural traditions (Raz-Krakotzkin 1993). The negation of exile was self-imposed cultural violence. All the more so given its association with the image of the 'new Jew' through which antisemitic stereotypes concerning the degenerate Jewish body and its corresponding traits of character (e.g. passivity, weakness, cowardliness, crookedness, and helplessness) were internalized and then repressed in the production of their antithesis: a hyper-masculine 'Spartan,' Jewish in name but gentile in form (Boyarin 1997).

The anarcho-diasporic negation of the negation of exile, in contrast, involved a comprehensive comportment toward Jewish history and the history of Jewishness characterized by openness and pride as opposed to shame and repression. The world as they experienced it, full of despotism and brutality, was not an aspirational goal but an object of deep disgust. If, therefore, Arendt (2009, 296–297) once condemned Jewish pariahood, proponents of anarcho-Judaism transvalued it. The stateless, powerless, Jewish pariah became the revolutionary *par excellence* by opposing the state and standing up to power. Thus, beyond the obvious fact (Lewin 2015) that de-territorializing Jewish identity would ease efforts to negotiate the exchange of land for peace between the river and the sea (if that is indeed the answer) it carries with it the promise of healing deep cultural wounds and revitalizing a damaged sense of Jewish idealism.

Pacifism was among the most radical expressions of utopian pariahood — and one that, in the shadow of the Holocaust, is perhaps most problematic. Here, a distinction between 'deontological' and 'consequentialist' approaches is pertinent. The latter object to violence because of its *effects*, the former in principle; the latter accept contingencies and justify certain types of violence in certain circumstances, the former do not (Fiala 2018). Basing themselves on a radical interpretation of the biblical injunction 'thou shalt not kill,' many members of our anarchist *minyan* were pacifists of the deontological variety. If, for a community still traumatized by genocide, such arguments are less than compelling, consequentialist concerns remain relevant. Apprehension as to the fundamental shift in Jewish values that military power would bring about permeate their work. To borrow a biblical idiom, Jacob might *once* don goat skins and play Esau while reasonably expecting to remove them later and return to his tent unchanged, but were he to wear them at all times, and also to carry with him Esau's weapons, the hands of Jacob would *truly* become the hands of Esau (Genesis 27:22). Such misgivings have been mirrored in Sigal Ben-Porath's (2009, 34–35) description of 'belligerent citizenship,' a return to a crude Hobbian model of the state in which safety needs dominate the public agenda, democratic commitments wither, and uncritical nationalistic tendencies thrive, thus leading to cultural and political stagnation. This coarsening of moral and political sentiment — which, as several figures considered in this volume insisted, are not limited to Israel but potentially extend also to the Jewish diaspora — constituted a core anxiety for Jewish anarcho-pacifists.

In closing our summary of critical-utopian contributions to discourse on the question of Zionism derivable from the sources of anarcho-Judaism, an important distinction must be made. The crucial difference separating Tamaret, for instance, from Satmar and Neturei Karta — ultra-orthodox anti-Zionist groups still active today — lies in a distinction between the *evil* and the *prohibited*. In books like Yoel Teitelbaum's *Vayoel Moshe*, or Amram Blau's *Torat Rabbi Amram*, which outline the doctrines of Satmar and Neturei Karta respectively, one will find elaborate and vehement invective against the Zionist idea drawing from a wide variety of traditional texts. However, their objections are strictly parochial. One will not find appeals to universal notions of justice, apprehensions about the moral and political dangers of nationalism, or patriotism, or statism; nor will one find denunciations of violence. It is true that in public statements like the one published by Daniel and Jonathan Boyarin (1993), representatives of Neturei Karta expressed concern over demonization of the Palestinian other among the 'Zionist faithful' and, by extension, for Palestinian human rights. However, I believe that far greater weight should be placed on their internal discourse, on materials intended for consumption within their own communities. For Satmar and Neturei Karta, Jewish nationalism is a *heresy*, while the establishment of a Jewish army or a pre-messianic Jewish state is sinful. Their objections to Zionism, cultural or political, arise from the contention that these things are *forbidden to Jews* (Lamm 1971; Nadler 1982), not that they are bad in themselves. It is for this reason that such groups do not shy away from collaboration with fascists and reactionaries of all stripes (Santos 2007; Elgot 2012) so long as they share a common antagonism to the State of Israel. While addressing his own community, Tamaret, in contrast, denounced nationalism, patriotism, statism, and militarism as *universal evils* (Gendler 2003). He did not single out the Jews; his 'anti-Zionism' was but one instance of a far more comprehensive critique that would extend equally to any and all national movements. In my opinion, this is the correct approach and it should serve to inform contemporary discourse on the subject at hand; either such things are morally or religiously objectionable *in themselves*, or they are not. They cannot be represented as suitable and even laudable for some and reprehensible for others — at least when forwarded by gentiles, this would be antisemitic.

In sum, then, anarcho-Judaism contributes a utopian critique around Zionism on five fronts. It expands the boundaries of Jewish identity, bridging the universal and the particular. It disambiguates sovereignty from attachment to the land in a way that cuts across contemporary factional lines. It restores diasporic consciousness in a way that does not simply facilitate flexibility in the drawing of borders, if borders are to be drawn, but addresses deep cultural wounds sustained by modern Jews. It raises important questions about the cultural and political impact of prolonged conflict. Finally, it provides resources for distinguishing between anti-Zionism and antisemitism.

Final remarks

At the start of this concluding chapter, I placed a rough translation of Eugen Relgis' 'El Nuevo Templo,' in which he describes the core insight that drove other Jewish anarchists, especially those discussed here. He described the way that Baal, the great idol — be it a nation, a state, a homeland, or an army — demands sacrifice and swallows up its worshippers. Above all, religious Jewish anarchists denounced the worship of this Baal. They did so, moreover, from the standpoint of faith. That is, they resisted what is in essence a religious drive by turning to religious tools. Above and beyond the specific ideas that they promoted, or the particular ways that they interpreted Jewish oral and written traditions, I believe that this was perhaps the most important aspect of their project. They battled darkness not by pretending to negate it, but by bringing light; instead of tearing down, they built up something they deemed better. They 'cast brimstone' not on worship, but on the *worship of Baal* and led the way out of his 'voracious mouth.' This *positive* effort to create a new order of things within the old, to displace rather than to destroy, is the essence of their revolutionary message.

Heshvan 29, 5780
Sigd

References

Quotations from the Hebrew Bible follow New Jewish Publication Society translation except when they appear within quotations from other texts. Quotations from the New Testament follow the English Standard translation. Quotations from the Babylonian talmud follow the Steinzaltz translation, and mishnaic quotations follow the Kulp translation. Mishnaic citations are indicated by the abbreviation 'M.' Talmudic citations follow the standard citation format: tractate, folio number, side of page (a or b). All talmudic citations refer to the Babylonian talmud unless preceded by a 'J.' to indicate the Jerusalem talmud. The following abbreviations are used for midrashic texts: 'GR' for Genesis Rabbah, 'ER' for Exodus Rabbah, 'LR' for Leviticus Rabba, and 'DR' for Deuteronomy Rabbah. Other midrashim are cited by name.

Unless otherwise noted, translations from Hebrew and Yiddish texts, including emphasis, are my own.

Abensour, Miguel (2011). *Democracy Against the State: Marx and the Machiavellian Movement*. Translated by Max Blechman and Martin Breaugh. Cambridge: Polity Press.

Adams, Matthew (2013). 'The Possibilities of Anarchist History: Rethinking the Canon and Writing History.' *Anarchist Developments in Cultural Studies* 1. https://journals.uvic.ca/index.php/adcs/article/view/17138 (accessed September 29, 2020).

— (2015). *Kropotkin, Read, and the Intellectual History of British Anarchism: Between Reason and Romanticism*. Dordrecht: Springer.

Adler, Eliyana R. (2011). *In Her Hands: The Education of Jewish Girls in Tsarist Russia*. Detroit: Wayne State University Press.

A. H. A. (1957). 'Ha-Rav Avraham Heyn Aynenu.' *Davar*, October 6, 6.

Alexandrov, Shmuel (undated). Letter to Shainboim. Eliezer Yitshak Ilaneh Collection, National Library of Israel Archives. Shelf 5, series 948, folder 01 4 and 02 38.

— (1886a). *Masekhet Nega'im*. Warsaw: Yosef Eisenshtadt.

— (1886b). 'Ma'amarei Madah: Ma'adanot Kima.' *Ha-Meylits*, December 15, 5.

— (1891a). 'Ha-Yonah le-et Erev: Hegyon le-Hanukkah.' *Ha-Zefira*, December 23, 1119–1120.

— (1891b). 'Esh-Da'at we-Ruah Le'umi (Chapter 9).' *Ha-Magid*, August 6, 246–247.

— (1891c). 'Esh-Da'at we-Ruah Le'umi (Chapters 7–8).' *Ha-Magid*, June 25, 193–195.

— (1891d). 'Esh-Da'at we-Ruah Le'umi (Chapter 6).' *Ha-Magid*, June 18, 185–186.

— (1891e). 'Esh-Da'at we-Ruah Le'umi (Chapter 2).' *Ha-Magid*, May 21, 155.

— (1892a). *Agadat Pakh ha-Shemen*. Warsaw: Defus Levinski.

— (1892b). '*Le-Torah we-le-Te'uda.*' *Ha-Magid*, November 18, 1–2.

— (1894). 'Letter to R. Yehudah Levik dated November 8.' *Talpiyot*. Edited by Yehuda Levik and Duberosh Yeruhamzohn. Berditchov: H. Y. Sheftil: 2.

— (1896). *Tel Tehiya al Masekhet Avot.* Vilna: Defus ha-Almana we-ha-Ahim Rom.

— (1898a). 'Ba-Sukkot Teshvu.' *Ha-Magid*, September 29, 2.

— (1898b). '*Hegyonot Kezarim.*' *Ha-Magid*, September 16, 292–293.

— (1898c). '*Hegyonot le-Yerah ha-Eytanim.*' *Ha-Magid*, September 15, 292–293.

— (1899a). '*Takhlit Ma'aseh Shamayim wa-Arez: Perek alef.* Ha-Eshkol.* Edited by A. Ginsburg. Krakow: Yosef Fisher: 192–197.

— (1899b). '*Hegyonot le-Tisha be-Av.*' *Ha-Magid*, July 15, 3–4.

— (1899c). '*Hegyonot le-Hanukkah.*' *Ha-Magid*, November 28, 402–403.

— (1899d). '*Higayon le-Pesah.*' *Ha-Magid*. March 23, 4–5.

— (1900a). *Resisei Tal.* Vilnius: Defus Re'em.

— (1900b). 'Higayon le-Pesah.' *Ha-Magid*, April 12, 177–178.

— (1900c). '*Zeman Matan Torateynu.*' *Ha-Magid,* May 31, 1–2.

— (1901). 'Hegyonot le-Hanukkah.' *Ha-Magid*, December 5, 1.

— (1902). '*Takhlit ma'aseh shamayim wa-arets: Perek beyt.*' *Ha-Eshkol.* Edited by A. Ginsburg. Krakow: Yosef Fisher: 265–270.

— (1905). '*Takhlit ma'aseh shamayim wa-arets: Perek gimel-vav.*' *Ha-Eshkol.* Edited by A. Ginsburg. Krakow: Yosef Fisher: 226–243.

— (1907). *Mikhtavei Mehkar u-Bikoret be-She'alot ha-Zeman u-be-Hokhmat Yisrael ha'Atikah we-ha-Hadasha.* Vilinius: Re'em.

— (1908). Letter to Shainboim, dated November. Eliezer Yitshak Ilaneh Collection, National Library of Israel Archives. Shelf 5, series 948, folder 01 4 and 02 38.

— (1909). 'Letter to R. Kook: Summer 1909.' In D. Shneor, 'Rabbi Abraham Kook and Rabbi Samuel Aleksandrov.' M. A. thesis. Touro College Jerusalem, 2002: 75–82.

— (1910a). *Mikhtavei Mehkar u-Bikoret be-Shitot ha-Zeman u-be-Hokhmat Yisrael ha'Atikah we-ha-Hadasha.* Cracow: Metsape.

— (1910b). 'Letter to Paltiel Katsnelson, dated January.' Notebook of transcribed correspondence, Alexandrov Collection, Genazim Archives, Folder 143.

— (1914a). Letter to Shainboim, dated January. Eliezer Yitshak Ilaneh Collection, National Library of Israel Archives. Shelf 5, series 948, folder 01 4 and 02 38.

— (1914b). Letter to Shainboim, dated March. Eliezer Yitshak Ilaneh Collection, National Library of Israel Archives. Shelf 5, series 948, folder 01 4 and 02 38.

— (1914c). Letter to Shainboim, dated May. Eliezer Yitshak Ilaneh Collection, National Library of Israel Archives. Shelf 5, series 948, folder 01 4 and 02 38.

— (1914d). Letter to Shainboim, dated June 9. Eliezer Yitshak Ilaneh Collection, National Library of Israel Archives. Shelf 5, series 948, folder 01 4 and 02 38.

— (1931). *Mikhtavei mehkar u-bikoret al davar ha-Yahadut we-ha-rabanut be-zeman ha-zeh.* Jerusalem: Defus Lipshitz.

— (1939). '*Ha-Torah, ha-safa, u-mizwot ma-asiyot.*' *Ramah: Yarhon Le-divrei Sifrut, Mada, we-She'alot ha-Zeman.* New York: Hever Ivrim.

Almagor, Laura (2015). 'Forgotten Alternatives: Jewish Territorialism as a Movement of Political Action and Ideology (1905–1965).' PhD diss., European University Institute.

— (2017). 'A Territory, but not a State.' *SIMON Shoah: Intervention. Methods. Documentation.* 4, no. 1: 93–108.

— (2018). 'Fitting the Zeitgeist: Jewish Territorialism and Geopolitics, 1934–1960.' *Contemporary European History* 27, no. 3: 351–369.

— (2019). 'Tropical Territorialism: Displaced Persons, Colonialism, and the Freeland League in Suriname (1946–1948).' In *New Perspectives on Jewish Cultural History*. Edited by Maja G. Zuckerman and Jacob E. Feldt. New York: Routledge: 73–95.

Alroey, Gur (2008). 'Journey to new Palestine: The Zionist Expedition to East Africa and the Aftermath of the Uganda Debate.' *Jewish Culture and History* 10, no. 1: 23–58.

— (2016). *Zionism without Zion: The Jewish Territorial Organization and Its Conflict with the Zionist Organization*. Detroit: Wayne State University Press.

A. M. K. (1953). 'Devarim Tamohim.' *Davar*, June 18.

Anidjar, Gil and Amos Funkenstein (1996). 'Jewish Mysticism Alterable and Unalterable: On Orienting Kabbalah Studies and the "Zohar of Christian Spain".' *Jewish Social Studies* 3, no. 1: 89–157.

Anonymous (1901). 'Behuz Learzaynu.' *Ha-Meyliz*, February 9, 2.

— (1905). 'The Jewish Territorial Movement.' *Jewish Chronicle*, September 8, 12.

— (1907). 'A Sermon by Dr. J. M. Salkind, Cardiff's New Jewish Minister.' *Cardiff Times*, April 6, 2.

— (1916). 'Jews' Protection Committee.' *Herald*, August 19, 16.

— (1917a). 'Mr. Scott Dickers.' *Daily Herald*, Saturday February 10, 2.

— (1917b). 'Russian-Born Aliens and Military Service.' *Jewish Chronicle*, March 30, 22.

— (1917c). 'A Jewish Minister!' *Jewish Chronicle*, August 24, 6.

— (1930). 'Koyft un Farshprayt di Letste Verke fun Hillel Zeitlin.' *Grodner Moment Ekspress*, July 4, 9.

— (1931a). 'Di Vegen un Umvegen fun a Rav a Kempfer: Nakhen Toyt fun ha-Rov Aaron Shmuel Tamares, Ehad ha-Rabanim ha-Margishim.' *Der Fraynd*, August 11.

— (1931b). 'Ver iz geven Ehad ha-Rabanim ha-Margishim.' *Grodner Moment Ekspress*, September 2, 4.

— (1932a). 'Naye Zamel Bikher fun Hillel Zaytlin.' *Unser Ekspress*, October 17, 4.

— (1932b). 'Fun Bikher Tish.' *Unser Ekspress*, November 4, 10.

— (1937). 'Dr. Yaakov Meir Zalkind.' *Ha-Zofeh*, December 27, 1.

— (1945). 'Mehusar Da'agot ke-Nireh.' *Ha-Boker*, August 19, 4.

— (1946). 'Sofrim u-Sefarim.' *Ha-Zofeh*, June 28, 6.

— (1948). 'Shnei Mishpatim Neged Mishtamtim me-Hakara.' *Davar*, May 24, 3.

— (1949). 'Ha-Memshala Kiblah le-Yadeha et Mahleket ha-Tarbut me-Yesodo shel ha-Wa'ad ha-Leumi.' *Ha-Zofeh*, June 17, 4.

— (1950). 'Ha-Yom Skirat Sharet be-Wa'adat ha-Huts.' *Ha-Tsofeh*, February 21, 1.

— (1952). 'Le-Tikun Hok ha-Ezrahut.' *Al ha-Mishmar*, July 10, 3.

— (1954a). 'Zikhroni Mamshikh be-Shevitat ha-Ra'av.' *Ha-Boker*, June 6, 7.

— (1954b). 'Mohim Neged Ma'asaro shel Sarvan ha-Milhama.' *Al ha-Mishmar*, June 8, 4.

— (1954c). 'Zikhroni Alul le-Hitmotet be-kol Rega: Toanat Agudat Sarvane ha-Milkhama be-Yisrael.' *Ha-Zofeh*, June 17, 4.

— (1954d). 'Zom Zikhroni le-Yomo ha-20.' *Al ha-Mishmar*, June 17, 1.

— (1954e). 'Ayn Nishkefet Sakana le-Briyuto she Zikhroni.' *Ha-Boker*, June 18, 1.

— (1954f). 'Wikuah be-Davar.' *Herut*, July 14, 2.

— (1954g). 'Der Fal Amon Zikroni.' *Lebens Fragen*, August 1, 2.

— (1954h). 'Eliezer Hirshauge.' *Lebens Fragen*, June 1, 18.

— (1961). 'Ha-Arabim Pat'hu be-Ma'arakha.' *Davar*, December 8, 13.

— (1965). 'Ba-Lev u-ba-Nefesh.' *Maariv*, May 14, 14.

Arendt, Hannah (2009). *The Jewish Writings*. New York: Schocken.

Aronson, Gregorii (1966). 'Ideological Trends among Russian Jews.' In *Russian Jewry, 1860–1917*. Edited by Jacob Frumkin, Gregor Aronson, and Alexis Goldenweiser. New York and London: Thomas Yoseloff Publishers: 144–172.

Asaf, M. (1965a). '*Ba-Lev u-Ba-Nefesh*.' *Davar*, July 8, 3.

— (1965b). '*Teshuva le-Natan Hofshi*.' *Davar*, July 26, 3.

Ashlag, Yehudah (undated). '*Ha-pitaron*.' www.kab.co.il/heb/content/view/frame/3812?/heb/content/view/full/3812&mai (accessed January 23, 2020).

— (1956). '*Histaklut penimit*.' In *Talmud Eser ha-Sefirot*: Vol. 1, part 1. Jerusalem: 13–27.

— (1961). *Zohar im Perush ha-Sulam*: Vol. 1. Jerusalem.

— (1995). *Matan Torah*. Jerusalem: Or ha-Ganuz.

— (1999). '*Ahavat Hashem we-Ahavat ha-Beriyot*.' *Pri hakham: Ma'amarim*. Bnei Brak: n.p.

— (2015). *The Writings of the Last Generation & the Nation*. Toronto: Laitman Kabbalah Publishers.

Astor, Mikhael (1967). *Geshichte fun der Frayland Lige on fun Teritoriyalistishen*. New York: Freeland League.

Auerbach, Sascha (2007). 'Negotiating Nationalism: Jewish Conscription and Russian Repatriation in London's East End, 1916–1918.' *Journal of British Studies* 46, no. 3: 594–620.

Avishai, Bernard (2008). *The Hebrew Republic: How Secular Democracy and Global Enterprise Will Bring Israel Peace at Last*. Boston: Houghton Mifflin Harcourt.

Avner, Ari and Naftali Prat (eds) (2001). '*Shtaynberg, Yitshak Nahman*.' In *Elektronaya Evreyskaya Ensyklopediya*. Vol. 10. Jerusalem: Obschestvo Po Issledovaniyu Yevreyskikh Obshchin.

Avrich, Paul (1990). *Anarchist Portraits*. Princeton: Princeton University Press.

— (2005). *Anarchist Voices: An Oral History of Anarchism in America*. Okland: AK Press.

— (2015). *Russian Anarchists*. Princeton: Princeton University Press.

Bakunin, M. (1971). 'Federalism, Socialism, Anti-Theologism.' In *On Anarchy*. Edited and translated by S. Dolgoff, New York: Vintage: 102–147.

Baldwin, Peter M. (1980). 'Liberalism, Nationalism, and Degeneration: The Case of Max Nordau.' *Central European History* 13, no. 2: 99–120.

Barclay, Harold (2010). 'Anarchist Confrontations with Religion.' In *New Perspectives on Anarchism*. Edited by Nathan J. Jun and Shane Wahl. Lanham: Rowman & Littlefield: 169–185.

Bar-On, Mordechai (1996). *In Pursuit of Peace: A History of the Israeli Peace Movement*. Washington DC: US Institute of Peace Press.

Bar-Yosef, Hamutal (1996). 'De-Romanticized Zionism in Modern Hebrew Literature.' *Modern Judaism* 16, no. 1: 67–79.

Bashevis Singer, Isaac (2000). *More Stories from My Father's Court: A Collection*. New York: Farrar, Straus and Giroux.

Bat-Yehuda, Geula (1987). 'Rabbi Shmuel Alexandrov.' *Sinai* 100: 195–221.

Bat-Yehuda, Geula and Yitshak Rafael (eds) (1965). 'Lewin, Binyamin Menashe.' *Ensyklopediya shel Ziyonut ha-Datit*. Vol. 3. Jerusalem: Mossad Harav Kook.

Bauer, Nicole (2019). 'The Kabbalah Centre and Spirituality of the Self.' *International Journal for the Study of New Religions* 10, no. 1: 49–65.

Beiser, Friedrich C. (2003). *The Romantic Imperative: The Concept of Early German Romanticism*. Cambridge, MA: Harvard University Press.

Belinson, Moshe E. (1893). *Yalkut Mishpahot. Iggeret Yuhasin le-Mishpahat Alexandrov*. Odessa: Belinson.

Benaroya, Abraham (1949). 'A Note on "The Socialist Federation of Saloniki".' *Jewish Social Studies* 11, no. 1: 69–72.

Ben-Ezra, A. (1978). *Demuyot: Ishim Yedu'im u-Balti Yedu'im*. Tel Aviv: he-Ashur.

Ben-Gurion, David (1950). 'On War and on Immigrant Absorption,' *Ner*, April 28.

Benjamin, Walter (1968). *Illuminations: Essays and Reflections*. Edited by Hannah Arendt and Harry Zohn. New York: Schocken.

— (2003). *Walter Benjamin: Selected Writings, 1938–1940*. Vol. 4. Edited by Michael W. Jennings. Cambridge, MA: Harvard University Press.

Bennett, Scott H. (2001). 'Radical Pacifism and the General Strike Against War: Jessie Wallace Hughan, the Founding of the War Resisters League, and the Socialist Origins of Secular Radical Pacifism in America.' *Peace & Change* 26, no. 3: 352–373.

Ben-Porath, Sigal R. (2009). *Citizenship Under Fire: Democratic Education in Times of Conflict*. Princeton: Princeton University Press.

Berdichevsky, Mikhal Y. (1888). '*Yediyat Soferim*.' *Ha-Zefira*, April 13, 10.

Berdyaev, Nicholas, Alan A. Spears, and Victor B. Kanter (1950). 'Christianity and Anti-Semitism.' *CrossCurrents* 1, no. 1: 43–54.

Berk, Stephen M. (1977). 'The Russian Revolutionary Movement and the Pogroms of 1881–1882.' *East European Jewish Affairs* 7, no. 2: 22–39.

Berkman, Alexander (2003). *What is Anarchism?* Oakland: AK Press.

Berkowitz, Michael (2012). 'Emma Goldman's Radical Trajectory: A Resiliant "Litvak" Legacy?' *Journal of Modern Jewish Studies* 11, no. 2: 243–263.

Berline, Paul (1947). 'Russian Religious Philosophers and the Jews (Soloviev, Berdyaev, Bulgakov, Struve, Rozanov and Fedotov).' *Jewish Social Studies*: 271–318.

Berti, Francesco (2010). 'Torah e Libertà.' *A/Rivista Anarchica* 40, no. 352 (April): 73–76.

Biagini, Furio (2008). *Studio sulle Corrispondenze tra Ebraismo e Anarchismo*. Lecce: Icaro.

Biale, David *et al.* (2017). *Hasidism: A New History*. Princeton: Princeton University Press.

Bick, Avraham (1940). *Kempfer un Hiter: Di Sotsial-Etishe Idea in der Yiddisher Religiezer Literatur un Leben*. New York: Atlantic.

Bielfeldt, Sigrun (2019). 'Schelling's Prehistory in Russia: The Legacy of Enlightenment.' *International Journal of Philosophy and Theology* 80, no. 1–2: 90–100.

Bing, Anthony G. (1990). *Israeli Pacifist: The Life of Joseph Abileah*. Syracuse: Syracuse University Press.

Birkenmaier, Willy (2014). *Jerusalem ist überall: Isaak Steinbergs Kritik am Zionismus*. Vol. 44. Eigenverlag.

Blatman, Daniel (2010). Bund. YIVO Encyclopedia of Jews in Eastern Europe. https://yivoencyclopedia.org/article.aspx/Bund (accessed July 8, 2020).

Blau, Yitzchak (2007). 'Rabbinic Responses to Communism.' *Tradition: A Journal of Orthodox Jewish Thought* 40, no. 4: 7–27.

Bloch, Ernst (1986). *The Principle of Hope*. Translated by Neville Plaice. Cambridge, MA: MIT Press.

Block, Irving (1963). 'Chabad Psychology and the "Beinoni" of the Tanya.' *Tradition: A Journal of Orthodox Jewish Thought* 6, no. 1: 30–39.

Borovoj, Aleksej A. (1989). *Anarchism and Law*. Buffalo: Friends of Malatesta.

Boshover, Joseph (1925). *Schriften*. New York: Farlag Arbeter Fraynd un Fraye Arbeter Shtime.

Bowie, A. (2016). 'Friedrich Wilhelm Joseph von Schelling.' *The Stanford Ency-clopedia of Philosophy* (Fall 2016 Edition), Edited by Edward N. Zalta. https://plato.stanford.edu/archives/fall2016/entries/schelling (accessed September 29, 2020).

Boyarin, Daniel (1997). *Unheroic Conduct: The Rise of Heterosexuality and the Invention of the Jewish Man.* Berkeley: University of California Press.

— (2015). *A Traveling Homeland: The Babylonian Talmud as Diaspora.* Philadelphia: University of Pennsylvania Press.

Boyarin, Daniel and Jonathan Boyarin (1993). 'Diaspora: Generation and the Ground of Jewish Identity.' *Critical Inquiry* 19, no. 4: 693–725.

Brill, Alan (2004). 'Judaism in Culture: Beyond the Bifurcation of Torah and Madda.' *The Edah Journal* 4, no. 1:1. www.edah.org/backend/JournalArticle/4_1_brill.pdf (accessed September 29, 2020).

— (2012). *Judaism and World Religions.* New York: Palgrave.

Brody, Samuel (2018). *Martin Buber's Theopolitics.* Bloomington: Indiana University Press.

Brown, Benjamin (2014). 'Jewish Political Theology: The Doctrine of "Da'at Torah" as a Case Study.' *The Harvard Theological Review* 107, no. 3: 255–289.

Buber, Martin (1996). *Paths in Utopia.* Syracuse: Syracuse University Press.

Buchan, Bruce (2018). 'Anarchism and Liberalism.' In *Brill's Companion to Anarchism and Philosophy.* Edited by Nathan Jun. Leiden: Brill: 51–80.

Bukiet, A. S. (2008). *Ha-Tanya: Nahalat ha-Am.* Kfar Habad: Ha-Hamisha.

Burmistrov, Konstantin (2007a). 'The Interpretation of Kabbalah in Early 20th-Century Russian Philosophy: Soloviev, Bulgakov, Florenskii, Losev.' *East European Jewish Affairs* 37, no. 2: 157–187.

— (2007b). 'Christian Orthodoxy and Jewish Kabbalah: Russian Mystics in the Search for Perennial Wisdom.' In *Polemical Encounters.* Leiden: Brill: 25–54.

Bush, Julia (1980). 'East London Jews and the First World War.' *The London Journal* 6, no. 2: 147–161.

Campbell, Michelle (2013). 'Voltairine de Cleyre and the Anarchist Canon.' *Anarchist Developments in Cultural Studies*: 64–81.

Carnochan, Peter Jack (1980). 'The Role of the Intelligentsia in the Political Thought of the Revolutionary Narodnik Strategists: Bakunin, Lavrov and Tkachev.' PhD diss., University of Birmingham.

Carr, Jessica (2020). 'Redefining Kabbalah: Combinative American Religion at the Kabbalah Centre.' *Shofar: An Interdisciplinary Journal of Jewish Studies* 38, no. 1: 76–108.

Cesarani, David (1989). 'An Embattled Minority: The Jews in Britain during the First World War.' *Immigrants & Minorities* 8, no. 1–2: 60–81.

Chatterjee, Margarett (1997). 'The Redemptive Role of Labor. In *Studies in Modern Jewish and Hindu Thought.* Basingstoke: Palgrave Macmillan.

Chernov, Victor (1948). *Yiddish Tuer in der Partey Sotsyalistn Revolutsiyonern.* New York: Shoulson Press.

Christoyannopoulos, Alexandre (2008). 'Leo Tolstoy on the State: A Detailed Picture of Tolstoy's Denunciation of State Violence and Deception.' *Anarchist Studies* 16, no. 1: 20–47.

— (ed.) (2009). *Religious Anarchism: New Perspectives.* Newcastle: Cambridge Scholars Publishing.

— (2019). *Tolstoy's Political Thought: Christian Anarcho-Pacifist Iconoclasm Then and Now.* New York: Routledge.

Christoyannopoulos, Alexandre and Mathew Adams (eds) (2017). *Essays in Anarchism and Religion: Volume I*. Stockholm: Stockholm University Press.

— (2018). *Essays in Anarchism and Religion: Volume II*. Loughborough University.

— (2020). *Essays in Anarchism and Religion: Volume III*. Stockholm: Stockholm University Press.

Christoyannopoulos, Alexandre and Lara Apps (2018). 'Anarchism and Religion.' In *Brill's Companion to Anarchism and Philosophy*. Edited by Nathan Jun. Leiden: Brill: 120–151.

Ciccariello-Maher, George (2011). 'An Anarchism that is Not Anarchism: Notes Toward a Critique of Anarchist Imperialism.' *How Not to be Governed*. Lanham, MD: Lexington Books.

Cohen, Aryeh (2015). '"The Foremost Amongst the Divine Attributes is to Hate the Vulgar Power of Violence": Aharon Shmuel Tamares and Recovering Nonviolence for Jewish Ethics.' *The Journal of Jewish Ethics* 1, no. 2: 233–252.

Cohn, Jesse (2009). 'Anarchism and Gender.' In *The International Encyclopedia of Revolution and Protest*. Edited by Immanuel Ness. Malden: Wiley-Blackwell: 1–5.

Cohn, Naftali S. (2008). 'The Ritual Narrative Genre in the Mishnah: The invention of the Rabbinic Past in the Representation of Temple Ritual.' PhD diss., University of Pennsylvania.

Confino, Michael and Daniel Rubinstein (1981). 'Anarchisme et internationalisme. Autour du "Manifeste des Seize." Correspondance inédite de Pierre Kropotkine et de Marie Goldsmith, janvier–mars 1916.' *Cahiers du monde russe et soviétique* (1981): 231–249.

— (1982). 'Kropotkine en 1914: La guerre et les congrès manqués des anarchistes russes. Lettres inédites de Pierre Kropotkine à Marie Goldsmith. 11 janvier–31 décembre 1914.' *Cahiers du Monde russe et soviétique*: 63–107.

— (1992). 'Kropotkine savant. Vingt-cinq lettres inédites de Pierre Kropotkine à Marie Goldsmith. 27 juillet 1901–9 juillet 1915.' *Cahiers du Monde russe et soviétique*: 243–301.

Conforti, Yitshak (2011a). 'The New Jew in the Zionist Movement: Ideology and Historiography.' *The Australian Journal of Jewish Studies* 25: 87–119.

— (2011b). 'Between Ethnic and Civic: The Realistic Utopia of Zionism.' *Israel Affairs* 17, no. 4: 563–582.

Crosby, Travis L (2014). *The Unknown Lloyd George: A Statesman in Conflict*. London: Tauris.

Daigin, Uri (2008). 'Kabbalah in Russian Religious Philosophy: The Impact of the Kabbalah on the Russian Sophiological Movement (during the Period from the Last Quarter of the Nineteenth Century to the Middle of the Twentieth Century).' PhD diss., Bar Ilan University.

Daniel, S. (1932). 'Hillel Zeitlin: Le-Yovlo ha-Shishim.' *Ha-Hed* 7, no. 9, 23.

Danzinger, Shelomo (1966). 'Modern Orthodoxy or Orthodox Modernism?' *Jewish Observer*: 3.

Davies, Helen M. (2016). *Emile and Isaac Pereire: Bankers, Socialists and Sephardic Jews in Nineteenth-Century France*. Manchester: Manchester University Press.

Deleuze, Gilles and Felix Guattari (1986). *Kafka: Toward a Minor Literature*. Translated by Dana Polan. Minneapolis: University of Minnesota Press.

De Oca, Rodolfo M. (2019). *Venezuelan Anarchism: The History of a Movement*. Tucson: See Sharp Press.

Deutsch, Karl (1969). *Nationalism and its Alternatives*. New York: Knopf.

Deutscher, Isaac (2017). *The Non-Jewish Jew and Other Essays*. New York: Verso.

Don-Yahiya, Shabtay (1932). *Rabbi Eliezer Don-Yahiya: Megilat Hayav*. Jerusalem: Defus Pinhas Eynav.

Don-Yahiya, Yehudah L. (1902). *Ha-Ziyonut me-Nekudat Hashkafat ha-Da'at*. Vilna: Shaarey Tsiyon.

— (c. 1914). 'Letter to Ahad Ha'am, dated 1914.' National Library of Israel. Ahad Ha'am Archive, ARC.4* 791 2 1194.

— (1930). *Bikurei Yehudah*. Vol. 1. Ludza: Defus Zev Wolf.

— (1933). *Bikurei Yehudah*. Vol. 1. Ludza: Defus Zev Wolf.

— (1939). *Bikurei Yehudah*. Vol. 2. Tel Aviv: Defus Y. Neiman & Yunish.

— (2004). '*Zikhronotai*.' *Yeshivat Lita: Pirkei Zikhronot*. Edited by Immanuel Etkes and S. Tikuchinsky. Jerusalem: Merkaz Zalman Shazar.

Dubnova-Erlich, Sofie (1991). *The Life and Work of S. M. Dubnov: Diaspora Nationalism and Jewish History*. Bloomington: Indiana University Press.

Dubnow, Arie M. (2011). 'Zionism on the Diasporic Front.' *Journal of Israeli History* 30, no. 2: 211–224.

Dubnow, Simon (1918). *History of the Jews in Russia and Poland, from the Earliest Times Until the Present Day Vol. 2*. Translated by Israel Friedlander. Philadelphia: Jewish Publication Society.

— (1920). *History of the Jews in Russia and Poland, from the Earliest Times Until the Present Day Vol. 3*. Translated by Israel Friedlander. Philadelphia: Jewish Publication Society.

— (2012). 'Jews as a Spiritual (Cultural-Historical) Nation Among Political Nations.' In *Jews and Diaspora Nationalism: Writings on Jewish Peoplehood in Europe and the United States*. Edited by Simon Rabinovitch. Waltham: Brandeis University Press: 23–44.

Duffy, Michael F. and Willard Mittelman (1988). 'Nietzsche's Attitudes toward the Jews.' *Journal of the History of Ideas*: 301–317.

Eisenstadt, Ben-Zion (1895). *Dor Rabanav we-Sofrav*. Warsaw: Halter & Eisenstadt.

Elazar, Daniel J. (ed.) (1983). *Kinship and Consent: The Jewish Political Tradition and Its Contemporary Uses*. Lanham: University Press of America.

Elgot, Jessica (2012). 'Strictly Orthodox Neturei Karta's New Alliance with Extreme Right.' *Jewish Chronicle*. www.thejc.com/news/uk-news/strictly-orthodox-neturei-karta-s-new-alliance-with-extreme-right-1.33770 (accessed September 29, 2020).

Eliav, Mordechai (1999). 'Pioneers of Modern Jewish and Religious Education for Girls: The First Schools in Germany in the 19th Century.' *Abiding Challenges. Research Perspectives on Jewish Education: Studies in Memory of Mordechai Bar-Lev, Ramat Gan*. Bar Ilan University: 145–159.

Engels, Freidrich (1892). *Socialism: Utopian and Scientific*. Translated by E. Aveling. New York: Scribner.

Epstein, Alek D. (1998). 'For the Peoples of the Promised Land: Intellectual and Social Origins of Jewish Pacifism in Israel.' *Journal of Israeli History* 19, no. 2: 5–20.

Eshel, Z. (1954). '*Sarvane ha-Milkhama: Mah Dinam be-Yisrael?*' Ha-Tsofe, June 24, 2.

Etkes, Immanuel (2010). 'Haskalah.' YIVO Encyclopedia of Jews in Eastern Europe. https://yivoencyclopedia.org/article.aspx/Haskalah (accessed July 3, 2020).

Evren, Sureyyya (2012). 'There Ain't No Black in the Anarchist Flag! Race.' *The Bloomsbury Companion to Anarchism*. Edited by Ruth Kinna. New York: Bloomsbury Publishing: 299.

Eynav, Moshe (1967). *Be-Sa'arat ha-Hayyim: Dr. Yitshak Nahman Shtaynberg, le-Demuto u-le-Derekh Hayav*. Tel Aviv: Me-Havrut le-Safrut.

Feinstein, Edward (2012). 'Kabbalah and the Spiritual Quest: The Kabbalah Centre in America.' *Conservative Judaism* 63, no. 4: 119–121.

Feldman, David E. (2004). *Pilgrimage from Darkness: Nuremberg to Jerusalem.* Jackson: University of Mississippi Press.

Fiala, A. (2018). 'Pacifism.' *The Stanford Encyclopedia of Philosophy* (Fall 2018 Edition). Edited by Edward N. Zalta. https://plato.stanford.edu/archives/fall2018/entries/pacifism/ (accessed September 29, 2020).

Fichte, Johann G. (2008). *Fichte: Addresses to the German Nation.* Cambridge: Cambridge University Press.

Fine, Lawrence (1989). 'Tikkun: A Lurianic Motif in Contemporary Jewish Thought.' *From ancient Israel to Modern Judaism: Intellect in Question of Understanding. Essays in Honor of Marvin Fox, Volume Four*: 35–55.

Firestone, Reuven (2012). *Holy War in Judaism: The Fall and Rise of a Controversial Idea.* New York: Oxford University Press.

Fisher, Edward (1828). *The Marrow of Divinity.* Edinburgh: John Boyd.

Fishman, Talya (1992). 'A Kabbalistic Perspective on Gender-Specific Commandments: On the Interplay of Symbols and Society.' *AJS Review* 17, no. 2: 199–246.

Fishman, William J. (2004). *East End Jewish Radicals: 1875–1914.* Nottingham: Five Leaves.

Forman, Michael (2010). *Nationalism and the International Labor Movement: The Idea of the Nation in Socialist and Anarchist Theory.* University Park: Penn State Press.

Foti, Veronique M. (2006). *Epochal Discordance: Hölderlin's Philosophy of Tragedy.* Albany: State University of New York Press.

Foxbrunner, Roman A. (1993). *Habad: The Hasidism of R. Shneur Zalman of Lyady.* Tuscaloosa: University of Alabama Press.

Frankel, Jonathan (1984). *Prophecy and Politics: Socialism, Nationalism, and the Russian Jews, 1862–1917.* Cambridge: Cambridge University Press.

— (2009). *Crisis, Revolution, and Russian Jews.* Cambridge: Cambridge University Press.

Franks, Benjamin (2006). Rebel Alliances: The Means and Ends of Contemporary British Anarchisms. London: AK Press.

— (2018). 'Prefiguration.' In *Anarchism: A Conceptual Approach.* Edited by Benjamin Franks, Nathan Jun, and Leonard Williams. New York: Routledge: 28–43.

Franks, Paul (2019). 'Mythology, Essence, and Form: Schellin p g's Jewish Reception in the Nineteenth Century.' *International Journal of Philosophy and Theology* 80, no. 1–2: 71–89.

Friedman, Menachem (1994). 'Habad as Messianic Fundamentalism: From Local Particularism to Universal Jewish Mission.' In *Accounting for Fundamentalism, the Dynamic Character of Movements.* Edited by Martin E. Marty and F. Scott Appbleby. Chicago: University of Chicago Press: 328–357.

Fromm, E. (undated). 'The Man of Faith: Dr. I. N. Steinberg.' Central Zionist Archives, A330/327.

Fuchs, Ilan (2013). *Jewish Women's Torah Study: Orthodox Religious Education and Modernity.* New York: Routledge.

Gamblin, Graham J. (2000). 'Russian Populism and its Relations with Anarchism 1870–1881.' PhD diss., University of Birmingham.

Gangulee, Nagendranath (2006). *Giuseppe Mazzini-Selected Writings.* Hong Kong: Hesperides Press.

Garb, Jonathan (2004). 'The Concept of Power in the Circle of Rabbi Kook.' *Jerusalem Studies in Jewish Thought*, 19: 753–770.

— (2009). *The Chosen Will Become Herds: Studies in Twentieth-Century Kabbalah*. Translated by Yaffa Berkovitz-Murciano. New Haven: Yale University Press.

Garcia, Renaud and Anatole Lucet (2019). 'Family and Society. Reflections on Gustav Landauer's "Conservative" Anarchism.' *Actuel Marx* 2: 115–131.

Gardiner, Michael (1992). 'Bakhtin's Carnival: Utopia as Critique.' *Utopian Studies* 3, no. 2: 21–49.

Gechtman, Roni (2005). 'Conceptualizing National-Cultural Autonomy: From the Austro-Marxists to the Jewish Labor Bund.' *Jahrbuch des Simon-Dubnow-Instituts* 4: 17–49.

— (2011). 'Creating a Historical Narrative for a Spiritual Nation: Simon Dubnow and the Politics of the Jewish Past.' *Journal of the Canadian Historical Association/ Revue de la Société historique du Canada* 22, no. 2: 98–124.

Gemie, Sharif (1996). 'Anarchism and Feminism: A Historical Survey.' *Women's History Review* 5, no. 3: 417–444.

Gendler, Everett (2003). 'Ancient Visions, Future Hopes: Rabbi Aaron Samuel Tamaret's Objection to Zionism As We Know It.' *Tikkun* 18 no. 4: 25–30.

— (2010). 'Elements of a Philosophy for Diaspora Judaism: An Introduction to Rabbi Aaron Samuel Tamaret's "The Exile of the Presence and the Presence of the Exile."' *Tikkun* 25, no. 6: 54–56.

Gerasimova, Inna (2007). 'The Opposition of the Belarusian Rabbis to the Anticlerical Policy of the Soviet Government in the 1920s and 30s: Repressive Policies of the Soviet Authorities in Belarus, *Memorial*: 230–252.

Gershuni, A. (1961). *Yahadut be-Rusiya ha-Soviyetit: Le-Korot Redifot ha-Da'at*. Jerusalem: Mossad Harav Kook.

Glatzer, N. N. (2009). *Essays in Jewish Thought*. Tuscaloosa: University of Alabama Press.

Goldman, Emma (1989). 'On Zionism.' In *British Imperialism and The Palestine Crisis: Selections from the Anarchist Journal 'Freedom' 1938–1948*. Edited by Vernon Richards. London: Freedom Press: 24–27.

— (2011). *Living My Life*. New York: Cosimo.

Goldshlag, Y. (1956). 'Ha-Rav Avraham Heyn we-Yetsirato.' *Or ha-Mizrah* 2, no. 10: 42–44, 47.

Goldwyn, Adam J (2015). 'Joseph Eliyia and the Jewish Question in Greece: Zionism, Hellenism, and the Struggle for Modernity.' *Journal of Modern Greek Studies* 33, no. 2: 365–388.

Golovic, R. (2020). 'The Sobornost: from the History of Russian Religious Social Thought.' *Sociological Studies* 5, no. 5: 121–125.

Goncharok, Moshe (2011). 'On the Question of the Relationship Between Certain Aspects of Judaism and Anarchism.' *Journal for the Study of Jewish History, Demography and Economy, Literature, Language and Ethnography* 6 (1): 8–22.

Gordin, Abba (1940). *Moral in Idishen Leben*. New York: Jewish Ethical Society.

Gordon, Adi (2017). *Toward Nationalism's End: An Intellectual Biography of Hans Kohn*. Waltham: Brandeis University Press, 142–158.

Gordon, Uri (2009). 'Anarchism, Israel and Palestine.' *The International Encyclopedia of Revolution and Protest*: 1–3.

— (2018a). 'Prefigurative Politics Between Ethical Practice and Absent Promise.' *Political Studies* 66, no. 2: 521–537.

— (2018b). 'Anarchism and Nationalism.' In *Brill's Companion to Anarchism and Philosophy*. Edited by Nathan Jun. Leiden: Brill: 196–215.

Gotlieb, S. N. (1912). *Ohaley Shem*. Pinsk: Defus Glouberman.

Graeber, David (2011). *Debt: The First 5000 Years*. New York: Melville House.

Grauer, Mina (1994). 'Anarcho-Nationalism: Anarchist Attitudes Towards Jewish Nationalism and Zionism.' *Modern Judaism*: 1–19.

Grill, Tobias (2014). 'Isaak Nachman Steinberg: "Als ich Volkskommissar war" oder "Eine soziale Revolution, die die Rechte ihrer Klassengegner verteidigt-das wäre eine große moralische Lehre der Menschlichkeit gewesen!"' *Nordost-Archiv: Zeitschrift für Regionalgeschichte* 23.

— (2015). 'Kampf für Sozialismus und Judentum auf vier Kontinenten: Isaac Nachman Steinberg's Rooted Cosmopolitanism.' *BIOS-Zeitschrift für Biographieforschung, Oral History und Lebensverlaufsanalysen* 28, no. 1–2: 41–65.

Gudemann, M. (1892). 'Spirit and Letter in Judaism and Christianity.' *The Jewish Quarterly Review* 4, no. 3: 345–356.

Guerin, Daniel (1970). *Anarchism: From Theory to Practice*. New York: Monthly Review Press.

Guy, A. (1949). '*Davar we-Hefukho: Ha-Safa ha_holandit hi Safa Mapai'it.*' *Herut*, April 14, 2.

Haaland, Bonnie (1993). *Emma Goldman: Sexuality and the Impurity of the State*. New York: Black Rose.

Ha'am, Ahad (1922). *Ahad Ha'am: Essays, Letters, Memoirs*. Translated by Leon Simon. London: Routledge.

Haberer, Erich (1992). 'Haskalah and the Roots of Jewish Radicalism in Nineteenth-Century Russia.' In *Jewish Sects, Religious Movements and Political Parties: Proceedings of the Third Annual Symposium of the Philip M. and Ethel Klutznick Chair in Jewish Civilization*: 123–147.

Hackett, Colleen (2015). 'Justice Through Defiance: Political Prisoner Support Work and Infrastructures of Resistance.' *Contemporary Justice Review* 18, no. 1: 68–75.

Hadas-Lebel, Mireille (1984). 'Jacob et Esau ou Israel et Rome dans le Talmud et le Midrash.' *Revue de l'histoire des religions*: 369–392.

Hafner, Lutz (1991). 'The Assassination of Count Mirbach and the "July Uprising" of the Left Socialist Revolutionaries in Moscow, 1918.' *The Russian Review* 50, no. 3: 324–344.

Halbertal, Moshe (1997). *People of the Book: Canon, Meaning, and Authority*. Cambridge, MA: Harvard University Press.

Hamburg, S. (1977). 'Der Varshaver anarkhist: Aaron Pinhas Gross.' *Fraye Arbeter Shtime*: 6.

Hartman, Daniel (1989). 'The Halakhic Hero: Rabbi Joseph Soloveitchik, Halakhic Man.' *Modern Judaism*: 249–273.

Hartman, Harriet and Moshe Hartman (2003). 'Gender and Jewish Identity.' *Journal of Contemporary Religion* 18, no. 1: 37–60.

Hartung, B. (1983). 'Anarchism and the Problem of Order.' *Mid-American Review of Sociology* 8, no. 1: 83–101.

Hattis, Susan L. (1970). *The Bi-National Idea in Palestine During Mandatory Times*. Jerusalem: Shikmona.

Hayes, Christine (2017). 'Law in Classical Rabbinic Judaism.' In *The Cambridge Companion to Judaism and Law*. Edited by Christine Hayes. Cambridge: Cambridge University Press: 76–127.

Hegel, G. F. W. (1975). *Aesthetics: Lectures on Fine Art*. Vol. 2. Translated by T. M. Knox. Oxford: Clarendon Press.

Hein-Shimoni, Leon (1968). '*Doktor Ya'akov Meir Zalkind Z'L.*' *Problemen* no. 50: 25–26.

Hellinger, Moshe (2012). 'Judaism: Historical Setting,' In *The Wiley-Blackwell Companion to Religion and Social Justice*. Edited by Michael D. Palmer and Stanley M. Burgess. Malden, MA: Wiley-Blackwell: 170–189.

Hermoni, Avraham (1948). '*Hastudent mibern: ziḥronot al Ya'kov Rabinoviz.*' *Al Hamishmar*, 6.

Heyn, Avraham (1931). *Lenahameyni*. Tel Aviv: Self published.

— (1958). *Be-Malkhut ha-Yahadut*. Vol. 1. Jerusalem: Mossad ha-Rav Kook.

— (1963). *Be-Malkhut ha-Yahadut*. Vol. 2. Jerusalem: Mossad ha-Rav Kook.

— (1970). *Be-Malkhut ha-Yahadut*. Vol. 3. Jerusalem: Mossad ha-Rav Kook.

Hirschauge, Eliezer (1964). *Farvirklekhung: Zikhronos-fartsaykhungen on Bamerkungen vegen der Anarkhistisher Bavegung in Polin* (Tel Aviv: Ha-Merkaz).

Hofshi, Natan (1920). '*Me-ha-Galil ha-Elyon.*' *Ha-Po'el ha-Za'ir*, 15–16.

— (1922). '*Mitokh ha-Prati Kol shel Ve'idat ha-Po'el ha-Tsa'ir.*' *Ha-Po'el ha-Za'ir*, 13.

— (1930). '*Mikhtave Haverim.*' *Davar*, 3.

— (1935). Hofshi, N. '*Mikhtav le-Ma'arekhet.*' *Davar*, 4.

— (1938). '*He'arot Ketanot le-Inyanim Gedolim.*' *Davar*, 6.

— (1939). '*Al Ketanot she-Nishkahu.*' *Davar*, 4.

— (1974). '*Be-Ad we-Neged Amdat Kaniyuk.*' *Davar*, 12.

— (1943a). '*Le-ma'an ha-Emet.*' *Davar*, 4.

— (1943b). '*Mikhtavim le-Ma'arekhet: Be-Inyan Dak Ehad.*' *Davar*, 4.

— (1950). '*She'alu Shalom.*' *Maariv*, 5.

— (1962). '*Be-Ta'uno she Professor Buber Mosif le-Hatif I-Teliyat Eichman.*' *Herut*, March 27, 2.

— (1964a). *Ba-Lev we-Nefesh: Be-Maavak be-Am we-Adam*. Tel Aviv: Strod & Sons.

— (1964b). '*Metsuka we-Shefa.*' *Davar*, 3.

— (1965a). '*Kashihut we-Tsedek.*' *Davar*, 3.

— (1965b). '*Melakha Kala we-Nekiya.*' *Davar*, 3.

— (1966). '*Ba-Lev we-Nefesh: Le-Zikhro shel Y.N. Steinberg.*' *Problemot* 40: 2–3.

— (1972). '*Shaalah Avrahamit.*' *Davar*, 10.

Hollerbach, Thomas (2006). 'Turnvater Jahn — Gouvernementalität der Ertüchtigung.' In *Gouvernementalität und Erziehungswissenschaft*. VS Verlag für Sozialwissenschaften: 265–280.

Honigmann, Peter (1992). 'Jüdische Studenten zwischen Orthodoxie und moderner Wissenschaft. Der Heidelberger Talmudistenkreis um Salman Baruch Rabinkow,' *Menora. Jahrbuch für deutsch-jüdische Geschichte*: 85–96.

Horkheimer, Max and Theodor W. Adorno (2002). *Dialectic of Enlightenment*. Translated by Gunzelin Noer. Redwood City: Stanford University Press.

Horrox, James (2009). *A Living Revolution: Anarchism in the Kibbutz Movement*. Oakland: AK Press.

Howe, Irving (2005). *World of Our Fathers*. New York: New York University Press.

Huskey, Eugene (2014). *Russian Lawyers and the Soviet State: The Origins and Development of the Soviet Bar, 1917–1939*. Vol. 107. Princeton: Princeton University Press.

Huss, Boaz (2004). '*Komunizm altruisiti,*' *Iyyunim be-tekumak Yisrael: Ma'asaf le-ba'ayot ha-Tsiyonut, ha-yishuv, u-Medinat Yisrael* 16: 109–130.

— (2005a). 'All you need is LAV: Madonna and Postmodern Kabbalah.' *Jewish Quarterly Review* 95, no. 4: 611–624.

— (2005b). 'Ask No Questions: Gershom Scholem and the Study of Contemporary Jewish Mysticism.' *Modern Judaism* 25, no. 2: 141–158.

— (2007). 'Authorized Guardians: The Polemics of Academic Scholars of Jewish Mysticism Against Kabbalah Practitioners.' In *Polemical Encounters: Esoteric*

Discourse and its Others. Edited by Olav Hammer and Kocku von Stuckrad. Leiden: Brill: 81–103.

— (2015). 'Kabbalah and the Politics of Inauthenticity: The Controversies over the Kabbalah Center.' *Numen* 62, no. 2–3: 197–225.

Ilicak, H. Sükrü (2002). 'Jewish Socialism in Ottoman Salonica.' *Southeast European and Black Sea Studies* 2, no. 3: 115–146.

Ish-Shalom, Benjamin (1993). *Rav Avraham Itzhak Hacohen Kook: Between Rationalism and Mysticism*. Syracuse: Syracuse: SUNY Press.

Ish-Shalom, Benjamin and S. Rosenberg (eds) (1991). *The World of Rav Kook's Thought*. Jerusalem: Avi-Chai.

Jacobson, Eric (2003). *Metaphysics of the Profane: The Political Theology of Walter Benjamin and Gershom Scholem*. New York: Columbia University Press.

Jost, I. M. (1824). *History of Israel*. Vol. 4. Berlin: Schlesingerschen.

Jun, Nathan (2013). 'Rethinking the Anarchist Canon: History, Philosophy, and Interpretation.' *Anarchist Developments in Cultural Studies* 1. https://journals.uvic.ca/index.php/adcs/article/view/17140 (accessed 25 September 2020).

Jung, Leo (1987). *Sages and Saints*. New York: Ktav.

Jutte, Daniel (2015). *The Age of Secrecy: Jews, Christians, and the Economy of Secrets, 1400–1800*. New Haven: Yale University Press.

Kaddish, Sharmen (2013). *Bolsheviks and British Jews: The Anglo-Jewish Community, Britain and the Russian Revolution*. New York: Routledge.

Kaplan, Eran (2005a). *The Jewish Radical Right: Revisionist Zionism and its Ideological Legacy*. Madison: University of Wisconsin Press.

— (2005b). 'A Rebel with a Cause: Hillel Kook, Begin and Jabotinsky's Ideological Legacy.' *Israel studies* 10, no. 3: 87–103.

— (2015). *Beyond Post-Zionism*. Albany: State University of New York Press.

Katz, Jacob (1997). 'Da'at Torah: The Unqualified Authority Claimed for Halakhists.' *Jewish History*: 41–50.

Keren, Michael (2002). *Zichroni V. State of Israel: The Biography of a Civil Rights Lawyer*. Lanham: Lexington.

Khuri-Makdisi, Ilham (2010). *The Eastern Mediterranean and the Making of Global Radicalism, 1860–1914*. Berkeley: University of California Press.

Kiel, Mark (1970). 'The Jewish Narodnik.' *Judaism* 19, no. 3: 295.

Kimelman, Reuven (1995). 'Abravanel and the Jewish Republican Ethos.' In *Commandment and Community: New Essays in Jewish Legal and Political Philosophy*. Edited by Daniel H. Frank. Albany: State University of New York Press: 195–216.

Kinna, Ruth (2005). *Anarchism: A Beginner's Guide*. Oxford: One World.

— (2016a). *Kropotkin: Reviewing the Classical Anarchist Tradition*. Edinburgh: Edinburgh University Press.

— (2016b). 'Utopianism and Prefiguration.' *Political Uses of Utopia: New Marxist, Anarchist, and Radical Democratic Perspectives*. Edited by S. D. Chrostowska and James Ingram. New York: Columbia University Press: 198–215.

Klarmen, Y. (1931). '*Der Velt-Tsuzamenfar fun Bris-Trumpeldor in Danzig: Jabotinsky's Groyser Ideologischer Report*.' *Haynt*, 4.

Klein, Charlotte (1978). 'Anti-Judaism in Christian Theology.' *Religious Studies Review* 4, no. 3: 161–168.

Kleinman, M. (1938). '*Ya'kov Meir Zalkind: Le-yom ha-shevi'i le-moto*.' *Davar*, 9.

Klieman, Aharon (2008). '*Shtadlanut* as Statecraft by the Stateless.' *Israel Journal of Foreign Affairs* 2, no. 3: 99–113.

Klier, John Doyle (2005). *Imperial Russia's Jewish Question, 1855–1881*. Vol. 96. Cambridge: Cambridge University Press.

Kloyzner, Y. (1959). 'Hibat Tsiyon be-Lita.' In *Yahadut Lita*. Vol. 1. Edited by Natan Goren, Leyb Garfunkle, Rafael Hasman, Dov Lipitz, Eliahu Segel, Israel Kaplan, and Reuben Rubinstein. Tel Aviv: Am ha-Sefer.

Knepper, Paul (2008). 'The Other Invisible Hand: Jews and Anarchists in London before the First World War.' *Jewish History* 22, no. 3: 295–315.

Kochan, Lionel (1977). 'The Apotheosis of History: Dubnow.' In *The Jew and His History*. London: Palgrave Macmillan: 88–98.

Kohn, Hans (1946). *The Idea of Nationalism: A Study in its Origins and Backgrounds*. New York: Macmillan: 330–331.

— (1949a). 'Father Jahn's Nationalism.' *The Review of Politics* 11, no. 4: 419–432.

— (1949b). 'The Paradox of Fichte's Nationalism.' *Journal of the History of Ideas*: 319–343.

— (1951). 'Ahad Ha'am: Nationalist with a difference.' *Commentary* 12: 558.

Kornblatt, Judith Deutsch (1991). 'Solov'ev's Androgynous Sophia and the Jewish Kabbalah.' *Slavic Review* 50, no. 3: 487–496.

Kosuch, Carolin (2019). 'The Secular–Religious Ambiguity in Nineteenth-Century German-Jewish Anarchism.' *Negotiating the Secular and the Religious in the German Empire: Transnational Approaches* 10: 147–170.

Krauskopf, J. (1911). *My Visit to Tolstoy: Five Discourses*. Philadelphia: Temple Keneset Yisrael.

Krauss, Chiara Russo (2019). *Wundt, Avenarius, and Scientific Psychology: A Debate at the Turn of the Twentieth Century*. Dordrecht: Springer.

Krier, Frédéric (2009). *Sozialismus für Kleinbürger: Pierre-Joseph Proudhon – Wegbereiter des Dritten Reiches*. Köln: Böhlau.

Kriloff, I. A. (1883). *Kriloff's Original Fables*. Translated by I. H. Harrison. London: Remington.

Kropotkin, Peter (1898). *Anarchist Morality*. San Francisco: Free Society.

— (1902). *Mutual Aid a Factor of Evolution*. London: McClure Phillips.

— (1907). 'On the Question of Nationalism.' *Arbeter Fraynd*. June 21, 6–7.

— (1995). '"Anarchism", from The Encyclopaedia Britannica.' In Kropotkin, *'The Conquest of Bread' and Other Writings*. Edited by Marshall S. Shatz. Cambridge Texts in the History of Political Thought. Cambridge: Cambridge University Press: 233–247.

— (1999). *Memoirs of a Revolutionist*. Mineola: Dover.

Laine, Alter E. (2013). *She'alot u-Teshuvot Avney Heyn*. New York: Kehot.

Lamm, Norman (1971). 'The Ideology of the Neturei Karta: According to the Satmarer Version.' *Tradition: A Journal of Orthodox Jewish Thought* 12, no. 2: 38–53.

Landauer, Gustav (2010). *Revolution and Other Writings: A Political Reader*. Edited and translated by Gabriel Kuhn. Oakland: PM Press.

Lavsky, Hagit (1996). 'German Zionists and the Emergence of Brit Shalom.' *Essential PAPERS on Zionism*. Edited by Jehuda Reinharz and Anita Shapira. New York: New York University Press: 171–172.

LeBlanc, Ronald D (2001). 'Vegetarianism in Russia: The Tolstoy(an) Legacy.' The Carl Beck Papers in Russian and East European Studies, No. 1507.

Lederhendler, Eli (1989). *The Road to Modern Jewish Politics: Political Tradition and Political Reconstruction in the Jewish Community of Tsarist Russia*. Oxford: Oxford University Press.

Ledesma, Manuel Pérez (2001). 'Studies on Anticlericalism in Contemporary Spain.' *International Review of Social History* 46, no. 2 (2001): 227–255.

Leeder, Elaine (1993). *The Gentle General: Rose Pesotta, Anarchist and Labor Organizer*. Syracuse: SUNY Press.

Leftwich, Joseph (1958). 'I. N. Steinberg: Profile of a Jewish Leader.' S. A. *Jewish Observer*.

Le Guerer, Annick (2002). 'Olfaction and Cognition: A Philosophical and Psycho-analytic View.' *Olfaction, Taste, and Cognition*: 3–15.

Leigh, Reuven (2013). 'Modern Orthodoxy or Orthodox Modernity? Rabbi Abraham Yehudah Chen and the Convergence of Rabbinic Traditionalism and Contemporary Thought.' M. A. thesis, Kings College.

Lenin, Vladimir L. (1977a). *Lenin: Collected Works. Volume 26: September 1917–February 1918*. Translated by Yuri Sidobnikov and George Hanna. Moscow: Progress Publishers.

— (1977b). *Lenin: Collected Works. Volume 42: October 1917–March 1923*. Translated by Bernard Isaacs. Moscow: Progress Publishers.

Levinas, Emanuel (1987). *Collected Philosophical Papers*. Dordrecht: Springer.

Levinson, Bernard M. (2008). '"The Right Chorale": Studies in Biblical Law and Interpretation.' *Forschungen zum Alten Testament* 54.

Levy, Carl (2004). 'Anarchism, Internationalism and Nationalism in Europe, 1860–1939.' *Australian Journal of Politics & History* 50, no. 3: 330–342.

— (2011). 'Anarchism and Cosmopolitanism.' *Journal of Political Ideologies* 16, no. 3: 265–278.

Lewin, Eyal (2015). 'The Disengagement from Gaza: Understanding the Ideological Background.' *Jewish Political Studies Review*: 15–32.

Likht, Zekharia (2016). 'Hayyim Zelig Slonimsky we-Pulmus Hanukkah: Mai Hanuk-kah.' https://seforimblog.com/2016/12/blog-pos-7/ (accessed December 28, 2016).

Lipshitz, H. A. (1991). *Eshkavta de-Tsadikaya: Te-or Histalkut shel Tsadikim me-Adam ha-Rishon ad Yamenu*. Jerusalem: Publisher unknown.

Lloyd, Anne (2009). 'Jews Under Fire: The Jewish Community and Military Service in World War I Britain.' PhD diss., University of Southampton.

— (2010). 'Between Integration and Separation: Jews and Military Service in World War I Britain,' *Jewish Culture and History* 12, no. 1–2: 41–60.

Lorberbaum, Yair (2011). *Disempowered King: Monarchy in Classical Jewish Literature*. New York: Continuum.

Lossky, Vladimir (1976). *The Mystical Theology of the Eastern Church*. St Vladimir's Seminary Press Crestwood: New York.

Louth, Andrew (1989). *Discerning the Mystery: An Essay on the Nature of Theology*. Oxford: Clarendon Press.

Löwy, Michael (2004). 'Jewish Nationalism and Libertarian Socialism in the Writings of Bernard Lazare.' *On the History of the Jews in the Diaspora*, no. 16: 9–20.

Luz, Ehud (1981). 'Spiritualism and Religious Anarchism in the Teaching of Shmuel Alexandrov.' *Daat*, no. 7: 121–138.

— (1987). 'The Moral Price of Sovereignty: The Dispute About the Use of Military Power Within Zionism.' *Modern Judaism*: 51–98.

— (2008). *Wrestling with an Angel: Power, Morality, and Jewish Identity*. New Haven: Yale University Press.

Luzzato, Moshe C. (2003). *The Knowing Heart*. Translated by Shraga Silverstein. Jerusalem: Feldheim.

Maciejko, Pawel, ed. (2017). *Sabbatian Heresy: Writings on Mysticism, Messianism, and the Origins of Jewish Modernity*. Waltham: Brandeis University Press.

Magid, Shaul (2004). *Hasidism on the Margin: Reconciliation, Antinomianism, and Messianism*. Madison: University of Wisconsin Press.

— (2017). 'Is "Land for Peace" Legitimate? Reflections on the Six-Day War, 50 Years Later,' *Tikkun* 32, no. 2: 29–32.

— (2019). 'Kahane Won: How the Radical Rabbi's Ideas and Disciples Took Over Israeli Politics, and Why it's Dangerous.' *Tablet*. www.tabletmag.com/jewish-news-and-politics/281388/kahane-won (accessed September 29, 2020).

Maimon, Y. L. (1999). *Shaar ha-Meya*. Vol. 2. Jerusalem: Mosad ha-Rav Kook.

— (2006). *Toldot ha-Gra*. Jerusalem: Mosad ha-Rav Kook.

Mannheim, Karl (2013). *Ideology and Utopia*. New York: Routledge.

Mar, H. (1942). '*Nekudot: Talmid Ra Mino le-Moreh.*'*Ha-Mashkif*, 2.

Margalith, D. (1958). 'Psychology and its place in Habad hasidism.' *Harofe haivri. The Hebrew Medical Journal* 2: 195–198.

Margolin, Ron (2020). 'Identity or Spirituality: The Resurgence of Habad, Neo Hasidism and Ashlagian Kabbalah in America.' In *Kabbalah in America*. Leiden: Brill: 377–390.

Margolis, Rebecca E. (2004). 'A Tempest in Three Teapots: Yom Kippur Balls in London, New York and Montreal.' In *The Canadian Jewish Studies Reader*. Edited by Richard Menkis and Norman Ravvin. Calgary: Red Deer Press: 141–163.

Marx, Karl (1973). *Grundrisse*. Translated by M. Nicolaus. New York: Penguin.

Mase, Aline (2012). 'Student Migration of Jews from Tsarist Russia to the Universities of Bern and Zürich, 1865–1914.' M. A. thesis, Utrecht University.

Maslanski, Z. H. (1929). *Kitve Maslanski: Ne'umim, Zikhronot, u-Ma'asiyot*. Vol. 3. New York: Hebrew Publishers.

May, Todd G. (1990). 'Kant the liberal, Kant the Anarchist: Rawls and Lyotard on Kantian Justice.' *The Southern Journal of Philosophy* 28, no. 4: 525–538.

— (2011). 'Kant via Ranciere: From Ethics to Anarchism.' In *How Not to Be Governed: Readings and Interpretations from the Critical Left*. Edited by J. C. Klausen and J. Martel. Lanham, MD: Lexington: 65–82.

McGrath, Sean J. (2010). 'Schelling on the Unconscious.' *Research in Phenomenology* 40, no. 1: 72–91.

Medzhibovskaya, Inessa (2013). "Tolstoy on Pogroms?' Publication, Translation and Commentary of the Newly Discovered Archival Document from the Memoirs by Isaak Teneromo.' *Tolstoy Studies Journal* 25: 78–82.

Meinecke, Friedrich (2015). *Cosmopolitanism and the National State*. Vol. 1343. Princeton: Princeton University Press.

Meir, Jonatan (2013). 'The Beginnings of Kabbalah in America: The Unpublished Manuscripts of R. Levi Isaac Krakovsky.' *Aries* 13, no. 2: 237–268.

— (2017). 'Reform Hasidism: The Image of Habad in Haskalah Literature.' *Modern Judaism — A Journal of Jewish Ideas and Experience* 37, no. 3: 297–315.

Mendes-Flohr, Paul and Anya Mali (eds) (2015). *Gustav Landauer: Anarchist and Jew*. Boston: De Gruyter.

Mendes-Flohr, Paul, Anya Mali, and Jehuda Reinharz (eds) (1995). *The Jew in the Modern World: A Documentary History*. Oxford: Oxford University Press.

Meyer, Michael A. (1987). *Ideas of Jewish History*. Detroit: Wayne State University Press.

— (1990). *Jewish Identity in the Modern World*. Seattle and London: University of Washington Press.

Michaelson, Jay (2017). 'Conceptualizing Jewish Antinomianism in the Teachings of Jacob Frank.' *Modern Judaism — A Journal of Jewish Ideas and Experience* 37, no. 3: 338–362.

Miller, M. A. (2008). 'Ordinary Terrorism in Historical Perspective.' *Journal for the Study of Radicalism* 2, no. 1: 125–154.

Milstein, Cindy (2010). *Anarchism and its Aspirations*. Oakland: AK Press.

Mokdoni, Alexander (2019). 'Abroad: My Encounters.' Translated by Hayyim Rothman. *In Geveb*. https://ingeveb.org/texts-and-translations/abroad-my-encounters (accessed September 29, 2020).

Mollov, Ben and Chaim Lavie (2018). 'Relationship Transformation between Israeli Settlers and West Bank Palestinians: The Case of "Roots".' *American Journal of Management* 18, no. 4. https://articlegateway.com/index.php/AJM/article/view/185/155 (accessed November 1, 2019).

Morris, Brian (2018). *Kropotkin: The Politics of Community*. Oakland: PM Press.

Mosse, George L. (1992). 'Max Nordau, Liberalism and the New Jew.' *Journal of Contemporary History* 27, no. 4: 565–581.

Moya, Jose C (2004). 'The Positive Side of Stereotypes: Jewish Anarchists in Early-Twentieth-Century Buenos Aires.' *Jewish History* 18, no. 1: 19–48.

Moylan, Tom (2014). *Demand the Impossible: Science Fiction and the Utopian Imagination*. Vol. 943. Bern: Peter Lang.

Muraskin, Bennett (2013). 'Jewish Alternatives to Zionism.' *New Politics* 14, no. 3: 49–55.

Myers, Jody (2007). *Kabbalah and the Spiritual Quest: The Kabbalah Centre in America*. Westport: Praeger Publishers.

— (2008). 'The Kabbalah Centre and Contemporary Spirituality.' *Religion Compass* 2, no. 3: 409–420.

— (2010). 'Marriage and Sexual Behavior in the Teachings of the Kabbalah Centre.' In *Kabbalah and Modernity*. Leiden: Brill: 259–281.

Nadler, Allan (1982). 'Piety and Politics: The Case of the Satmar Rebbe.' *Judaism* 31, no. 2: 135–152.

— (1999). *The Faith of the Mithnagdim: Rabbinic Responses to Hasidic Rapture*. Baltimore: JHU Press.

Nagorski, R. (1977). 'History of the Anarchist Movement in Poland,' *Cienfuegos Press Anarchist Review* 2: 20–22.

Nalimov, V. V. (2001). 'On the History of Mystical Anarchism in Russia.' *International Journal of Transpersonal Studies* 20, no. 1: 9.

Nedava, Joseph (1974). 'Abba Gordin: A Portrait of a Jewish Anarchist.' *Soviet Jewish Affairs* 4 no. 2: 73–79.

Neuburger, Mary (1996). 'The Russo-Turkish War and the "Eastern Jewish question": Encounters Between Victims and Victors in Ottoman Bulgaria, 1877–8.' *East European Jewish Affairs* 26, no. 2: 53–66.

Neufeld, Ernest (1994). 'The Sins of the Census.' *Judaism* 43, no. 2: 196–204.

Neusner, Jacob (2007). *The Rabbinic Utopia*. Lanham: University Press of America.

Nordau, Max (1887). *The Conventional Lies of Our Civilization*. Chicago: L. Schick.

— (1895). *Degeneration*. New York: Appleton.

— (1896). *Paradoxes*. Portsmouth: William Heinemann.

— (1909). *Zionistische Schriften*. Cologne: Juedischer Verlag.

— (1913). 'Of What Value is Gymnastics to Us Jews?' Translated by G. Jeshurun, *The Maccabean*: 313–315, 333.

— (1922). *Morals and the Evolution of Man*. New York: Funk and Wagnalls.

Nussbaum, Martha (1994). 'Patriotism and Cosmopolitanism.' *The Cosmopolitan Reader*: 155–162.

Ofek, Adina (1993). 'Cantonists: Jewish Children as Soldiers in Tsar Nicholas's Army.' *Modern Judaism*: 277–308.

Ohana, David (2012). *Modernism and Zionism*. New York: Palgrave.

Ohana, David and Liran Shia Gordon (2019). 'Restorative Utopias: The Settlers and the Bible.' *Modern Theology*.

Orend, Brian (1999). 'Kant's Just War Theory.' *Journal of the History of Philosophy* 37, no. 2: 323–353.

Orwell, George (1968). *The Collected Essays, Journalism, and Letters of George Orwell*. Vol. 3. Edited by S. Orwell and I. Angus. New York: Secker & Warburg.

Pannekoek, Anton (1948). *Lenin as Philosopher: A Critical Examination of the Philosophical Foundations of Leninism*. New York: New Essays.

Parush, Iris (2004). *Reading Jewish Women: Marginality and Modernization in Nineteenth-Century Eastern European Jewish Society*. Vol. 5. Upne.

Pedler, Anne (1927). 'Going to the People: The Russian Narodniki in 1874–5.' *The Slavonic Review*: 130–141.

Pelletier, Madeleine (1934). 'Religion.' In *L'Encyclopedie Anarchiste*. Edited by Sebastian Faure Paris: International Library.

Pelli, Moshe (1970). 'Intimations of Religious Reform in the German Hebrew Haskalah Literature.' *Jewish Social Studies* 32, no. 1: 3–13.

Penkower, Monty Noam (2004). 'The Kishinev Pogrom of 1903: A Turning Point in Jewish History.' *Modern Judaism* 24, no. 3: 187–225.

Persico, Tomer (2014). 'Neo-Hasidic Revival: Expressivist Uses of Traditional Lore.' *Modern Judaism — A Journal of Jewish Ideas and Experience* 34, no. 3: 287–308.

— (2017). 'The End Point of Zionism: Ethnocentrism and the Temple Mount.' *Israel Studies Review* 32, no. 1: 104–122.

— (2019). 'Tokhnit ha-Hakhra'ah shel Smotrich: Ha-Tsiyonit ha-Datit u-Fundamentalizm.' https://tomerpersico.com/2017/05/15/smut_fund/ (accessed November 17, 2019).

Pickhan, Gertrude (2009). 'Yiddishkayt and Class Consciousness: The Bund and its Minority Concept.' *East European Jewish Affairs* 39, no. 2: 249–263.

Polland, Annie (2007). 'May a Freethinker Help a Pious Man? The Shared World of the "Religious" and the "Secular" among Eastern European Jewish Immigrants to America.' *American Jewish History* 93, no. 4: 375–407.

Polonsky, Anthony (2003). 'The New Jewish Politics and its Discontents.' In *The Emergence of Modern Jewish Politics: Bundism and Zionism in Eastern Europe*. Edited by Zvi Gitelman. Pittsburgh: University of Pittsburgh Press: 35–53.

Presner, Todd S. (2003). 'Clear Heads, Solid Stomachs, and Hard Muscles: Max Nordau and the Aesthetics of Jewish Regeneration.' *Modernism/modernity* 10, no. 2: 269–296.

— (2007). *Muscular Judaism: the Jewish Body and the Politics of Regeneration*. New York: Routledge.

Prichard, Alex (2010). 'Deepening Anarchism: International Relations and the Anarchist Ideal.' *Anarchist Studies* 18, no. 2: 29–57.

Proudhon, Pierre J. (2011). *Property is Theft! A Pierre-Joseph Proudhon Anthology*. Edited by Iain McKay Oakland: AK Press.

— (2012). 'God is Evil, Man is Free.' In *Essential Proudhon*. Edited by J. Bates, 1–15. n.p.: CreateSpace Independent Publishing Platform.

Rabinkow, Zalman (1929). 'Individuum und Gemeinschaft im Judentum.' In Die Biologie der Person. Ein Handbuch der allgemeinen und speziellen Konstitution-slehre, herausgegeben von Th. Brugsch und F.H. Lewy, Band 4: Soziologie der Person, Berlin/Wien, S. 799–824. Urban und Schwarzenberg.

Rabinovitch, A. Z. (1937). 'Ish Segula.' *Ha-Hed.* Nisan, 7.

Rabkin, Yakov M. (2006). *A Threat from Within: A History of Jewish Opposition to Zionism.* London: Zed Books.

Rakovsky, Puah (2003). *My Life as a Radical Jewish Woman: Memoirs of a Zionist Feminist in Poland.* Bloomington: Indiana University Press.

Ram, Uri (2000). 'National, Ethnic or Civic? Contesting Paradigms of Memory, Identity and Culture in Israel.' *Studies in Philosophy and Education* 19, no. 5–6: 405–422.

Rapp, John A (2012). *Daoism and Anarchism: Critiques of State Autonomy in Ancient and Modern China.* New York: Bloomsbury Publishing.

Rappaport, Yossef (2017). 'Two States in One Homeland: Solving the Riddle of Resolution 2334.' Open Democracy. January 8. www.opendemocracy.net/en/two-states-in-one-homeland-solving-riddle-of-resolution-2334/ (accessed September 29, 2020).

Ratzabi, Shalom (1995). 'The Polemic about the "Negation of the Diaspora" in the 1930s and its Roots.' *Journal of Israeli History* 16, no. 1: 19–38.

— (2011). *Anarchy in Zion: Between Martin Buber and AD Gordon.* Tel-Aviv: Am Oved Press.

Ravid, Y. (2013). 'Rav, mekubal, kommunist: Darko shel HRY'L Ashlag.' *Alon Igud Safrane ha-Yahadut.* Vol. 23. https://safranim.com/קומוניסט-דרכו-של-הריל-אשלג-/גליון-כג-2/ב-רב-מקובל/ (accessed April 15, 2019).

Ravitch, Melekh (ed.) (1960). *Yitshak Nahman Steinberg: Der Mentsh, Zayn Vort, Zayn Oyftu 1888–1957.* New York: I. N. Steinberg Book Committee.

Raz-Krakotzkin, Amnon (1993). 'Exile Within Sovereignty: A Critique of "the Negation of Exile" in Israeli Culture.' *Theory and Criticism* 3: 23–55.

Reichman, Edward and Fred Rosner (1996). 'The Bone called Luz.' *Journal of the History of Medicine and Allied Sciences* 51, no. 1: 52–65.

Reinharz, Jehuda (1993). 'The Conflict between Zionism and Traditionalism before World War I.' *Jewish History* 7, no. 2: 59–78.

Reisen, Zalman (1926a). 'Dr. Yaakov Meir Zalkind.' *Lexicon of Yiddish Literature and Philology: Vol. 1.* Vilna: Klezkin: 1030–1034.

— (1926b). *Lexicon of Yiddish Literature and Philology: Vol. 4.* Vilna: Klezkin.

Reizbaum, Marilyn (2005). 'Yiddish Modernisms: Red Emma Goldman.' *Modern Fiction Studies* 51, no. 2: 456–481.

Rendle, Matthew (2013). 'Defining the "Political" Crime: Revolutionary Tribunals in Early Soviet Russia.' *Europe-Asia Studies* 65, no. 9: 1771–1788.

Rezvykh, P. (2003). 'The Reception of Schelling's Philosophy in Russia.' *Philosophisches Jahrbuch* 110, no 2: 347–358.

Rocker, Rudolf (1942). 'Kropotkin and the Jewish Labour Movement in England.' *Centennial Expressions on Peter Kropotkin 1842–1942.* Los Angeles: Rocker Publications Committee: 17–19.

— (1998). *Nationalism and Culture.* Montreal: Black Rose.

Rose, Herbert H. (1964). *The Life and Thought of A. D. Gordon: Pioneer, Philosopher, and prophet of Modern Israel.* New York: Bloch.

Rosenthal, Bernice Glatzer (1977). 'The Transmutation of the Symbolist Ethos: Mystical Anarchism and the Revolution of 1905.' *Slavic Review* 36, no. 4: 608–627.

— (1993). 'Lofty Ideals and Worldly Consequences: Visions of Sobornost'in Early Twentieth-Century Russia.' *Russian History* 20, no. 1/4: 179–195.

— (2006). 'Remarkable Parallels: Mystical Anarchism in Russia and the United States.' *Dialogue and Universalism* 16, no. 3/4: 109–131.

Rovner, Adam (2014). *In the Shadow of Zion: Promised Lands before Israel*. New York: NYU Press.

Ruderman, David B. (1997). 'Was there a "Haskalah" in England? Reconsidering an Old Question.' *Zion* 62: 109–131.

Salant, Yankl (2010). 'Frayland-lige. YIVO Encyclopedia of Jews in Eastern Europe.' https://yivoencyclopedia.org/article.aspx/Frayland-lige (accessed December 19 2019).

Salmon, Yosef (1991). 'The Emergence of a Jewish Nationalist Consciousness in Europe during the 1860s and 1870s.' *AJS Review* 16, no. 1/2: 107–132.

Sanborn, Joshua A. (2005). 'Unsettling the Empire: Violent Migrations and Social Disaster in Russia during World War I.' *The Journal of Modern History* 77, no. 2: 290–324.

Sanders, Ed P. (1983). *Paul, the Law, and the Jewish People*. Minneapolis: Fortress Press.

Santos, Fernanda (2007). 'New York Rabbi Finds Friends in Iran and Enemies at Home.' *New York Times*, January 15, 2007. www.nytimes.com/2007/01/15/nyregion/15rabbi.html (accessed September 29, 2020).

Schacter, Jacob J. (1990). 'Haskalah, Secular Studies and the Close of the Yeshiva in Volozhin in 1892.' *The Torah U-Madda Journal* 2: 76–133.

Schapiro, Leonard (1961). 'The Role of the Jews in the Russian Revolutionary Movement.' *The Slavonic and East European Review*: 148–167.

Schechtman, Joseph B. (1955). 'The Jabotinsky-Slavinsky Agreement: A Chapter in Ukrainian-Jewish Relations.' *Jewish Social Studies*: 289–306.

Schefski, Harold K. (1982). 'Tolstoi and the Jews.' *The Russian Review* 41, no. 1: 1–10.

Schelling, Freidrich W. J. (1980). *The Unconditional in Human Knowledge: Four Early Essays*. Translated by F. Marti Cranbury: Lewisburg: Associated University Presses.

— (1989). *The Philosophy of Art*. Translated by D. W. Stott. Minneapolis: University of Minnesota Press.

— (1993). *System of Transcendental Idealism (1800)*. Translated by P. Heath. Richmond: University of Virginia Press.

Schick, Shana Strauch (2017). 'Mitzvot Eyn Tzerikhot Kavvanah: The Radical Reconceptualization of Ritual.' *Jewish Studies Quarterly* 24, no. 1: 1–22.

Schnaber, Mordechai (1784). *Tokhahat Megillah*. Hamburg: Erdman.

Schneerson, Menahem (1994). *Likkutei Sichos Vol 17*. New York: Kehot.

Schneersohn, Yosef Y. (1983). *Igrot Kodesh Moreynu ha-Rayats*. Vol. 1. New York: Kehot.

— (1993). *Igrot Kodesh Moreynu ha-Rayats*. Vol. 13. New York: Kehot.

Schneider, Stanley and Joseph. H. Berke (2000). 'Sigmund Freud and the Lubavitcher Rebbe.' *Psychoanalytic Review* 87, no. 1: 39–59.

Schoeman, Marinus (2007). 'Generosity as a Central Virtue in Nietzsche's Ethics.' *South African Journal of Philosophy* 26, no. 1: 41–54.

Scholem, Gershom (1976). 'Issac Luria: A Central Figure in Jewish Mysticism.' *Bulletin of the American Academy of Arts and Sciences* 29, no. 8: 8–13.

— (1990). *Origins of the Kabbalah*. Princeton: Princeton University Press.

— (1991). '"Sitra ahra": Good and Evil in the Kabbalah.' *On the Mystical Shape of the Godhead: Basic Concepts in the Kabbalah* (1991): 56–87.

— (1995a). *The Messianic Idea in Judaism and Other Essays on Jewish Spirituality.* Translated by H. Halkin. New York: Schocken.

— (1995b). *Major Trends in Jewish Mysticism.* New York: Pantheon.

Schopenhauer, Arthur (1893). 'The Christian System.' *In Religion: A Dialogue, and Other Essays.* Translated by B. Saunders. New York: Macmillan: 103–118.

— (1958). *The World as Will and Representation.* Vol. 2. Translated by E. Payne. New York: Dover.

— (1971). 'On Jurisprudence and Politics.' In *Parerga and Paralipomena.* Vol. 2. Translated by E. Payne. Oxford: Clarendon Press: 261–264.

— (1998). *On the Basis of Morality.* Indianapolis: Hackett Publishing.

Schrøder-Simonsen, Cecilie S. (2016). 'A Spatial Expansion of a Pocket-Size Homeland: Heinrich Heine's Construction of Jewish Space.' *Journal of Literature and the History of Ideas* 14, no. 2: 303–321.

Schwartz, Dov (2000). 'The Revolutionary Consciousness of the Religious Zionist Movement since 1902.' *Review of Rabbinic Judaism* 3, no. 1: 175–184.

Schwarzschild, Steven S. (2018). *The Tragedy of Optimism: Writings on Hermann Cohen.* New York: SUNY Press.

— (2002). *Faith at the Crossroads: A Theological Profile of Religious Zionism.* Translated by B. Stein. Boston: Brill.

Seemann, Birgit (2008). 'Anarcha-féminisme et judaïsme: Quelques questions.' In *Juifs et anarchistes: Histoire d'une rencontre.* Edited by Amedeo Bertolo. Paris: Editions de l'Éclat: 207–212.

Seltzer, Robert (2013). *Simon Dubnow's 'New Judaism': Diaspora Nationalism and the World History of the Jews.* Leiden: Brill.

Shabbatay, D. (1938). 'Hareyni Mitkabel le-Hatsig: Ha-Rav Yehudah Don-Yahiya.' *Ha-Tsofeh,* August 19: 2–3.

Shapira, Amnon (2013). 'Ha-rabanim Ashlag we-Yakobs: Kommunizm dati, hazon shel tikkun olam.' In *Sihot Shiga'on we-Hazon: Hibitim Histori'im be-Peni'a el Tehume Da'at Shonim.* Edited by Z. Feldman. Ariel: University of Ariel Press: 10–39.

— (2015). *Anarkhizm Yehudi Dati: Iyyun Panorami ba-Gilgulo shel Rayon mi-Yemey ha-Mikra we-Hazal, Derekh Abarbanel, we-ad ha-Et ha-Hadash.* Ariel: Hotseyt Universitat Ariel.

Shapiro, Mark (2011). *The Limits of Orthodox Theology: Maimonides' Thirteen Principles Reappraised.* Liverpool: Liverpool University Press.

— (2017). 'The Hanukkah Miracle.' *Seforim blog.* April 23. https://seforimblog.com/2017/04/the-hanukkah-miracle/ (accessed April 23, 2017).

Shatz, Marshall (ed.) (1990). *Bakunin: Statism and Anarchy.* Cambridge: Cambridge University Press.

Shepherd, Naomi (1994). *A Price below Rubies: Jewish Women as Rebels and Radicals.* Cambridge, MA: Harvard University Press.

Shmuel, B. (1994). *Meorey Yisrael.* Jerusalem: Makhon Ohaley Yosef.

Shneor, David (2002). 'Rabbi Abraham Kook and Rabbi Samuel Aleksandrov.' M. A. thesis. Touro College Jerusalem.

Sholom, S. (1932). '*Reshimot Hatufot.*' *Davar* June 7, 2.

Shone, Steve J. (2019). 'Rose Pesotta, the Working Anarchist.' In *Women of Liberty.* Leiden: Brill: 282–304.

Shoro, H. (1967). '*Lo le-Geniza.*' *Davar*, 3.

Shuchat, B. Raphael (1998). 'The Debate Over Secular Studies Among the Disciples of the Vilna Gaon.' *The Torah U-Madda Journal* 8: 283–294.

Shumsky, Dmitri (2018). *Beyond the Nation-State: The Zionist Political Imagination from Pinsker to Ben-Gurion.* New Haven: Yale University Press.

Silberstein, Lawrence J. (1990). *Martin Buber's Social and Religious Thought: Alienation and the Quest for Meaning.* New York: New York University Press.

Simha (1977). '*Yitshak Nahman Shtaynberg.*' *Problemen* 98: 7–8.

Sinclair, Clive (2009). 'The Kimberley Fantasy: An Alternative Zion.' *Wasafiri* 24, no. 1: 33–43.

Singer, Isaac B. (2000). 'Father Becomes an Anarchist.' *More Stories from my Father's Court.* Translated by C. Leviant. New York: Farrar, Straus, & Giroux.

Skartveit, Hanna (2010). 'Science is Just Catching Up: The Kabbalah Centre and The Neo-Enlightenment.' In *Handbook of Religion and the Authority of Science.* Leiden: Brill: 453–481.

Slater, Isaac (2014). 'Universal Nationalism: Religion and Nationalism in the Thought of Shmuel Alexandrov.' M. A. thesis, Ben-Gurion University.

— (2016). 'Those Who Yearn for the Divine: Rabbi Shmuel Alexandrov and the Russian Religious-Philosophical Renaissance.' *Judaica Petropolitana* 5: 55–68.

— (2019). '"To Purify Religion": Nationalism, Individualism and Mysticism in the Thought of Shmuel Alexandrov.' PhD diss., Ben-Gurion University of the Negev.

Slodki, M. R. (1938). 'Al Hitnagdut shel R. Hayyim Soloveitchik le-Tsiyonut.' *Davar*, November 2, 4.

Slutsky, Y. (1967). 'Shemuel Aleksandrov.' In *Sefer-Zikaron le-Kehilat Babruysk u-Benoteha.* Edited by Y. Slutsky. Tel Aviv: Tarbut we-Hinukh: 319–324.

Soker, Y. (1937). '*Be-Beyt Midrash ha-Rambam.*' *Ha-Hed* 12 no. 9: 16–17.

Solovyov, Vladimir (2016). *The Burning Bush: Writings on Jews and Judaism.* Edited and translated by G. Glazov. Notre Dame: University of Notre Dame Press.

Sorel, Georges (1999). *Sorel: Reflections on Violence.* Translated by Jeremy Jennings. Cambridge: Cambridge University Press.

Stanislawski, Michael (2001). *Zionism and the Fin de siècle: Cosmopolitanism and Nationalism from Nordau to Jabotinsky.* Berkeley: University of California Press.

Starr, Joshua (1945). 'The Socialist Federation of Saloniki.' *Jewish Social Studies* 7, no. 4: 323–336.

Steinberg, Y. N. (undated A). *Vegen dem Makor fun Moral*, undated, YIVO Steinberg Collection, Series 15, Box 52, folder 955a.

— (undated B). *Vegen Yiddisher Religiyositet.* YIVO Steinberg Collection, Series 15, Box 52, folder 955.

— (undated C). *Reformizm on Sotsyalizm.* YIVO Archives, 52–953.

— (undated D). '*Oyf Barukh Rivkin's Artikel, Doktor Zhitlovsky on zayne Talmidim.*' YIVO Archives, 52–953.

— (undated E). *Am ha-Artsut le-Gabe Yisrael: Brief fun Nyu York.* YIVO Archives, 52–953.

— (1910). *Die Lehre vom Verbrechen im Talmud: Eine Juristisch-Dogmatische Studie.* Union deutsche Verlagsgesellschaft.

— (1921). '*Tezisy o Gosudarstve.*' *Znamya.* No. 7(9).

— (1925). *Der Maximalizm in der Yidisher Velt.* Berlin: Verlag Nachmin Horwitz.

— (1926). 'Alter Verter Oyfsnay.' *Fraye Schriftn*: 5–12.

— (1927a). *Der Moralisher Ponem fun der Revolyutsye.* Translated by S. Friedman. Warsaw: Farlag Bzhoza.

— (1927b). '*Vegen dem Sotsyalen Bazis fun Yiddishen Sotsializm.*' *Fraye Schriftn*: 2–21.

— (1929a). '*Di Role fun Anarchistishe Princip in Revolutsiyonaren Sotsyalizm.*' *Zhitlovsky Zamelbukh.* Edited by Yitshak N. Steinberg and Y. Rubin. Warsaw: Bzhoza: 317–334.

— (1929b). '*Derinerungen on Farflikhtungen.*' *Fraye Arbeter Schriften*: 5–25.

— (1929c). '*Politik un Moral by Yidden.*' *Fraye Arbeter Schriften*: 3–43.

— (1931). *Zikhronos fun a Folks Kommisar.* Warsaw: Bzhoza.

— (1932). '*Mayne Sotsyalistisher Ani Ma'amin.*' *Fraye Arbeter Shtime*: 2.

— (1934). '*Leyvik, Niger, Pinski, Vos Tut Ihr?*' *Fraye Vort.* Friday: 2.

— (1935a). Spiridonova: Revolutionary Terrorist. Translated by G. David and E. Mosbacher. London: Methuen.

— (1935b). *Draysik Yor Sotsyalistishe Ideen in Rusland.* Warsaw: Farlag Bzhoza.

— (1935c). *Sotsyalizm* oh Meshikhizm: A Dispute with Hillel Zeitlin.' *Dos Freie Wort.* Friday, January 25: 2.

— (1944). *A Land Far Yidn in Oystralye.* New York: Freeland League.

— (1945). *Gelebt un Gekholemt in Oystralye.* New York: Freeland League.

— (1946). 'Statement by Dr. I. N. Steinberg and Discussion before the Anglo-American Committee on Palestine.' [TNA DO 35/1140].

— (1947). *Nider mit der Milhome.* New York: Freeland League.

— (1948). *Australia, the Unpromised Land: In Search of a Home.* London: Victor Gollancz.

— (1950). 'Vilna on Yerushalayim.' *Oyfen Shvel* 3 no. 4: 1–4.

— (1951a). *Mit Ayn Fus in Amerike: Perzonen, Geshenishen, on Ideen.* Mexico City: Centro Cultural Israelita en Mexico.

— (1951b). 'The Way of Freeland.' *Freeland*: 2–5.

— (1952). *In Kampf far Mentsh un Yid.* Buenos Aires: Comite de Reception de I. N. Steinberg.

— (1953a). *In the Workshop of the Revolution.* New York: Reinhart.

— (1953b). 'The Jubilee of an Idea.' *Freeland.* November–December: 2–3.

— (1954). 'Kerosene or Electricity.' *Freeland*: 4–5.

— (1955). Yavneh or Jerusalem? *Judaism* 4 no. 1: 235–242.

— (1956a). 'The Mountain Peaks.' *Freeland*: 9–11.

— (1956b). 'Vilno and Jerusalem.' *Freeland* 9 no. 2: 5–6.

— (1960). 'Du Hast Gezigt Makhnachov!' In *Yitshak Nahman Steinberg: Der Mentsh, Zayn Vort, Zayn Oyftu 1888–1957.* Translated by Y. Rappaport. Edited by M. Ravich. New York: I.N. Steinberg Book Committee: 451–505.

— (1966). '*Politika u-Musar.*' Translated by A. Lisod. *Problemot* 37: 2–3.

Stern, Eliahu (2018). *Jewish Materialism: The Intellectual Revolution of the 1870s.* New Haven: Yale University Press.

Stirner, Max (2005). *The Ego and His Own: The Case of the Individual Against Authority.* Translated by Steven T. Byington. Mineola: Dover.

Strauss, Leo (1996). *Spinoza's Critique of Religion.* Chicago: University of Chicago Press.

Tamaret, A. S. (1900a). 'Shelomim le-Riv Tsiyon.' *Ha-Meylits,* January 30, 1.

— (1900b). 'Shelomim le-Riv Tsiyon.' *Ha-Meylits,* January 31, 1.

— (1900c). 'Shelomim le-Riv Tsiyon.' *Ha-Meylits,* February 6, 1.

— (1900d). 'Shelomim le-Riv Tsiyon.' *Ha-Meylits,* February 13, 1.

— (1900e). 'Shelomim le-Riv Tsiyon.' *Ha-Meylits*, February 14, 1.

— (1900f). 'Ezrat Soferim: Ada'ata de-Hakhi lo Hitnatsalti.' *Ha-Melits*, March 23, 1.

— (1900g). 'El ha-Dirshu le-Tsiyon.' *Ha-Meylits*, May 24, 1.

— (1900h). 'Ezrat Soferim: El ha-Doresh le-Tsiyon.' *Ha-Meylits*, May 31, 1.

— (1900i). 'El ha-Doresh le-Tsiyon.' *Ha-Meylits*, June 10, 1.

— (1900j). 'Da'at ha-Rabanim.' *Ha-Meylits*, July 25, 1.

— (1900k). 'Da'at ha-Rabanim.' *Ha-Meylits*, July 27, 1.

— (1900l). 'Da'at ha-Rabanim.' *Ha-Meylits*, July 31, 1.

— (1901a). '*Ha-Kongress ha-Revi'i.*' *Ha-Meylits*. 1.

— (1901b). '*Ha-Kongress ha-Revi'i.*' *Ha-Meylits*. 1.

— (1905). *Ha-Yahadut we-ha-Herut*. Odessa: Defus H. N. Bialik we-S. Boriskin.

— (1912). *Musar ha-Torah we-ha-Yahadut*. Vilnius: Graber.

— (1913a). 'Abgebrent a Shtetle.' *Der Fraynd*, July 22, 1.

— (1913b). 'Milaytshitser Nisrafim.' *Der Fraynd*, July 29, 3.

— (1913c). 'Milaytsits.' *Ha-Tsefira*, July 30, 4.

— (1920a). *Keneset Yisrael we-Milkhamot ha-Goyim*.Warsaw: Pimeni i Szawbi.

— (1920b). 'Savlanut ha-Da'at ve-Gezerat Shmad al ha-Torah.' *Ha-Tsefira*, April 19, 3.

— (1920c). 'Savlanut ha-Da'at ve-Gezerat Shmad al ha-Torah.' *Ha-Tsefira*, August 4, 3.

— (1923). *Yad Aharon*. Piotrkow: H. H. Folman.

— (1926a). '*Vegen der Faerung fun der Fan fun Yiddishen Legion.*' *Vilner Tog.* February 12, 3.

— (1926b). '*Vegen der Faerung fun der Fan fun Yiddishen Legion.*' *Vilner Tog.* February 17, 2.

— (1926c). '*Vegen der Faerung fun der Fan fun Yiddishen Legion.*' *Vilner Tog.* February 26, 3.

— (1929). *Shelosha Zivugim Balti Hagunim*. Piotrkow: H. H. Folman.

— (1968). 'Passover and Non-Violence.' Translated by E. E. Gendler, *Judaism* 17, no. 2: 203–210.

— (1985). *Igrot ha-Rav Aaron Shmuel Tamaret.' K'tav Et le-Haker ha-Tsiyonut ha-Datit we-ha-Aliyot le-Erets Yisrael*. Vol. 2. Edited by Y. Rafael. Jerusalem: Mosad ha-Rav Kook.

— (1986). 'He-Azilut me-Hokhmat ha-Torah: Keta'im me-Devaraw.' In *Shana be-Shana 5746*. Edited by A. Pichnik. Jerusalem: Hekhal Shelomo.

— (1992). 'Ha-Emunah ha-Tehora we-ha-Dat ha-Hamonit.' *Pacifism le-Or ha-Torah*. Edited by E. Luz. Jerusalem: Merkaz Dinor.

— (1993). '*Autobiyografiya shel ha-Rav Aaron Shmuel Tamaret, Ehad ha-Rabanim ha-Margishim.' K'tav Et le-Haker ha-Tsiyonut ha-Datit we-ha-Aliyot le-Erets Yisrael*. Vol. 4. Edited by Y. Rafael. Jerusalem: Mosad ha-Rav Kook.

Teller, Judd L. (1954). *Scapegoat of the Revolution*. New York: Scribner.

— (1957). *The Kremlin, the Jews, and the Middle East*. New York: Yoseloff.

Thorin, A. (1966). 'Y. N. Steinberg: Vegen Rudolf Rocker.' *Problemot* no. 40: 13–14.

Tidhar, David (1958). '*Doktor Ya'akov Meir Zalkind.*' In *Encyclopedia of the Founders and Builders of Israel*, Vol. 9. Tel Aviv: 3354–3355.

Tirosh-Samuelson, Hava (2003). 'Philosophy and Kabbalah: 1200–1600.' In *The Cambridge Companion to Medieval Jewish Philosophy*. Edited by Daniel H. Frank and Oliver Leaman. Cambridge: Cambridge University Press: 218–257.

Torres, Anna E. (2016). 'Any Minute Now the World's Overflowing Its Border: Anarchist Modernism and Yiddish Literature.' PhD. diss., University of California, Berkeley.

— (2019). 'The Anarchist Sage/*Der Goen Anarkhist*: Rabbi Yankev-Meir Zalkind and Religious Genealogies of Anarchism.' *In geveb*. https://ingeveb.org/articles/the-anarchist-sage-der-goen-anarkhist (accessed September 29, 2020).

Trachtenberg, Barry (2008). *The Revolutionary Roots of Modern Yiddish, 1903–1917*. Syracuse: Syracuse University Press.

Tropp, Asher (1988). 'Russian Jews in Britain during the First World War.' M. A. thesis, University College London.

Tsirkin-Sadan, Rafi (2012). 'Tolstoy, Zionism, and the Hebrew Culture.' *Tolstoy Studies Journal* 24: 26–35.

Turk, Lillian and Jesse Cohn (2018). 'Yiddish Radicalism, Jewish Religion: Controversies in the *Fraye Arbeter Shtime*.' In *Essays in Anarchism and Religion: Volume II*. Edited by Alexandre Christoyannopoulos and Matthew Adams. Stockholm: Stockholm University Press: 20–57.

Turnbull, G. H. (1923). 'Fichte on Education.' *The Monist* 33, no. 2: 184–201.

Ungerfeld, M. (1954). '*Yevul Sifruteynu be-Shenat 5714*.' *Ha-Zofeh*, October 10, 5.

Vasilyev, Tikhon (2019). 'Aspects of Schelling's Influence on Sergius Bulgakov and Other Thinkers of the Russian Religious Renaissance of the Twentieth Century.' *International Journal of Philosophy and Theology* 80, no. 1–2: 143–159.

Vassilikou, Maria (1999). 'Politics of the Jewish Community of Salonika in the Interwar Years: Party Ideologies and Party Competition.' PhD diss., University College London.

Viernik, P. (1921). '*Unser Fil-Shprakhtige Literature*.' *Der Morgen Journal*, 6.

Waldstreicher, David (1990). 'Radicalism, Religion, Jewishness: The Case of Emma Goldman.' *American Jewish History* 80, no. 1: 74–92.

Wallat, Henrik (2013). *Oktoberrevolution oder Bolschewismus: Studien zu Leben un Werk von Isaak N. Steinberg*. Berlin: Edition Assemblage.

— (2014). '*Isaak Steinberg Sozialrevolutionar und Judischer Intellektueller*.' In *Intellektuelle in Heidelberg 1910–1933. Ein Lesebuch*. Edited by Markus Bitterolf, Oliver Schlaudt, and Stefan Schöbel. Heidelberg: Verlag der Buchhandlung Schöbel.

Weinberg, Z. Z. (1967). 'Hillel Zeitlin: Twenty Five Years After his Murder.' *Davar*, September 29, 7.

Weinstein, Stephen L. (1978). 'Galut (Exile): A Mission or a Curse? The Writings of Aharon Shmuel Tamares, 1869–1931.' *Jewish Quarterly* 26 no. 2: 21–26.

Wertheimer, Jack (1987). *Unwelcome Strangers: East European Jews in Imperial Germany*. Oxford: Oxford University Press.

White, Elizabeth (2010). *The Socialist Alternative to Bolshevik Russia: The Socialist Revolutionary Party, 1921–39*. new York: Routledge.

White, Stephen (1974). 'Labour's Council of Action 1920.' *Journal of Contemporary History* 9, no. 4: 99–122.

Wicks, Robert (2019). 'Arthur Schopenhauer.' *The Stanford Encyclopedia of Philosophy* (Spring 2019 Edition). Edited by Edward N. Zalta. https://plato.stanford.edu/archives/spr2019/entries/schopenhauer/ (accessed September 29, 2020).

Wiley, A. Terrance (2014). *Angelic Troublemakers: Religion and Anarchism in America*. New York: Bloomsbury.

Wilson, Nelly (1978). *Bernard-Lazare*. Cambridge: Cambridge University Press.

Wokenfield, David (2007). 'Pacifism, the Jewish Mission, and Religious Anti-Zionism: Rabbi Aaron Samuel Tamares in Context.' *Milin Havivin* 3. https://library.yctorah.org/journals/milin-havivin-vol-3-beloved-words/ (accessed September 29, 2020).

Wolf, Siegbert and Jürgen Mümken (eds) (2013). '*Antisemit, das geht nicht unter Menschen*'. *Anarchistische Positionen zu Antisemitismus, Zionismus und Israel. Band 1: Von Proudhon bis zur Staatsgründung* Lich/Hessen: Edition AV.

— (2014). '*Antisemit, das geht nicht unter Menschen*'. *Anarchistische Positionen zu Antisemitismus, Zionismus und Israel. Band 2: Von der Staatsgründung bis heute.* Lich/Hessen: Edition AV.

Wolff, Robert P. (1970). *In Defense of Anarchism.* Berkeley: University of California Press.

Wolfson, Elliot R. (1992). 'Images of God's FEET: Some observations on the Divine Body in Judaism.' *People of the Body: Jews and Judaism From an Embodied Perspective*: 143–181.

— (2006). *Venturing Beyond – Law and Morality in Kabbalistic Mysticism.* New York: Oxford University Press.

— (2010). 'The Status of the (Non) Jewish Other in the Apocalyptic Messianism of Menahem Mendel Schneerson.' In *Kabbalah and Modernity.* Leiden: Brill: 221–257.

— (2015). 'Eternal Duration and Temporal Compresence: The Influence of Ḥabad on Joseph B. Soloveitchik.' In *The Value of the Particular: Lessons from Judaism and the Modern Jewish Experience.* Leiden: Brill: 195–238.

Woodcock, George (2004). *Anarchism: A History of Libertarian Ideas and Movements.* Ontario: Broadview.

Yeyushson, B. (1932). 'Ha-Rav Avraham Heyn.' *Haynt*, 4.

Zagoria-Moffet, Adam (2017). 'The Communist Kabbalist: The Political Theology of Rav Yehudah Ashlag.' M. A. thesis, Jewish Theological Seminary.

Zalkind, Yaakov M. (1900). 'Nouvelle de la Vie Juive.' *L'Echo Sioniste.* 30.

— (1904). (Mibney Heykhalah), '*Mikhtavim me-Angliyah.*' *Ha-Zefirah.* 3.

— (1906). '*Avadim Hayinu.*' *Ha-Mitspah.* 3.

— (1914). '*Bemakom hakdama: A brief fun Dr. Y. M. Zalkind.*' In Y. Pozikov, *Di Milkhome un di Idden Frage.* London: Defus Noroditsky.

— (1916a). '*Di Idishe Shtime.*' *Di Idishe Shtime.* 9.

— (1916b). (Baal Madrega). '*Unzer Teshuva*' *Di Idishe Shtime.* 8.

— (1916c). '*Stam Makhshoves.*' *Di Idishe Shtime.* 10–11.

— (1916d). '*Heshbon ha-Nefesh.*' *Di Idishe Shtime.* 8–9.

— (1916e). '*Fun Vokh tsu Vokh: Trade Yunyon Kongress.*' *Di Idishe Shtime.* 3.

— (1917). *Wa-Yomer Ya'akov: Be'urim ba-Mikra we-Hidushim ba-Gemara.* London: Vainberg.

— (1920a). '*Tesen far a Konferens.*' *Arbeter Fraynd.* 1–2.

— (1920b). '*Glaykhheit Ader Gezetsen.*' *Arbeter Fraynd.* 6–7.

— (1920c). '*Tesen far a Konferens.*' *Arbeter Fraynd.* 1–2.

— (1920d). '*Gedanken-Punken.*' *Arbeter Fraynd.* May, 7.

— (1920e). '*Bolshevism on Anarkhism.*' *Arbeter Fraynd.* November 1, 6.

— (1920f). '*Bolshevism on Anarkhism.*' *Arbeter Fraynd.* October 15, 6.

— (1920g). '*Natitsen: Fihrer-Farfihrers.*' *Arbeter Fraynd.* 2.

— (1920h). '*Bolshevism on Anarkhism.*' *Arbeter Fraynd.* September 30, 6.

— (1920i). '*Natitsen: Der Yiddisher Garibaldi.*' *Arbeter Fraynd.* 2.

— (1920j). '*Bolshevism on Anarkhism.*' *Arbeter Fraynd.* September 15, 3.

— (1920k). '*Bolshevism on Anarkhism.*' *Arbeter Fraynd.* September 1, 5.

— (1920l). '*Gegen di Piavkes.*' *Arbeter Fraynd.* 1.

— (1920m). '*Vi Mir Kolonisiren?*' *Arbeter Fraynd.* 4–5.

— (1920n). '*Bolshevism on Anarkhism.*' *Arbeter Fraynd.* August 14, 5.

— (1920o). '*Di Ershte Probe.*' *Arbeter Fraynd.* 1–2.

— (1920p). 'Natisen: An Antfer.' *Arbeter Fraynd.* 2.
— (1920q). 'Vi Mir Koloniziren?' *Arbeter Fraynd.* 4.
— (1920r). 'Der Kleyne Kongress.' *Arbeter Fraynd.* 1.
— (1920s). 'A Likht in Abgrund.' *Arbeter Fraynd.* 7.
— (1920t). 'Natitsen: Di Rekonstrukters by der Arbet.' *Arbeter Fraynd.* 3.
— (1920u). 'Der Emes fun Erets Yisroel.' *Arbeter Fraynd.* 2.
— (1920v). 'Gedanken-Punken.' *Arbeter Fraynd.* 3.
— (1920w). 'Natitsen: Der Nekster Shrit.' *Arbeter Fraynd.* 3.
— (1920x). 'A Religiyah ahen Religiyah.' *Arbeter Fraynd.* 7–8.
— (1920y). 'Tsu Unser Leyser.' *Arbeter Fraynd.* 1–2.
— (1921a). *Talmud Babli: Berakhot, Gemore in Idish Vol. 1.* London: Vainberg.
— (1921b). 'Natitsen: Horror Vakyui.' *Arbeter Fraynd.* 2.
— (1921c). 'Brief un Barikhten: Antfer fun di Redaktor.' *Arbeter Fraynd.* December 31, 7.
— (1921d). 'Nakh Amal Jabotinski.' *Arbeter Fraynd.* December 17, 1–2.
— (1921e). 'Tsu der Agenda Fun Unser Kongress.' *Arbeter Fraynd.* 1–2.
— (1921f). 'Klarhayt.' *Arbeter Fraynd.* 1–2.
— (1921g). 'Das Letste Vort fun Individualizm.' *Arbeter Fraynd.* 4.
— (1921h). 'Vider Vegen der Imigraziyes Frage.' *Arbeter Fraynd.* 1–2.
— (1921i). 'Natitsen: Der Tsiyonistisher Kongress.' *Arbeter Fraynd.* 3.
— (1921j). 'Gedanken-Punken.' *Arbeter Fraynd.* 5.
— (1921k). 'Natitsen: Unser Shayni le-Melekh.' *Arbeter Fraynd.* 2.
— (1921l). 'Vider Vegen Organizitsiya.' *Arbeter Fraynd.* 1–2.
— (1921m). 'Vos Uns Shaydet.' *Arbeter Fraynd.* 1.
— (1921n). 'Anarkhism un Schmerts.' *Arbeter Fraynd.* 4–5.
— (1921o). 'Vi Kumen Mir tsu Rekht un Gerehtigkeyt?' *Arbeter Fraynd.* 4–5.
— (1921p). 'Antfer fun der Redaktor.' *Arbeter Fraynd.* 3.
— (1921q). 'In A Falshe Pozitsiya.' *Arbeter Fraynd.* 1–2.
— (1922a). 'Refleksiyon: Poesy un Heshbon.' *Arbeter Fraynd.* November 24, 5–6.
— (1922b). 'Vider a Sakh ha-Kol.' *Arbeter Fraynd.* September 29, 1–2.
— (1922c). 'A Vort tsu Genossen un Lezers.' *Arbeter Fraynd.* September 21, 2.
— (1922d). 'Lamir Shafen a Shtarke Organizitsiya.' *Arbeter Fraynd.* August 26, 1–2.
— (1922e). 'Gedanken Punken.' *Arbeter Fraynd.* July 29, 8.
— (1922f). 'Der Zig fun Moskova un Abisele Musar Haskel.' *Arbeter Fraynd.* 1–2.
— (1922g). 'Herschaftslosen Socialism.' *Arbeter Fraynd.* June 3, 1–2.
— (1922h). 'Fareynigter Front.' *Arbeter Fraynd.* April 22, 1–2.
— (1922i). 'Revolutsyes Makhen Ader Farbarayten: A Vort Vegen Itstigen Politisch Ekonomisch Matsav.' *Arbeter Fraynd.* 1–2.
— (1922j). 'Der Internatsiyonal Anarkhisten Kongress.' *Arbeter Fraynd.* 5.
— (1922k). 'Natitsen: Ven Kritik iz Lakherlikh.' *Arbeter Fraynd.* 3.
— (1923a). 'Natitsen: Maks Nordau.' *Arbeter Fraynd.* 2.
— (1923b). 'Natitsen: Real Politik un Mah Yafisa.' *Arbeter Fraynd.* 2.
Zeitlin, H. (1913). 'Vos es Muz Getun Veren.' *Der Moment.* 2.
— (1926a). 'Aber Taki Gar Shtile Verter.' *Der Moment,* May 17, 4.
— (1926b). 'Mayn Fraynd un Zayn Musar Brief.' *Der Moment,* June 18, 4.
— (1930a). 'Serafim.' *Der Moment,* November 28, 4.
— (1930b). 'Vegen Dray Nisht Gerantene Zivugim.' *Der Moment,* November 7, 4.
— (1961). 'Le-Demuto shel Ehad ha-Rabanim ha-Margishim.' *Ha-Tsafa,* November 17, 6.

Zerubavel, Yael (1991). 'The Politics of Interpretation: Tel Hai in Israel's Collective Memory.' *AJS Review* 16, no. 1–2: 133–160.

Zevin, S. Y. (1957). '*Yayin Mefahe.*' November 8, 5.

Zevuloni, N. (1962). '*Anshe Ihud Darshu Pegisha im Ben-Gurion le-Hafsik ha-Aliyah.*' *Herut*, Junen 25, 2.

Ziegler, Robert (1988). 'The Elitist Metaphysic of Joséphin Péladan.' *Nineteenth-Century French Studies* 16, no. 3/4: 361–371.

Zimmer, Kenyon (2015). *Immigrants Against the State: Yiddish and Italian Anarchism in America*. Chicago: University of Illinois Press.

Zionist Anarchist (1903). 'Letter to the Editor.' *Arbeter Fraynd.* 7.

Zohar, H. (2003). '*Mosad ha-Rav Kook: Reyshito u-Meyasdaw, Terumato le-Haker Erets Yisrael we-ha-Tsiyonut ha-Datit.*' *Sinai: Ma'amarim u-Mehakrim be-Torah u-be-Mada'ai ha-Yahadut*. Edited by Y. E. Movshovits. Tammuz-Elul 5763.

Index

9 781526 149039